A Man's Skin

HUBERT   ZANZIM

Publisher's Cataloging-in-Publication data

Names: Hubert, 1971- author. | Zanzim, artist.
Title: A man's skin / Hubert ; Zanzim.
Description: Portland, OR:
Ablaze Publishing, 2021
Identifiers: ISBN: 978-1-950912-48-3
Subjects: LCSH Renaissance-Italy-Comic books, strips, etc. | Romance-Comic books, strips, etc. | Sex role-Comic books, strips, etc. | Feminism-Comic books, strips, etc. | Arranged marriage-Comic books, strips, etc. | Homosexuality-Comic books, strips, etc. | Graphic novels. | BISAC COMICS & GRAPHIC NOVELS / Historical Fiction | COMICS & GRAPHIC NOVELS / LGBTQ+
Classification: LCC PN6747.H83P43 M36 2021 | DDC 741.5-dc23

A MAN'S SKIN. Published by Ablaze Publishing, 11222 SE Main St. #22906 Portland, OR 97269.

10 9 8 7 6 5 4 3 2 1

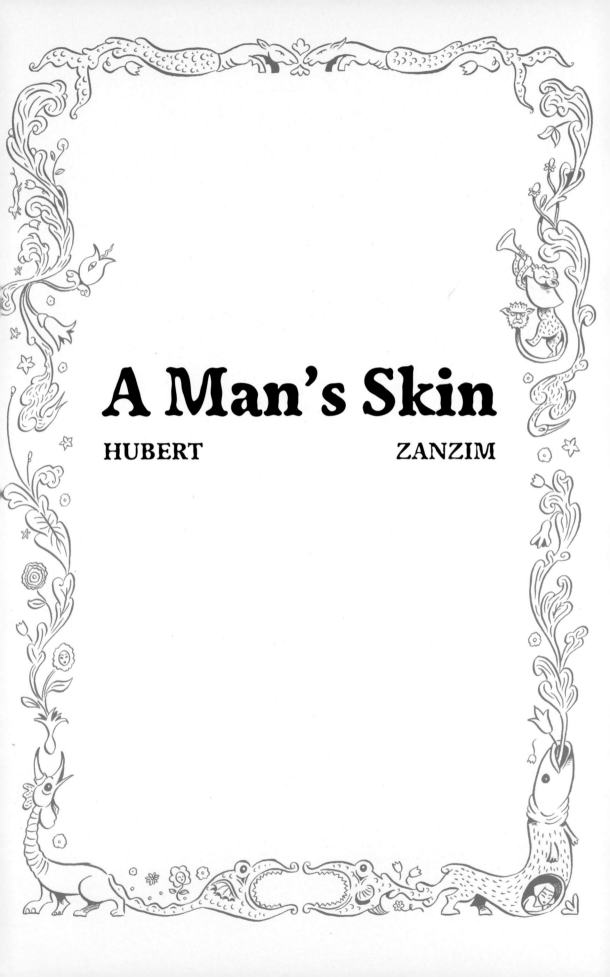

A Man's Skin

HUBERT   ZANZIM

FOR ABLAZE

Managing Editor
Rich Young
Editor
Kevin Ketner
Design
Rodolfo Muraguchi

Chapter 1

A real young woman

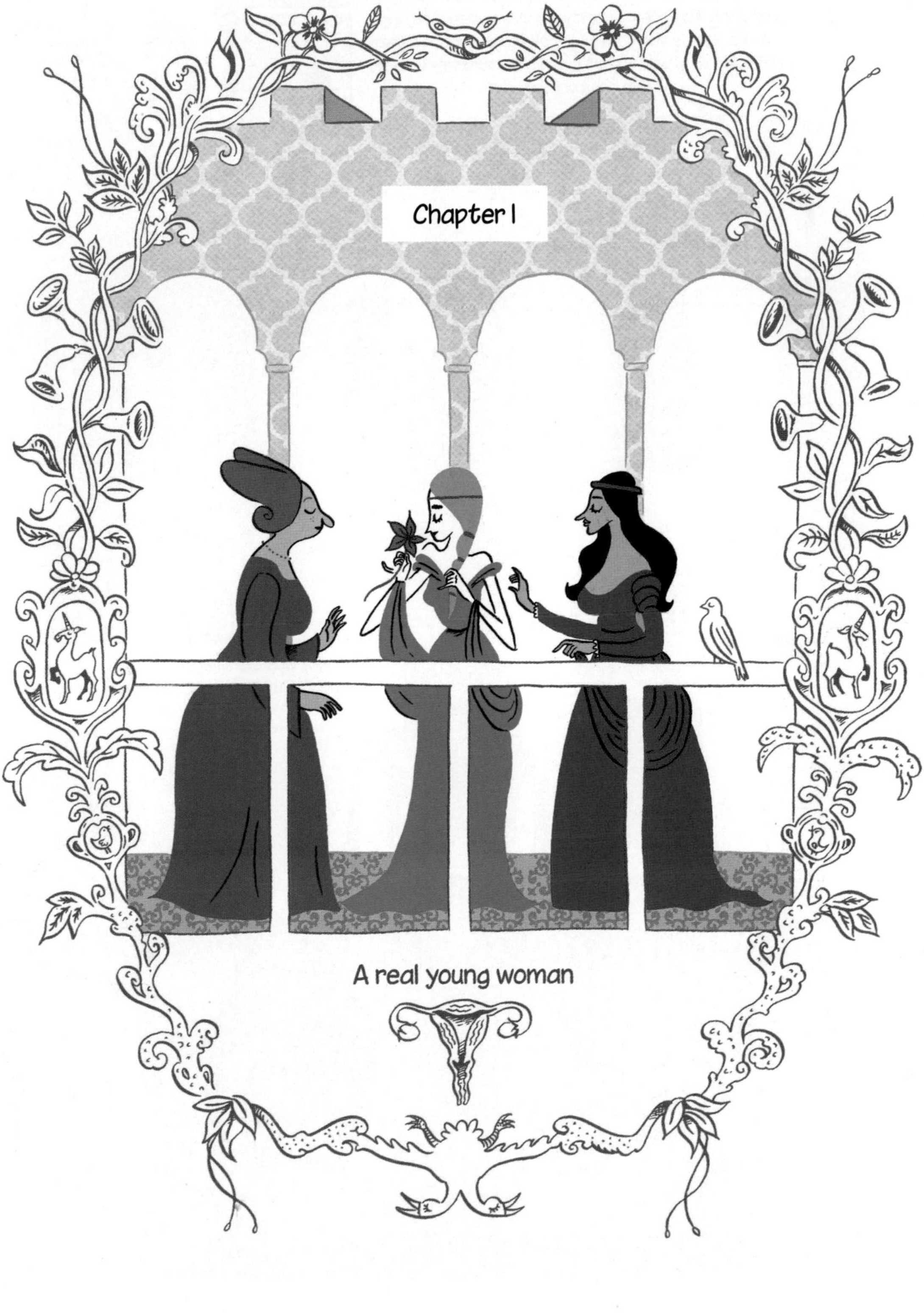

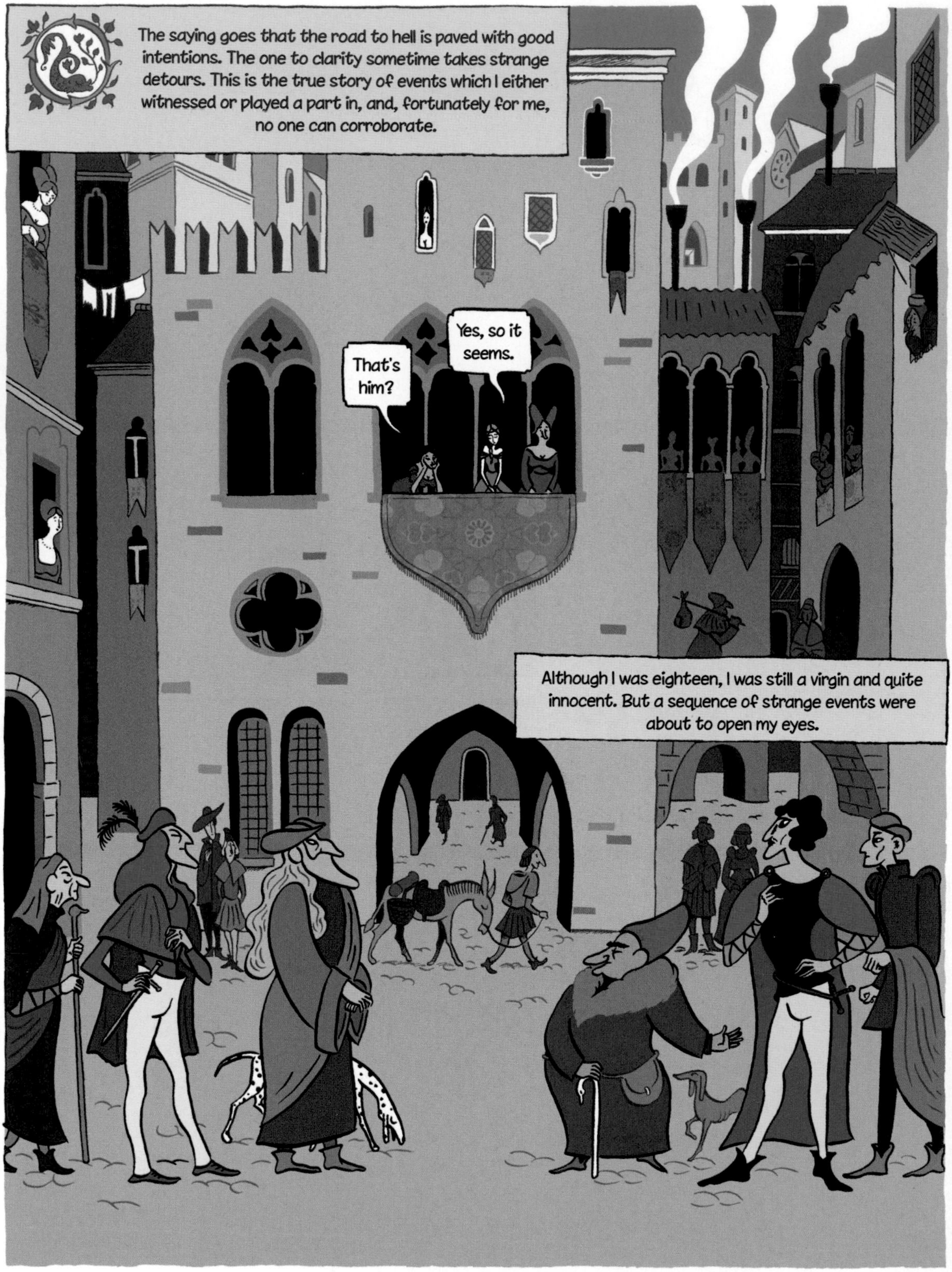
The saying goes that the road to hell is paved with good intentions. The one to clarity sometime takes strange detours. This is the true story of events which I either witnessed or played a part in, and, fortunately for me, no one can corroborate.
That's him?
Yes, so it seems.
Although I was eighteen, I was still a virgin and quite innocent. But a sequence of strange events were about to open my eyes.

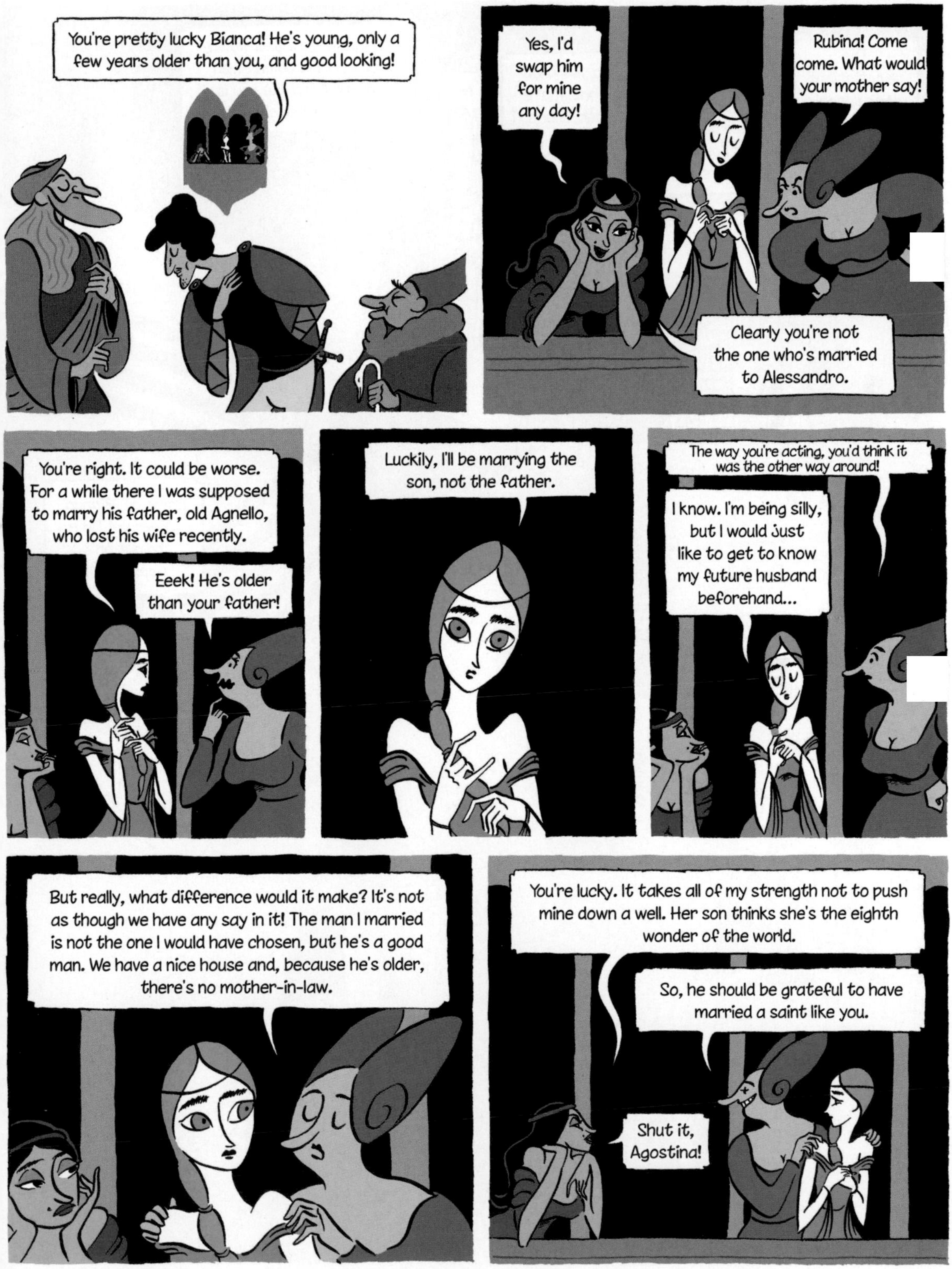

You're pretty lucky Bianca! He's young, only a few years older than you, and good looking!
Yes, I'd swap him for mine any day!
Rubina! Come come. What would your mother say!
Clearly you're not the one who's married to Alessandro.
You're right. It could be worse. For a while there I was supposed to marry his father, old Agnello, who lost his wife recently.
Eeek! He's older than your father!
Luckily, I'll be marrying the son, not the father.
The way you're acting, you'd think it was the other way around!
I know. I'm being silly, but I would just like to get to know my future husband beforehand...
But really, what difference would it make? It's not as though we have any say in it! The man I married is not the one I would have chosen, but he's a good man. We have a nice house and, because he's older, there's no mother-in-law.
You're lucky. It takes all of my strength not to push mine down a well. Her son thinks she's the eighth wonder of the world.
So, he should be grateful to have married a saint like you.
Shut it, Agostina!

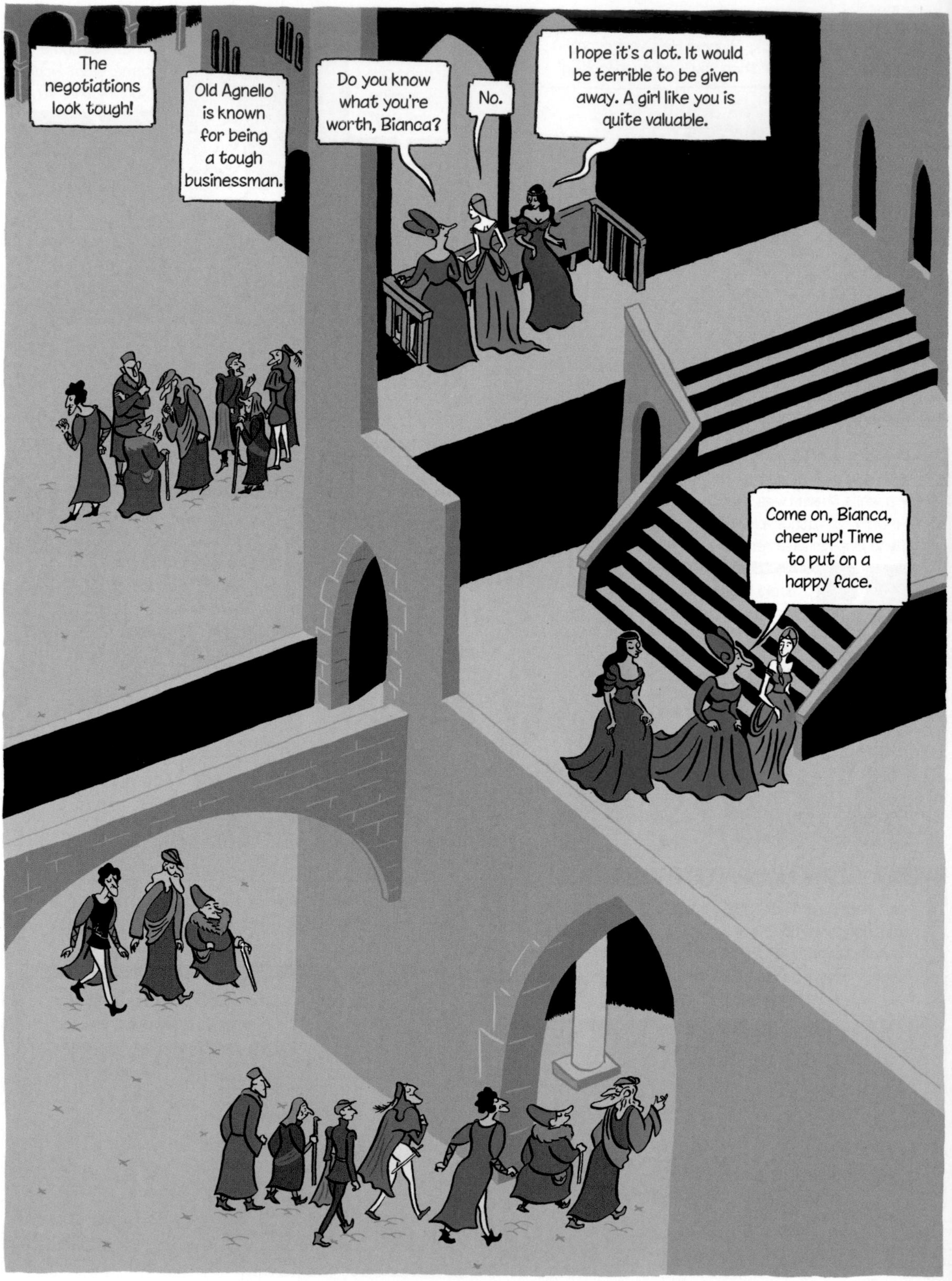
The negotiations look tough!
Old Agnello is known for being a tough businessman.
Do you know what you're worth, Bianca?
No.
I hope it's a lot. It would be terrible to be given away. A girl like you is quite valuable.
Come on, Bianca, cheer up! Time to put on a happy face.

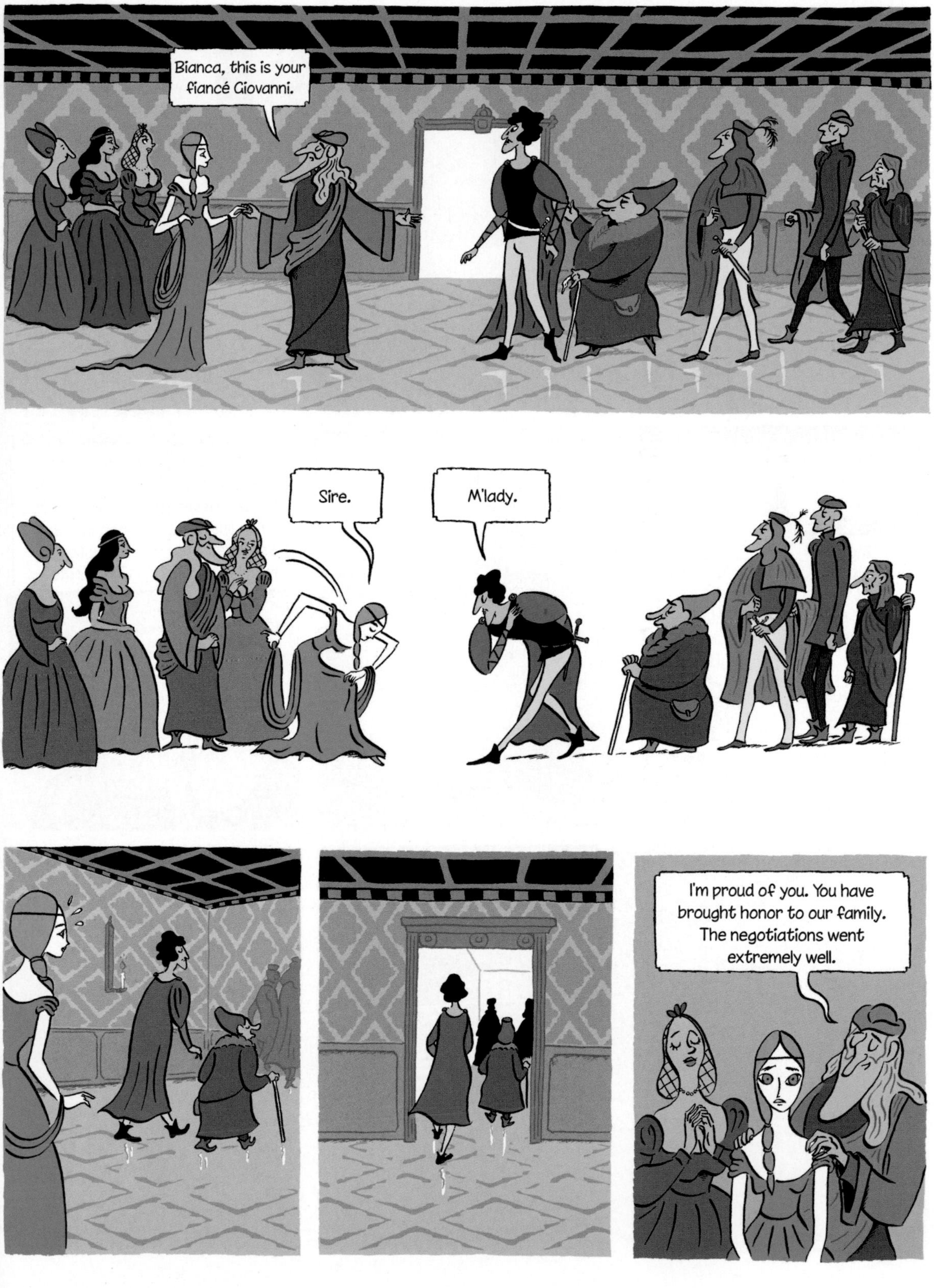
Bianca, this is your fiancé Giovanni.
Sire.
M'lady.
I'm proud of you. You have brought honor to our family. The negotiations went extremely well.

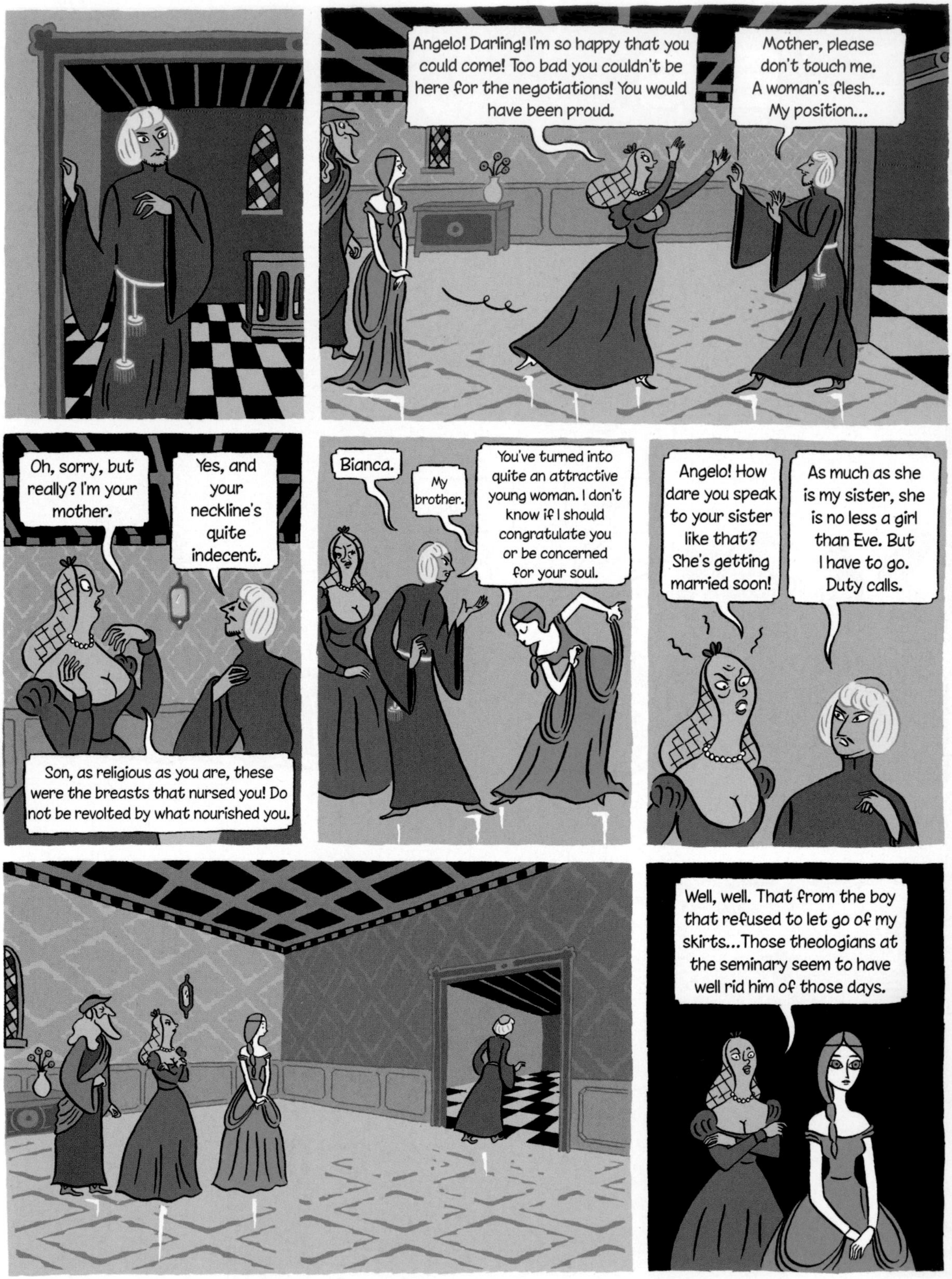
Angelo! Darling! I'm so happy that you could come! Too bad you couldn't be here for the negotiations! You would have been proud.
Mother, please don't touch me. A woman's flesh... My position...
Oh, sorry, but really? I'm your mother.
Yes, and your neckline's quite indecent.
Son, as religious as you are, these were the breasts that nursed you! Do not be revolted by what nourished you.
Bianca.
My brother.
You've turned into quite an attractive young woman. I don't know if I should congratulate you or be concerned for your soul.
Angelo! How dare you speak to your sister like that? She's getting married soon!
As much as she is my sister, she is no less a girl than Eve. But I have to go. Duty calls.
Well, well. That from the boy that refused to let go of my skirts...Those theologians at the seminary seem to have well rid him of those days.

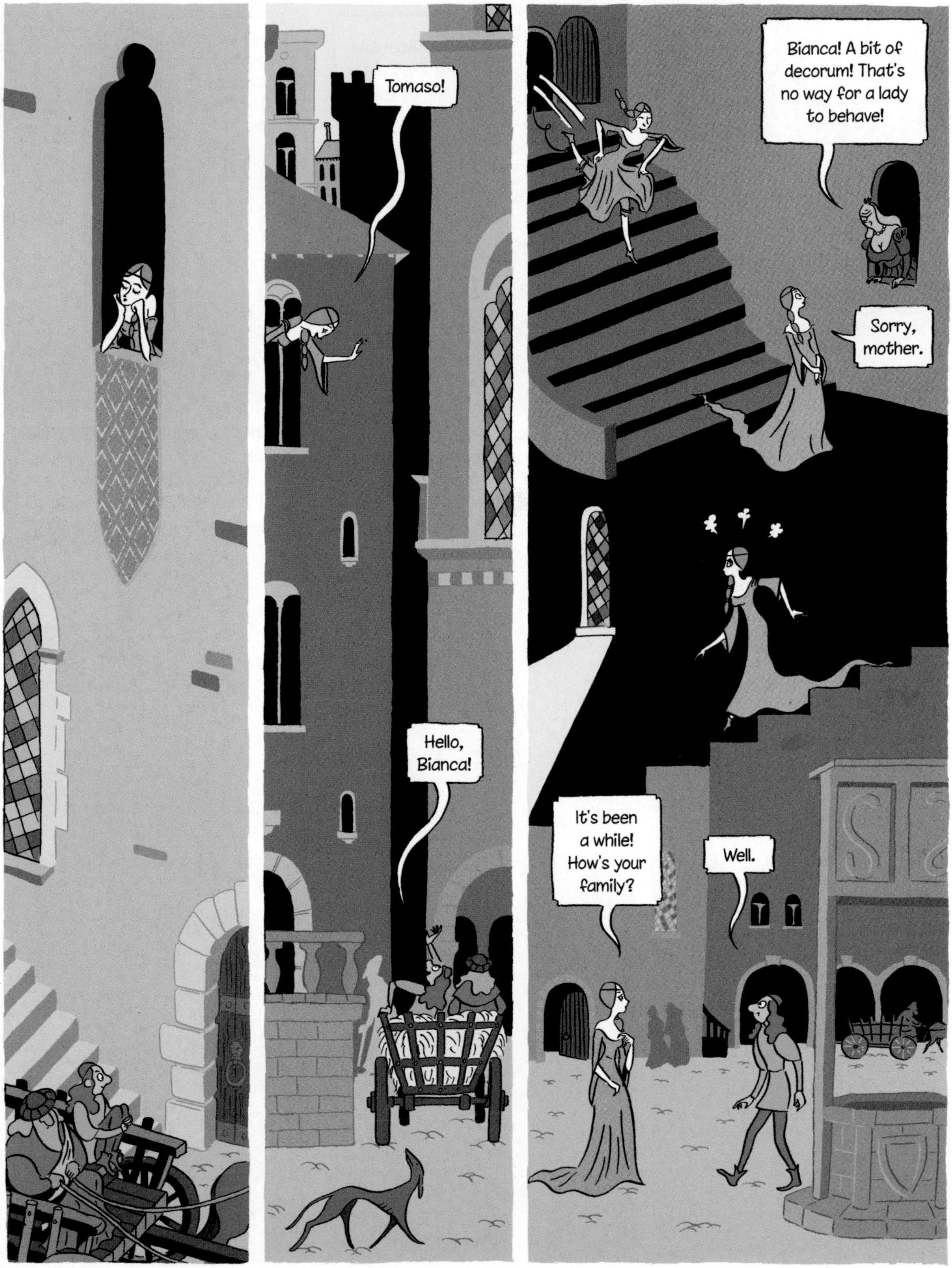
Tomaso!
Hello, Bianca!
Bianca! A bit of decorum! That's no way for a lady to behave!
Sorry, mother.
It's been a while! How's your family?
Well.

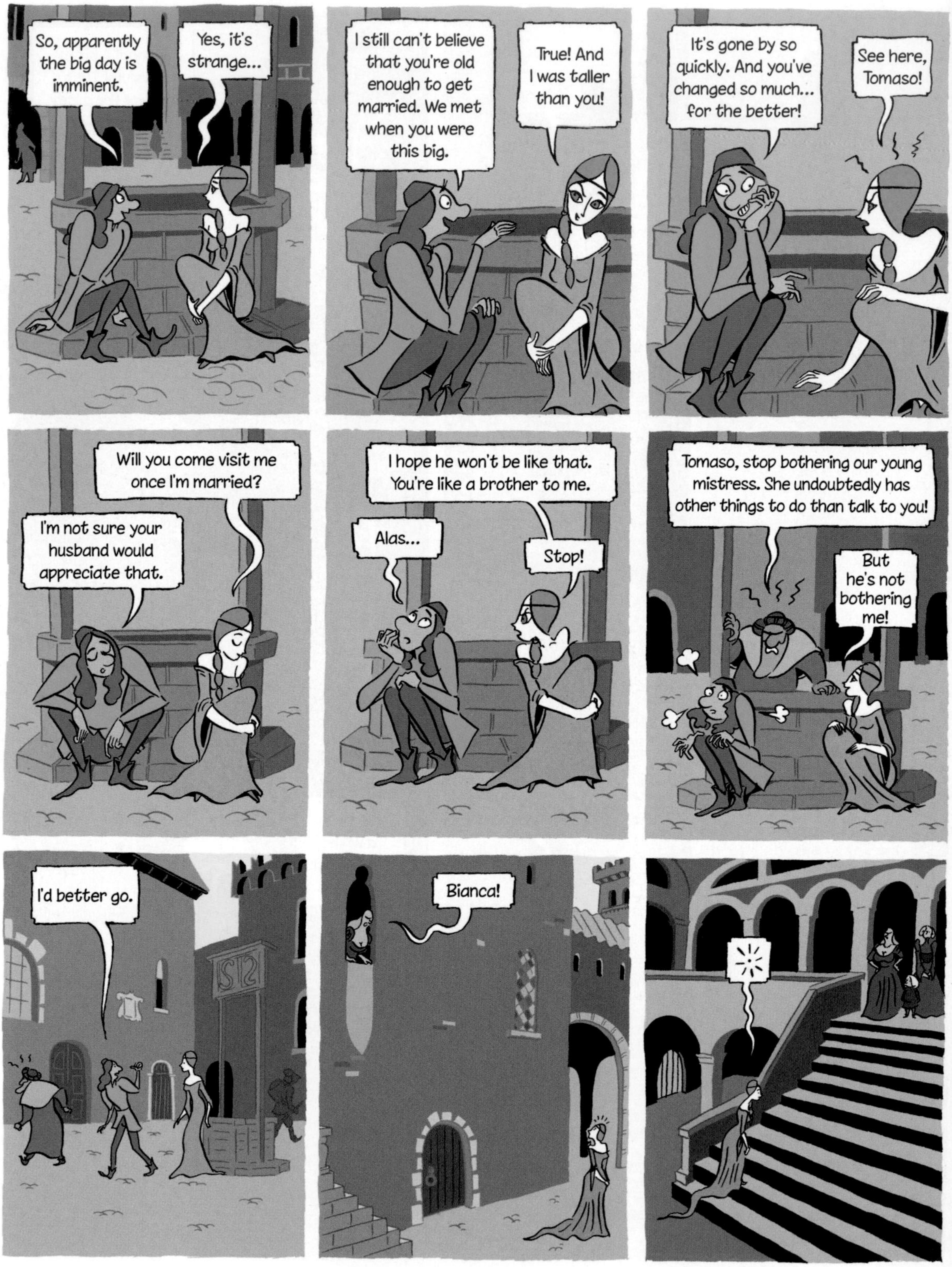
So, apparently the big day is imminent.
Yes, it's strange...
I still can't believe that you're old enough to get married. We met when you were this big.
True! And I was taller than you!
It's gone by so quickly. And you've changed so much... for the better!
See here, Tomaso!
Will you come visit me once I'm married?
I'm not sure your husband would appreciate that.
I hope he won't be like that. You're like a brother to me.
Alas...
Stop!
Tomaso, stop bothering our young mistress. She undoubtedly has other things to do than talk to you!
But he's not bothering me!
I'd better go.
Bianca!

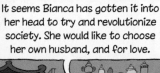

It seems Bianca has gotten it into her head to try and revolutionize society. She would like to choose her own husband, and for love.

Luigi darling, stop. Momma's busy.

Mother! I would just like to get to know him before we're married and not after!

And if you don't like him we cancel it. Is that it? We tell his family that we're sorry but Bianca doesn't like him.

Can you imagine the scandal? Our family honor is at stake.

That's not what I said! I'll marry who you want me to marry!

What difference would it make if you got to know him before hand? You think that I knew your father? Oh, youth today and their crazy ideas!

Luigi! Leave that vase alone or you'll break it!

Why not let Bianca come and stay with me for a while? It'll take her mind off things.

Smash!

LUIGI!

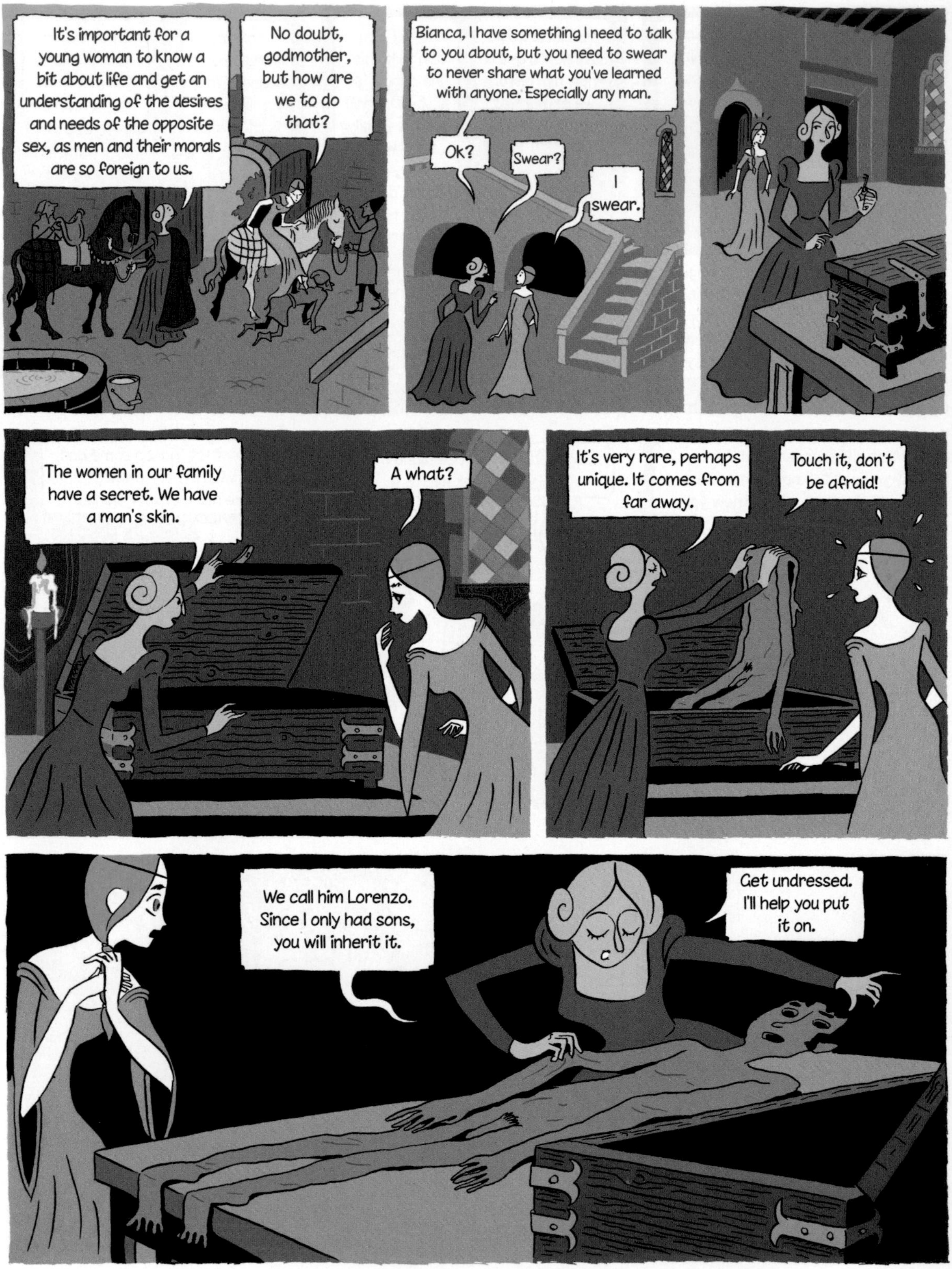
It's important for a young woman to know a bit about life and get an understanding of the desires and needs of the opposite sex, as men and their morals are so foreign to us.
No doubt, godmother, but how are we to do that?
Bianca, I have something I need to talk to you about, but you need to swear to never share what you've learned with anyone. Especially any man.
Ok?
Swear?
I swear.
The women in our family have a secret. We have a man's skin.
A what?
It's very rare, perhaps unique. It comes from far away.
Touch it, don't be afraid!
We call him Lorenzo. Since I only had sons, you will inherit it.
Get undressed. I'll help you put it on.

Once you've put it on, no one will doubt that you're a man.

It'll allow you to be incognito in the world of men.

That way you can get to know your fiancé in his world!

It's really tight around the chest.

Don't complain, young lady. Can you imagine how it was for your aunt Theresa?

Theresa? The one who's in a convent?

Yes! Before she took the veil, she wore this. She left a trail of broken hearts and several teary young ladies when she took off Lorenzo and took her vows.

She wanted to take it with her, but I dissuaded her. Imagine if she'd been caught! She would have found herself up in front of the inquisition!

And mother? Did she...

Your mother found she was a bit too rigid for a stunt like this.

And you?

I'll never tell. Not even if I'm tortured!

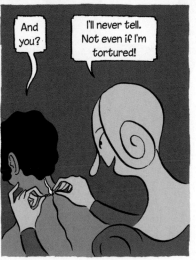

But try to avoid your mother seeing you as Lorenzo. You never know.

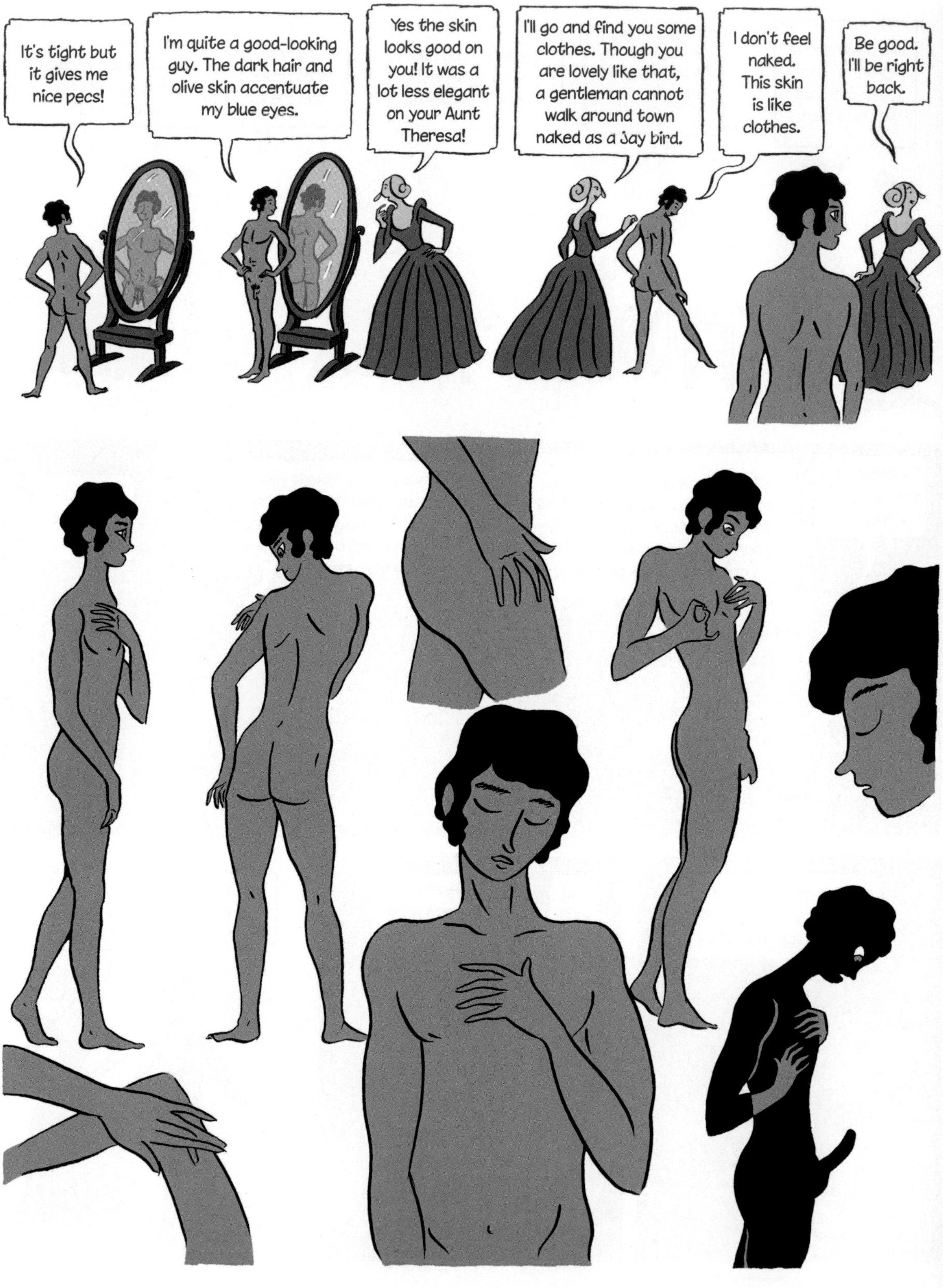
It's tight but it gives me nice pecs!
I'm quite a good-looking guy. The dark hair and olive skin accentuate my blue eyes.
Yes the skin looks good on you! It was a lot less elegant on your Aunt Theresa!
I'll go and find you some clothes. Though you are lovely like that, a gentleman cannot walk around town naked as a Jay bird.
I don't feel naked. This skin is like clothes.
Be good. I'll be right back.

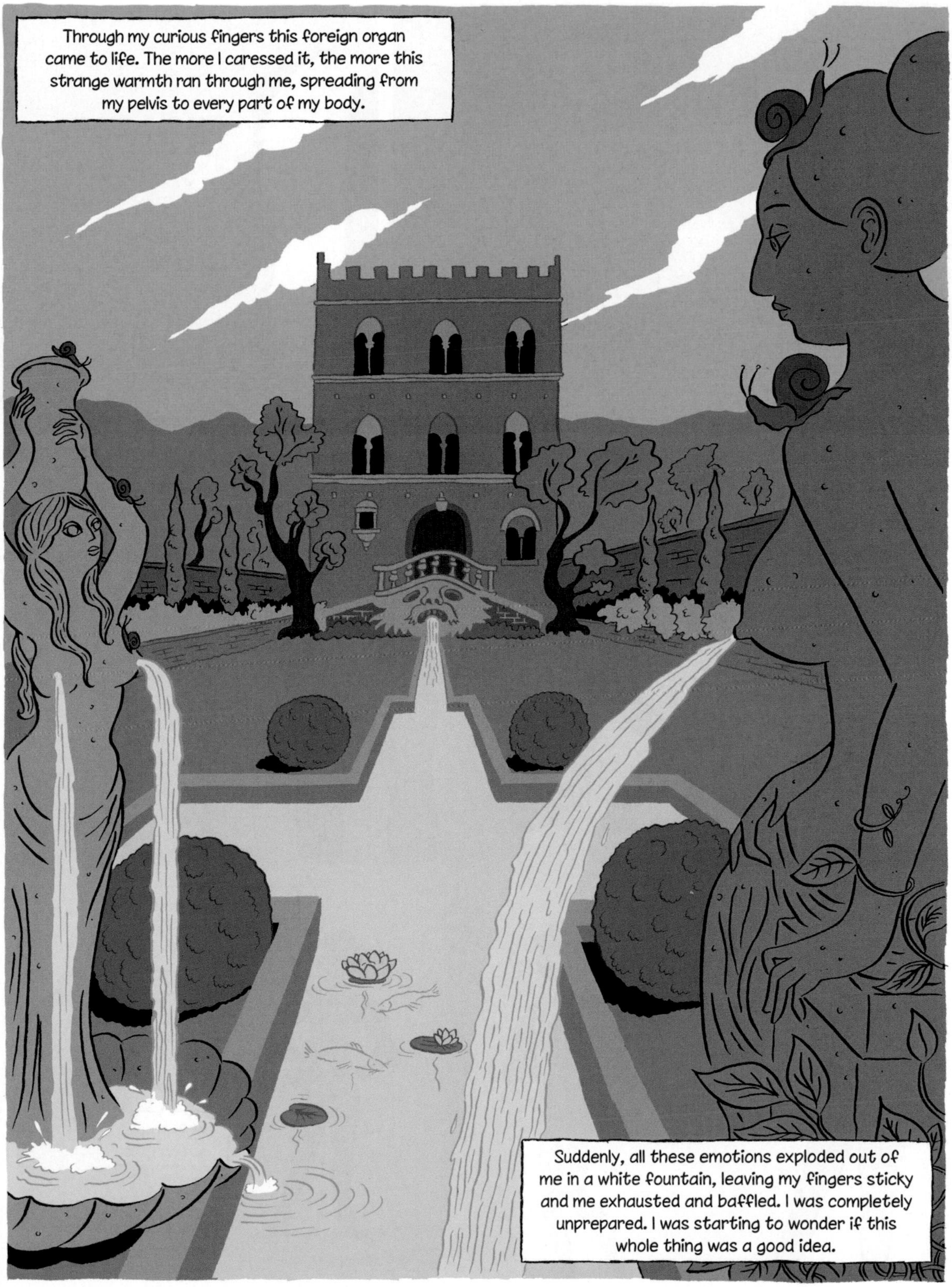
Through my curious fingers this foreign organ came to life. The more I caressed it, the more this strange warmth ran through me, spreading from my pelvis to every part of my body.
Suddenly, all these emotions exploded out of me in a white fountain, leaving my fingers sticky and me exhausted and baffled. I was completely unprepared. I was starting to wonder if this whole thing was a good idea.

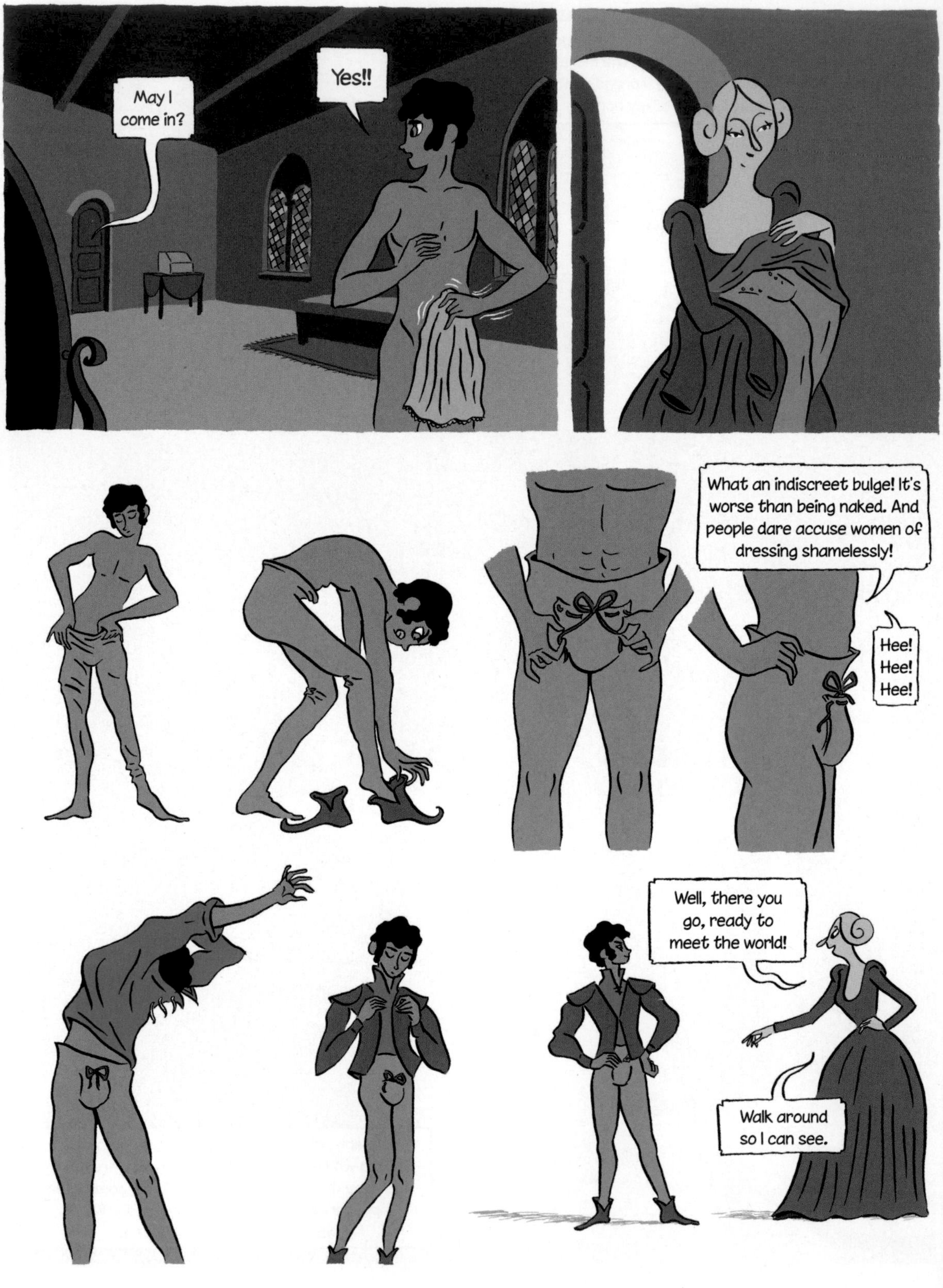
May I come in?
Yes!!
What an indiscreet bulge! It's worse than being naked. And people dare accuse women of dressing shamelessly!
Hee! Hee! Hee!
Well, there you go, ready to meet the world!
Walk around so I can see.

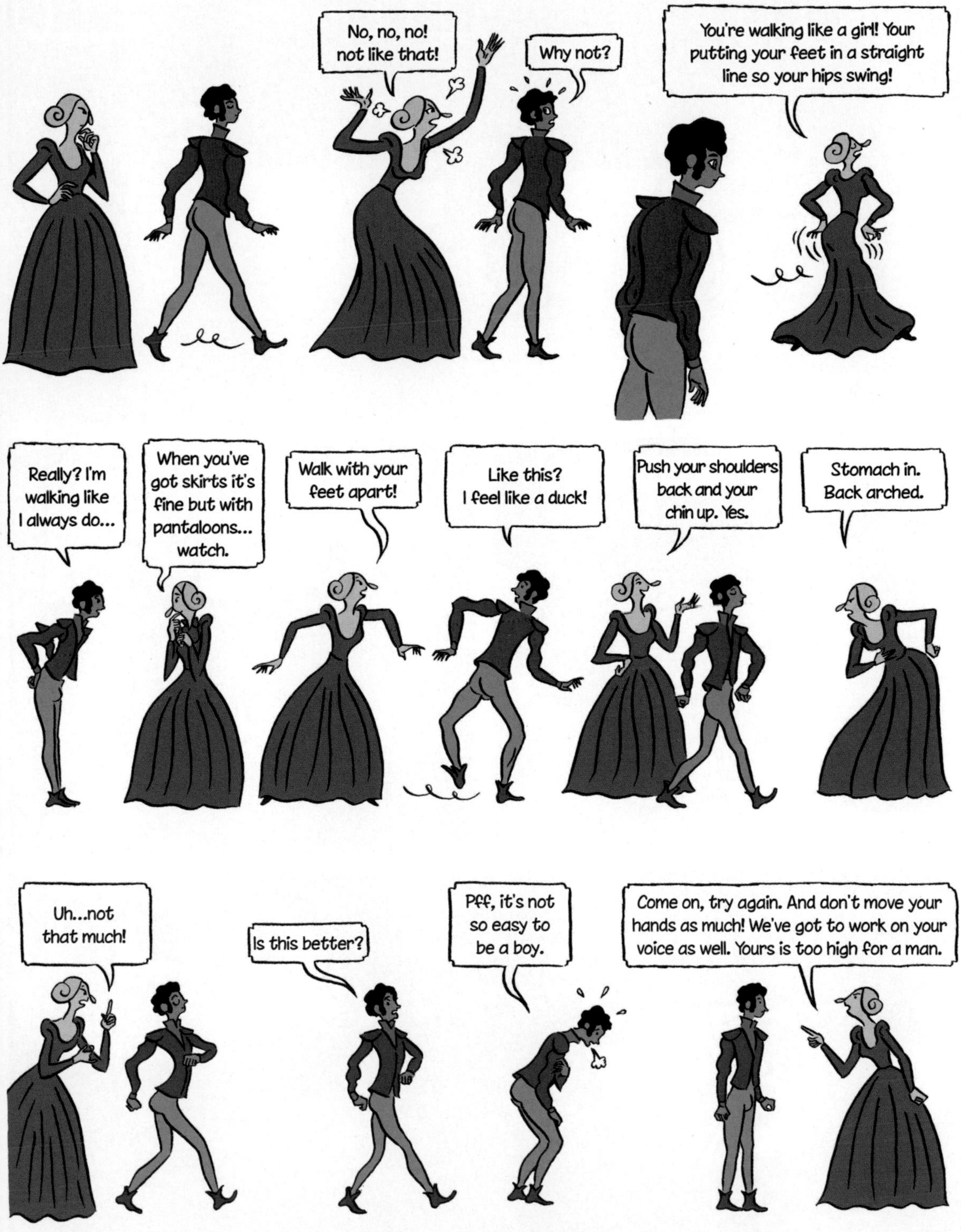
No, no, no! not like that!
Why not?
You're walking like a girl! Your putting your feet in a straight line so your hips swing!
Really? I'm walking like I always do...
When you've got skirts it's fine but with pantaloons... watch.
Walk with your feet apart!
Like this? I feel like a duck!
Push your shoulders back and your chin up. Yes.
Stomach in. Back arched.
Uh...not that much!
Is this better?
Pff, it's not so easy to be a boy.
Come on, try again. And don't move your hands as much! We've got to work on your voice as well. Yours is too high for a man.

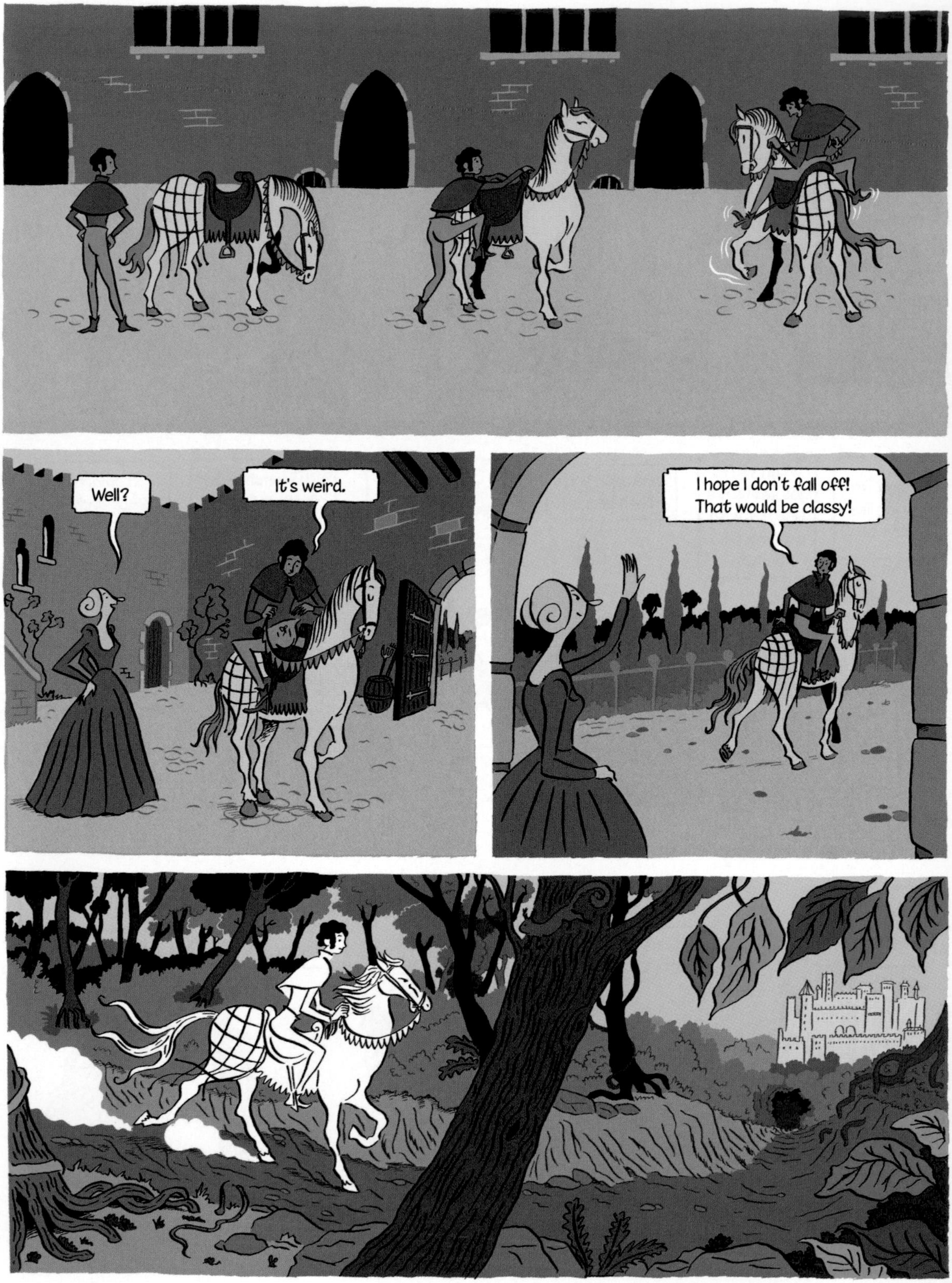
Well?
It's weird.
I hope I don't fall off! That would be classy!

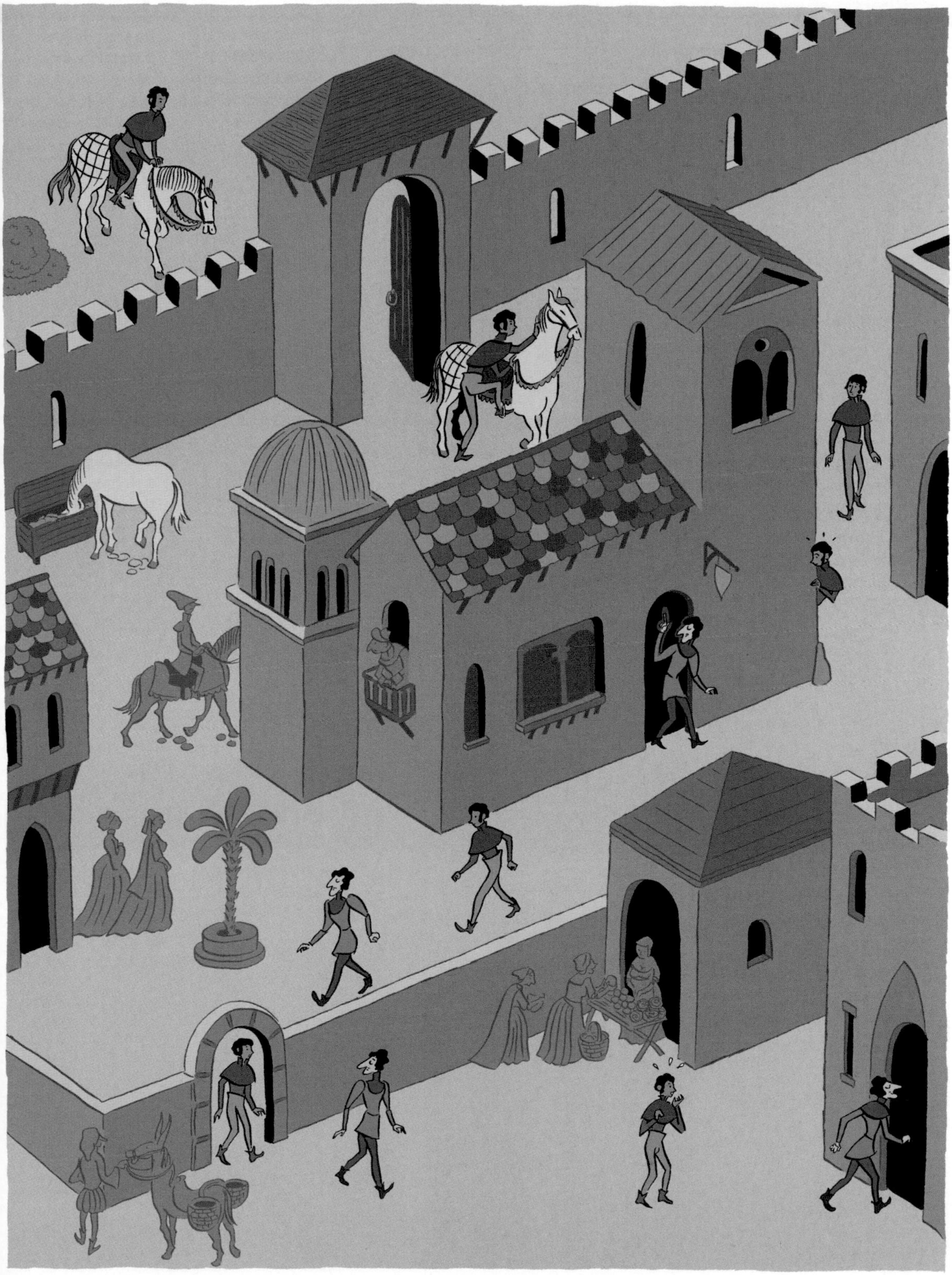

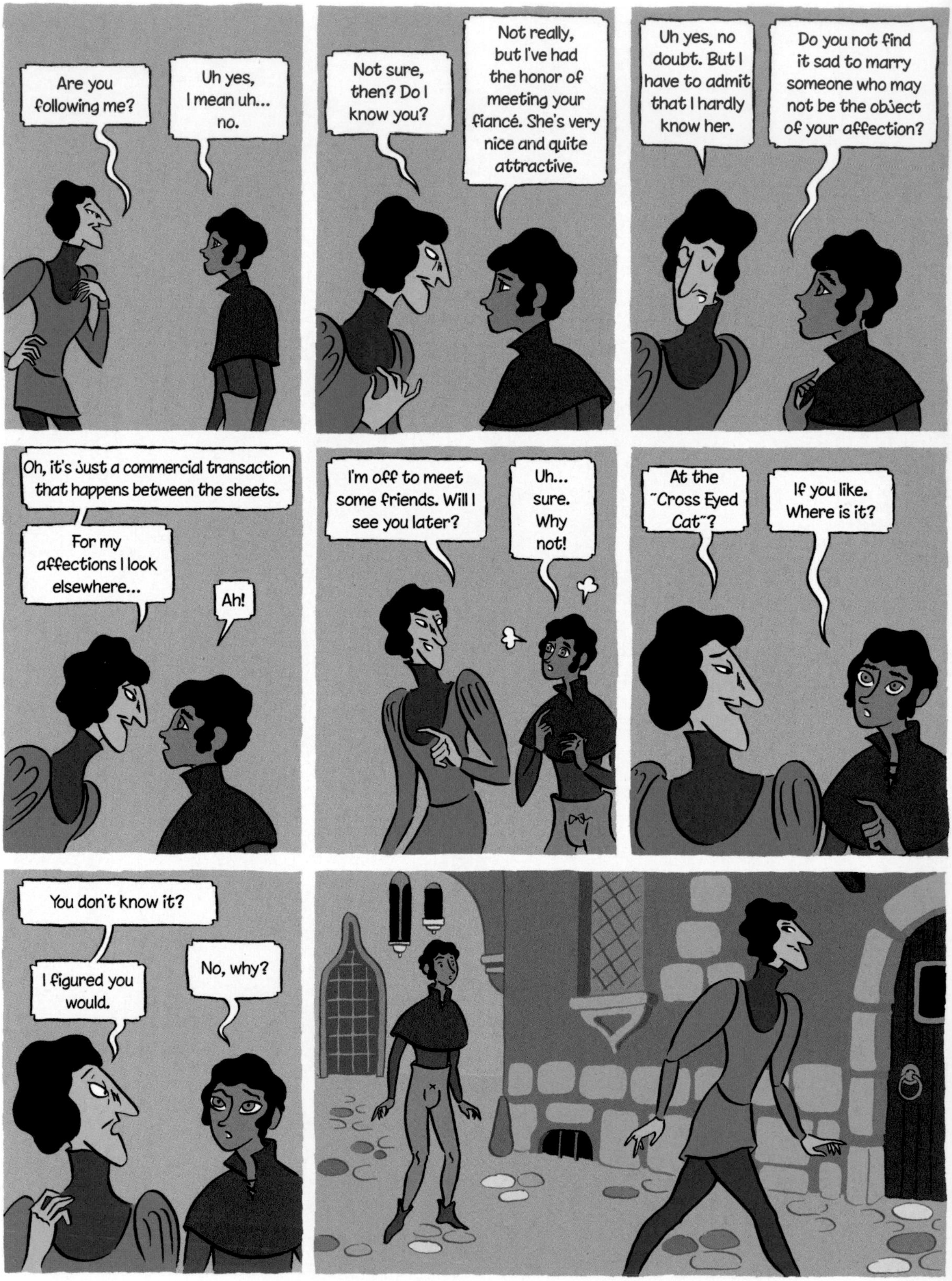
Are you following me?
Uh yes, I mean uh... no.
Not sure, then? Do I know you?
Not really, but I've had the honor of meeting your fiancé. She's very nice and quite attractive.
Uh yes, no doubt. But I have to admit that I hardly know her.
Do you not find it sad to marry someone who may not be the object of your affection?
Oh, it's just a commercial transaction that happens between the sheets.
For my affections I look elsewhere...
Ah!
I'm off to meet some friends. Will I see you later?
Uh... sure. Why not!
At the "Cross Eyed Cat"?
If you like. Where is it?
You don't know it?
I figured you would.
No, why?

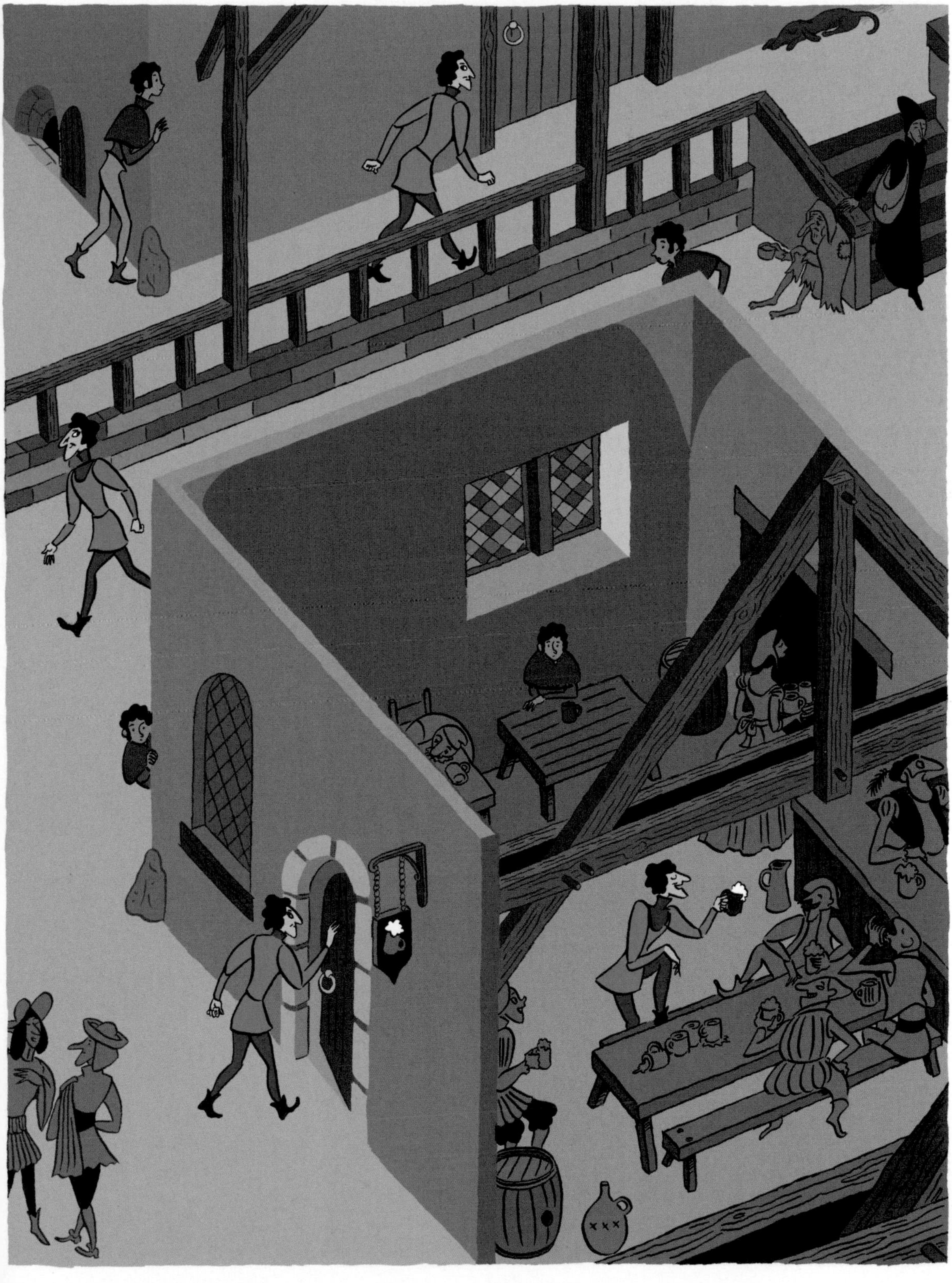

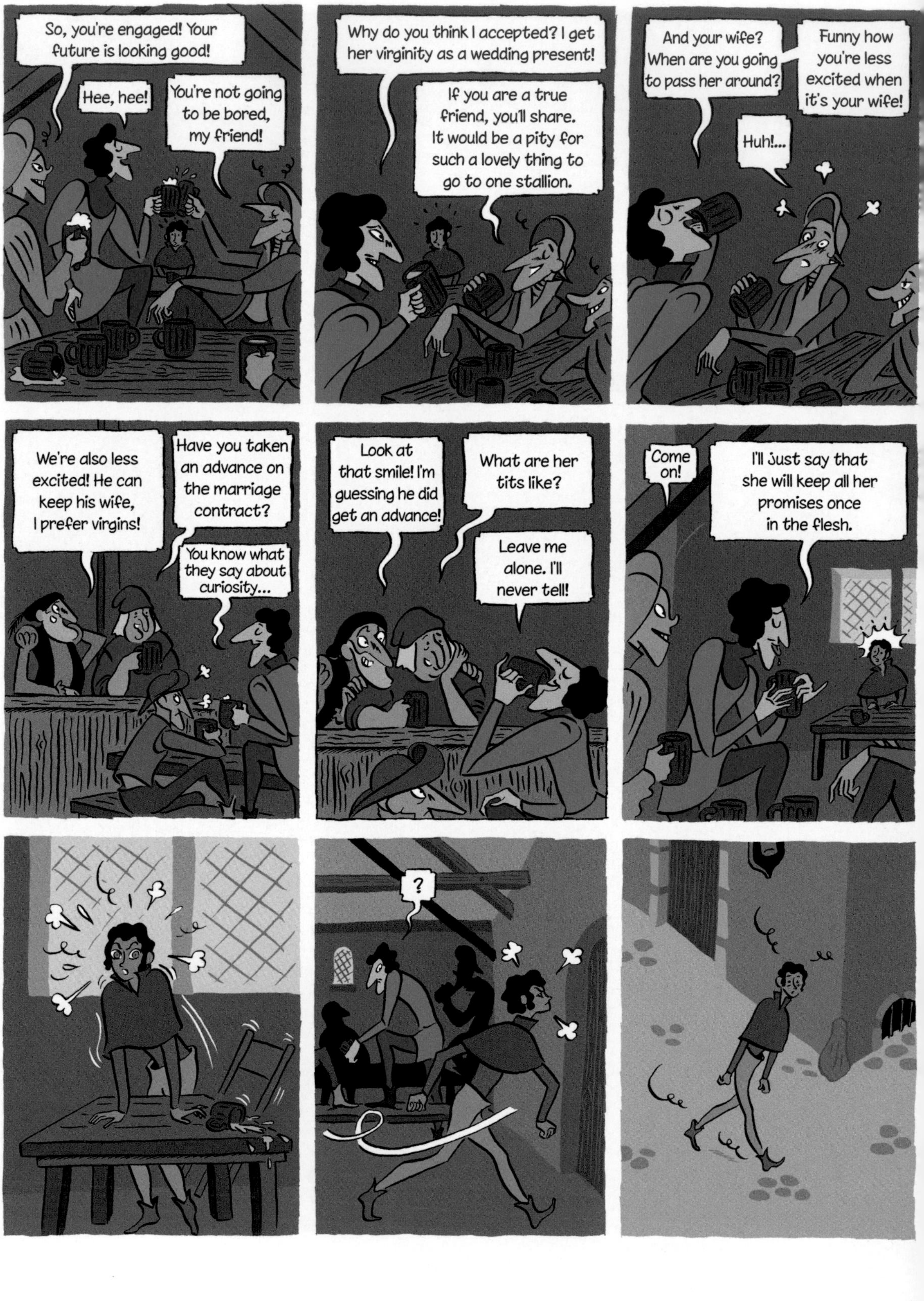

So, you're engaged! Your future is looking good!
Hee, hee!
You're not going to be bored, my friend!
Why do you think I accepted? I get her virginity as a wedding present!
If you are a true friend, you'll share. It would be a pity for such a lovely thing to go to one stallion.
And your wife? When are you going to pass her around?
Funny how you're less excited when it's your wife!
Huh!...
We're also less excited! He can keep his wife, I prefer virgins!
Have you taken an advance on the marriage contract?
You know what they say about curiosity...
Look at that smile! I'm guessing he did get an advance!
What are her tits like?
Leave me alone. I'll never tell!
Come on!
I'll just say that she will keep all her promises once in the flesh.
?

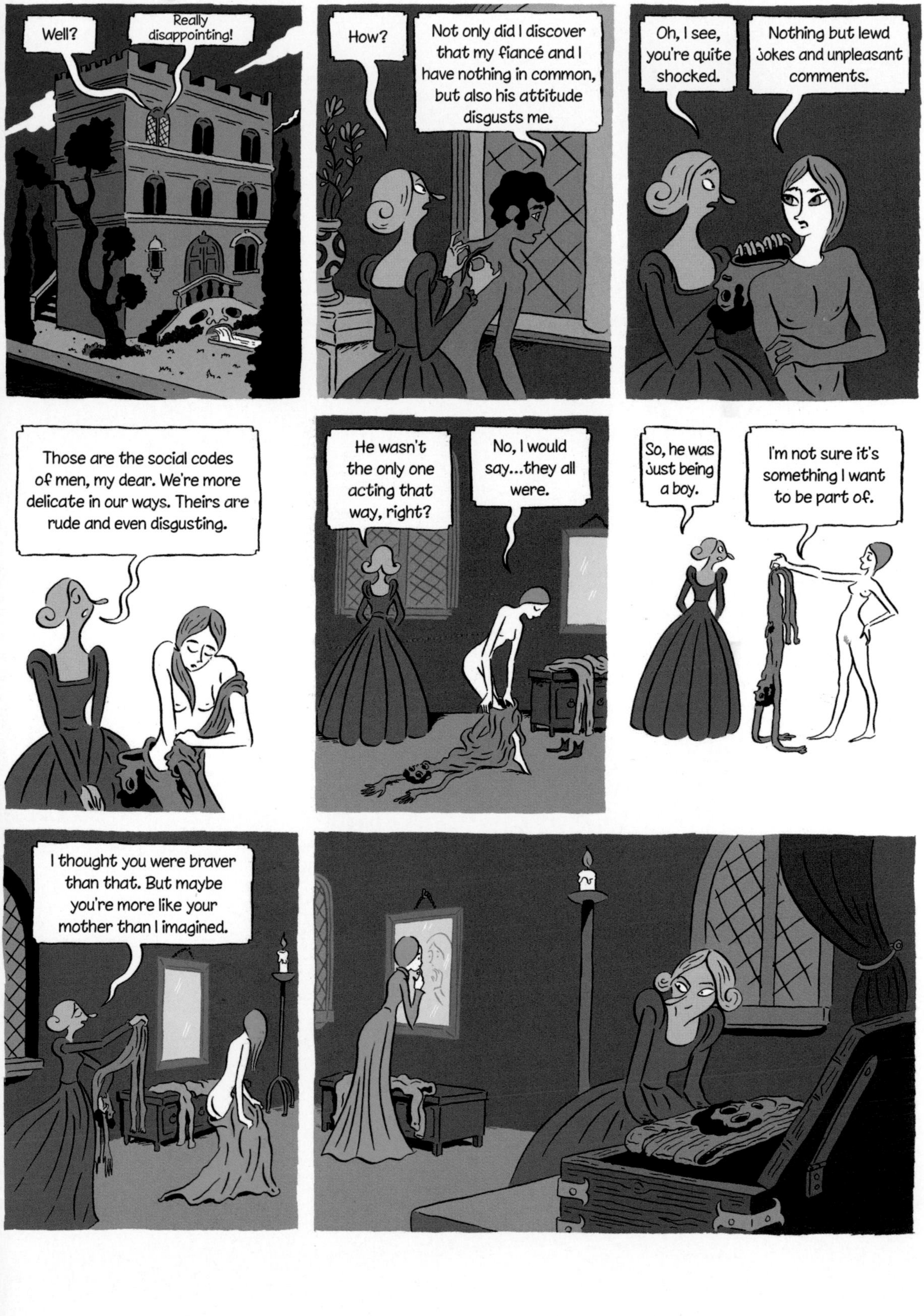
Well?
Really disappointing!
How?
Not only did I discover that my fiancé and I have nothing in common, but also his attitude disgusts me.
Oh, I see, you're quite shocked.
Nothing but lewd jokes and unpleasant comments.
Those are the social codes of men, my dear. We're more delicate in our ways. Theirs are rude and even disgusting.
He wasn't the only one acting that way, right?
No, I would say...they all were.
So, he was just being a boy.
I'm not sure it's something I want to be part of.
I thought you were braver than that. But maybe you're more like your mother than I imagined.

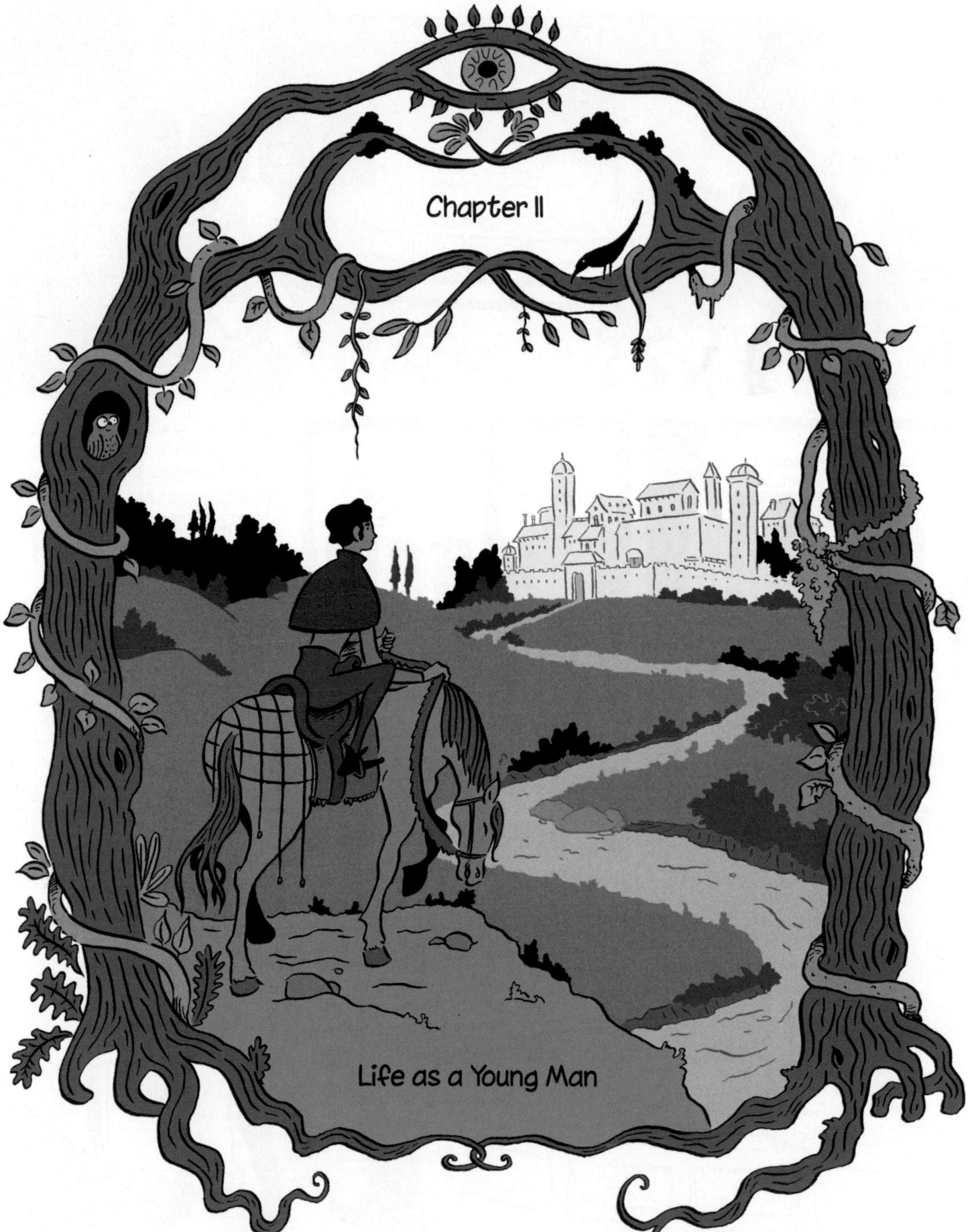
Chapter II
Life as a Young Man

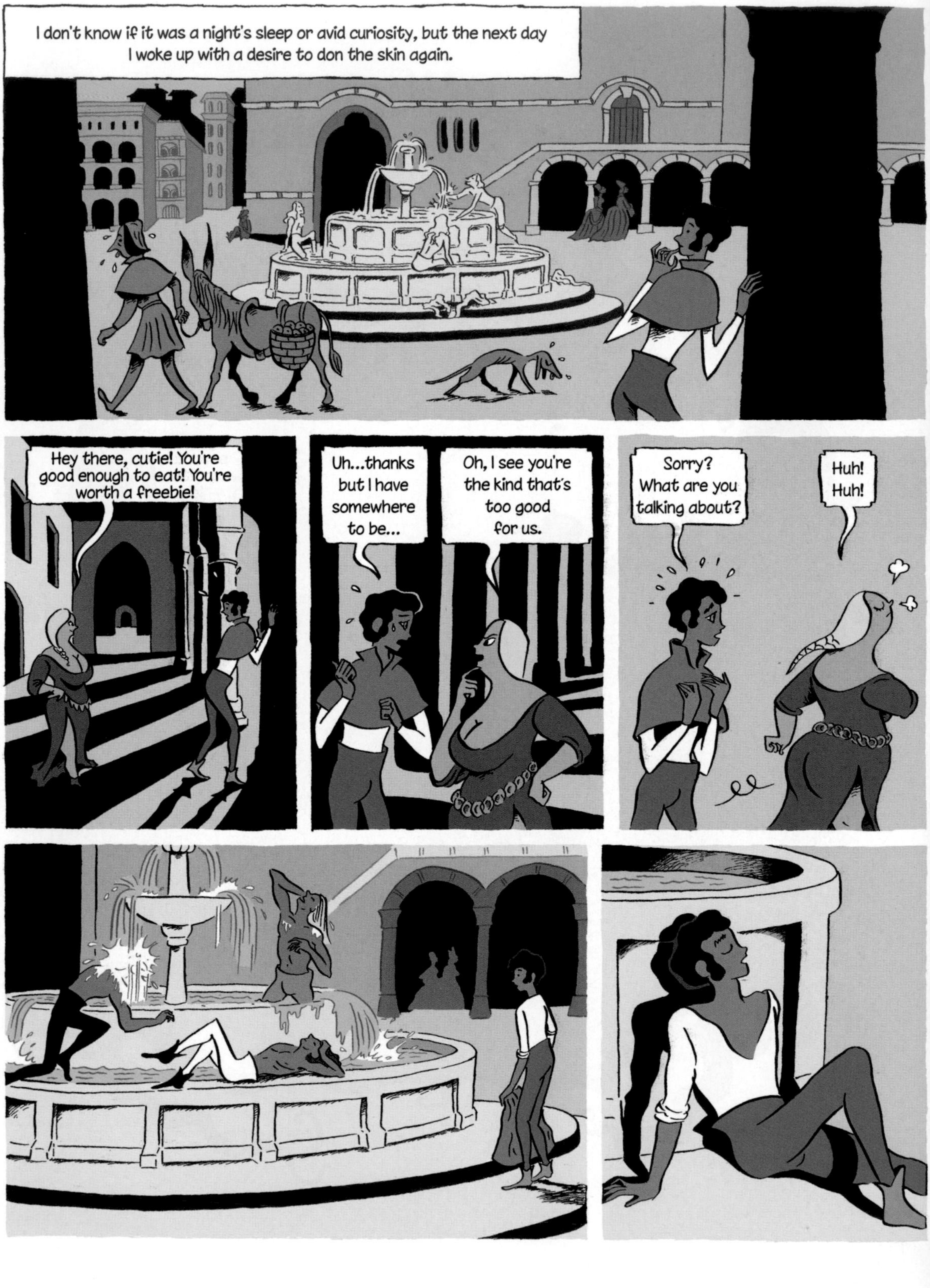
I don't know if it was a night's sleep or avid curiosity, but the next day I woke up with a desire to don the skin again.
Hey there, cutie! You're good enough to eat! You're worth a freebie!
Uh...thanks but I have somewhere to be...
Oh, I see you're the kind that's too good for us.
Sorry? What are you talking about?
Huh! Huh!

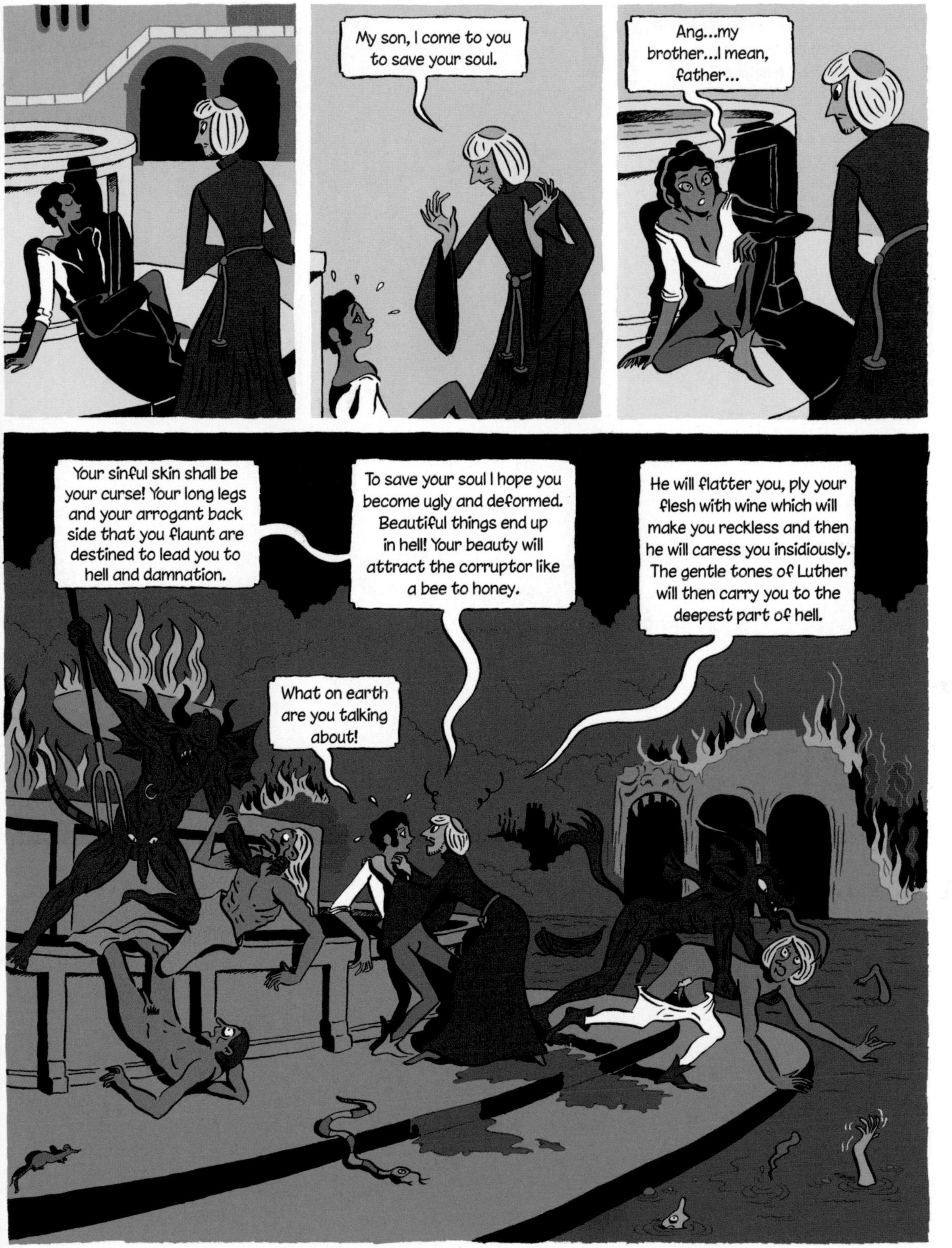
My son, I come to you to save your soul.
Ang...my brother...I mean, father...
Your sinful skin shall be your curse! Your long legs and your arrogant back side that you flaunt are destined to lead you to hell and damnation.
To save your soul I hope you become ugly and deformed. Beautiful things end up in hell! Your beauty will attract the corruptor like a bee to honey.
He will flatter you, ply your flesh with wine which will make you reckless and then he will caress you insidiously. The gentle tones of Luther will then carry you to the deepest part of hell.
What on earth are you talking about!

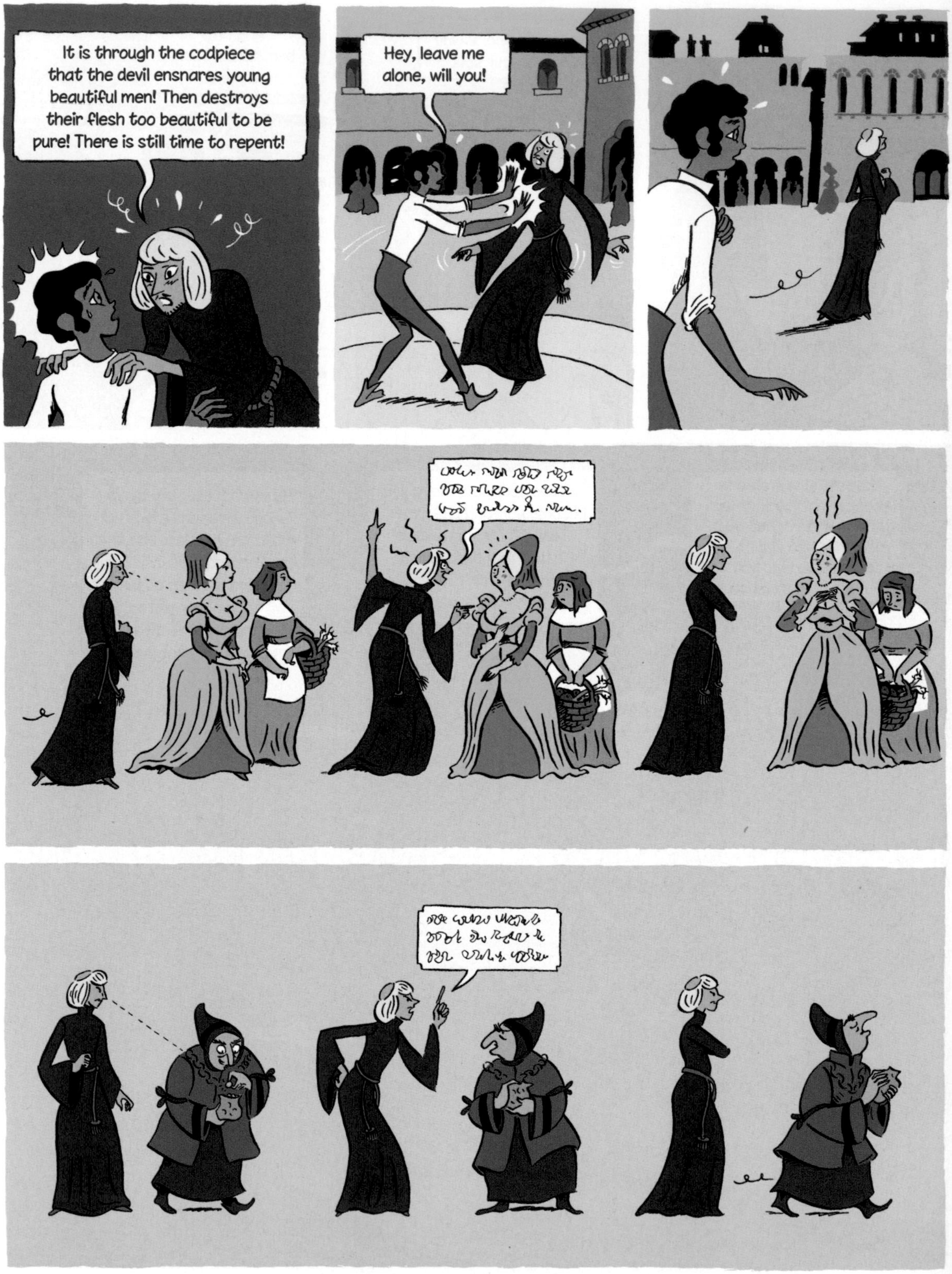
It is through the codpiece that the devil ensnares young beautiful men! Then destroys their flesh too beautiful to be pure! There is still time to repent!
Hey, leave me alone, will you!

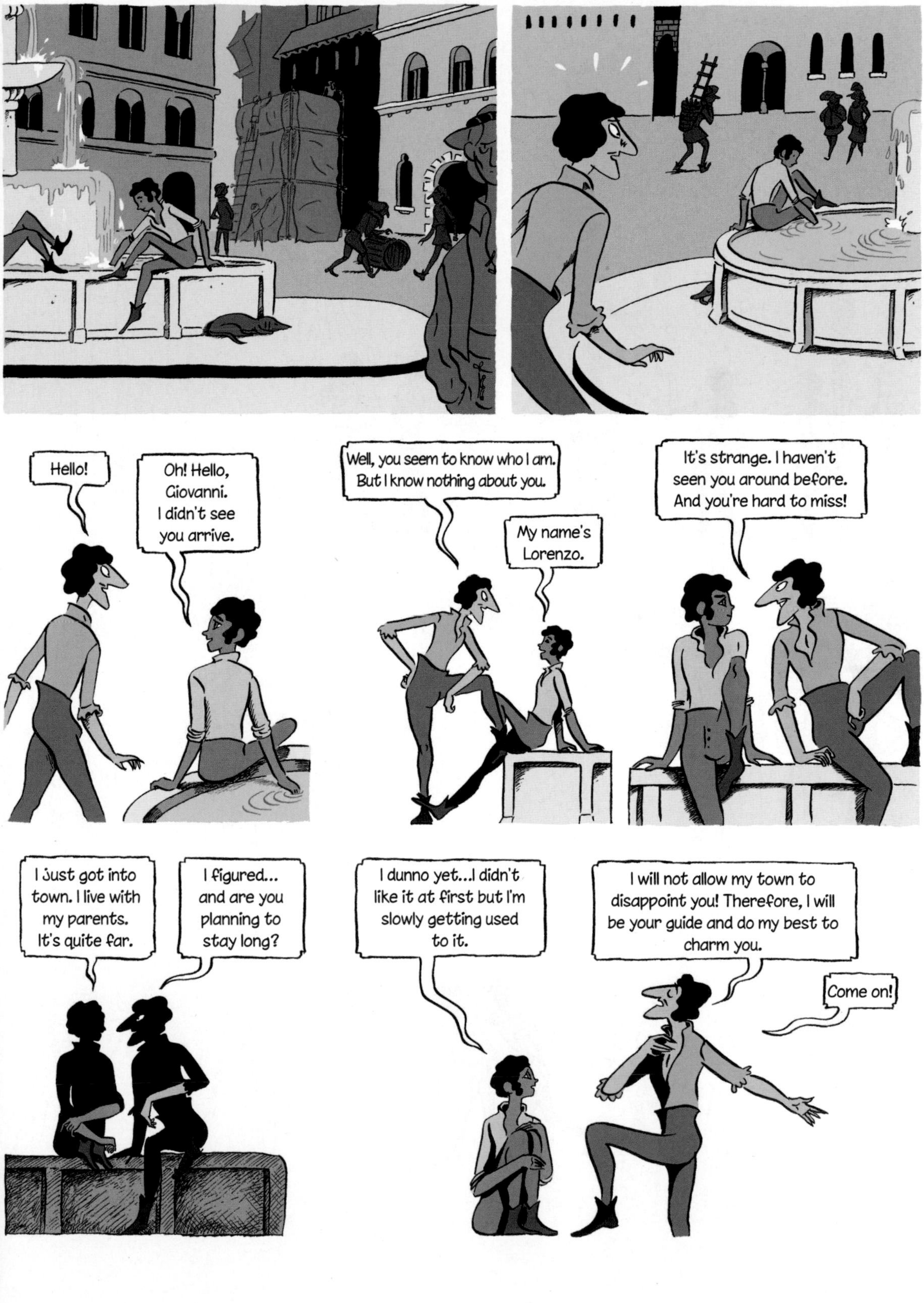
Hello!
Oh! Hello, Giovanni. I didn't see you arrive.
Well, you seem to know who I am. But I know nothing about you.
My name's Lorenzo.
It's strange. I haven't seen you around before. And you're hard to miss!
I just got into town. I live with my parents. It's quite far.
I figured... and are you planning to stay long?
I dunno yet...I didn't like it at first but I'm slowly getting used to it.
I will not allow my town to disappoint you! Therefore, I will be your guide and do my best to charm you.
Come on!

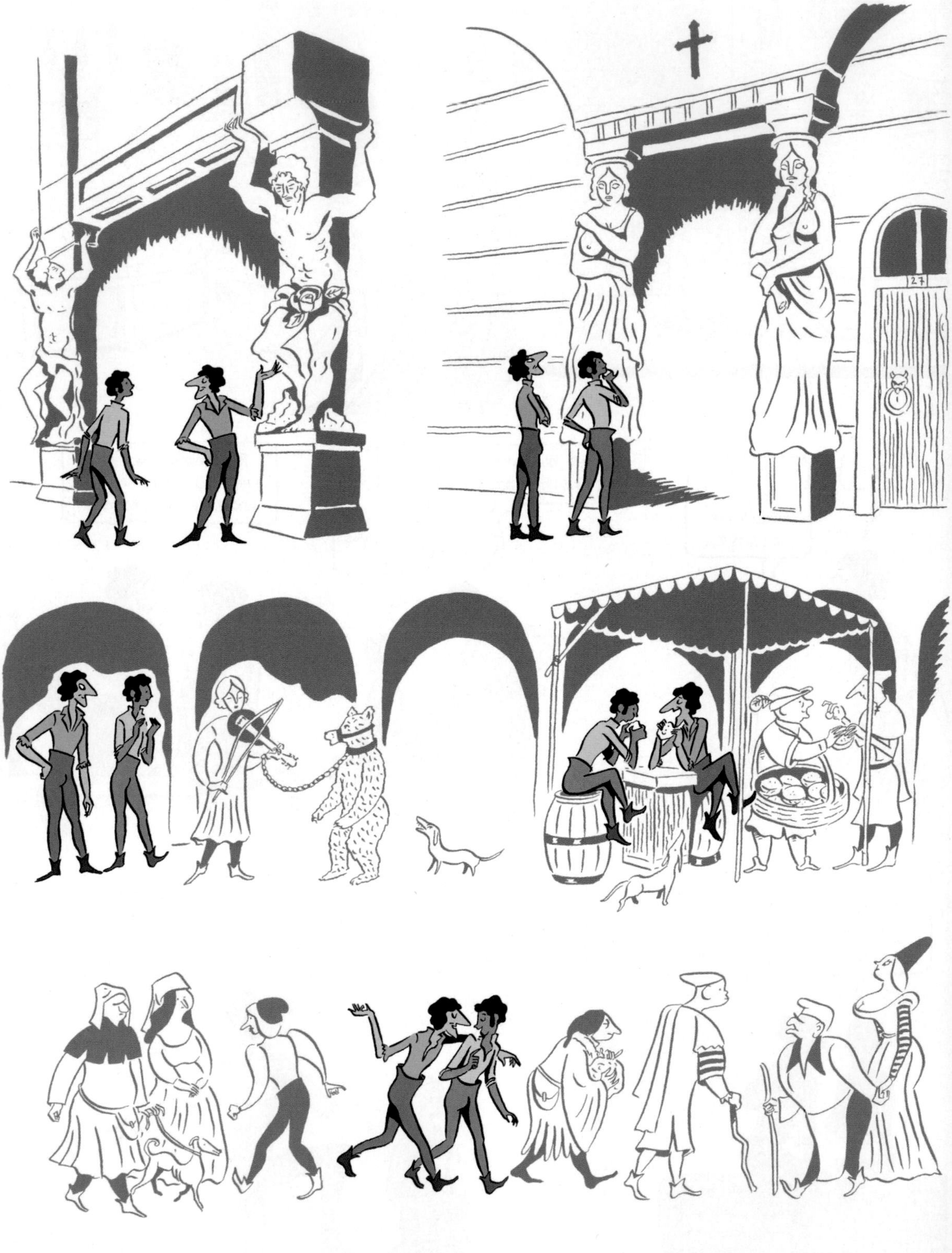
27

The Cross Eyed Cat

D'you wanna go in?

I dunno. It looks a bit grungy, no?

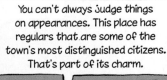

You can't always judge things on appearances. This place has regulars that are some of the town's most distinguished citizens. That's part of its charm.

Really?

You'll never see a woman here. Not even the solicitous type. It's more a Socratic gathering place than a Bacchanalian one.

?

Don't look at me like that! Go on in!

Hey, I thought that there weren't going to be any women?

Her? That's Peccorina! But during the day every-one calls him Peccorino.

The painter?

Herself! At your service, fair squire.

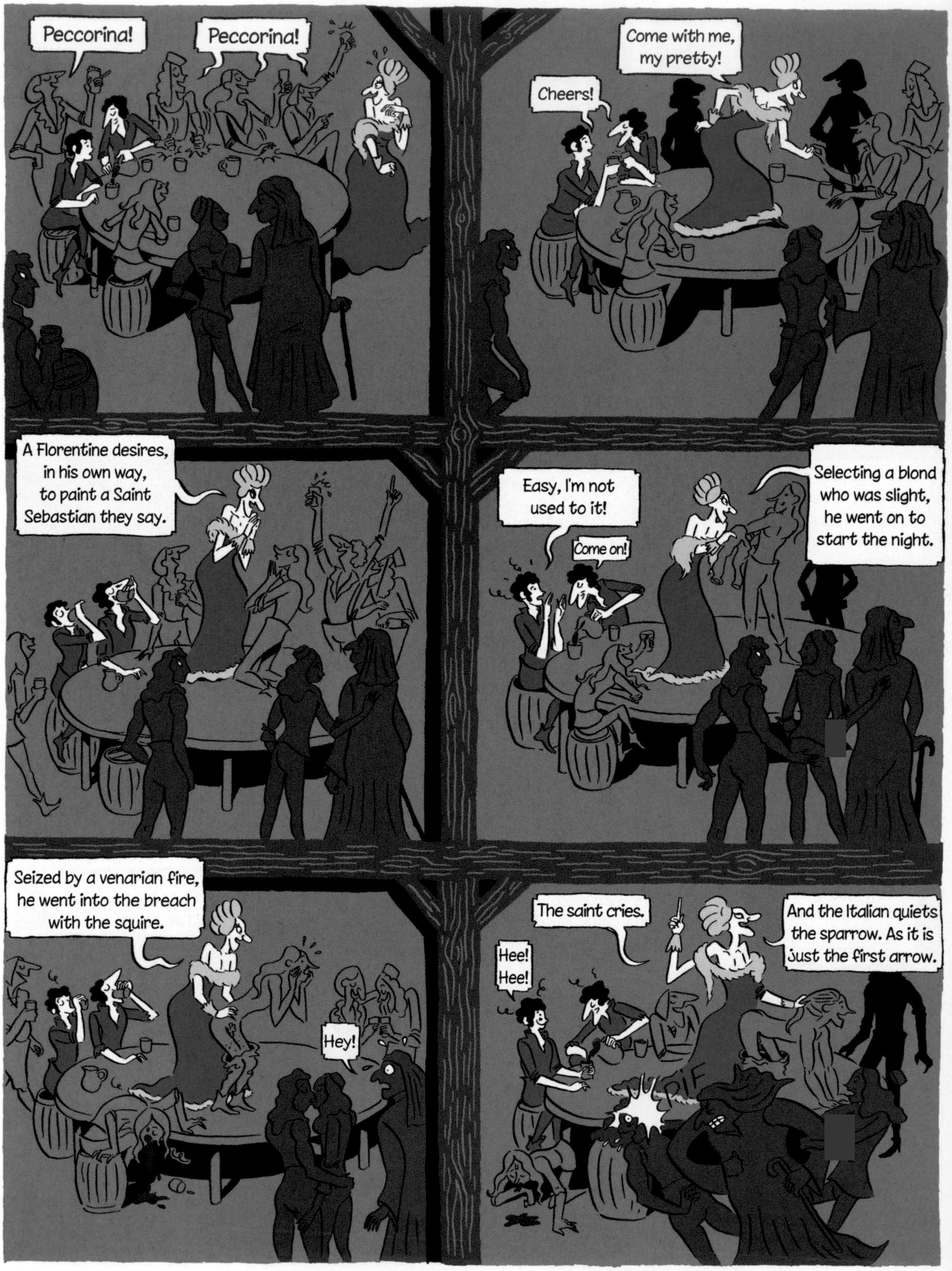
Peccorina!
Peccorina!
Come with me, my pretty!
Cheers!
A Florentine desires, in his own way, to paint a Saint Sebastian they say.
Easy, I'm not used to it!
Come on!
Selecting a blond who was slight, he went on to start the night.
Seized by a venarian fire, he went into the breach with the squire.
Hey!
The saint cries.
Hee! Hee!
And the Italian quiets the sparrow. As it is just the first arrow.
PIF

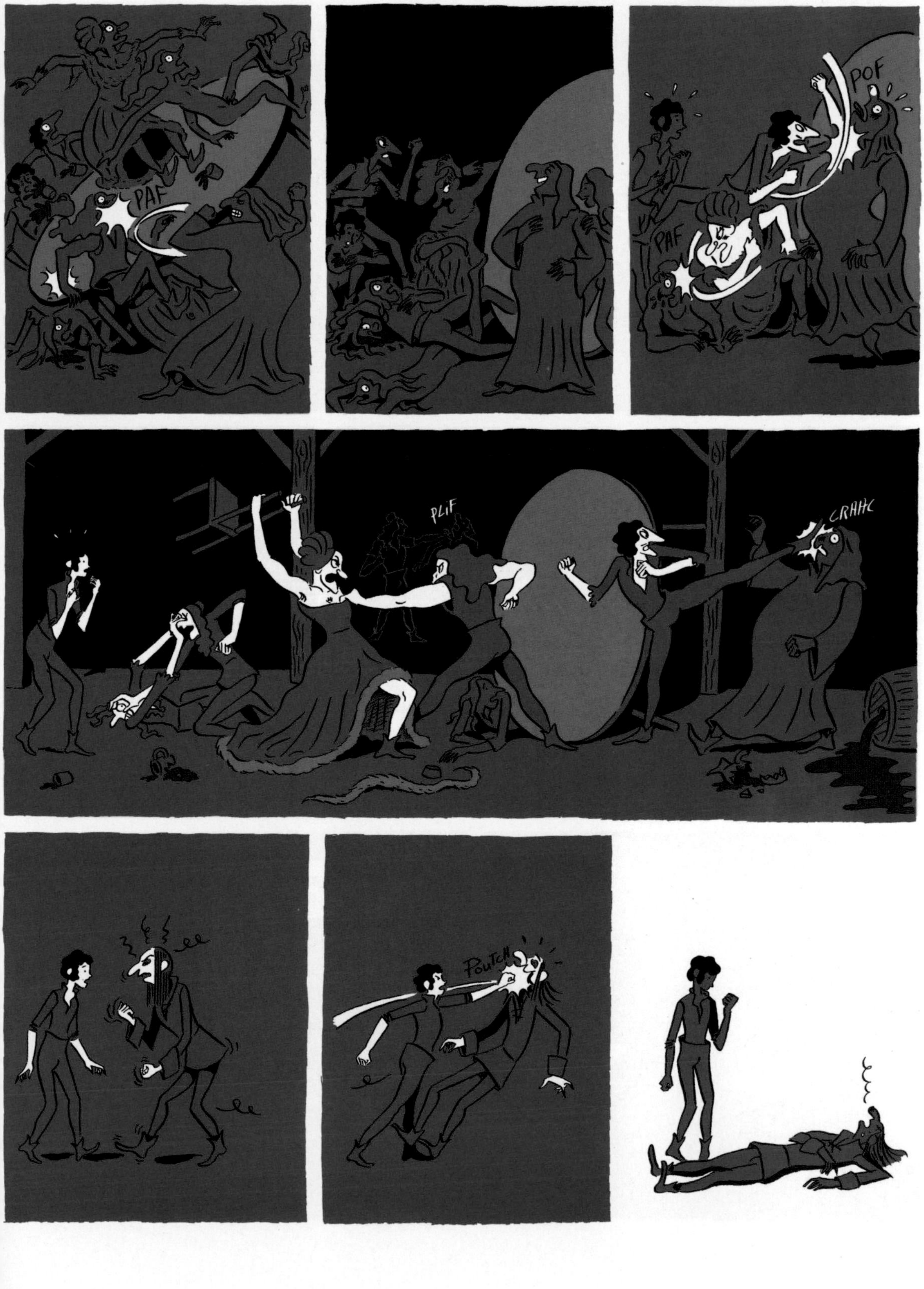
PAF
POF
PAF
PLIF
CRAHC
POUTCH

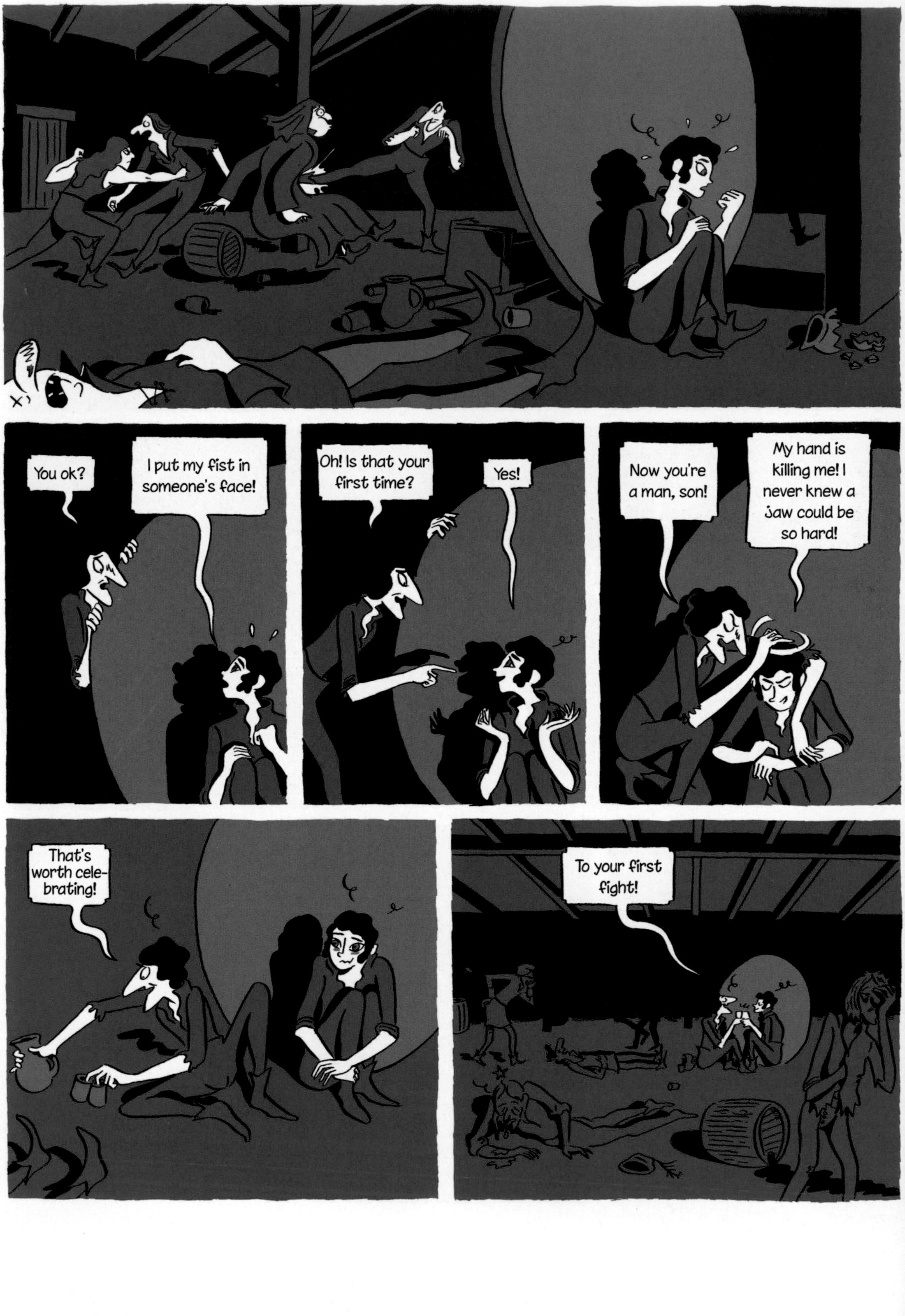
You ok?
I put my fist in someone's face!
Oh! Is that your first time?
Yes!
Now you're a man, son!
My hand is killing me! I never knew a jaw could be so hard!
That's worth cele-brating!
To your first fight!

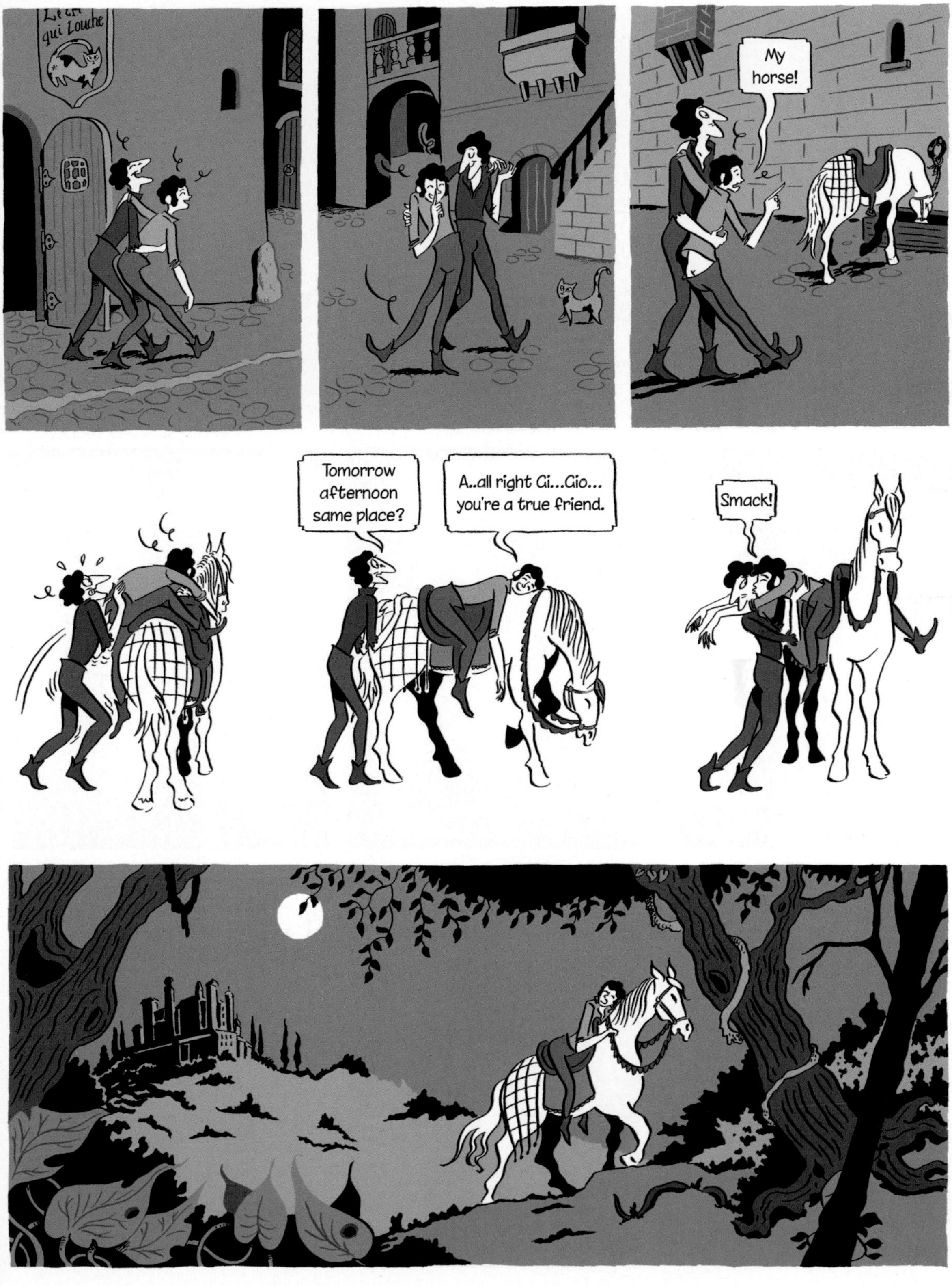
qui Louche
My horse!
Tomorrow afternoon same place?
A..all right Gi...Gio... you're a true friend.
Smack!

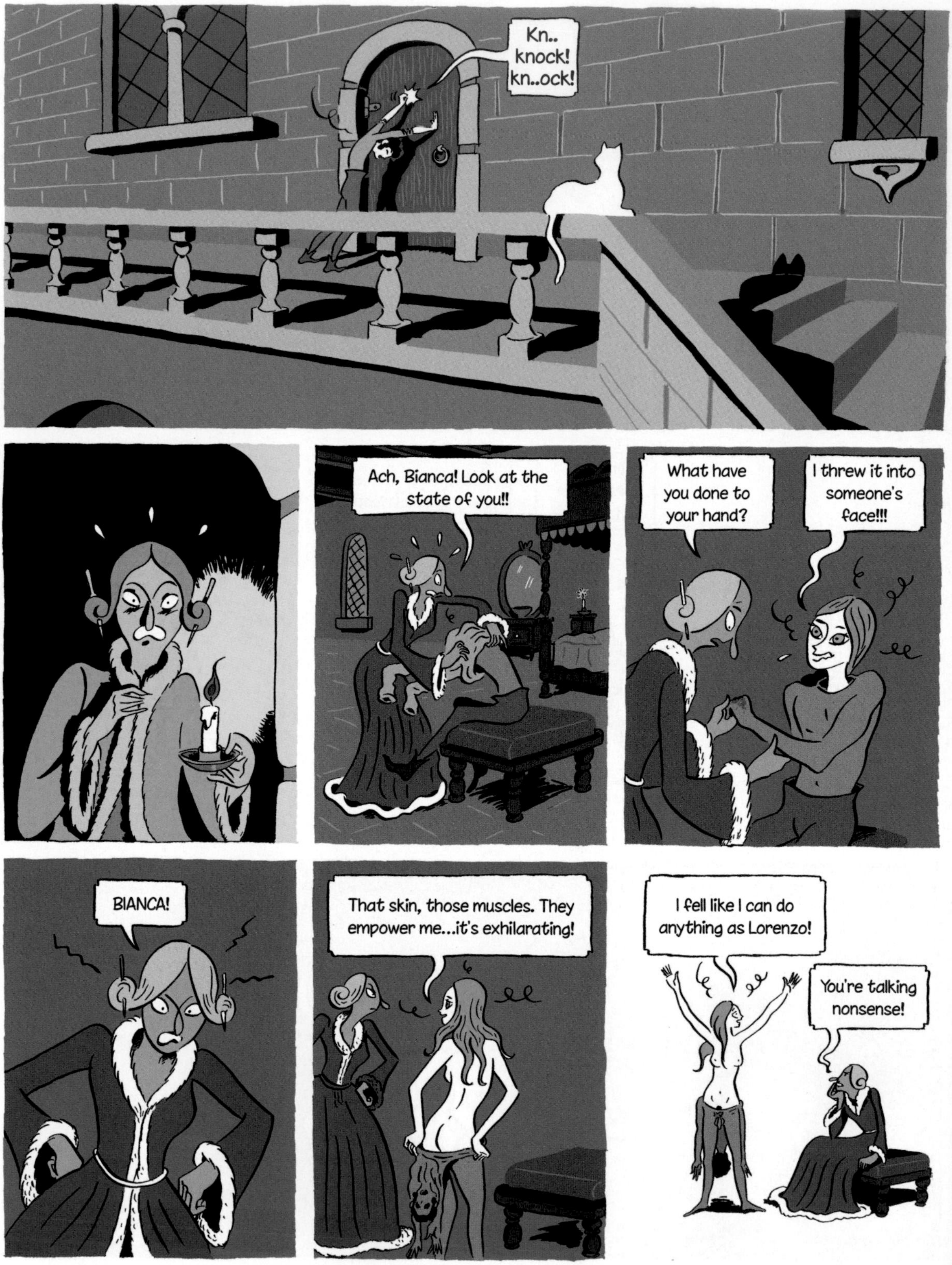
Kn..
knock!
kn..ock!
Ach, Bianca! Look at the state of you!!
What have you done to your hand?
I threw it into someone's face!!!
BIANCA!
That skin, those muscles. They empower me...it's exhilarating!
I fell like I can do anything as Lorenzo!
You're talking nonsense!

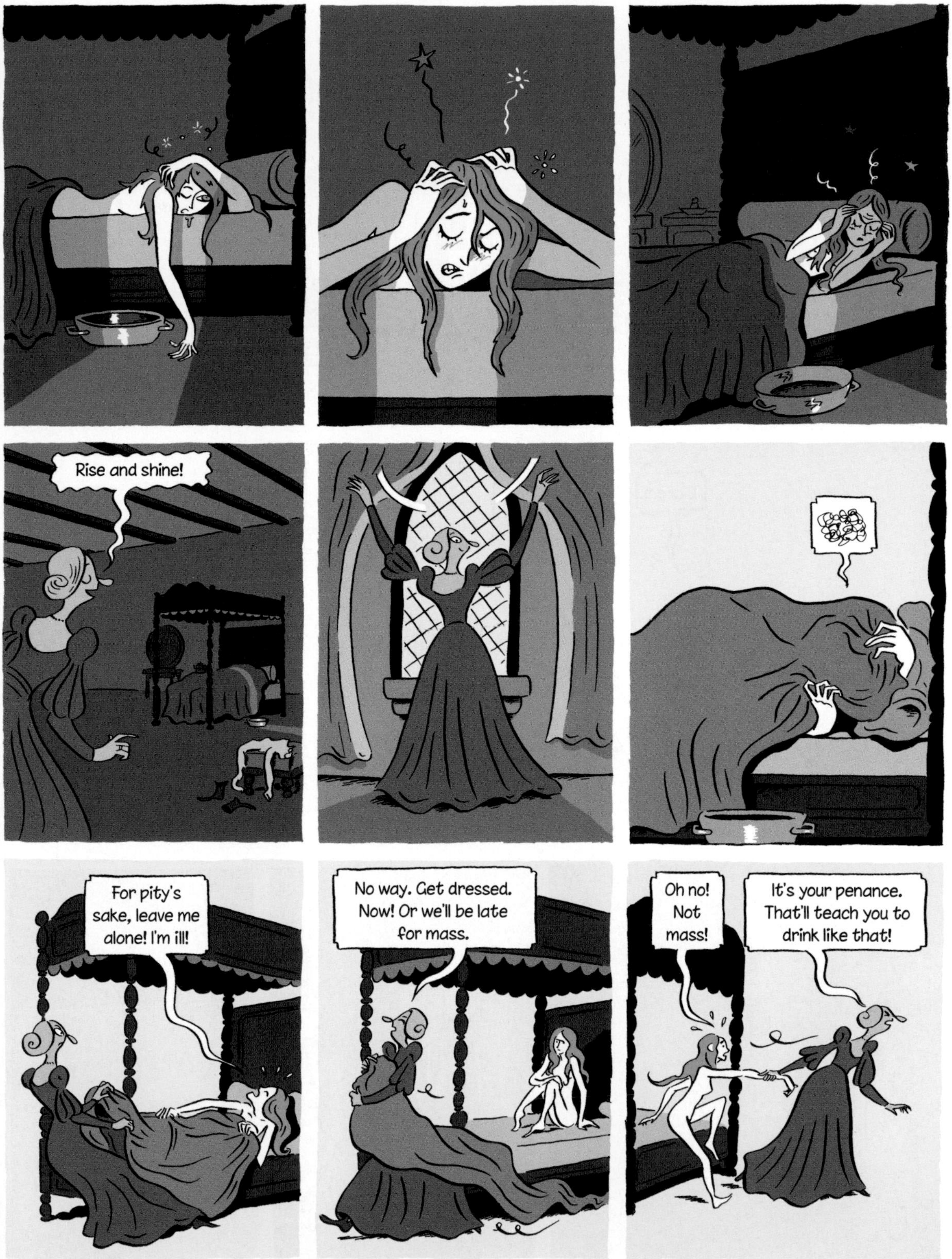

Rise and shine!
For pity's sake, leave me alone! I'm ill!
No way. Get dressed. Now! Or we'll be late for mass.
Oh no! Not mass!
It's your penance. That'll teach you to drink like that!

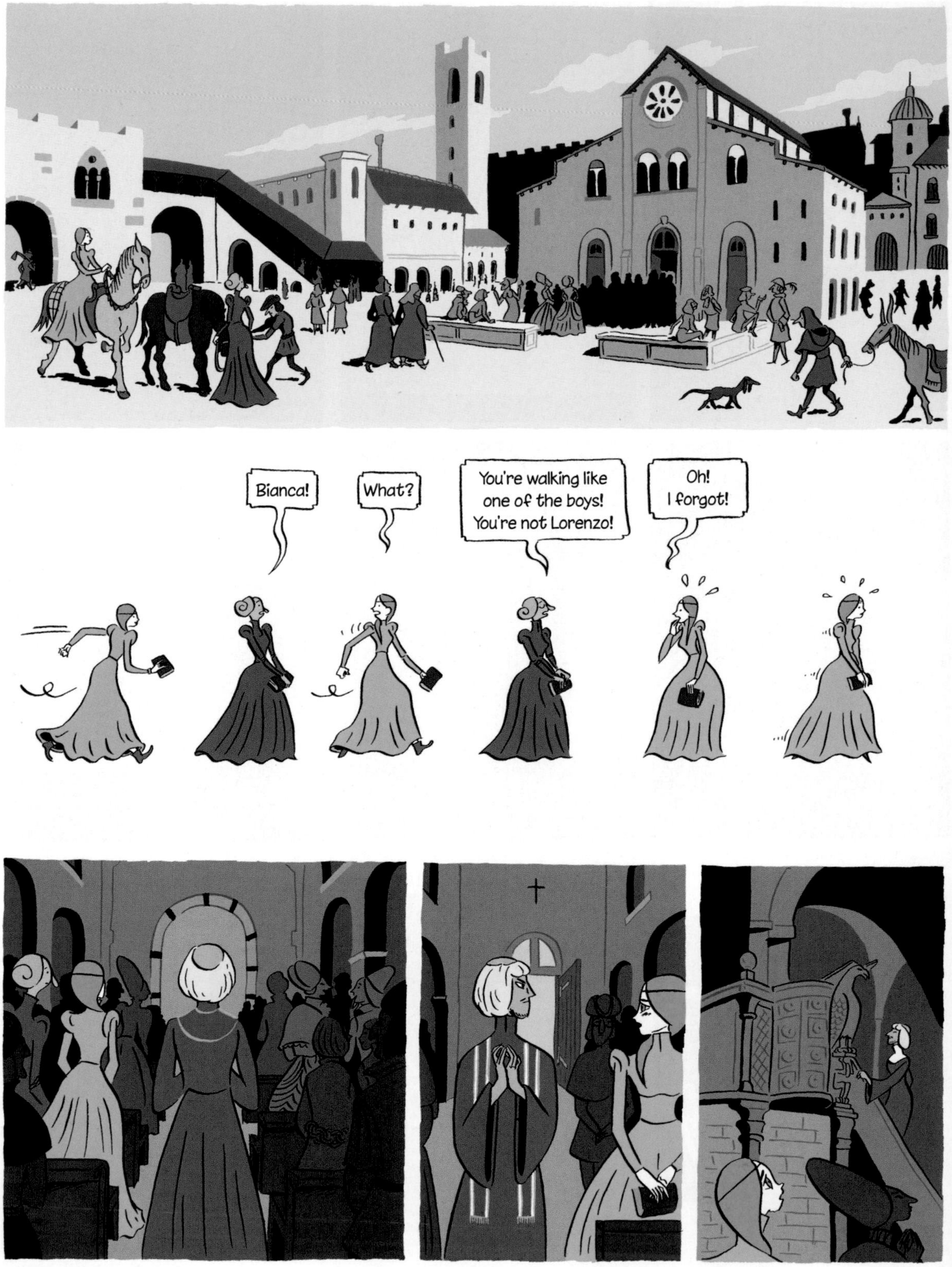
Bianca!
What?
You're walking like one of the boys! You're not Lorenzo!
Oh! I forgot!

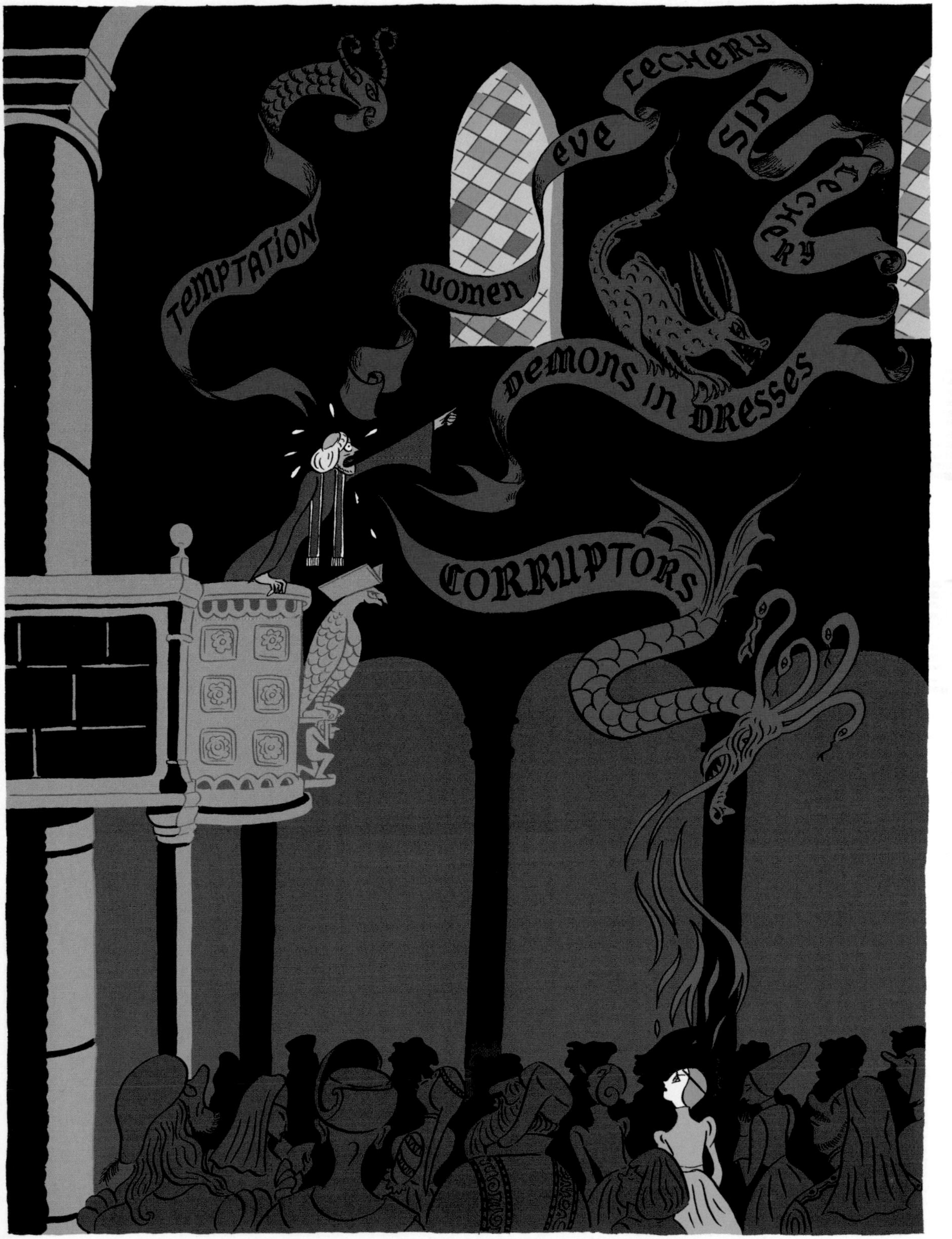

TEMPTATION
women
eve
LECHERY
SIN
LECHERY
DEMONS IN DRESSES
CORRUPTORS

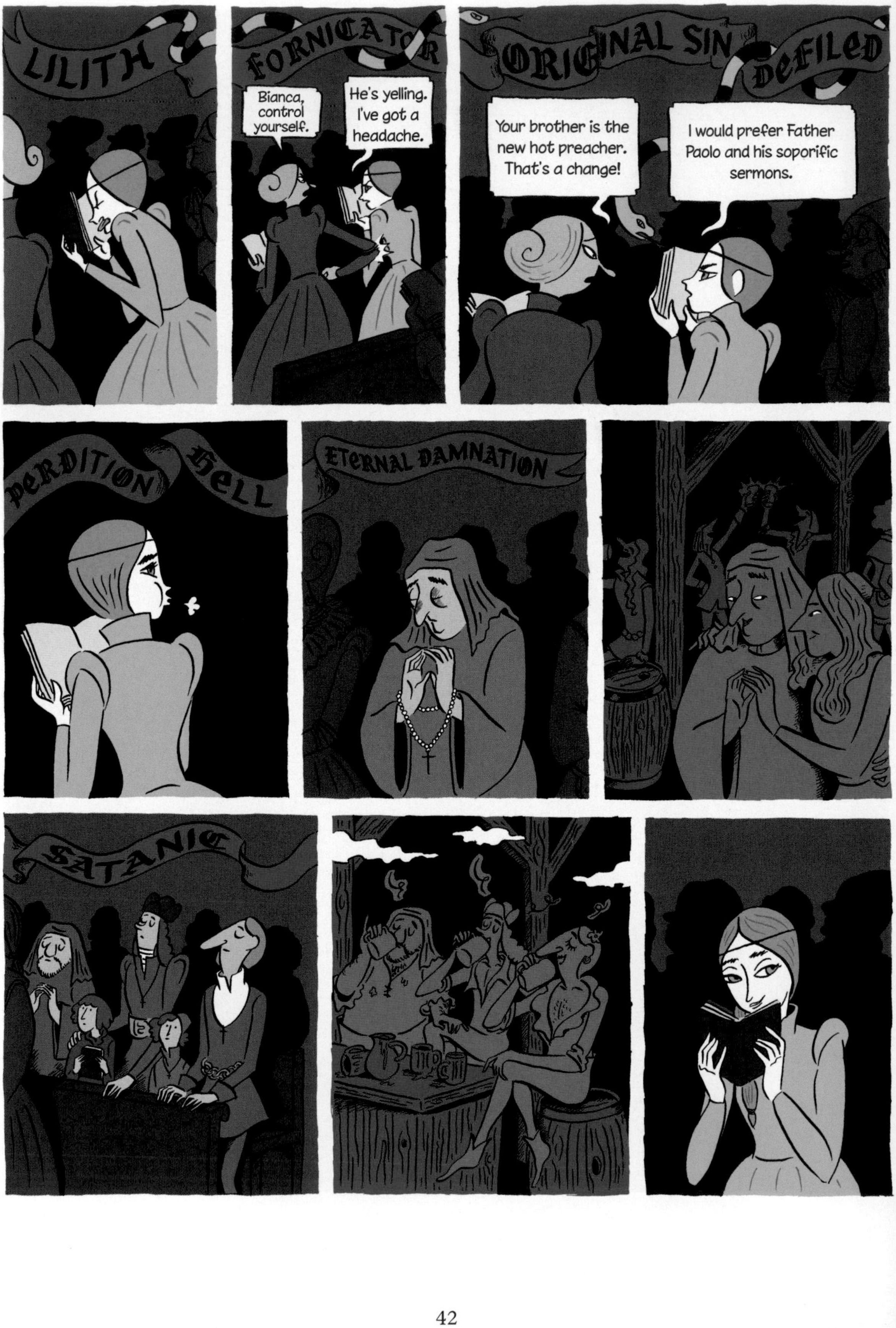
LILITH
FORNICATOR
Bianca, control yourself.
He's yelling. I've got a headache.
ORIGINAL SIN
DEFILED
Your brother is the new hot preacher. That's a change!
I would prefer Father Paolo and his soporific sermons.
PERDITION
HELL
ETERNAL DAMNATION
SATANIC

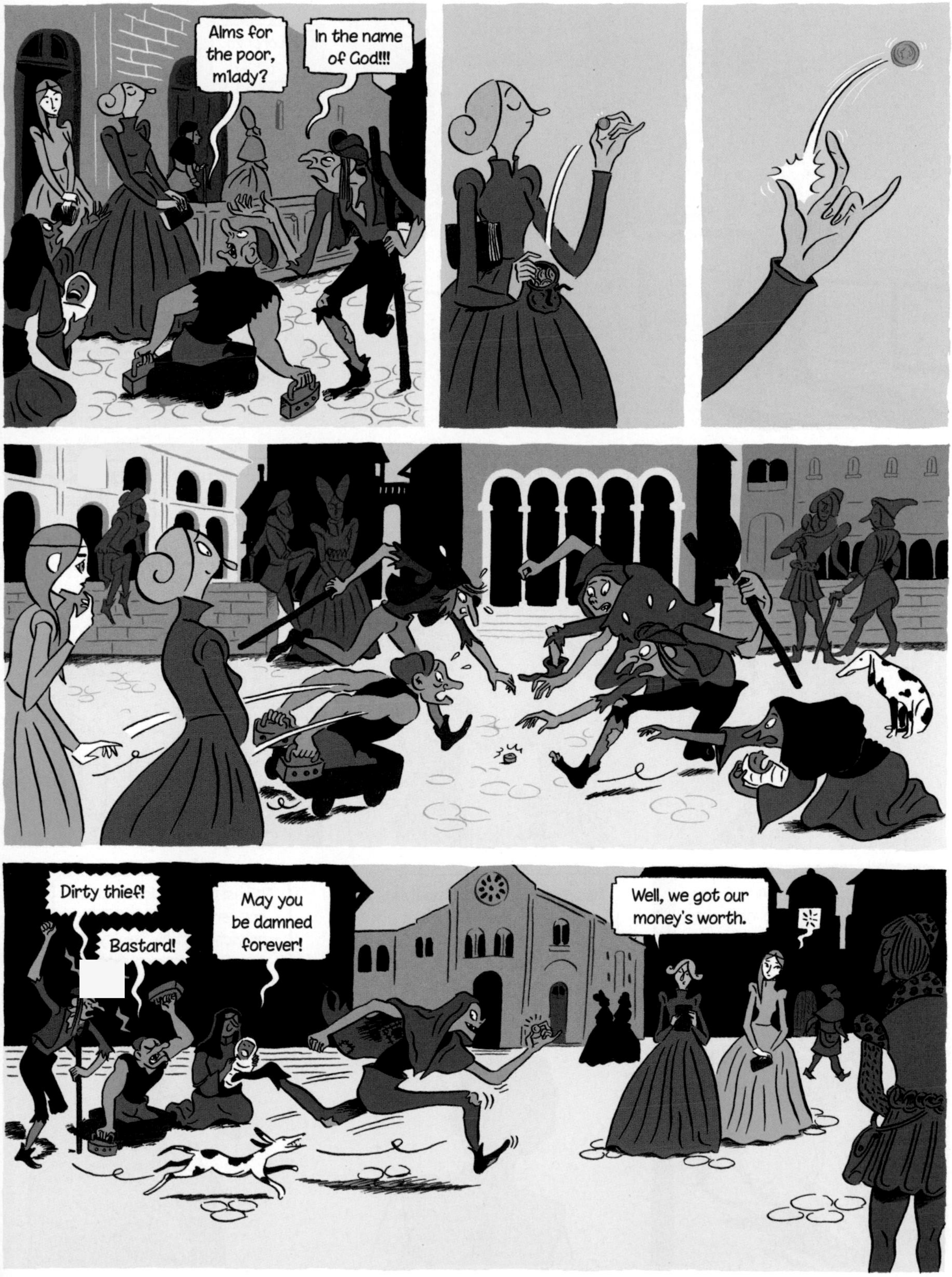
Alms for the poor, m'lady?
In the name of God!!!
Dirty thief!
Bastard!
May you be damned forever!
Well, we got our money's worth.
!

Lorenzo, finally!

Hello, Giovanni!

You're really late! I thought you weren't coming.

I'm hung over.

Not surprising! You were pretty far gone last night.

I don't know how I got home.

You could have just stayed. I would have put you up for the night...

I'll consider it next time.

And this morning at mass, it was terrible.

Mass? The morning after such a night? You're crazy!

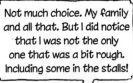

Not much choice. My family and all that. But I did notice that I was not the only one that was a bit rough. Including some in the stalls!

Ah yes! Our religious leaders are very ecumenical! They preach the holy trinity by day, Bacchus by night and Mammon at all times!

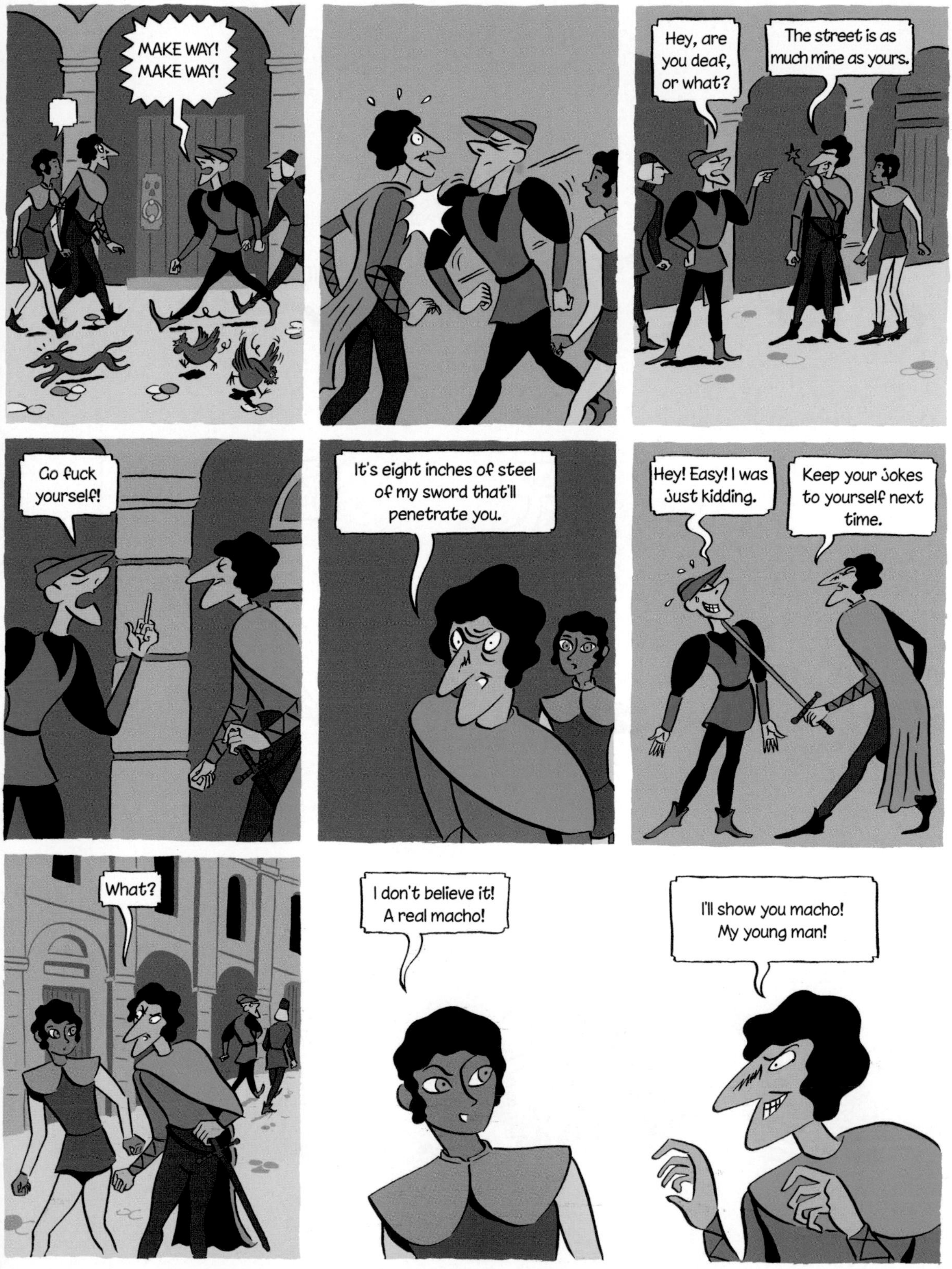
MAKE WAY!
MAKE WAY!
Hey, are you deaf, or what?
The street is as much mine as yours.
Go fuck yourself!
It's eight inches of steel of my sword that'll penetrate you.
Hey! Easy! I was just kidding.
Keep your jokes to yourself next time.
What?
I don't believe it! A real macho!
I'll show you macho! My young man!

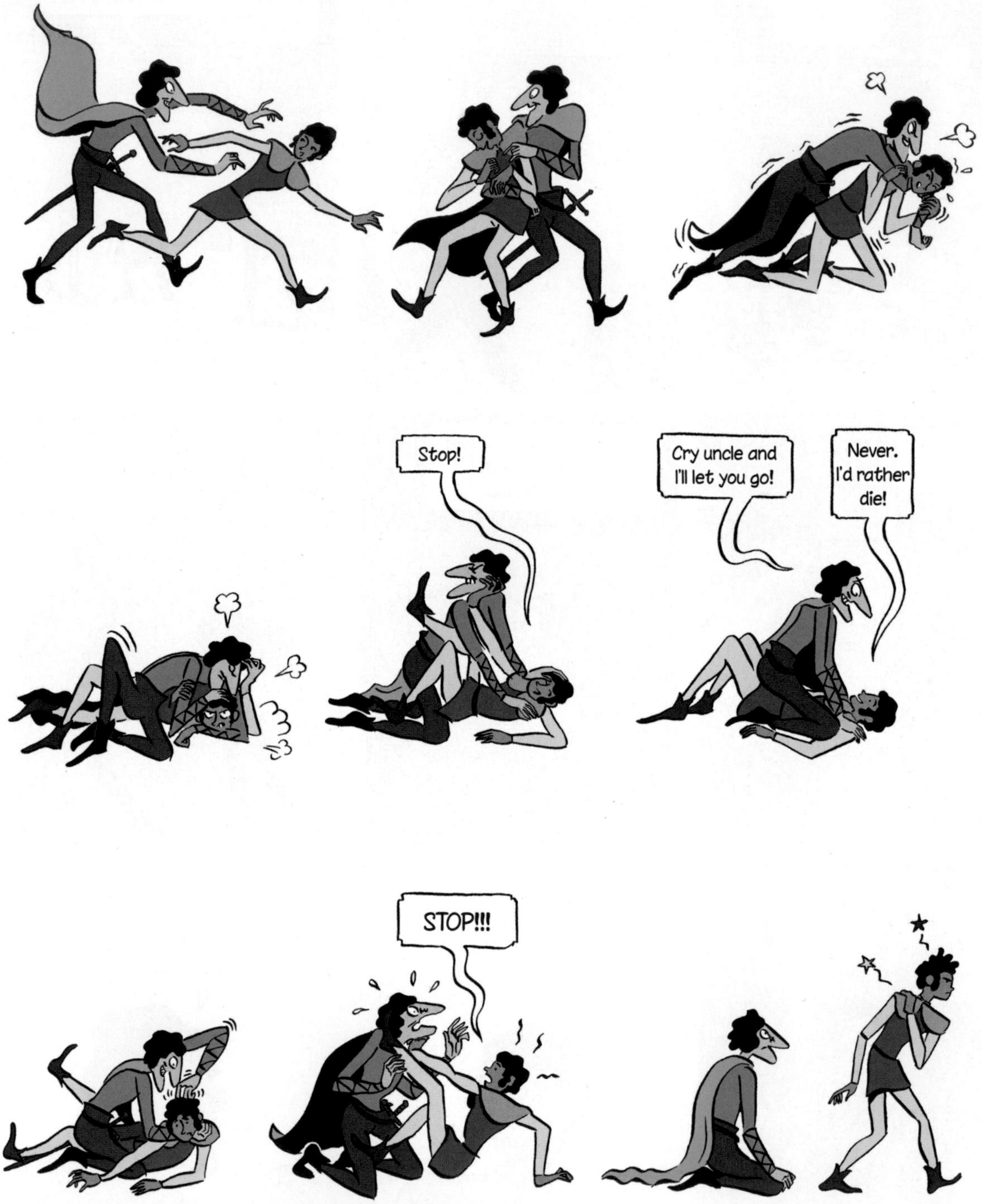
Stop!
Cry uncle and I'll let you go!
Never. I'd rather die!
STOP!!!

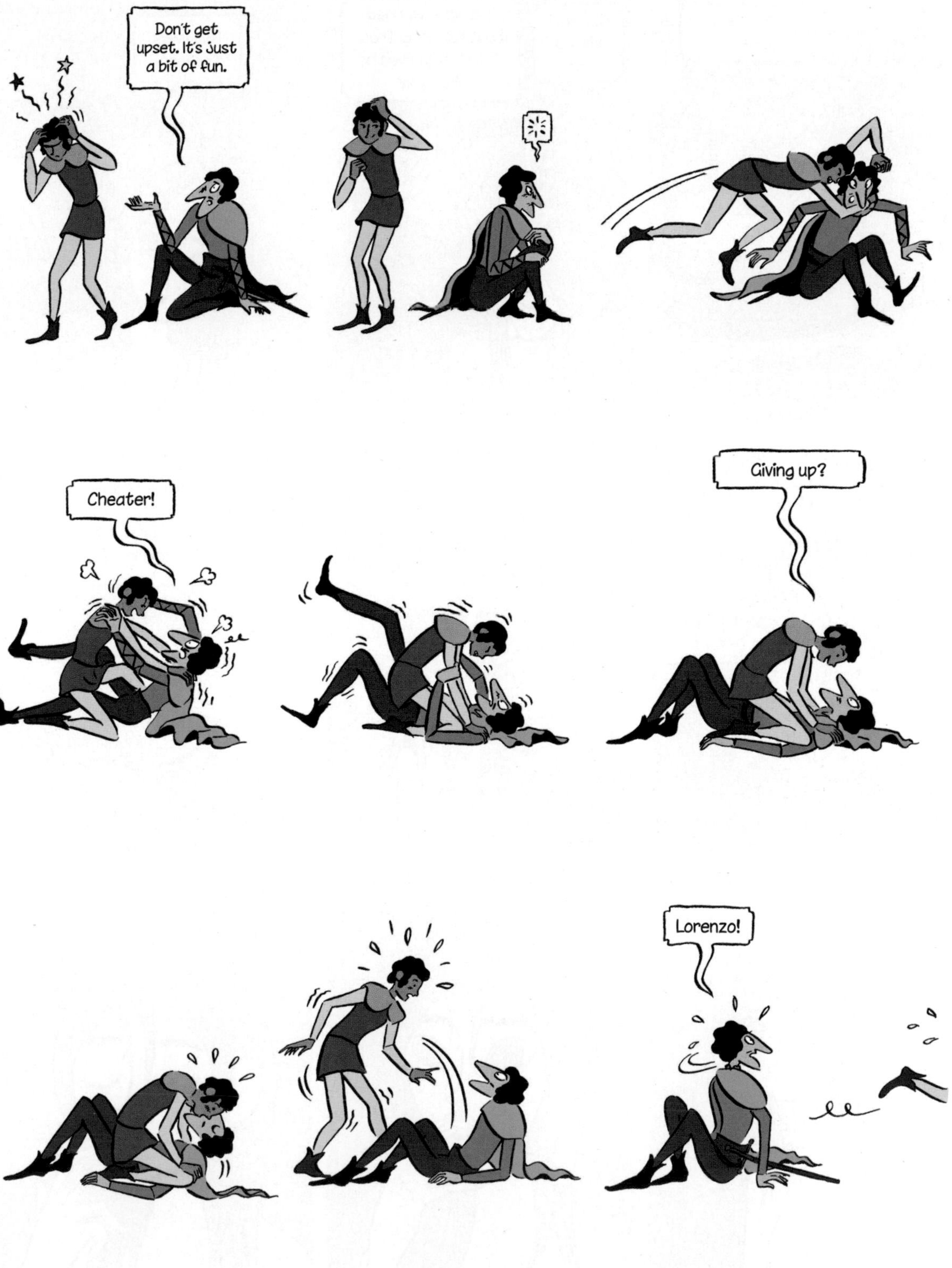
Don't get upset. It's just a bit of fun.
Cheater!
Giving up?
Lorenzo!

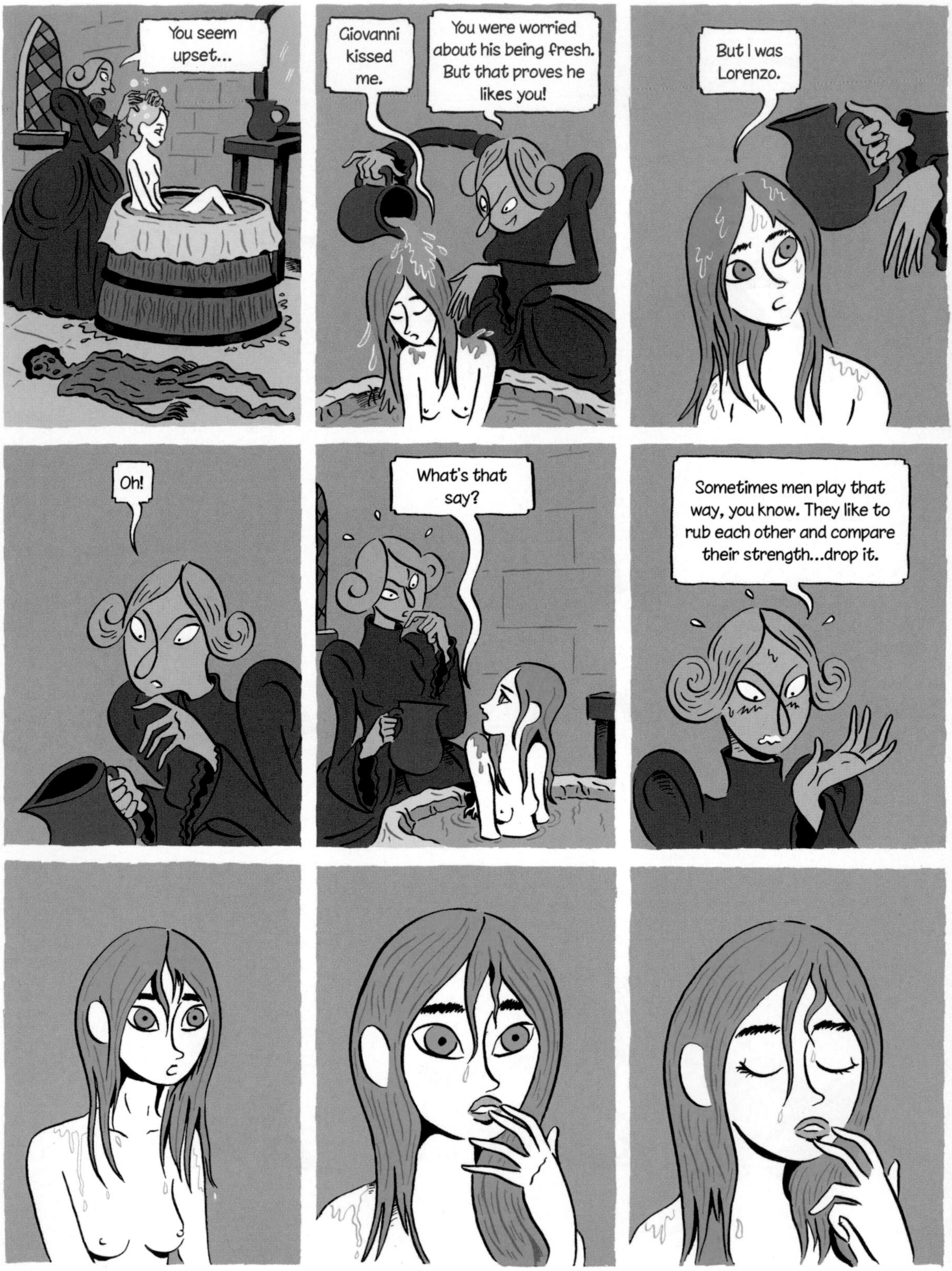
You seem upset...
Giovanni kissed me.
You were worried about his being fresh. But that proves he likes you!
But I was Lorenzo.
Oh!
What's that say?
Sometimes men play that way, you know. They like to rub each other and compare their strength...drop it.

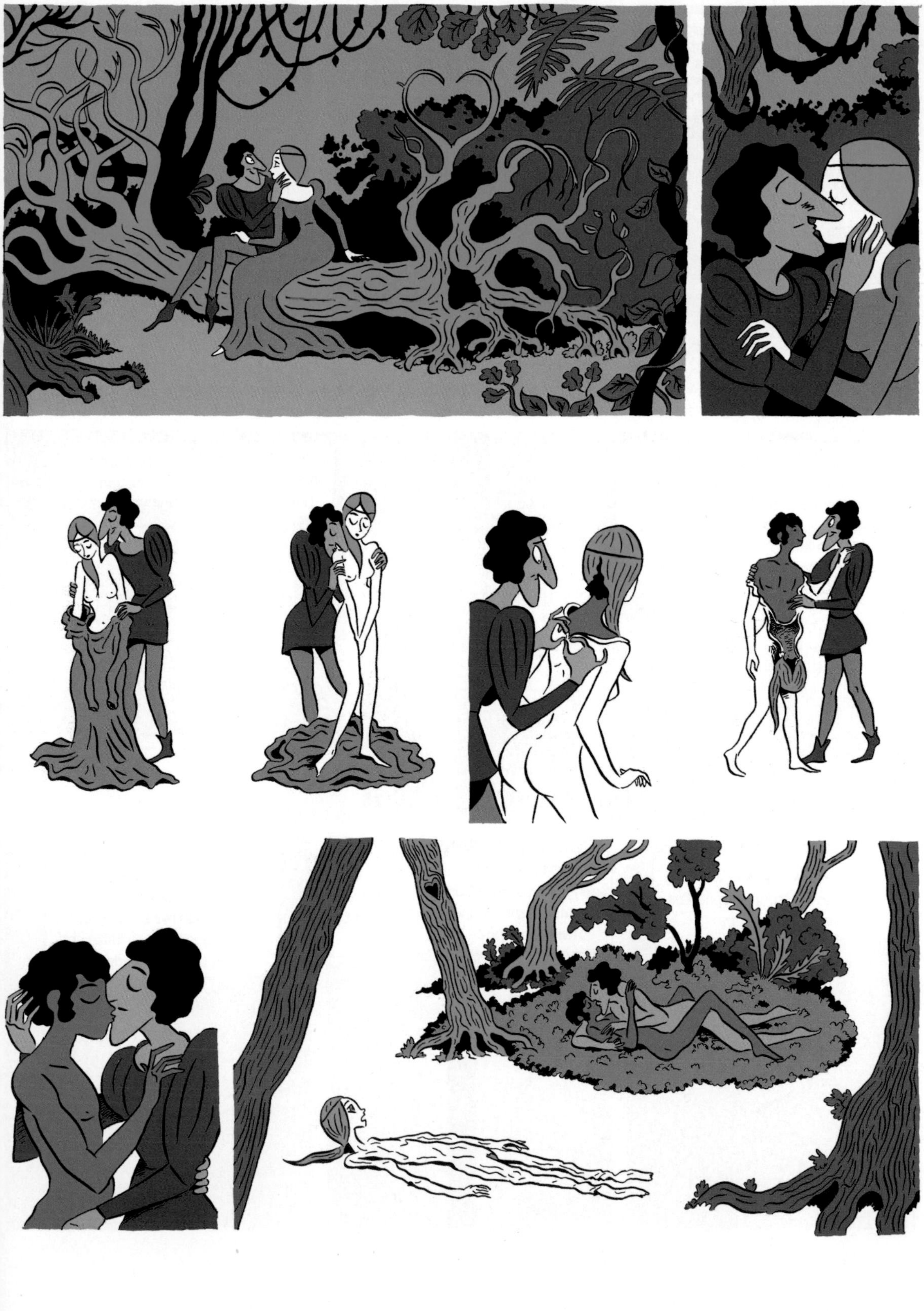

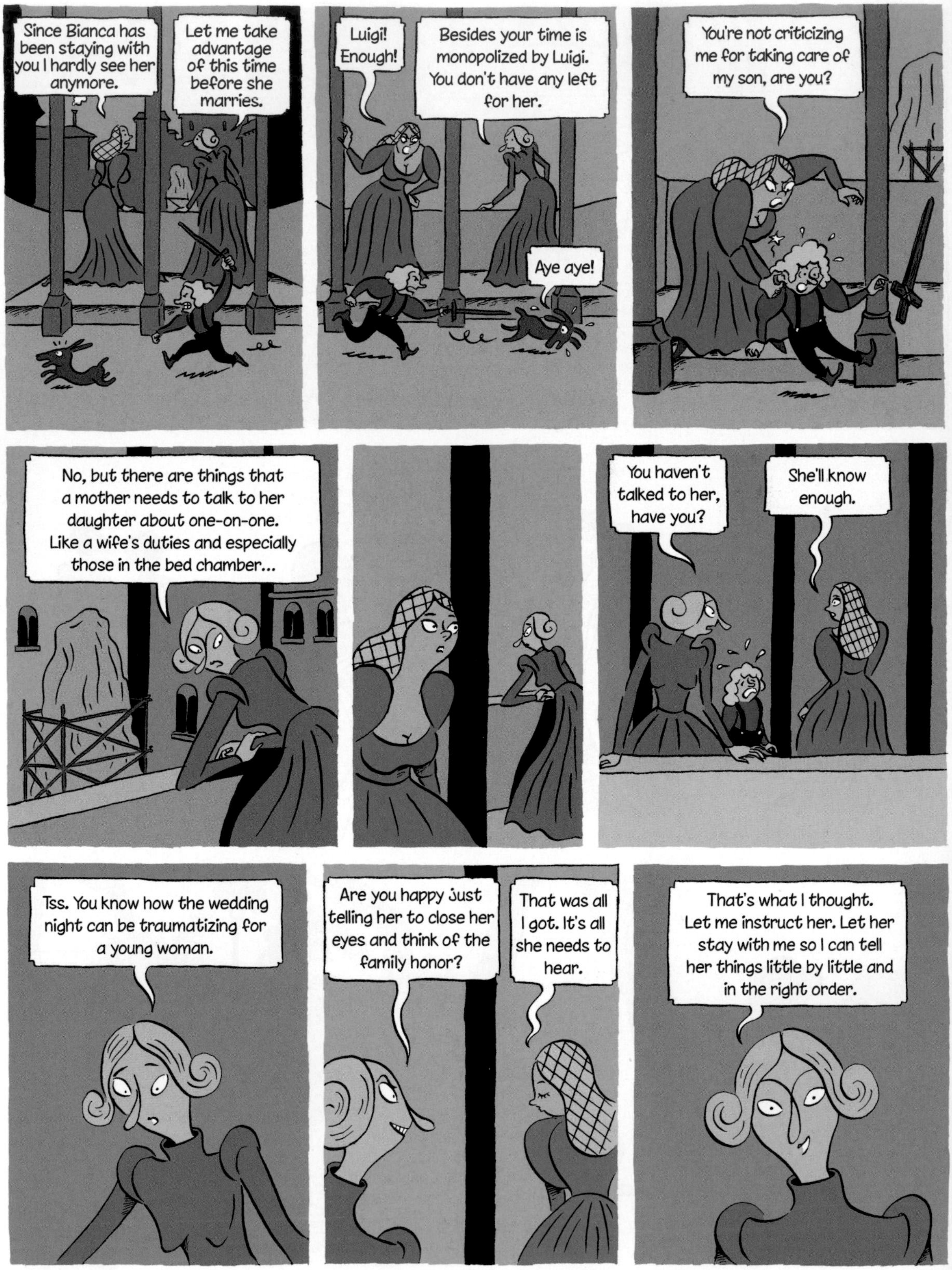
Since Bianca has been staying with you I hardly see her anymore.
Let me take advantage of this time before she marries.
Luigi! Enough!
Besides your time is monopolized by Luigi. You don't have any left for her.
Aye aye!
You're not criticizing me for taking care of my son, are you?
No, but there are things that a mother needs to talk to her daughter about one-on-one. Like a wife's duties and especially those in the bed chamber...
You haven't talked to her, have you?
She'll know enough.
Tss. You know how the wedding night can be traumatizing for a young woman.
Are you happy just telling her to close her eyes and think of the family honor?
That was all I got. It's all she needs to hear.
That's what I thought. Let me instruct her. Let her stay with me so I can tell her things little by little and in the right order.

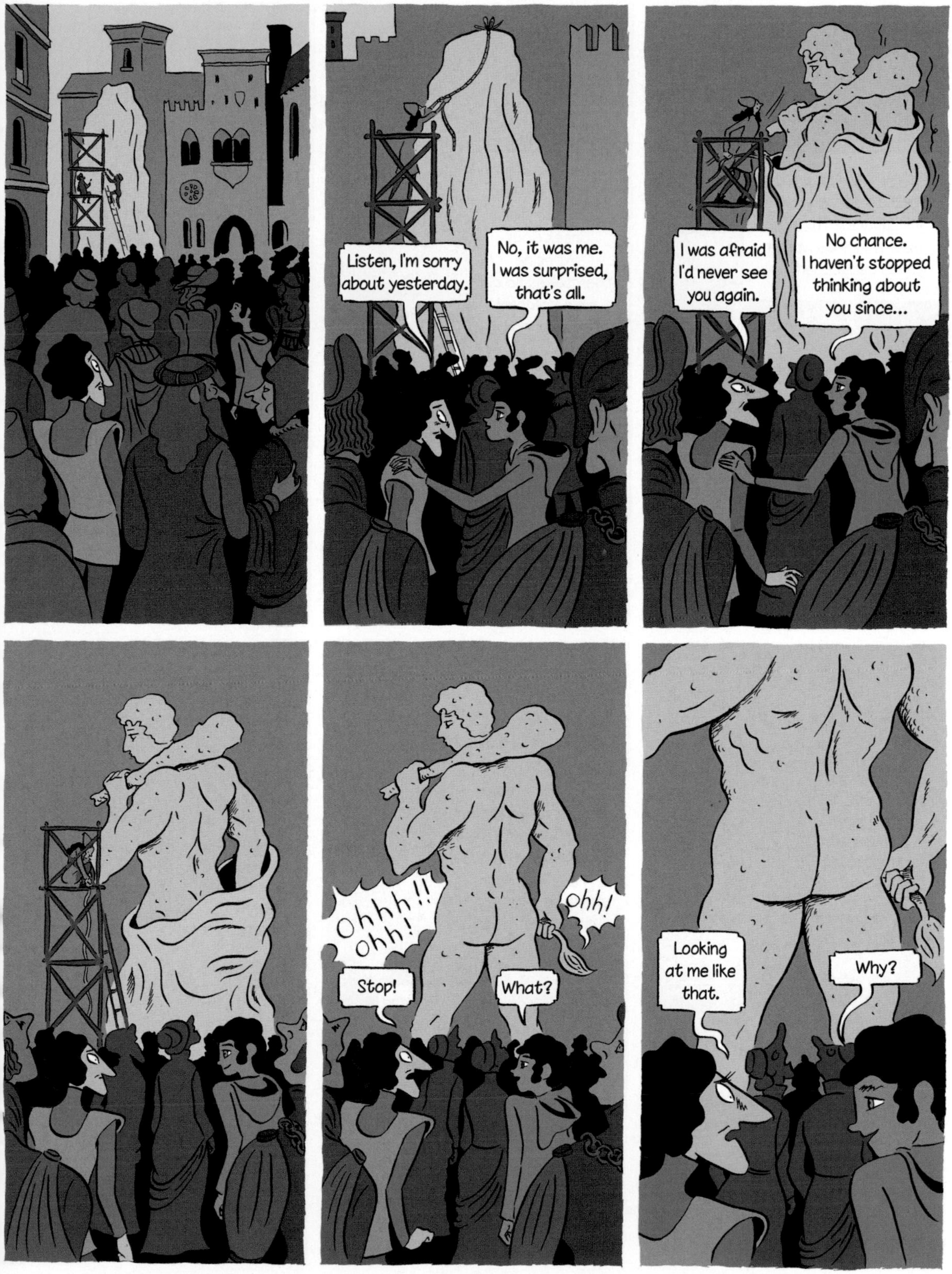
Listen, I'm sorry about yesterday.
No, it was me. I was surprised, that's all.
I was afraid I'd never see you again.
No chance. I haven't stopped thinking about you since...
Ohhh!! ohh!
Ohh!
Stop!
What?
Looking at me like that.
Why?

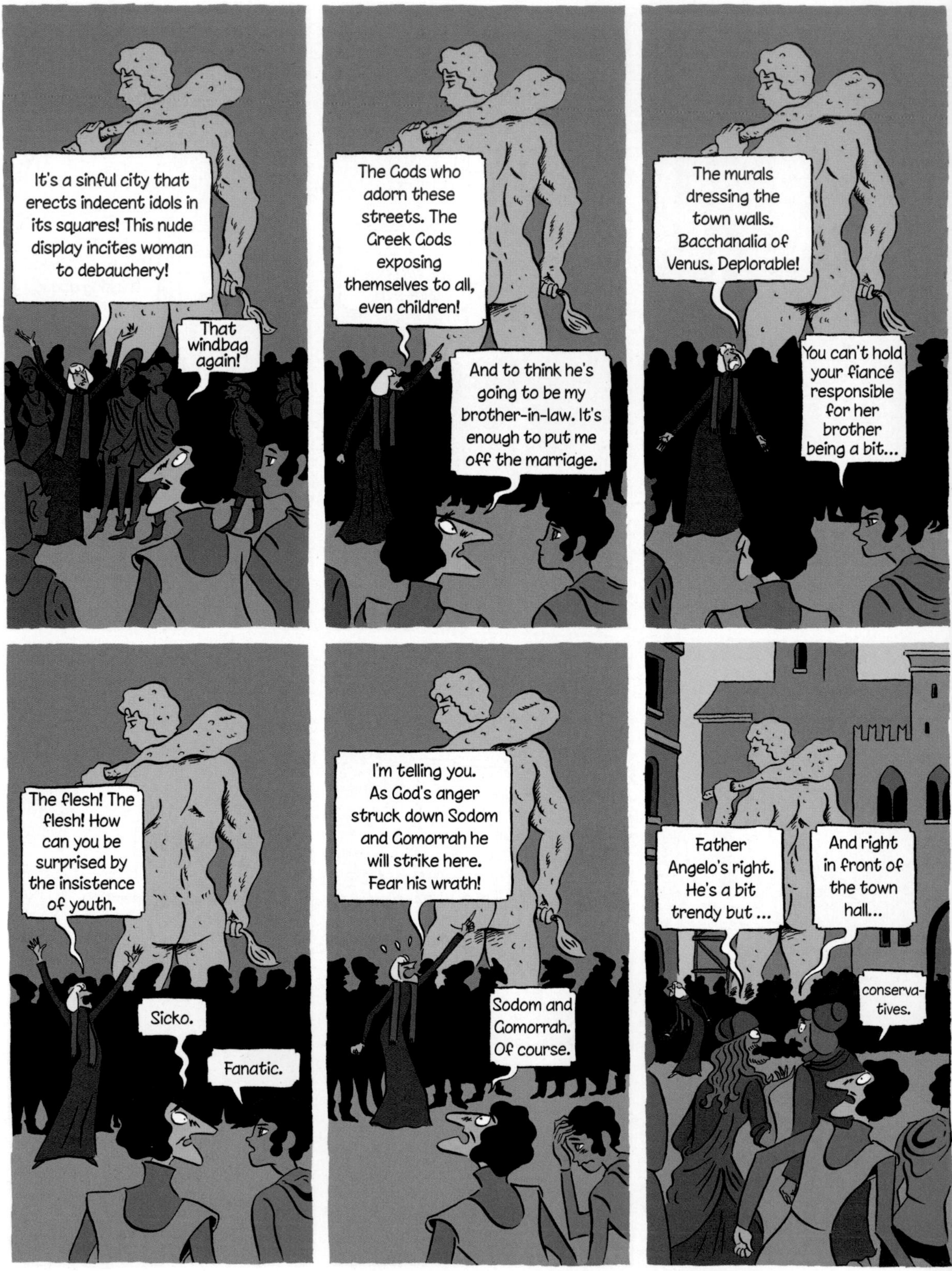
It's a sinful city that erects indecent idols in its squares! This nude display incites woman to debauchery!
That windbag again!
The Gods who adorn these streets. The Greek Gods exposing themselves to all, even children!
And to think he's going to be my brother-in-law. It's enough to put me off the marriage.
The murals dressing the town walls. Bacchanalia of Venus. Deplorable!
You can't hold your fiancé responsible for her brother being a bit...
The flesh! The flesh! How can you be surprised by the insistence of youth.
Sicko.
Fanatic.
I'm telling you. As God's anger struck down Sodom and Gomorrah he will strike here. Fear his wrath!
Sodom and Gomorrah. Of course.
Father Angelo's right. He's a bit trendy but ...
And right in front of the town hall...
conserva-tives.

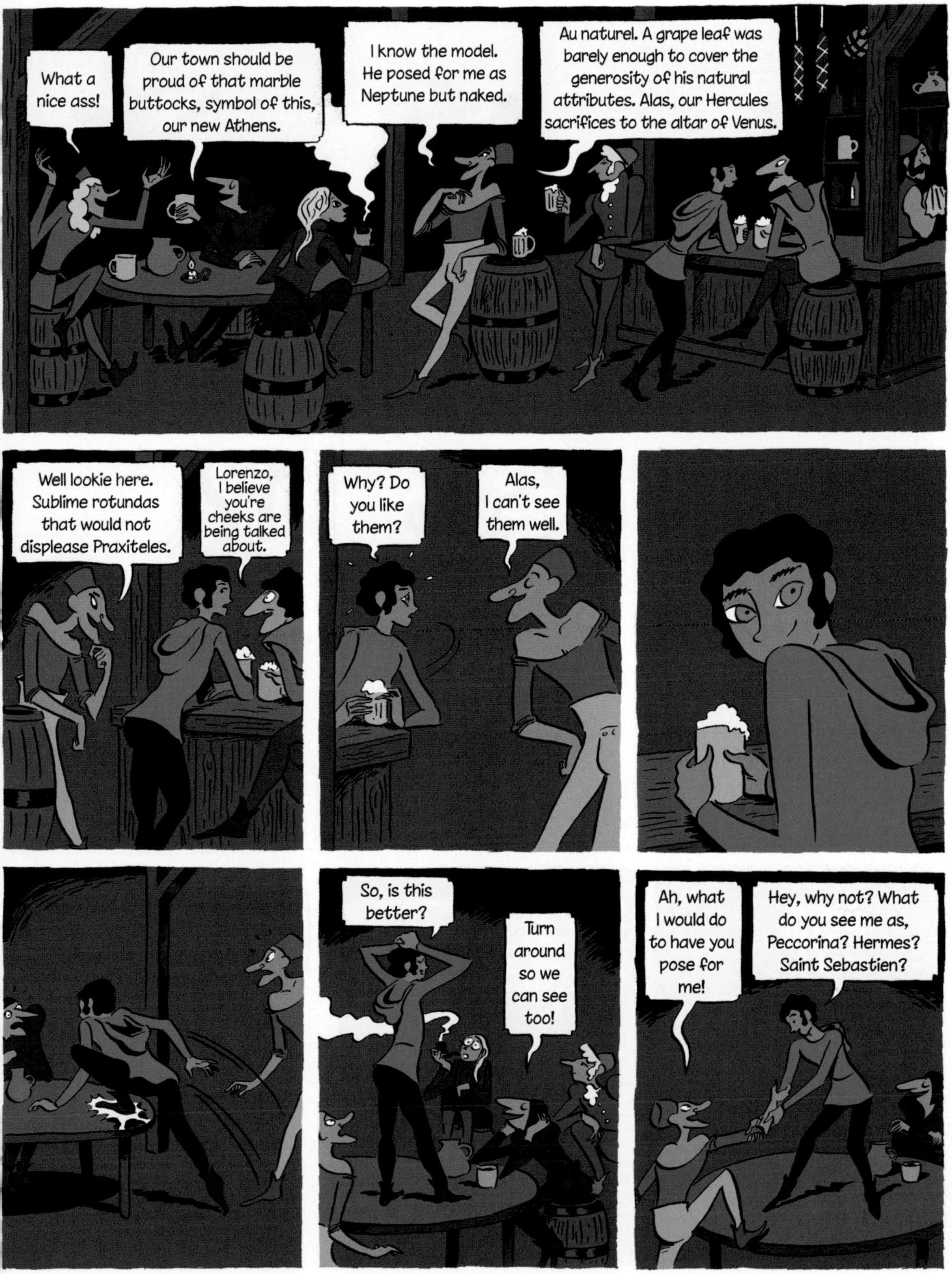
What a nice ass!
Our town should be proud of that marble buttocks, symbol of this, our new Athens.
I know the model. He posed for me as Neptune but naked.
Au naturel. A grape leaf was barely enough to cover the generosity of his natural attributes. Alas, our Hercules sacrifices to the altar of Venus.
Well lookie here. Sublime rotundas that would not displease Praxiteles.
Lorenzo, I believe you're cheeks are being talked about.
Why? Do you like them?
Alas, I can't see them well.
So, is this better?
Turn around so we can see too!
Ah, what I would do to have you pose for me!
Hey, why not? What do you see me as, Peccorina? Hermes? Saint Sebastien?

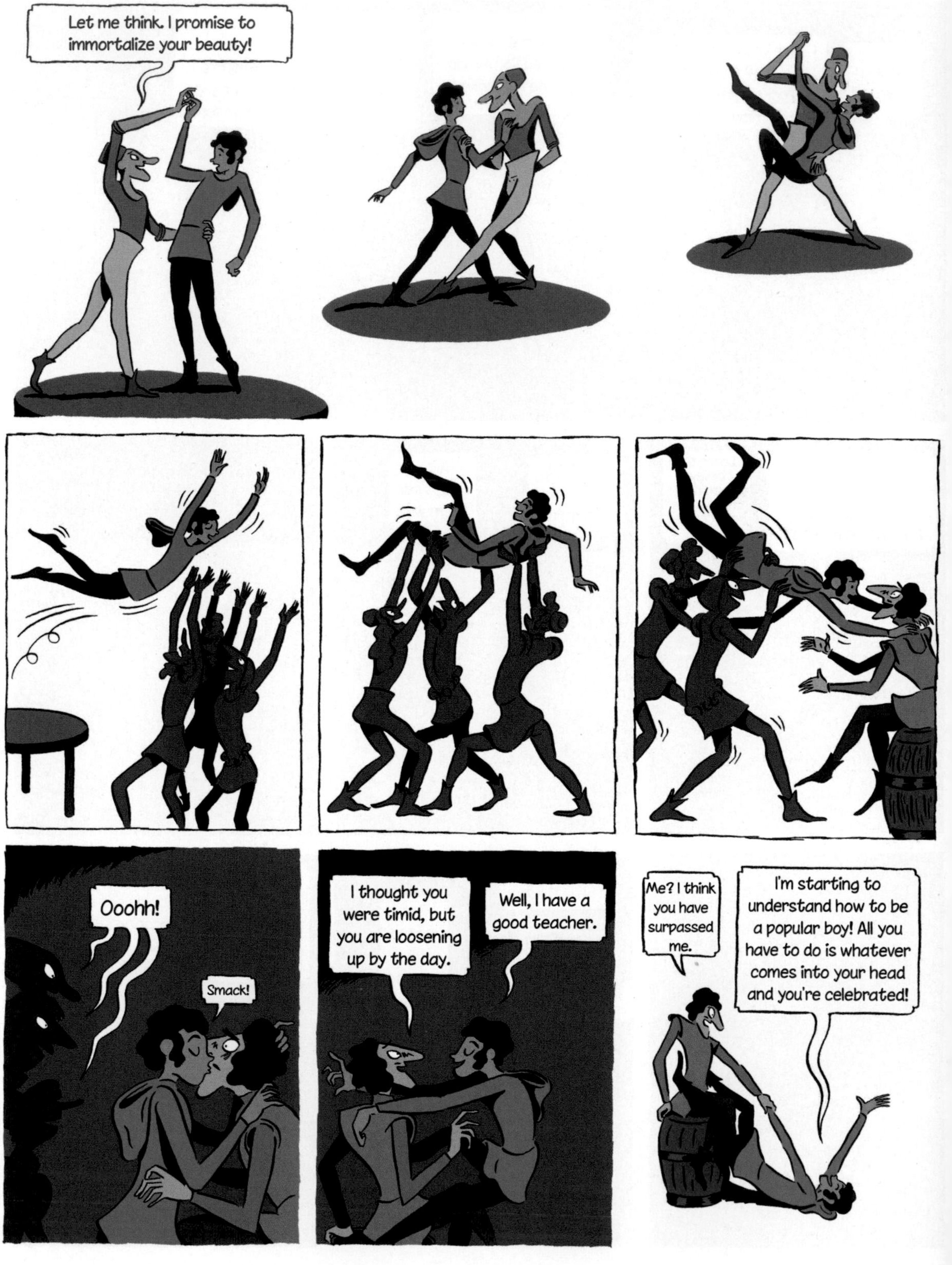
Let me think. I promise to immortalize your beauty!
Ooohh!
Smack!
I thought you were timid, but you are loosening up by the day.
Well, I have a good teacher.
Me? I think you have surpassed me.
I'm starting to understand how to be a popular boy! All you have to do is whatever comes into your head and you're celebrated!

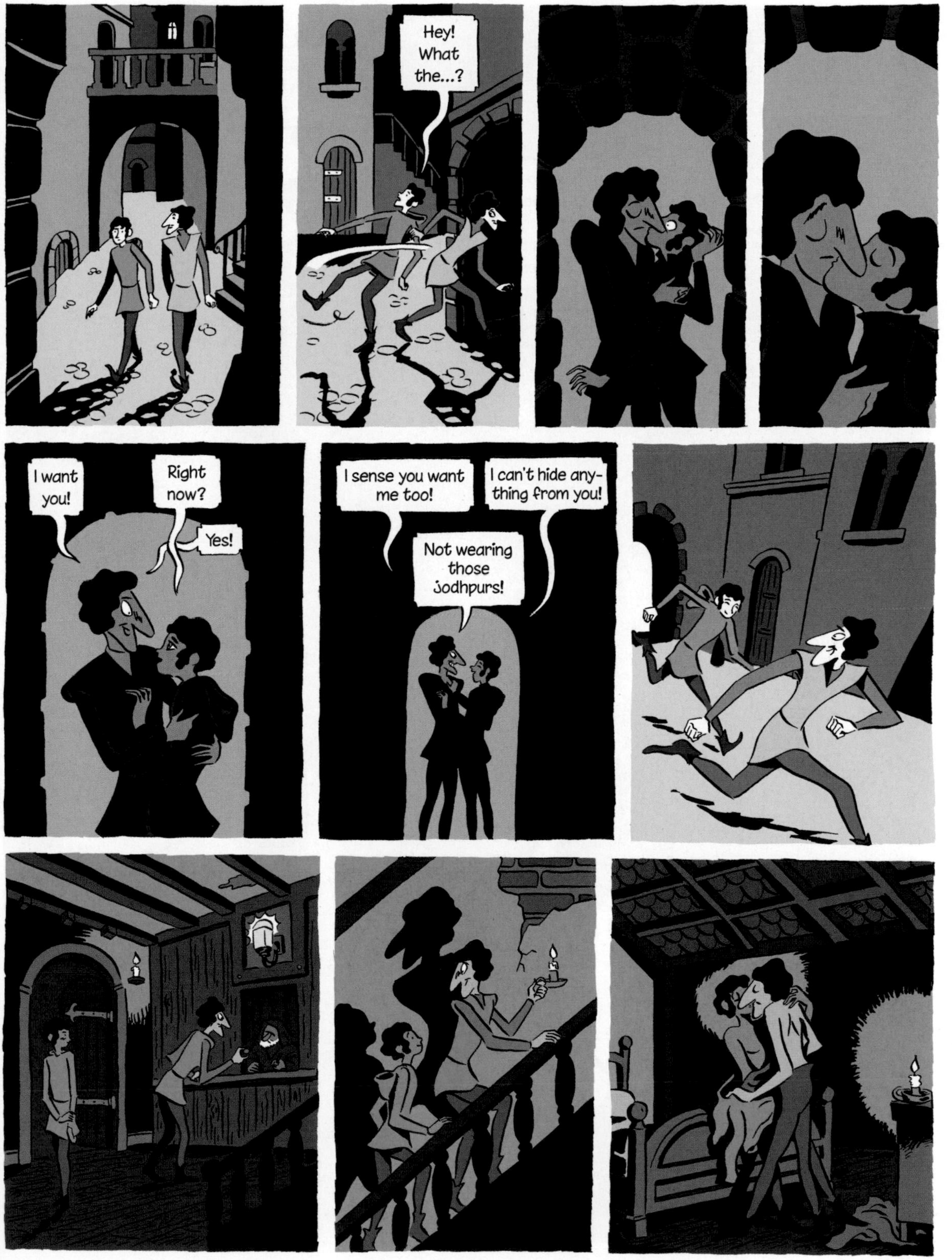
Hey! What the...?
I want you!
Right now?
Yes!
I sense you want me too!
I can't hide anything from you!
Not wearing those jodhpurs!

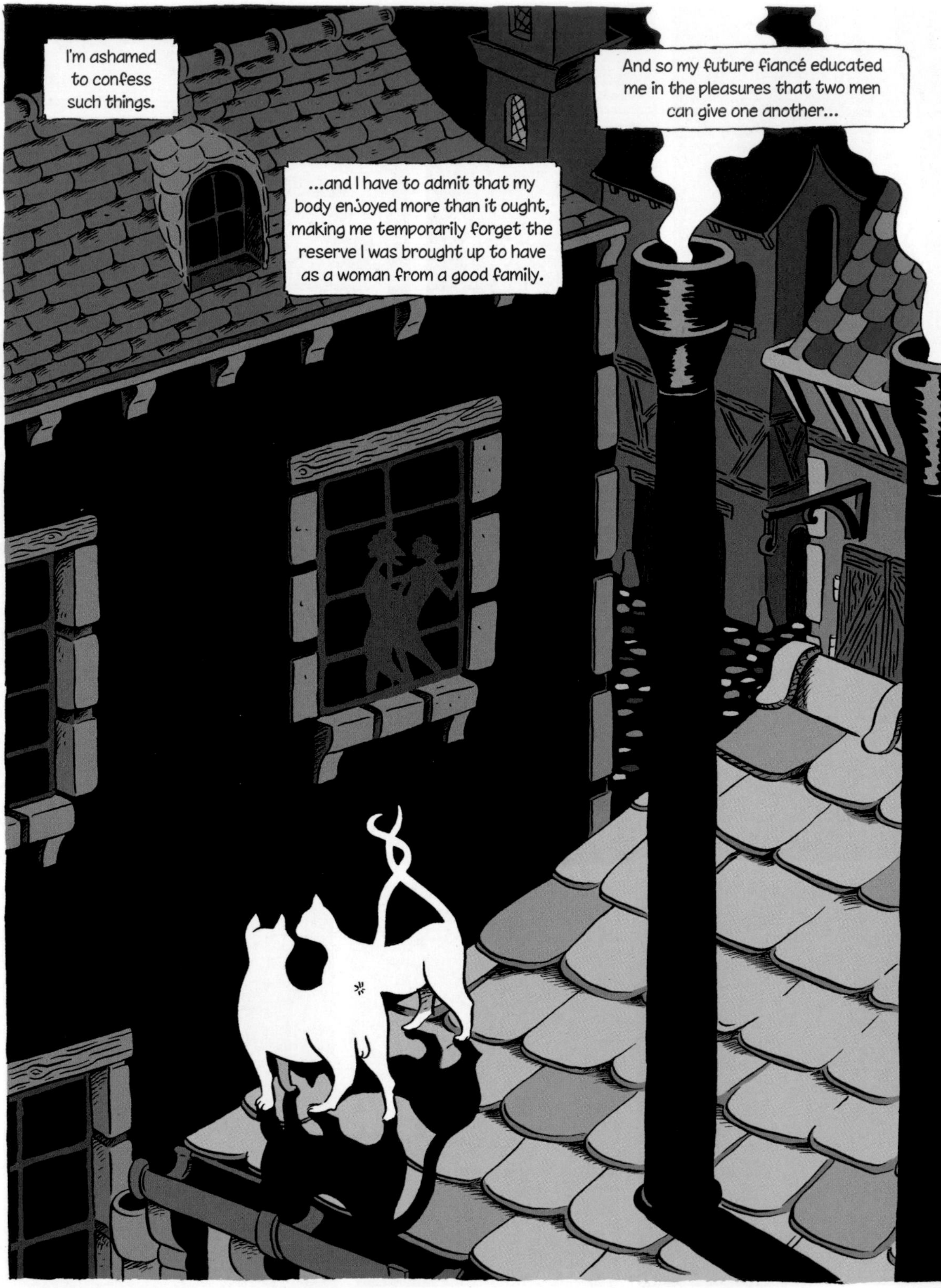
I'm ashamed to confess such things.
...and I have to admit that my body enjoyed more than it ought, making me temporarily forget the reserve I was brought up to have as a woman from a good family.
And so my future fiancé educated me in the pleasures that two men can give one another...

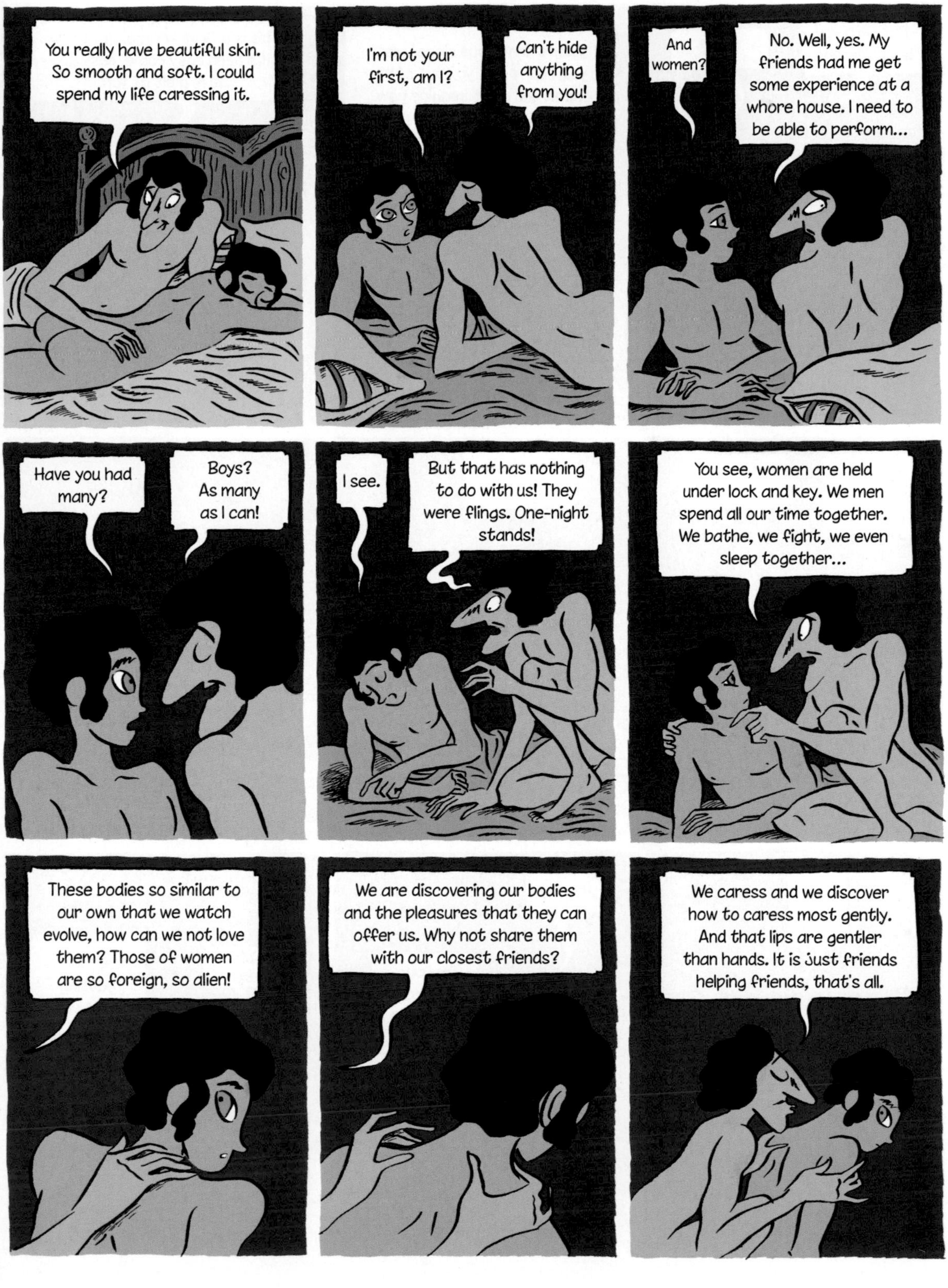
You really have beautiful skin. So smooth and soft. I could spend my life caressing it.
I'm not your first, am I?
Can't hide anything from you!
And women?
No. Well, yes. My friends had me get some experience at a whore house. I need to be able to perform...
Have you had many?
Boys? As many as I can!
I see.
But that has nothing to do with us! They were flings. One-night stands!
You see, women are held under lock and key. We men spend all our time together. We bathe, we fight, we even sleep together...
These bodies so similar to our own that we watch evolve, how can we not love them? Those of women are so foreign, so alien!
We are discovering our bodies and the pleasures that they can offer us. Why not share them with our closest friends?
We caress and we discover how to caress most gently. And that lips are gentler than hands. It is just friends helping friends, that's all.

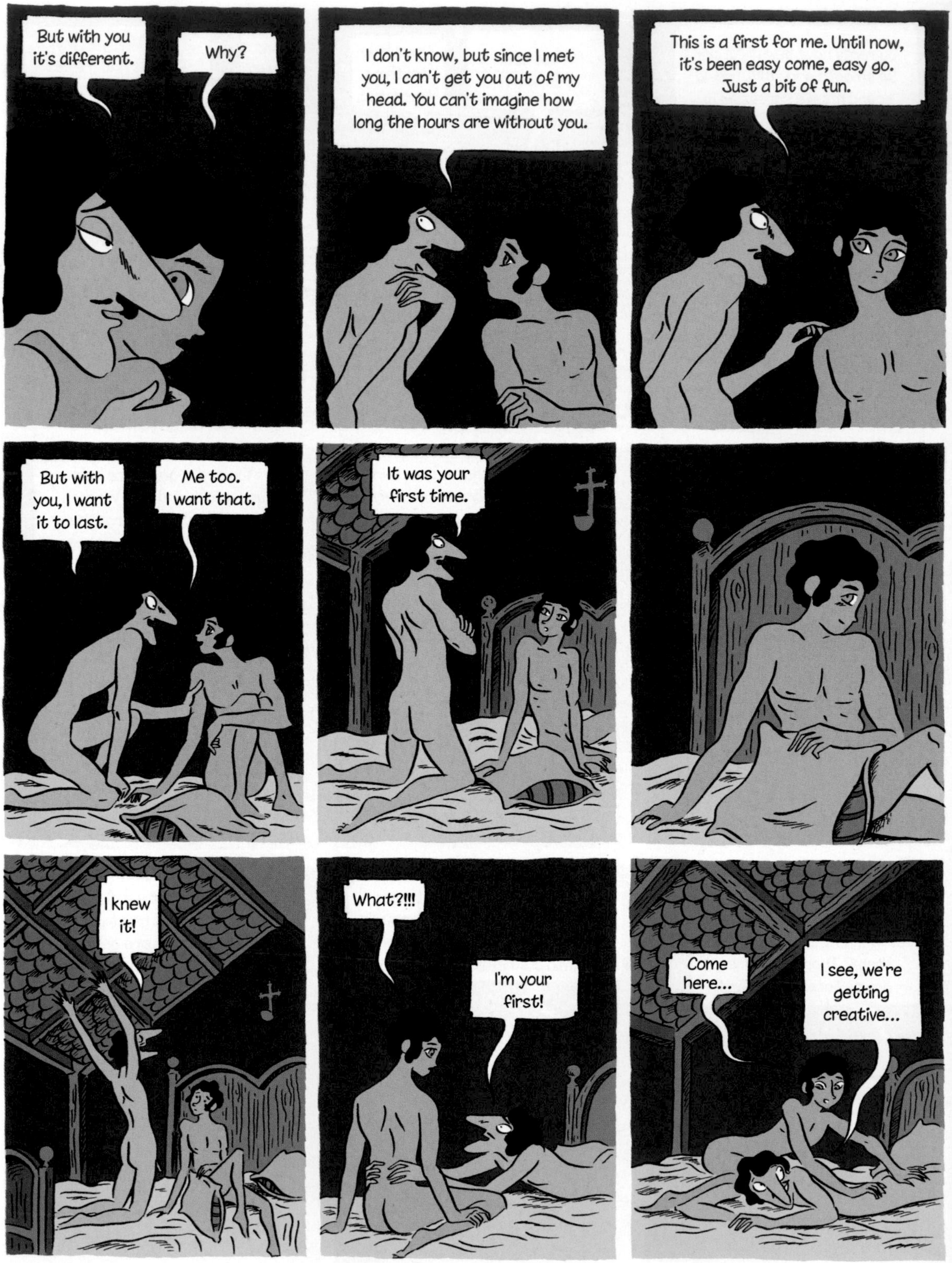
But with you it's different.
Why?
I don't know, but since I met you, I can't get you out of my head. You can't imagine how long the hours are without you.
This is a first for me. Until now, it's been easy come, easy go. Just a bit of fun.
But with you, I want it to last.
Me too. I want that.
It was your first time.
I knew it!
What?!!!
I'm your first!
Come here...
I see, we're getting creative...

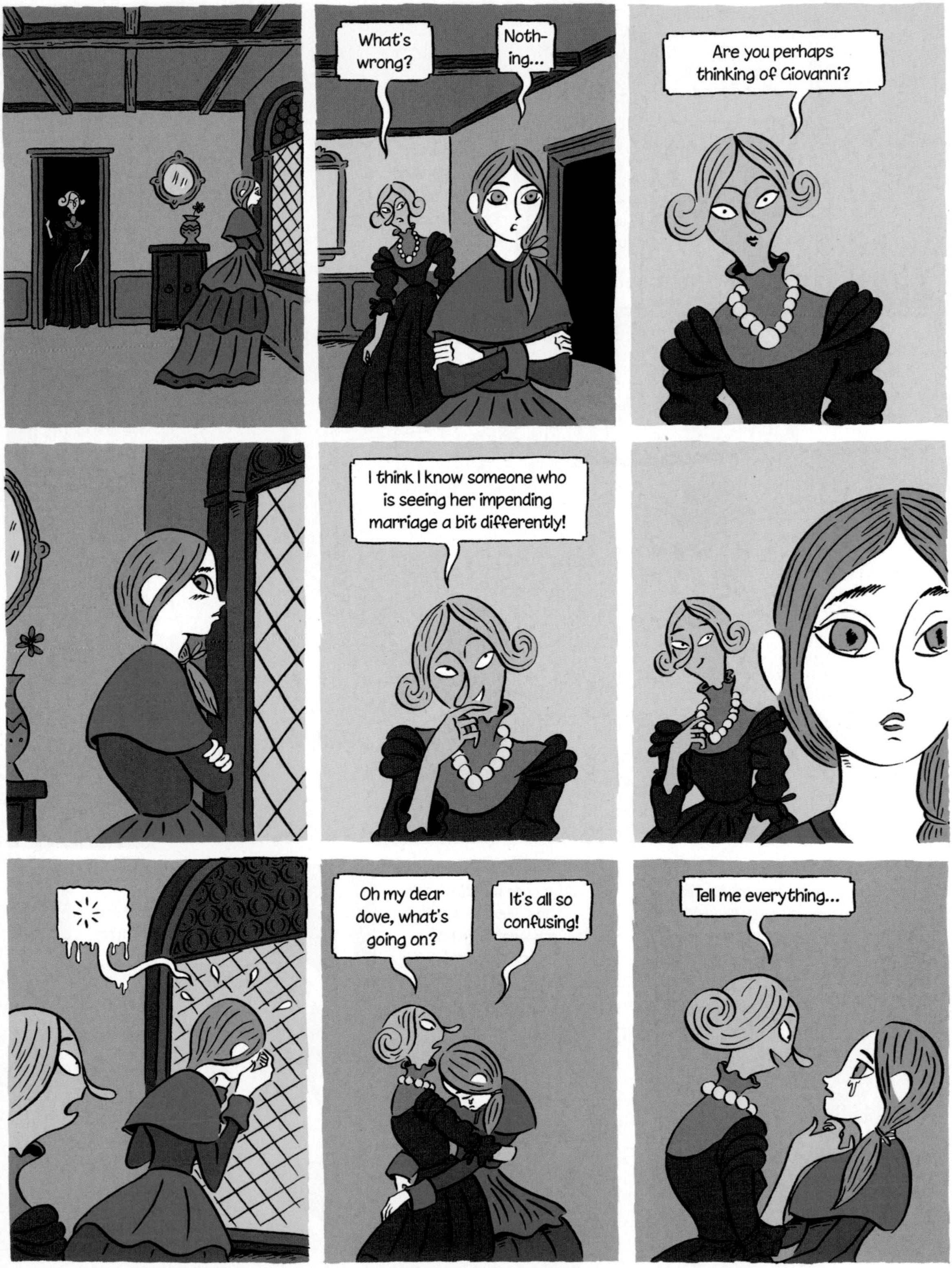
What's wrong?
Noth-ing...
Are you perhaps thinking of Giovanni?
I think I know someone who is seeing her impending marriage a bit differently!
Oh my dear dove, what's going on?
It's all so confusing!
Tell me everything...

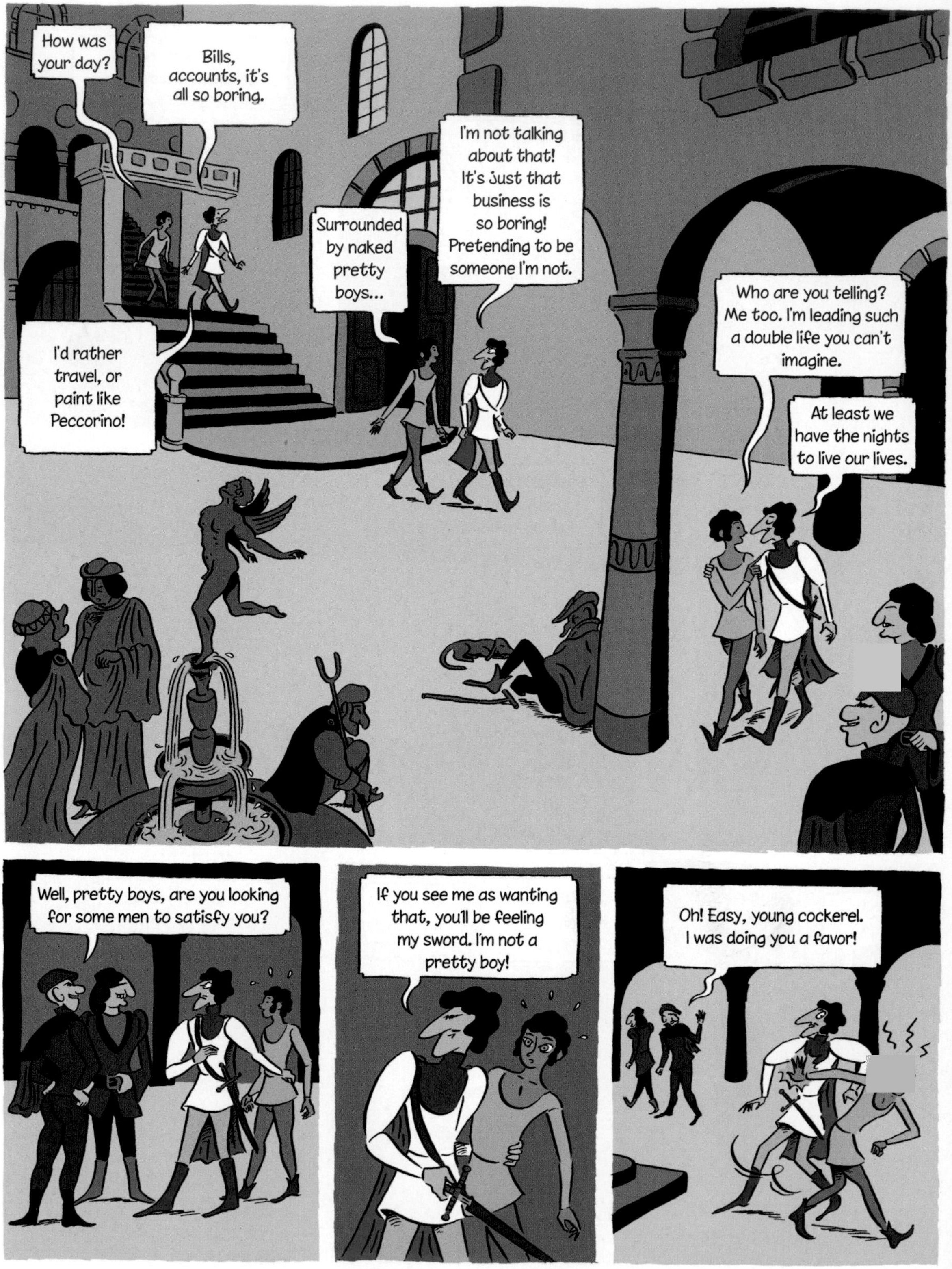
How was your day?
Bills, accounts, it's all so boring.
I'd rather travel, or paint like Peccorino!
Surrounded by naked pretty boys...
I'm not talking about that! It's just that business is so boring! Pretending to be someone I'm not.
Who are you telling? Me too. I'm leading such a double life you can't imagine.
At least we have the nights to live our lives.
Well, pretty boys, are you looking for some men to satisfy you?
If you see me as wanting that, you'll be feeling my sword. I'm not a pretty boy!
Oh! Easy, young cockerel. I was doing you a favor!

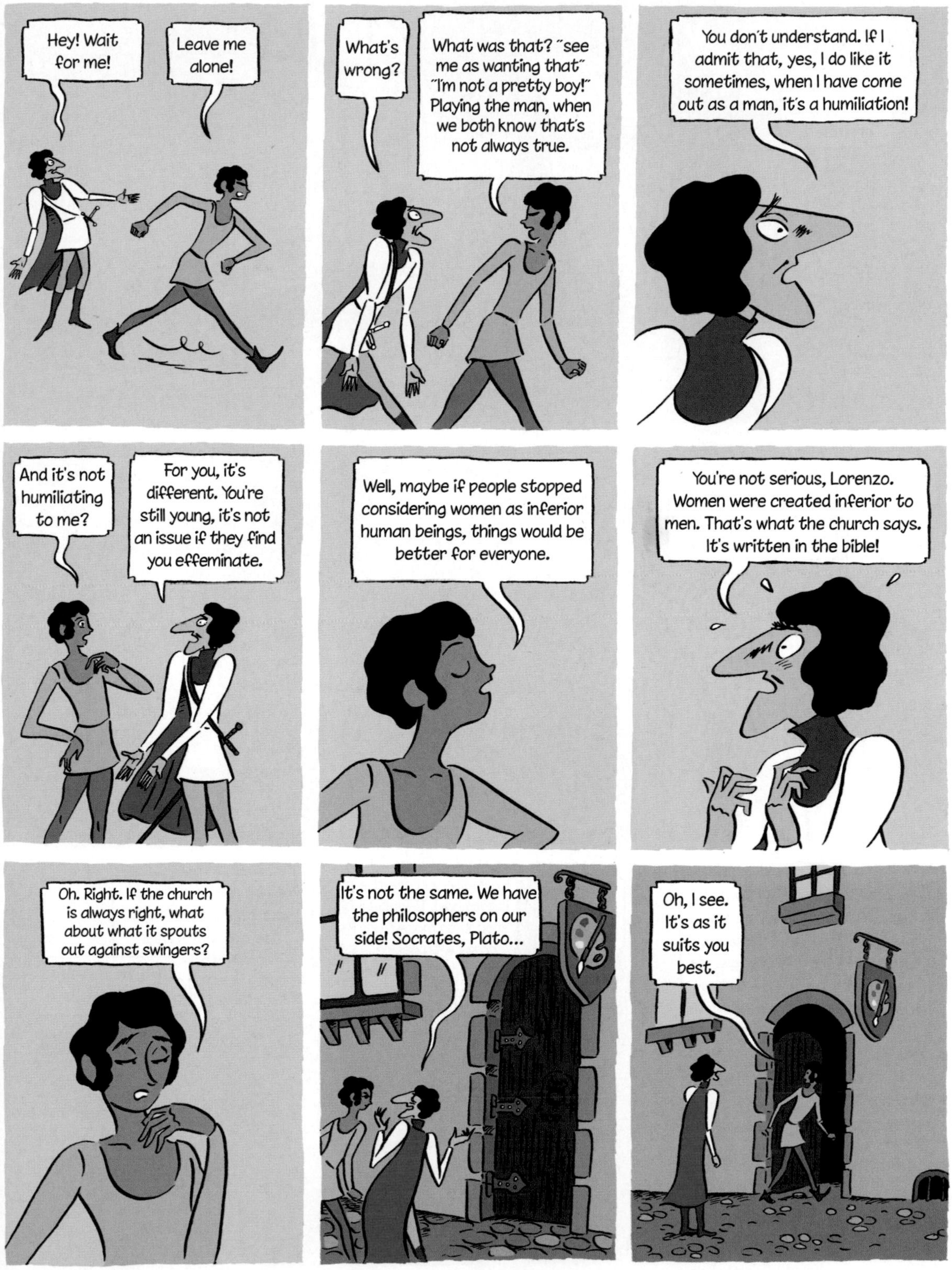
Hey! Wait for me!
Leave me alone!
What's wrong?
What was that? "see me as wanting that" "I'm not a pretty boy!" Playing the man, when we both know that's not always true.
You don't understand. If I admit that, yes, I do like it sometimes, when I have come out as a man, it's a humiliation!
And it's not humiliating to me?
For you, it's different. You're still young, it's not an issue if they find you effeminate.
Well, maybe if people stopped considering women as inferior human beings, things would be better for everyone.
You're not serious, Lorenzo. Women were created inferior to men. That's what the church says. It's written in the bible!
Oh. Right. If the church is always right, what about what it spouts out against swingers?
It's not the same. We have the philosophers on our side! Socrates, Plato...
Oh, I see. It's as it suits you best.

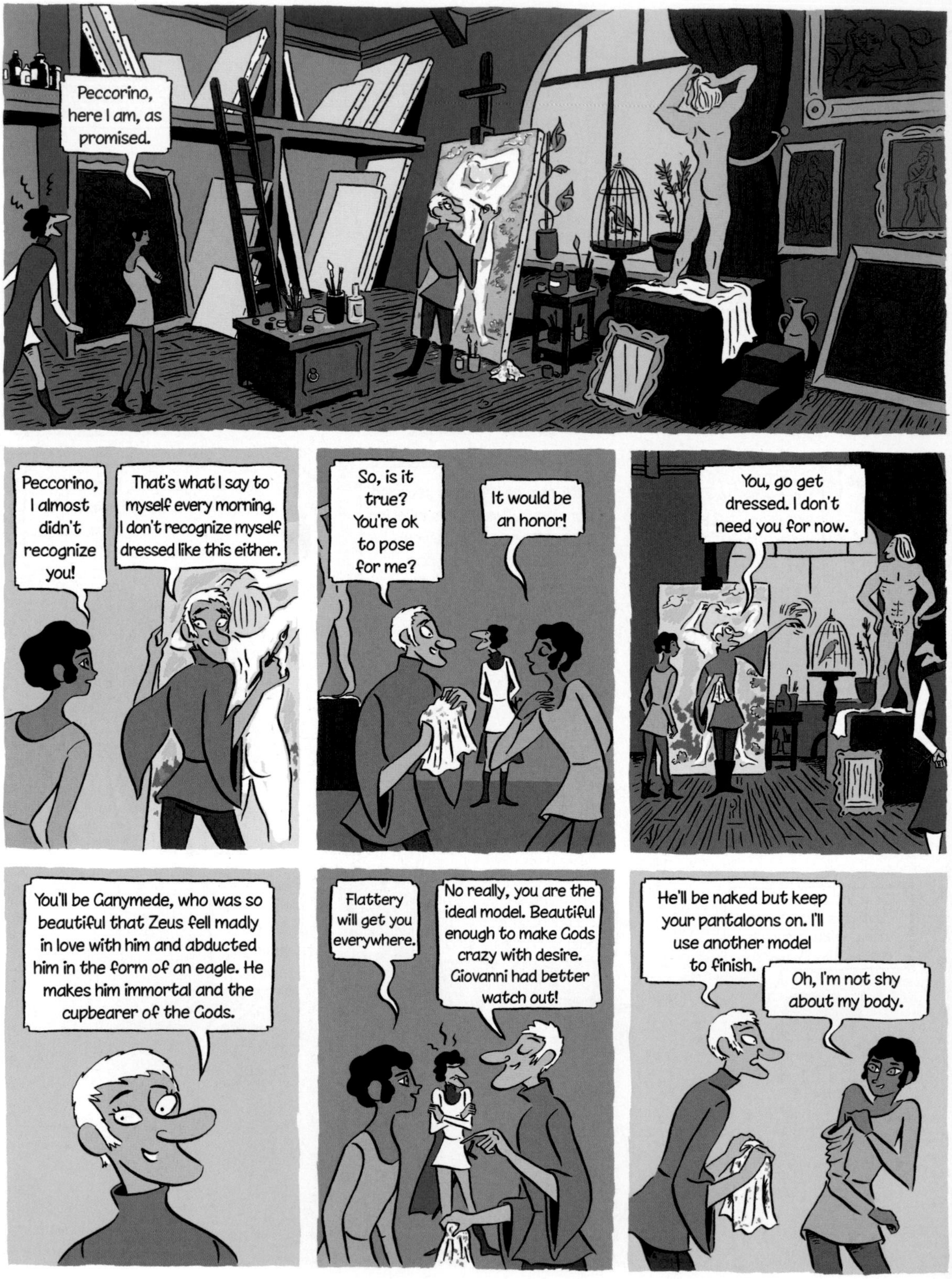
Peccorino, here I am, as promised.
Peccorino, I almost didn't recognize you!
That's what I say to myself every morning. I don't recognize myself dressed like this either.
So, is it true? You're ok to pose for me?
It would be an honor!
You, go get dressed. I don't need you for now.
You'll be Ganymede, who was so beautiful that Zeus fell madly in love with him and abducted him in the form of an eagle. He makes him immortal and the cupbearer of the Gods.
Flattery will get you everywhere.
No really, you are the ideal model. Beautiful enough to make Gods crazy with desire. Giovanni had better watch out!
He'll be naked but keep your pantaloons on. I'll use another model to finish.
Oh, I'm not shy about my body.

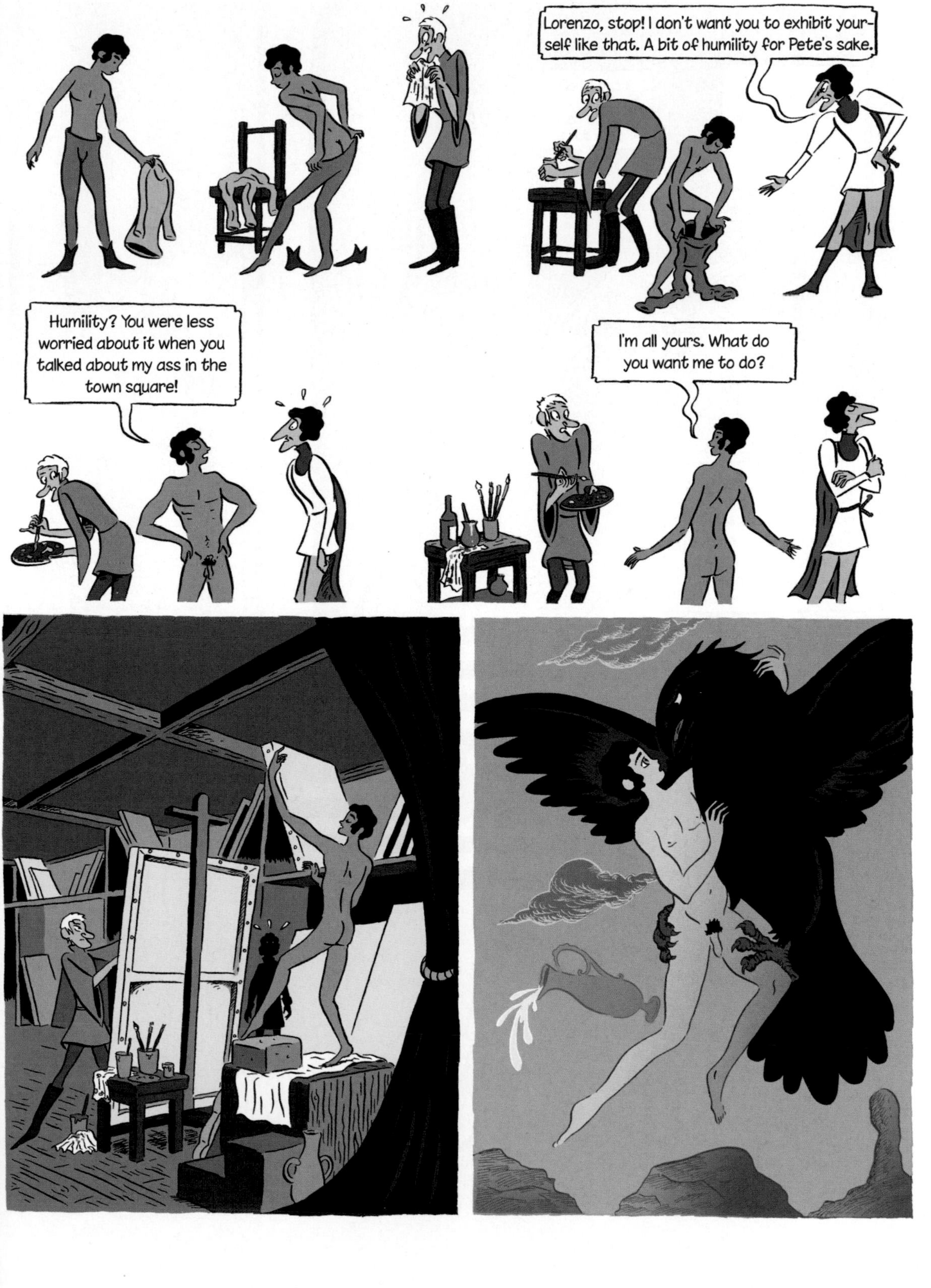
Lorenzo, stop! I don't want you to exhibit yourself like that. A bit of humility for Pete's sake.
Humility? You were less worried about it when you talked about my ass in the town square!
I'm all yours. What do you want me to do?

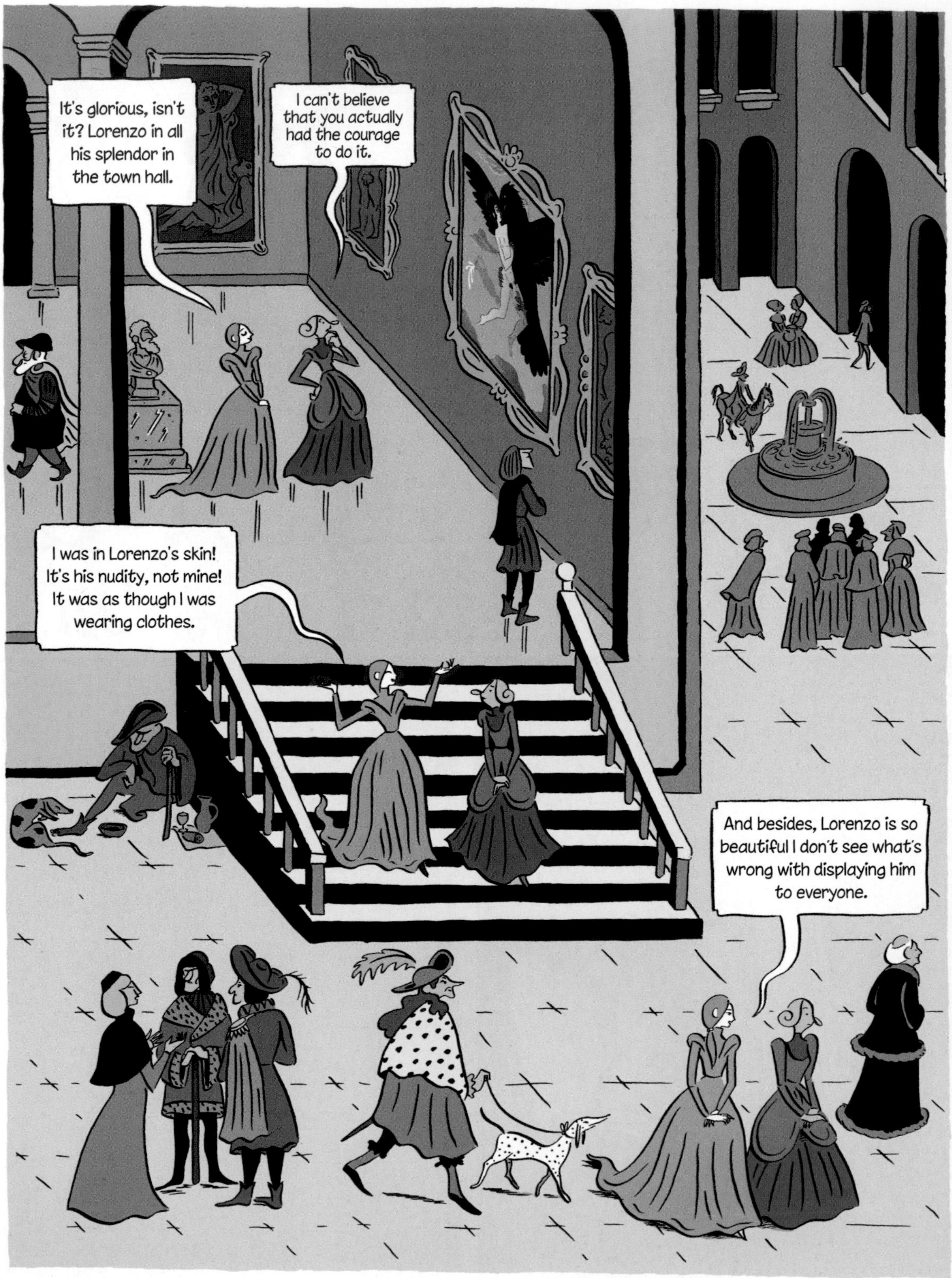
It's glorious, isn't it? Lorenzo in all his splendor in the town hall.
I can't believe that you actually had the courage to do it.
I was in Lorenzo's skin! It's his nudity, not mine! It was as though I was wearing clothes.
And besides, Lorenzo is so beautiful I don't see what's wrong with displaying him to everyone.

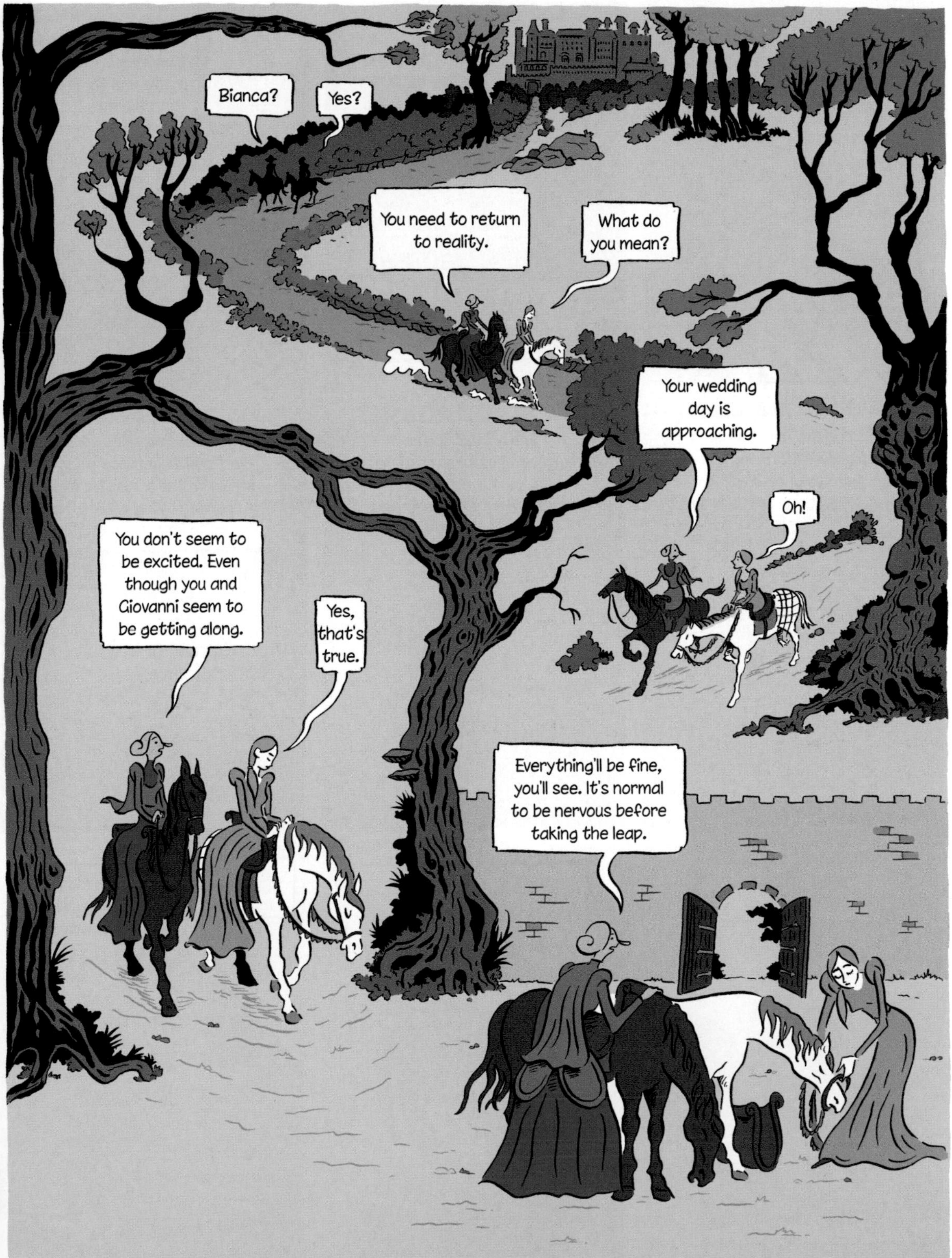
Bianca?
Yes?
You need to return to reality.
What do you mean?
Your wedding day is approaching.
Oh!
You don't seem to be excited. Even though you and Giovanni seem to be getting along.
Yes, that's true.
Everything'll be fine, you'll see. It's normal to be nervous before taking the leap.

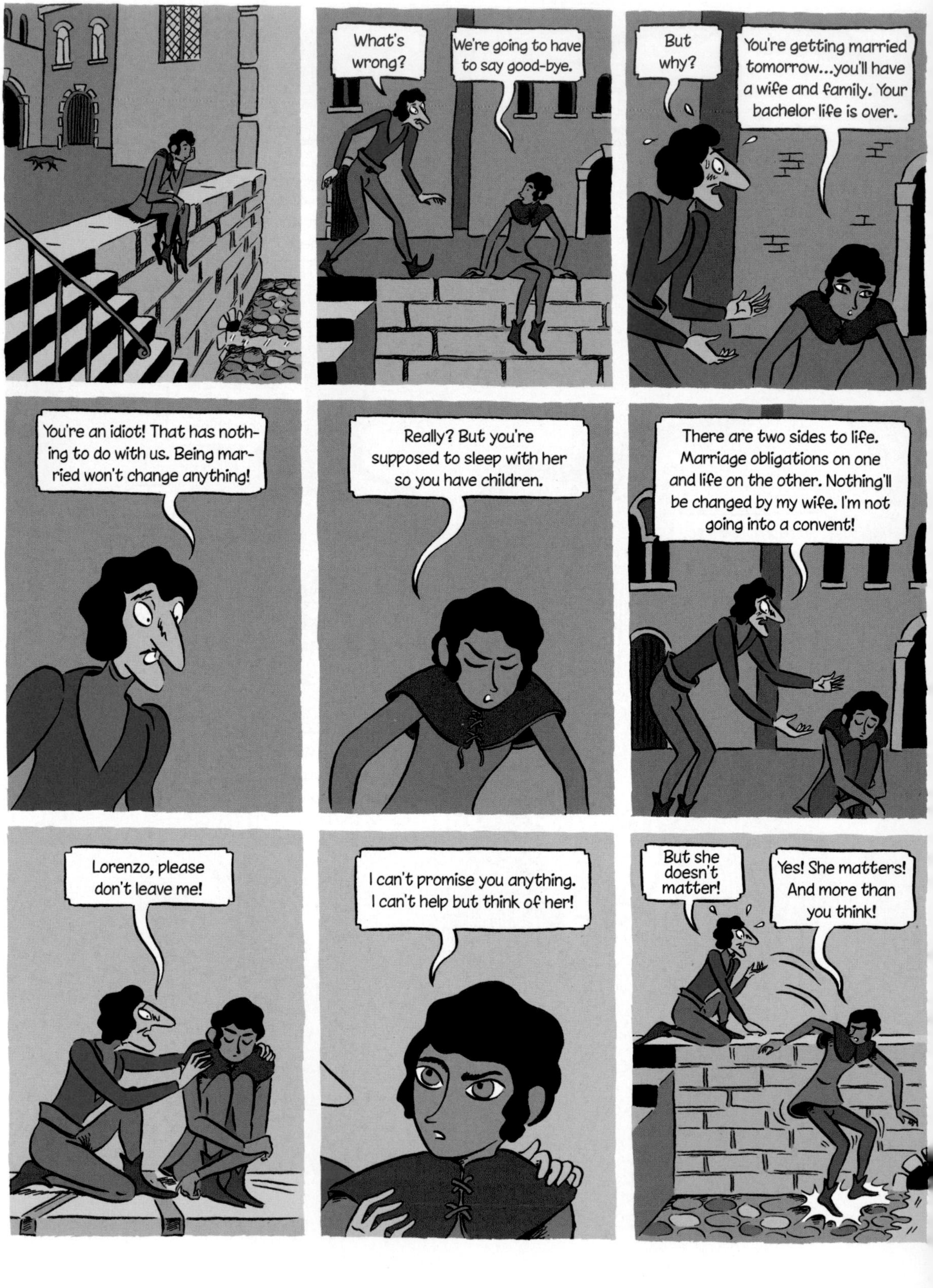
What's wrong?
We're going to have to say good-bye.
But why?
You're getting married tomorrow...you'll have a wife and family. Your bachelor life is over.
You're an idiot! That has nothing to do with us. Being married won't change anything!
Really? But you're supposed to sleep with her so you have children.
There are two sides to life. Marriage obligations on one and life on the other. Nothing'll be changed by my wife. I'm not going into a convent!
Lorenzo, please don't leave me!
I can't promise you anything. I can't help but think of her!
But she doesn't matter!
Yes! She matters! And more than you think!

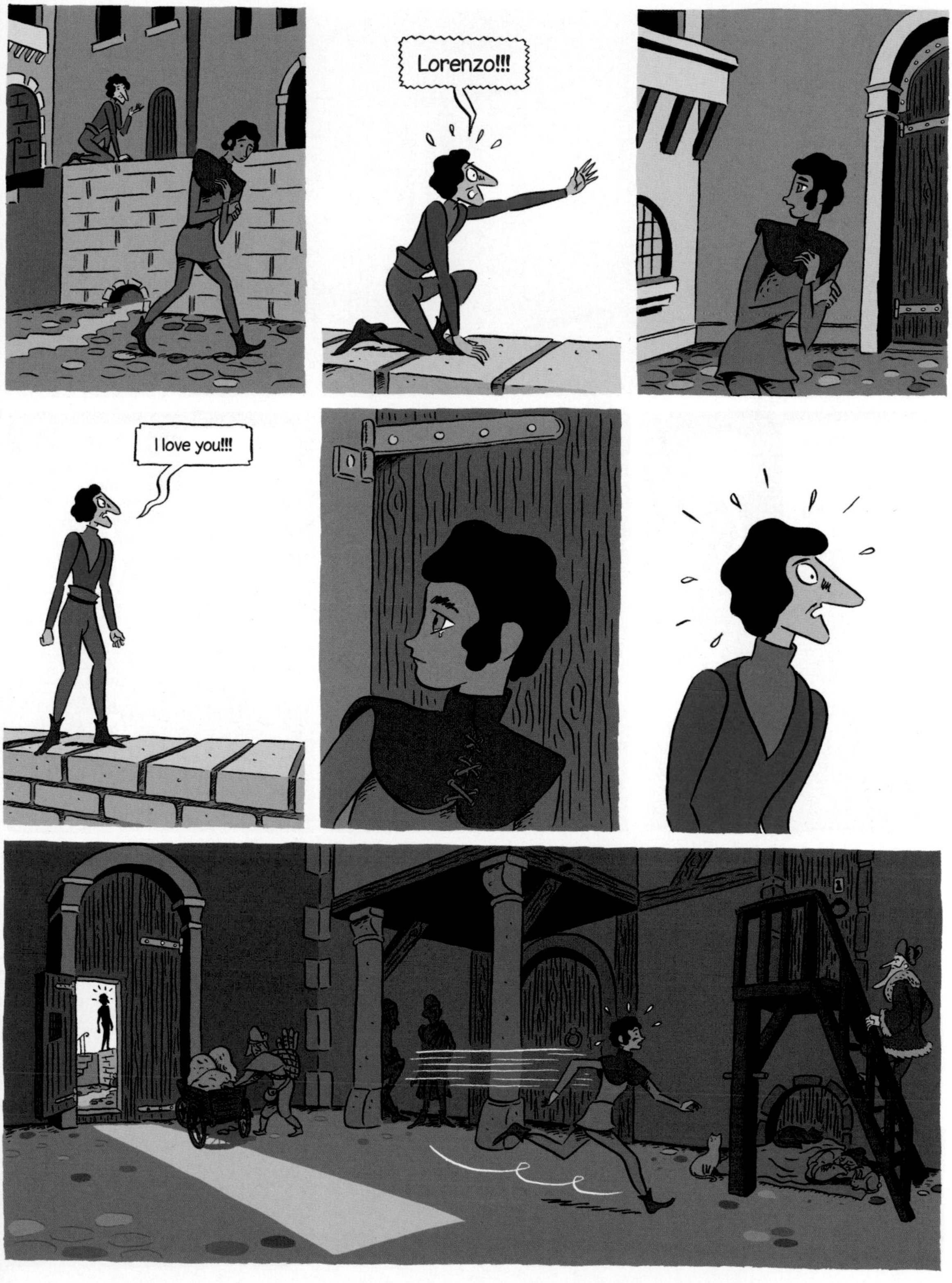
Lorenzo!!!
I love you!!!

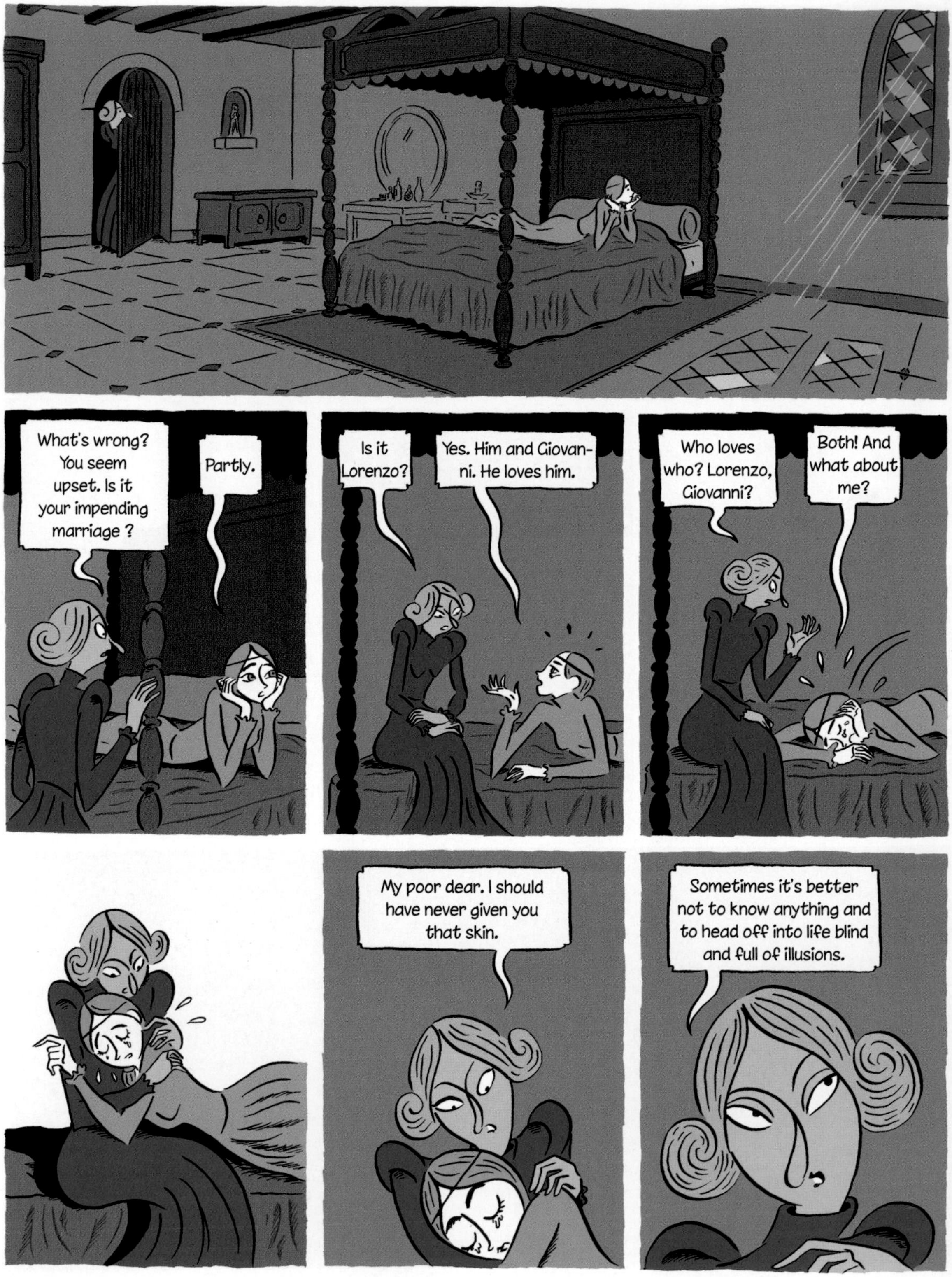
What's wrong? You seem upset. Is it your impending marriage ?
Partly.
Is it Lorenzo?
Yes. Him and Giovanni. He loves him.
Who loves who? Lorenzo, Giovanni?
Both! And what about me?
My poor dear. I should have never given you that skin.
Sometimes it's better not to know anything and to head off into life blind and full of illusions.

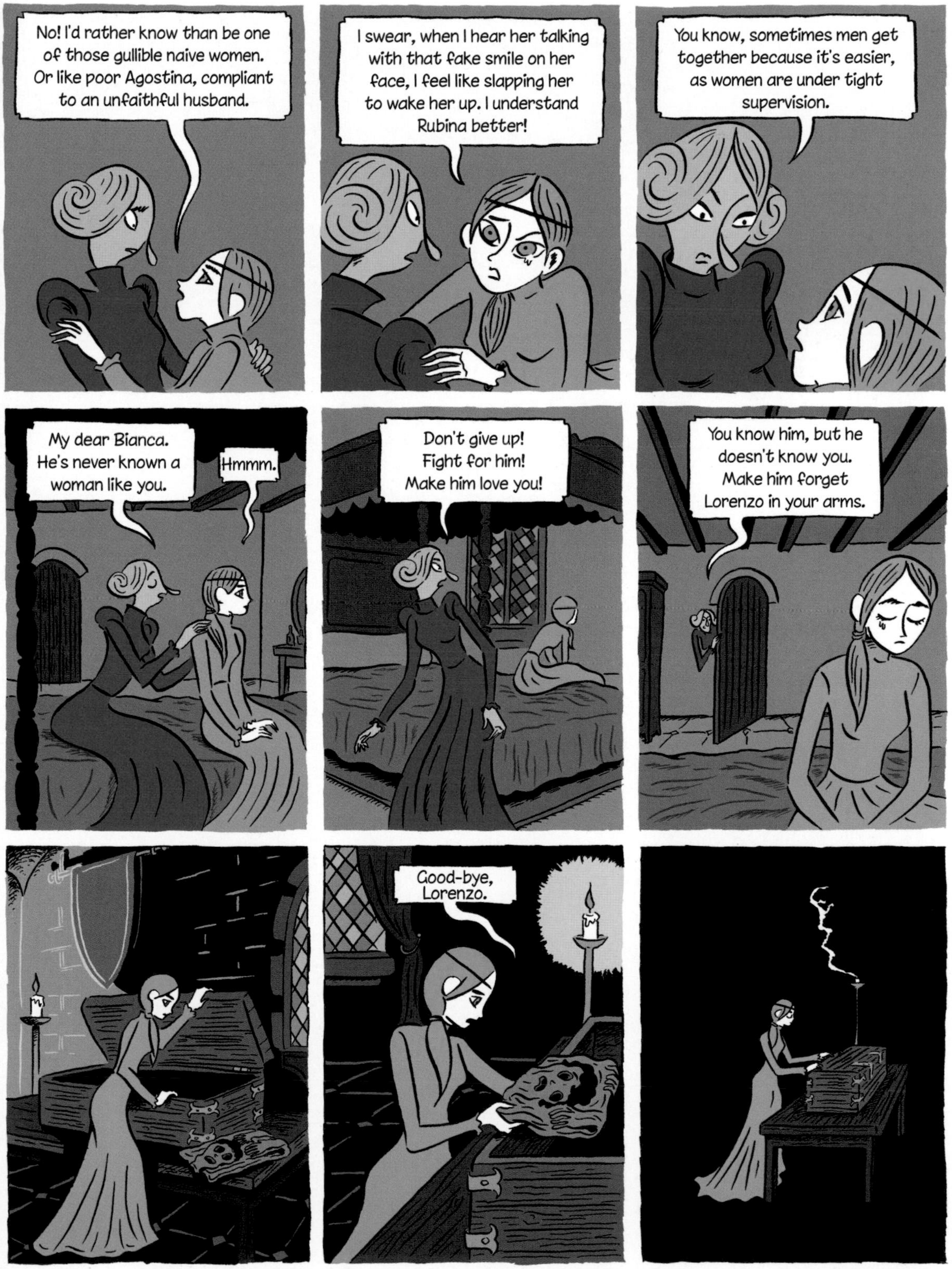
No! I'd rather know than be one of those gullible naive women. Or like poor Agostina, compliant to an unfaithful husband.
I swear, when I hear her talking with that fake smile on her face, I feel like slapping her to wake her up. I understand Rubina better!
You know, sometimes men get together because it's easier, as women are under tight supervision.
My dear Bianca. He's never known a woman like you.
Hmmm.
Don't give up! Fight for him! Make him love you!
You know him, but he doesn't know you. Make him forget Lorenzo in your arms.
Good-bye, Lorenzo.

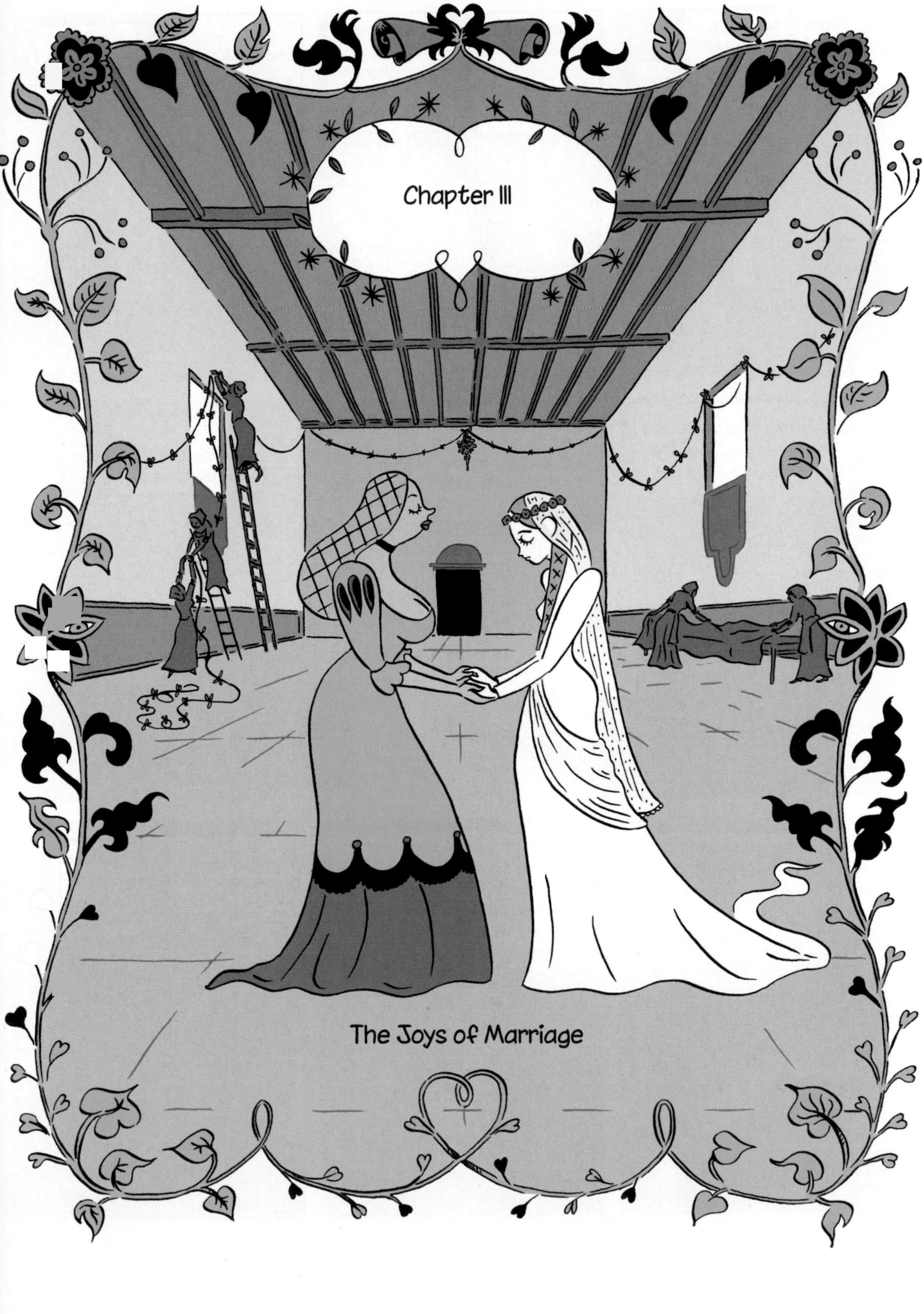
Chapter III
The Joys of Marriage

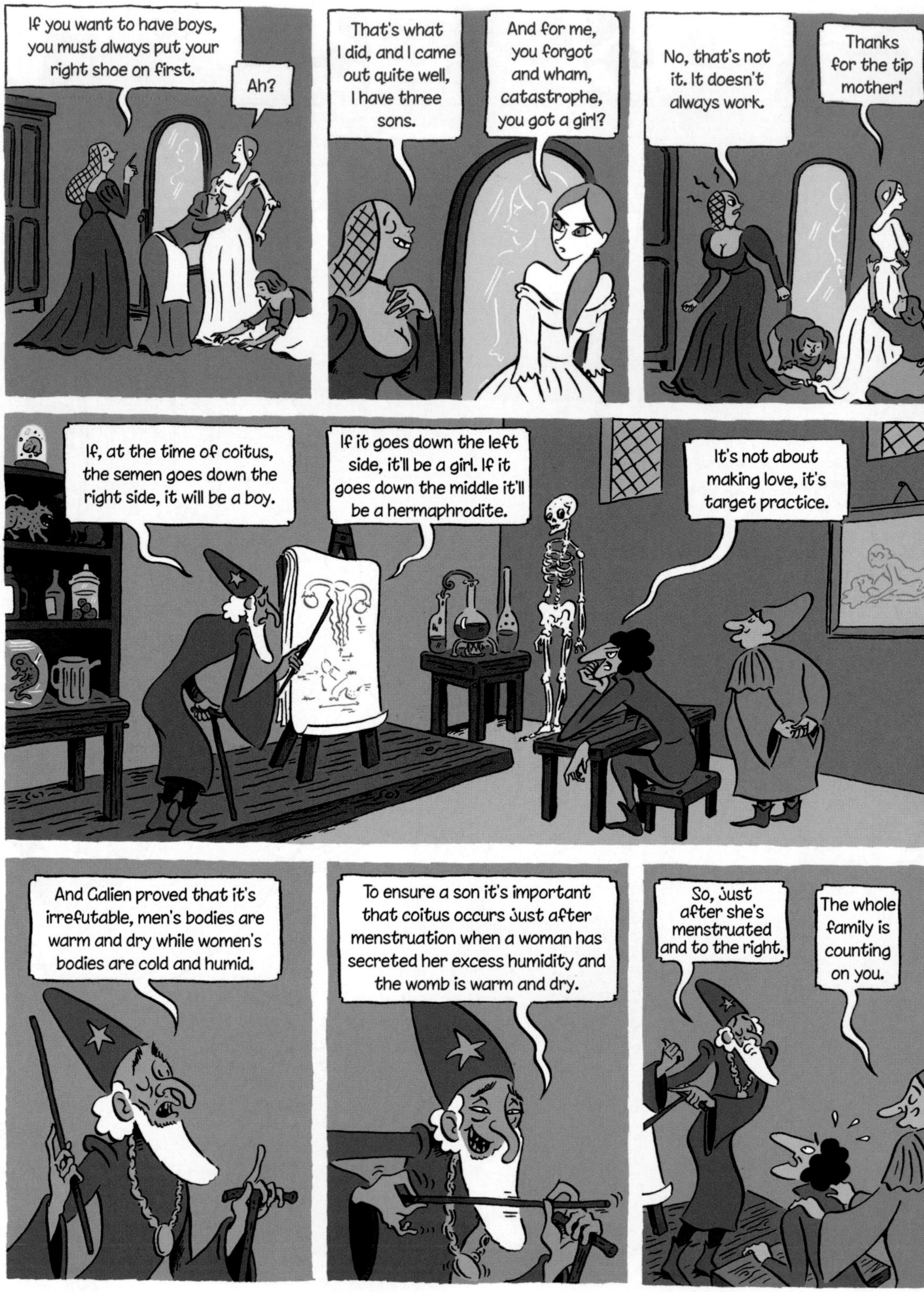
If you want to have boys, you must always put your right shoe on first.
Ah?
That's what I did, and I came out quite well, I have three sons.
And for me, you forgot and wham, catastrophe, you got a girl?
No, that's not it. It doesn't always work.
Thanks for the tip mother!
If, at the time of coitus, the semen goes down the right side, it will be a boy.
If it goes down the left side, it'll be a girl. If it goes down the middle it'll be a hermaphrodite.
It's not about making love, it's target practice.
And Galien proved that it's irrefutable, men's bodies are warm and dry while women's bodies are cold and humid.
To ensure a son it's important that coitus occurs just after menstruation when a woman has secreted her excess humidity and the womb is warm and dry.
So, just after she's menstruated and to the right.
The whole family is counting on you.

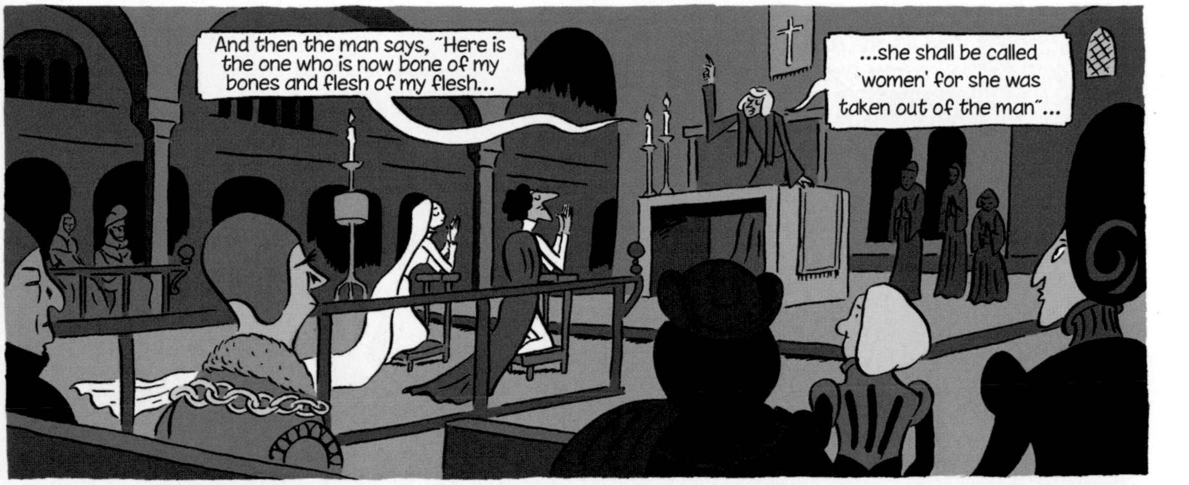
And then the man says, "Here is the one who is now bone of my bones and flesh of my flesh...
...she shall be called 'women' for she was taken out of the man"...

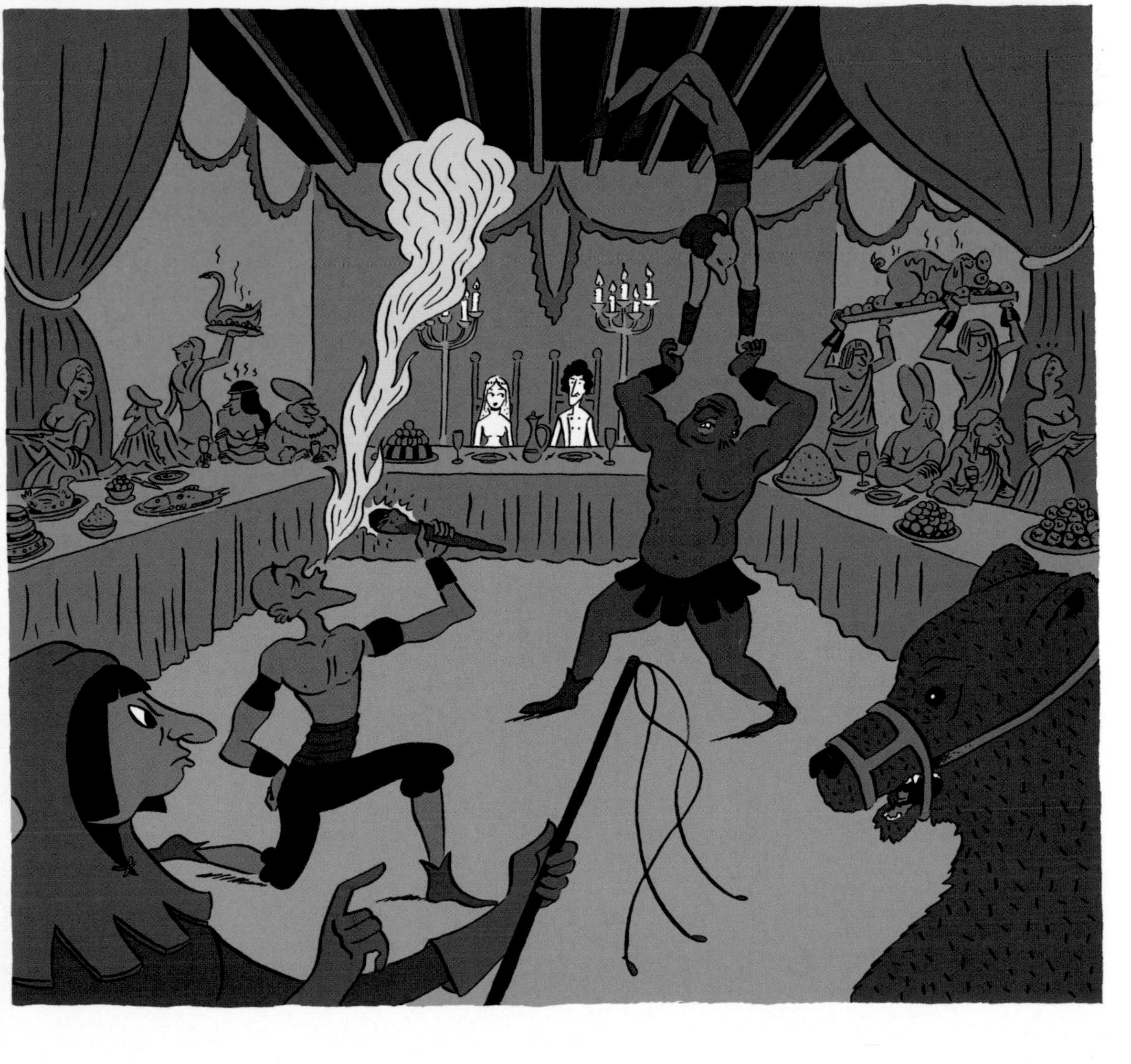

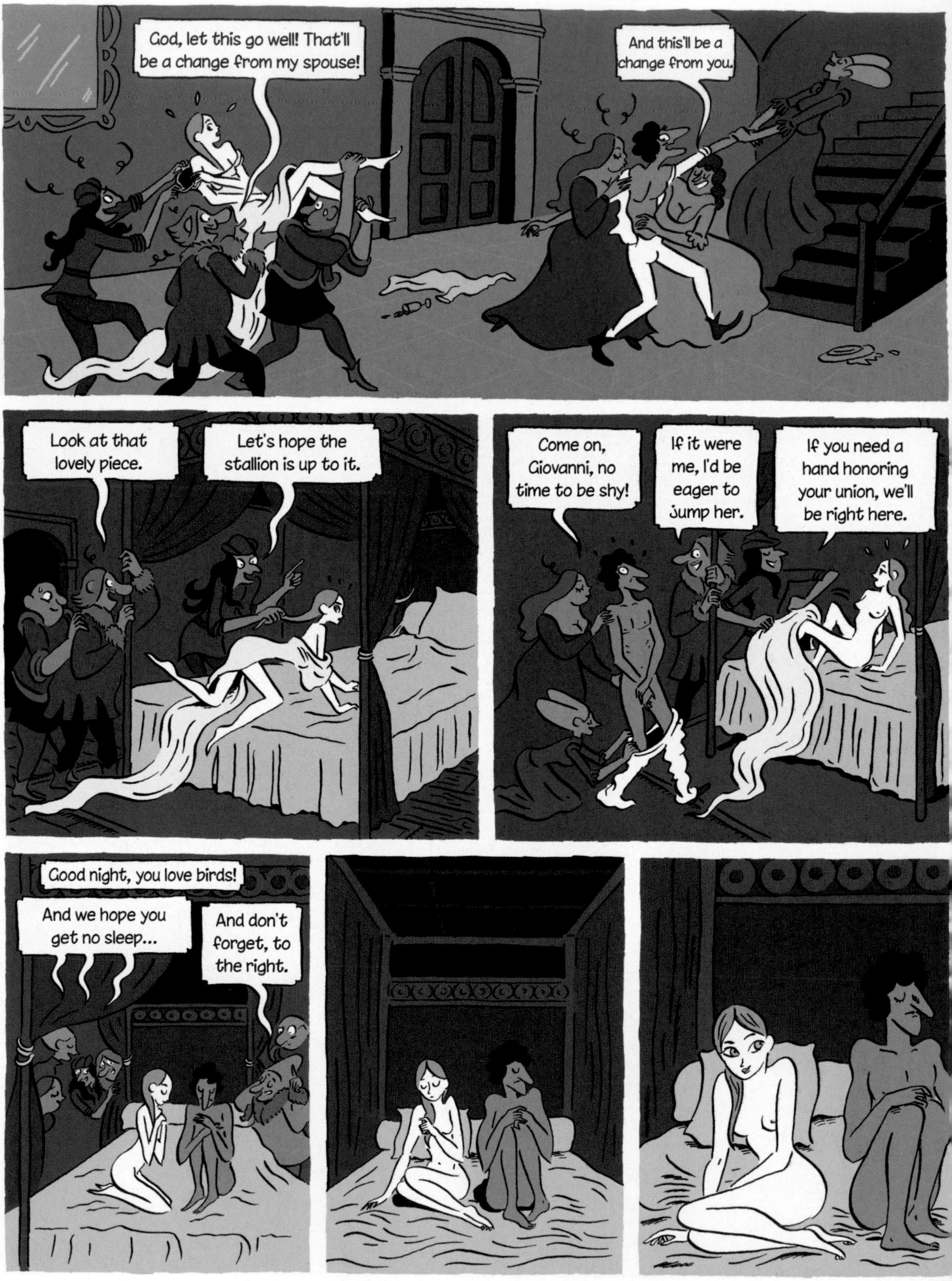
God, let this go well! That'll be a change from my spouse!
And this'll be a change from you.
Look at that lovely piece.
Let's hope the stallion is up to it.
Come on, Giovanni, no time to be shy!
If it were me, I'd be eager to jump her.
If you need a hand honoring your union, we'll be right here.
Good night, you love birds!
And we hope you get no sleep...
And don't forget, to the right.

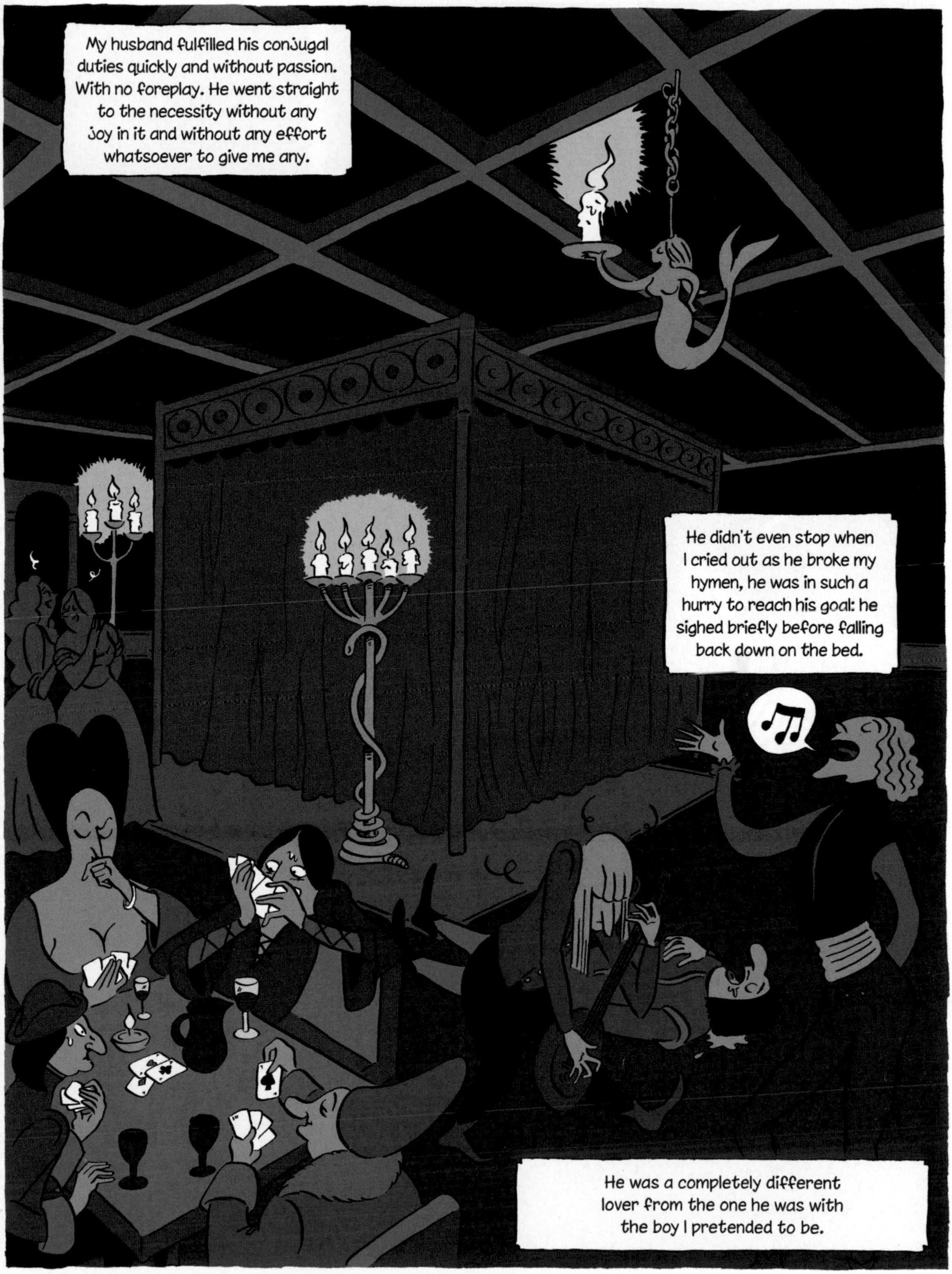
My husband fulfilled his conjugal duties quickly and without passion. With no foreplay. He went straight to the necessity without any joy in it and without any effort whatsoever to give me any.
He didn't even stop when I cried out as he broke my hymen, he was in such a hurry to reach his goal: he sighed briefly before falling back down on the bed.
He was a completely different lover from the one he was with the boy I pretended to be.

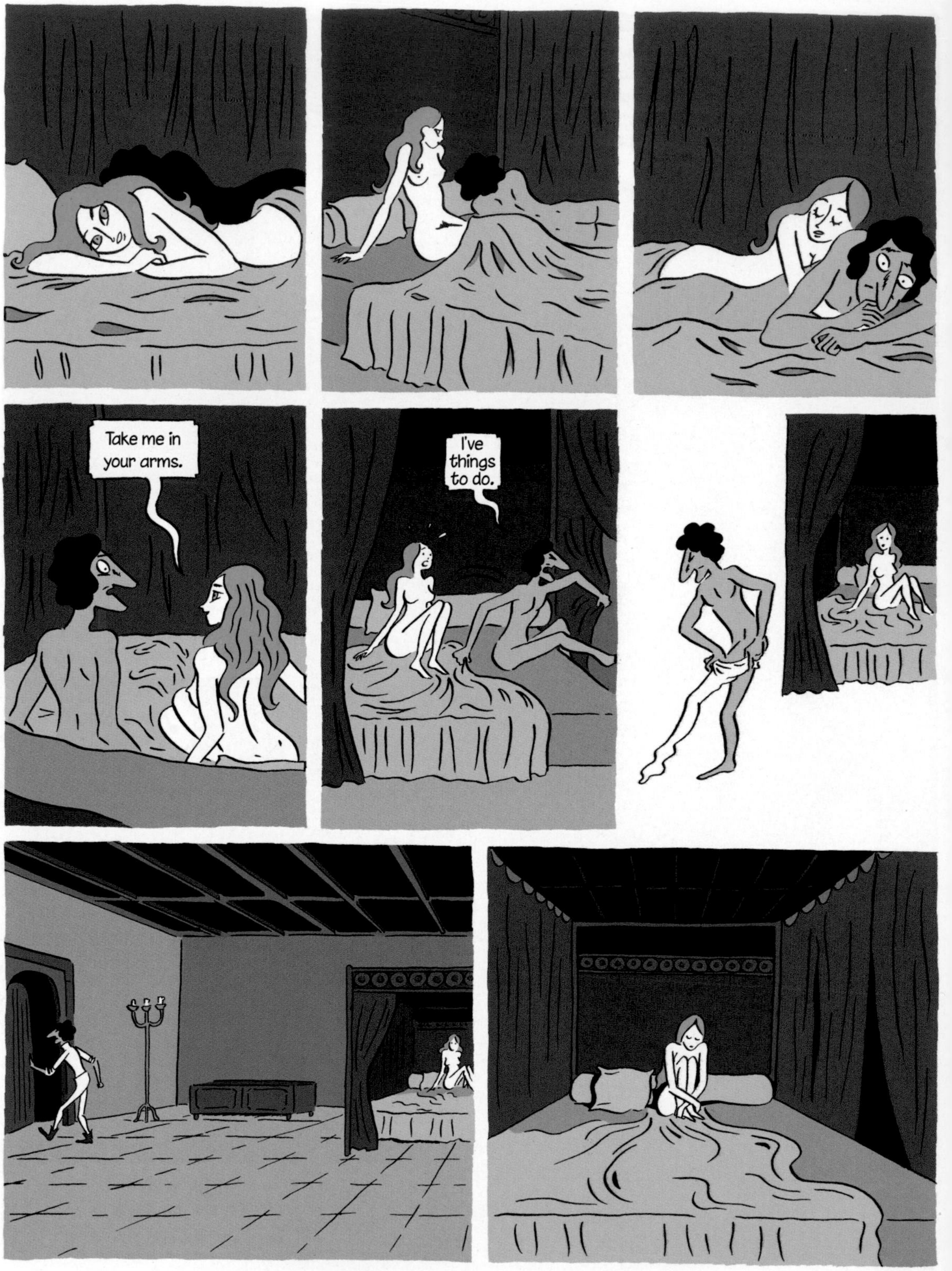
Take me in your arms.
I've things to do.

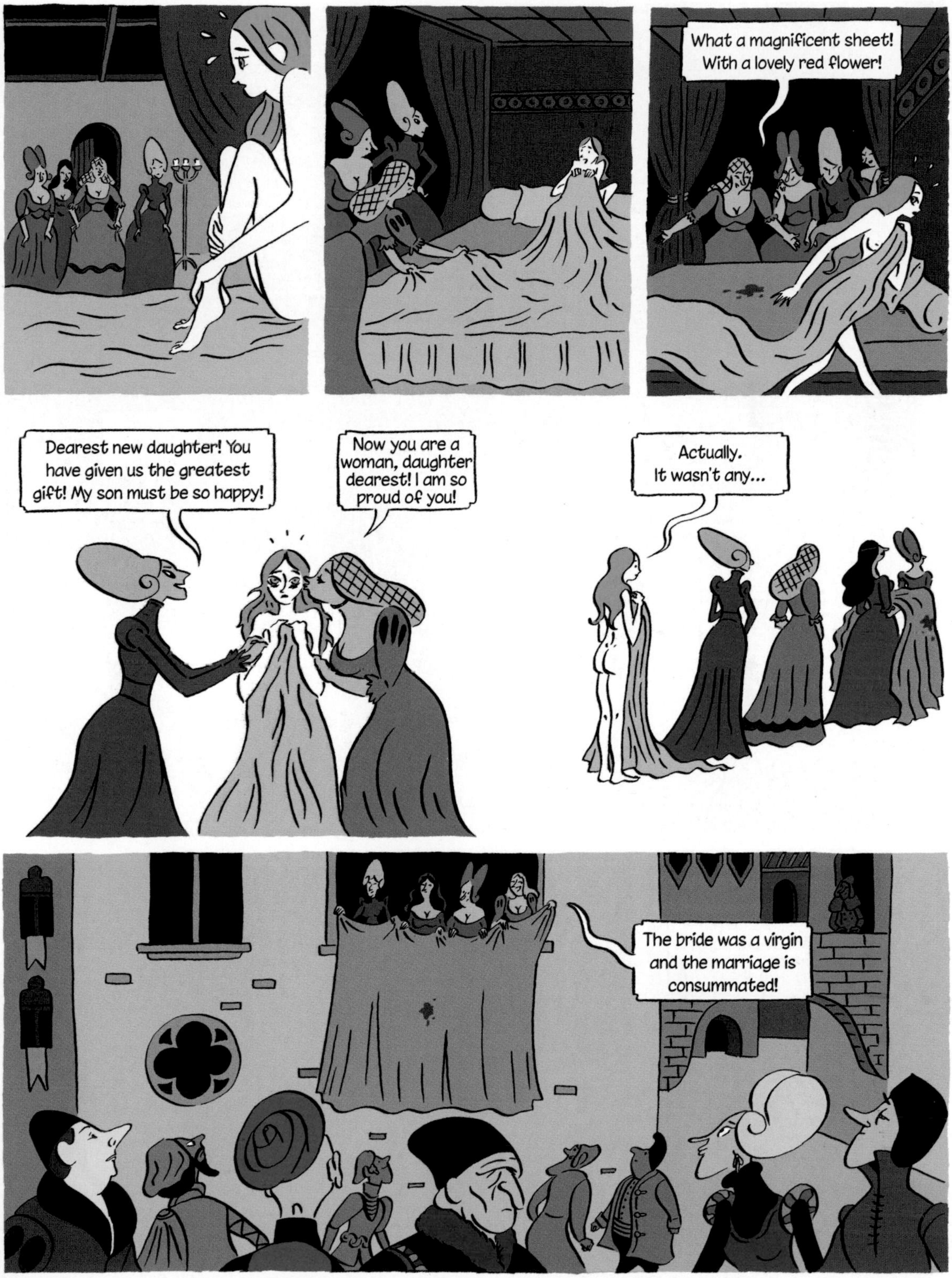
What a magnificent sheet! With a lovely red flower!
Dearest new daughter! You have given us the greatest gift! My son must be so happy!
Now you are a woman, daughter dearest! I am so proud of you!
Actually. It wasn't any...
The bride was a virgin and the marriage is consummated!

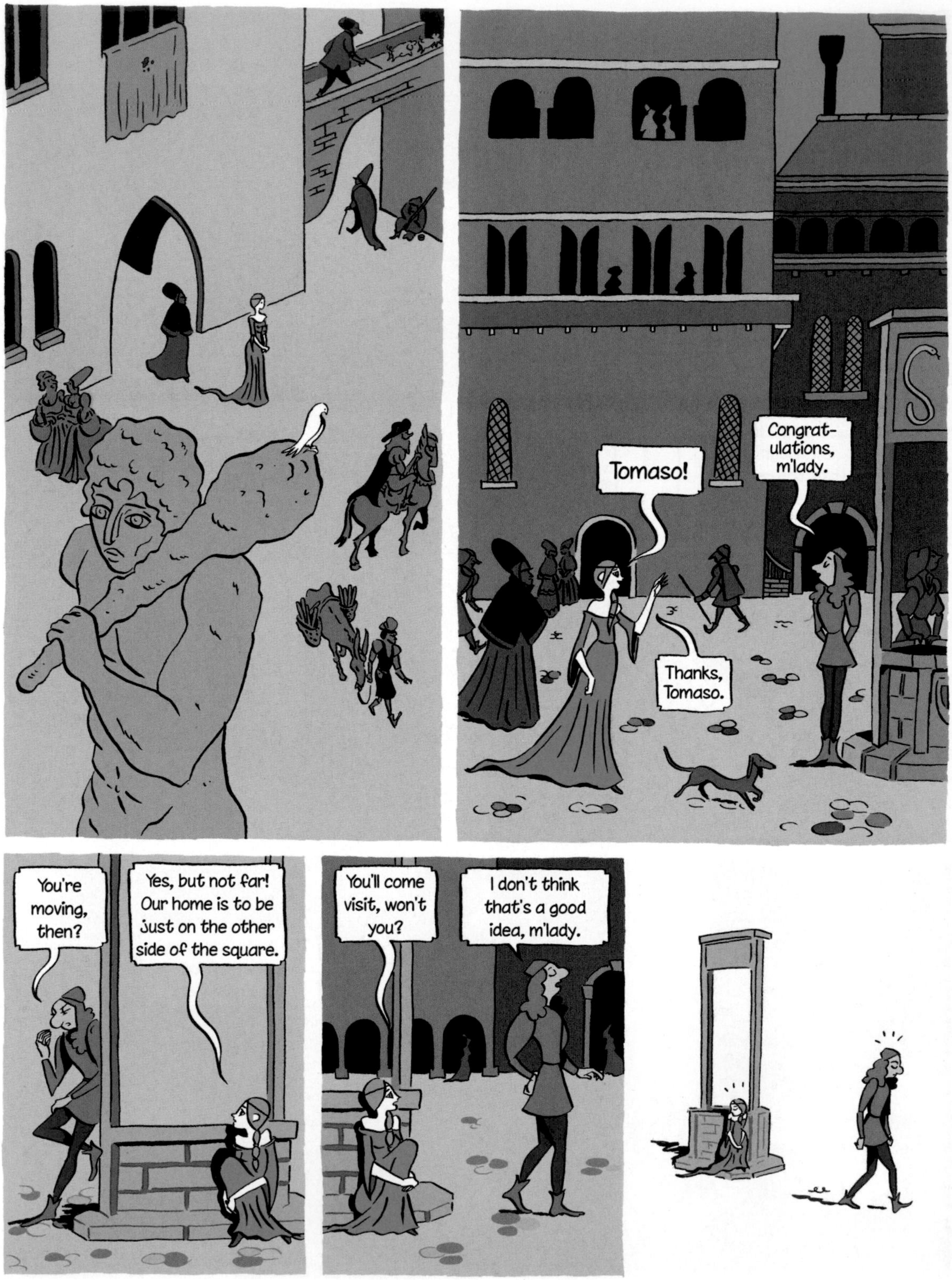
Tomaso!
Congrat-ulations, m'lady.
Thanks, Tomaso.
You're moving, then?
Yes, but not far! Our home is to be just on the other side of the square.
You'll come visit, won't you?
I don't think that's a good idea, m'lady.

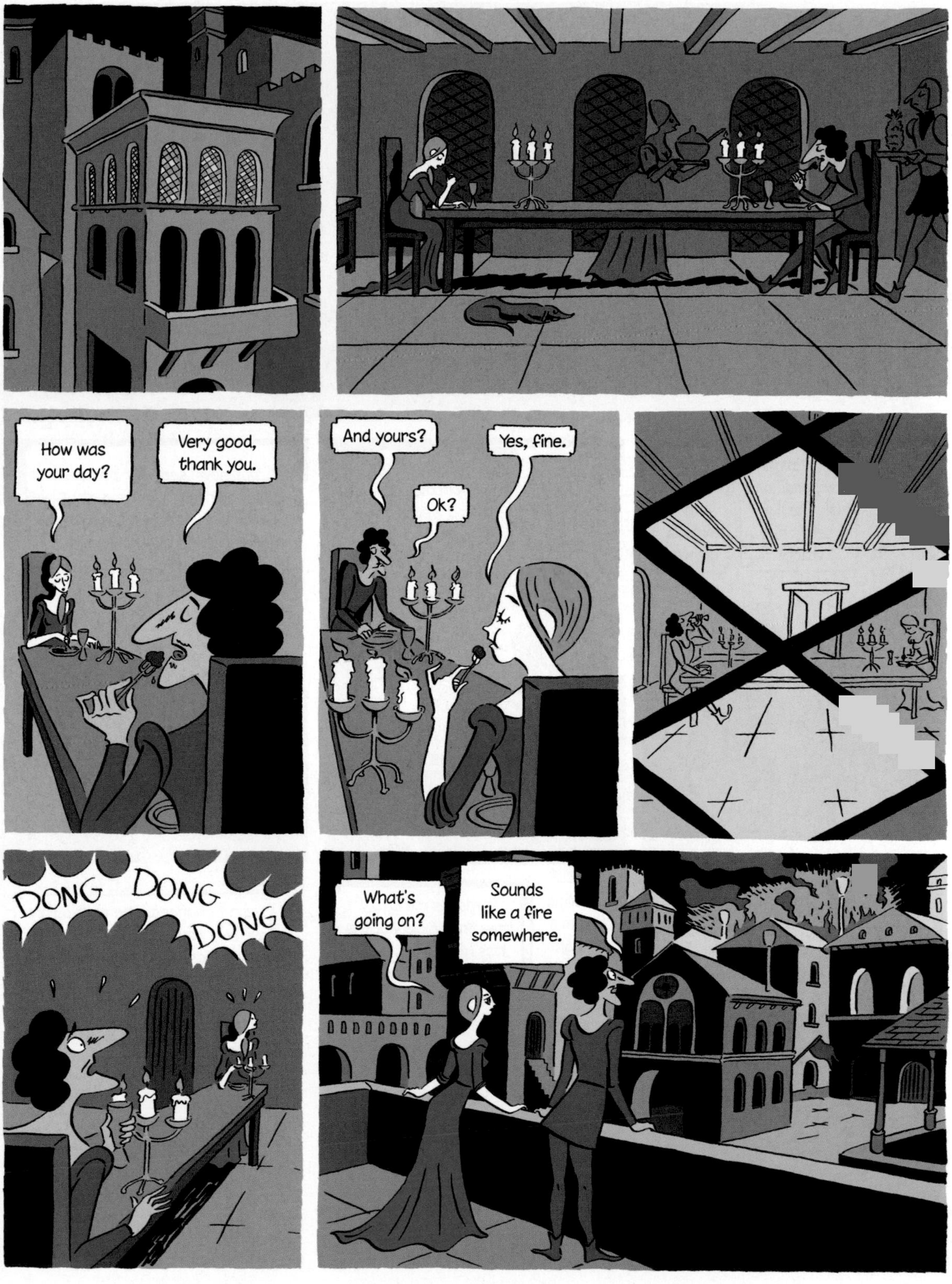
How was your day?
Very good, thank you.
And yours?
Ok?
Yes, fine.
DONG DONG DONG
What's going on?
Sounds like a fire somewhere.

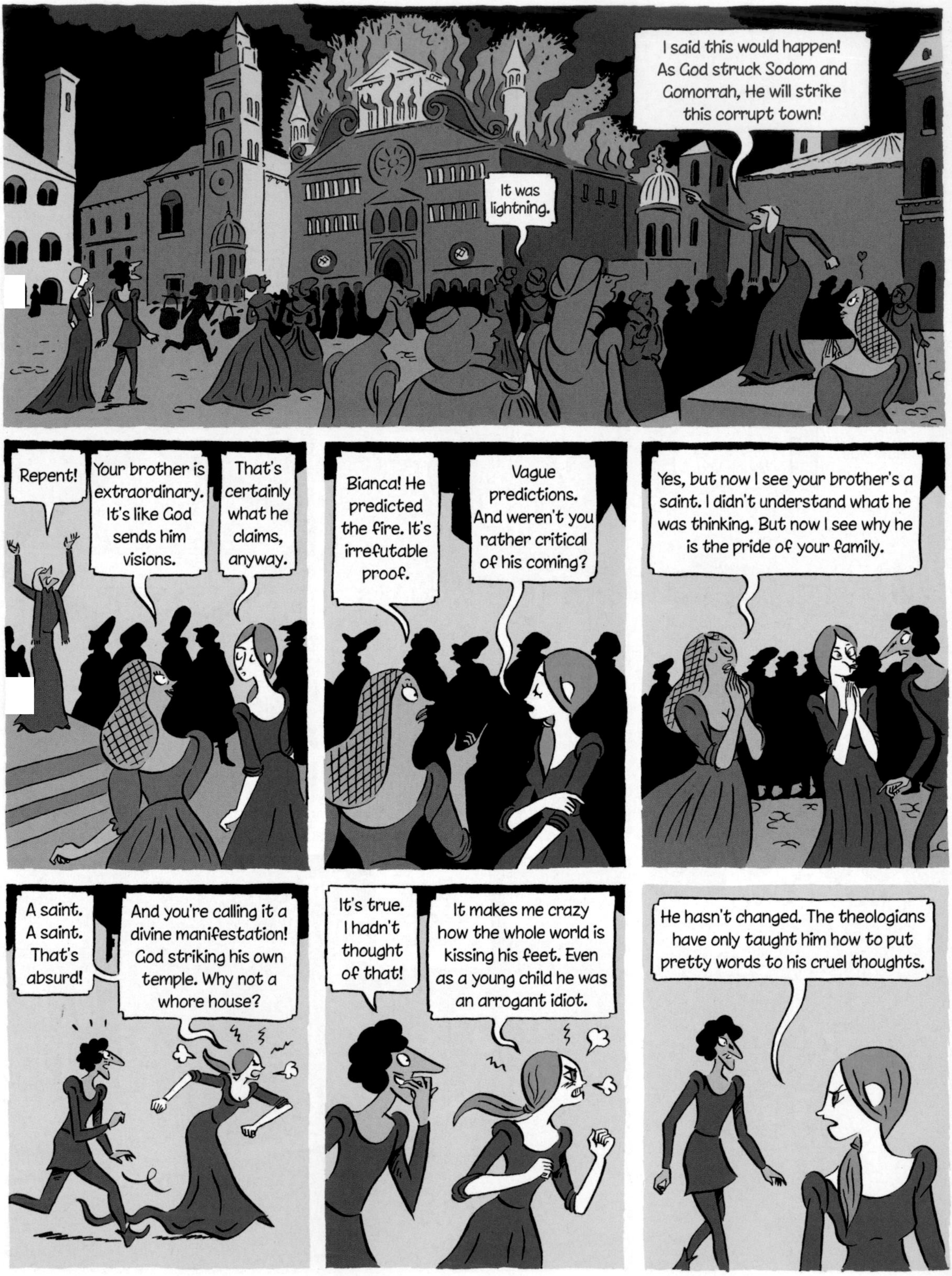
I said this would happen! As God struck Sodom and Gomorrah, He will strike this corrupt town!
It was lightning.
Repent!
Your brother is extraordinary. It's like God sends him visions.
That's certainly what he claims, anyway.
Bianca! He predicted the fire. It's irrefutable proof.
Vague predictions. And weren't you rather critical of his coming?
Yes, but now I see your brother's a saint. I didn't understand what he was thinking. But now I see why he is the pride of your family.
A saint. A saint. That's absurd!
And you're calling it a divine manifestation! God striking his own temple. Why not a whore house?
It's true. I hadn't thought of that!
It makes me crazy how the whole world is kissing his feet. Even as a young child he was an arrogant idiot.
He hasn't changed. The theologians have only taught him how to put pretty words to his cruel thoughts.

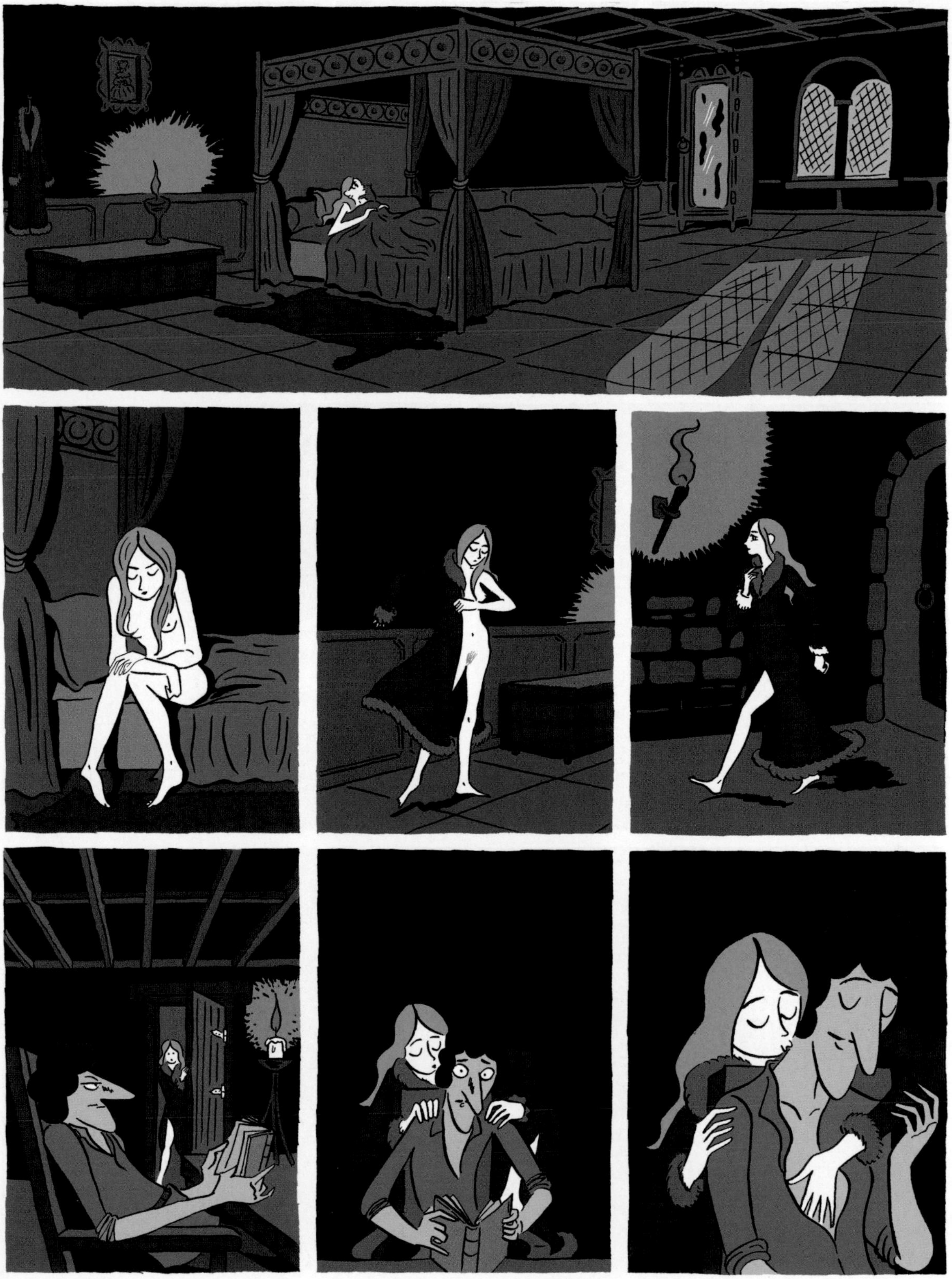

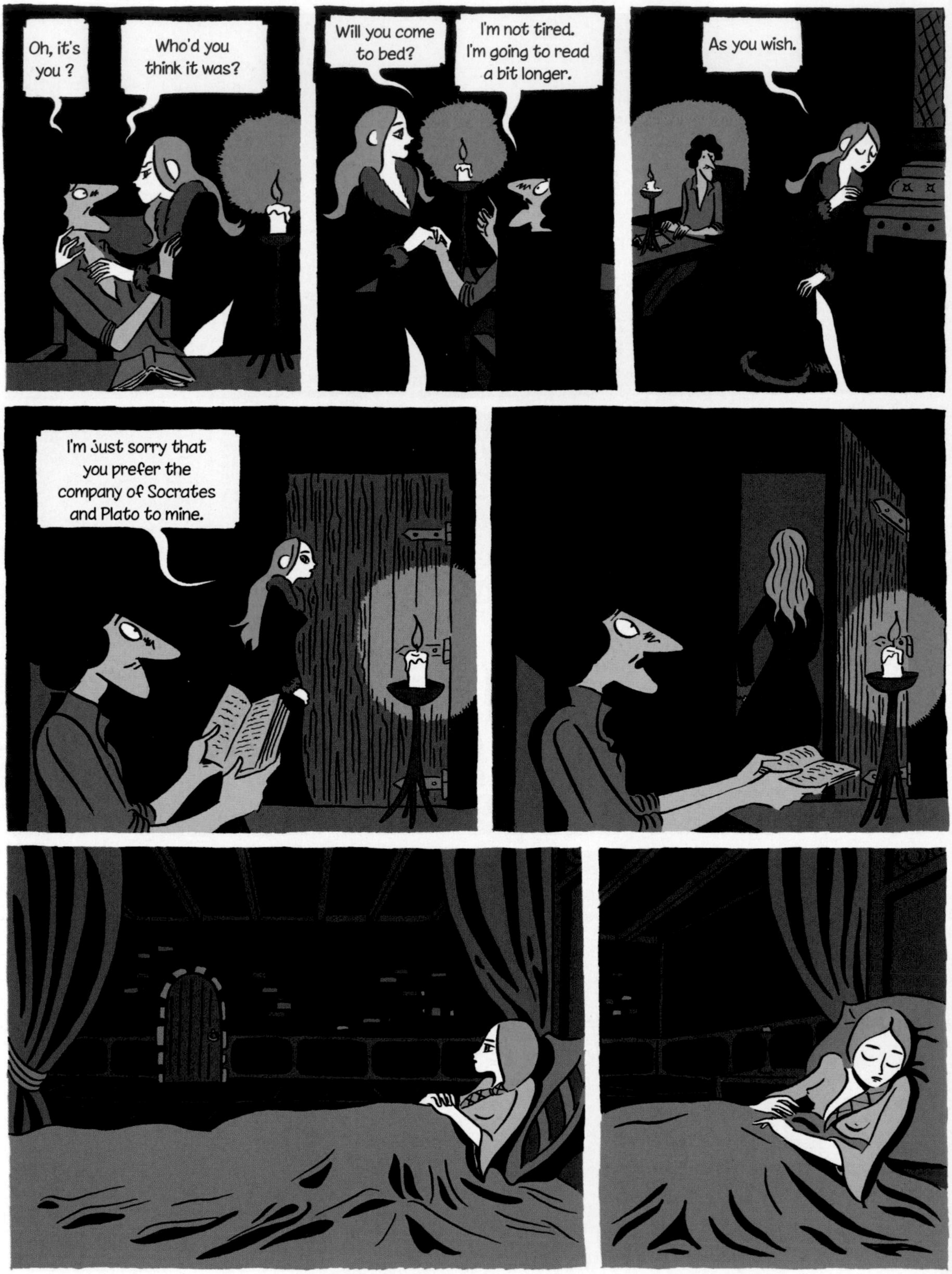
Oh, it's you ?
Who'd you think it was?
Will you come to bed?
I'm not tired. I'm going to read a bit longer.
As you wish.
I'm just sorry that you prefer the company of Socrates and Plato to mine.

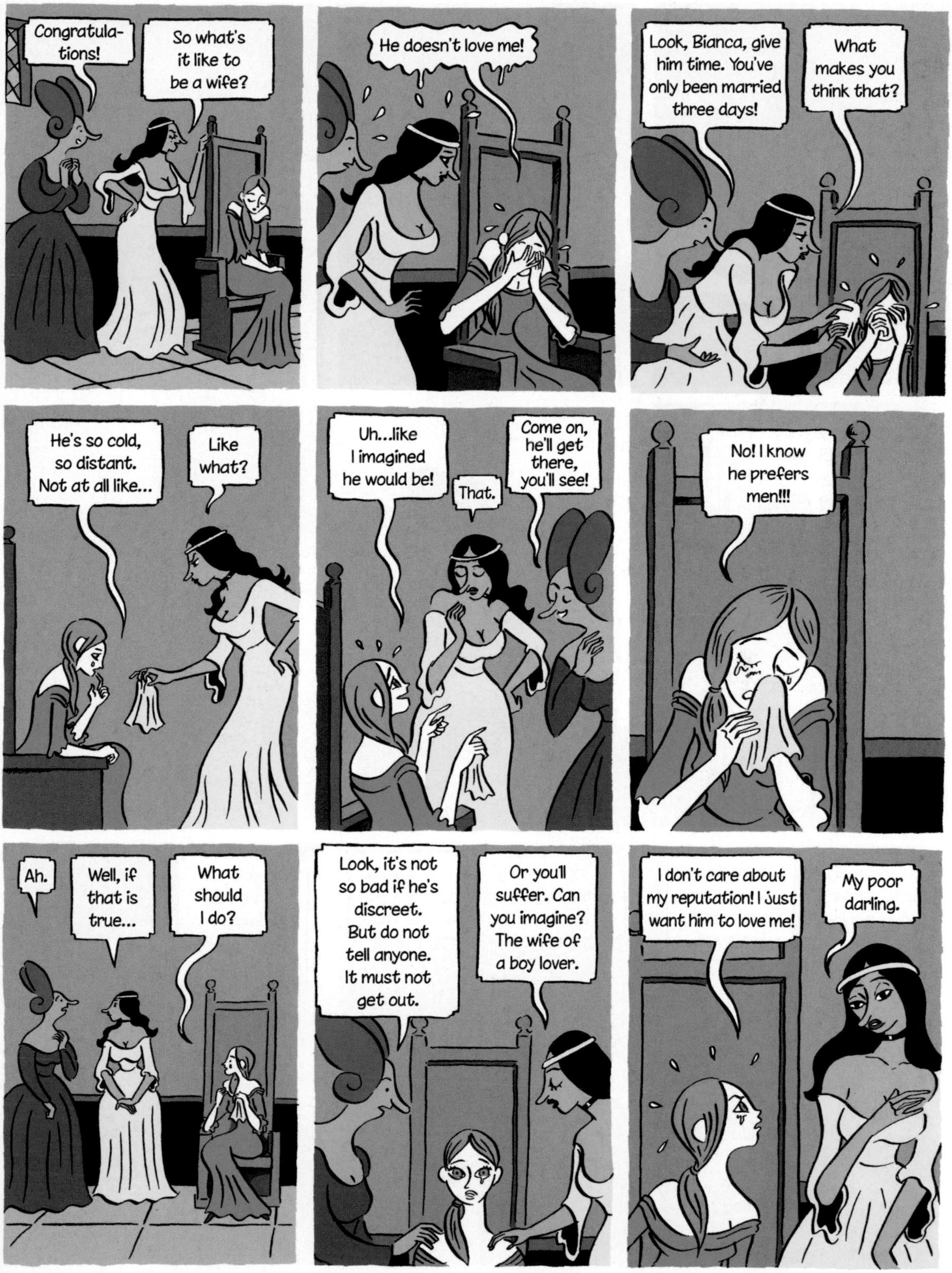
Congratula-tions!
So what's it like to be a wife?
He doesn't love me!
Look, Bianca, give him time. You've only been married three days!
What makes you think that?
He's so cold, so distant. Not at all like...
Like what?
Uh...like I imagined he would be!
That.
Come on, he'll get there, you'll see!
No! I know he prefers men!!!
Ah.
Well, if that is true...
What should I do?
Look, it's not so bad if he's discreet. But do not tell anyone. It must not get out.
Or you'll suffer. Can you imagine? The wife of a boy lover.
I don't care about my reputation! I just want him to love me!
My poor darling.

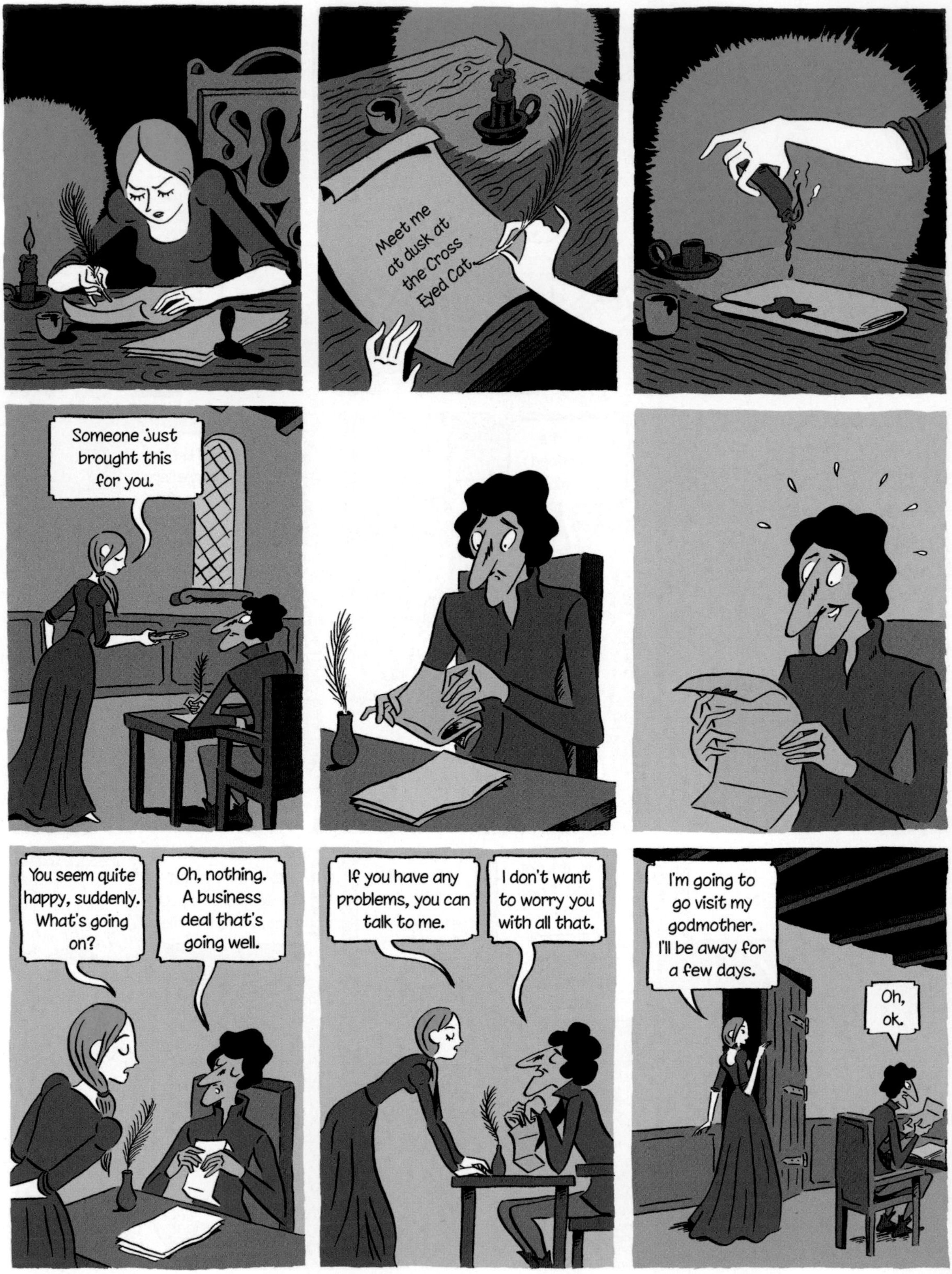
Meet me at dusk at the Cross Eyed Cat.
Someone just brought this for you.
You seem quite happy, suddenly. What's going on?
Oh, nothing. A business deal that's going well.
If you have any problems, you can talk to me.
I don't want to worry you with all that.
I'm going to go visit my godmother. I'll be away for a few days.
Oh, ok.

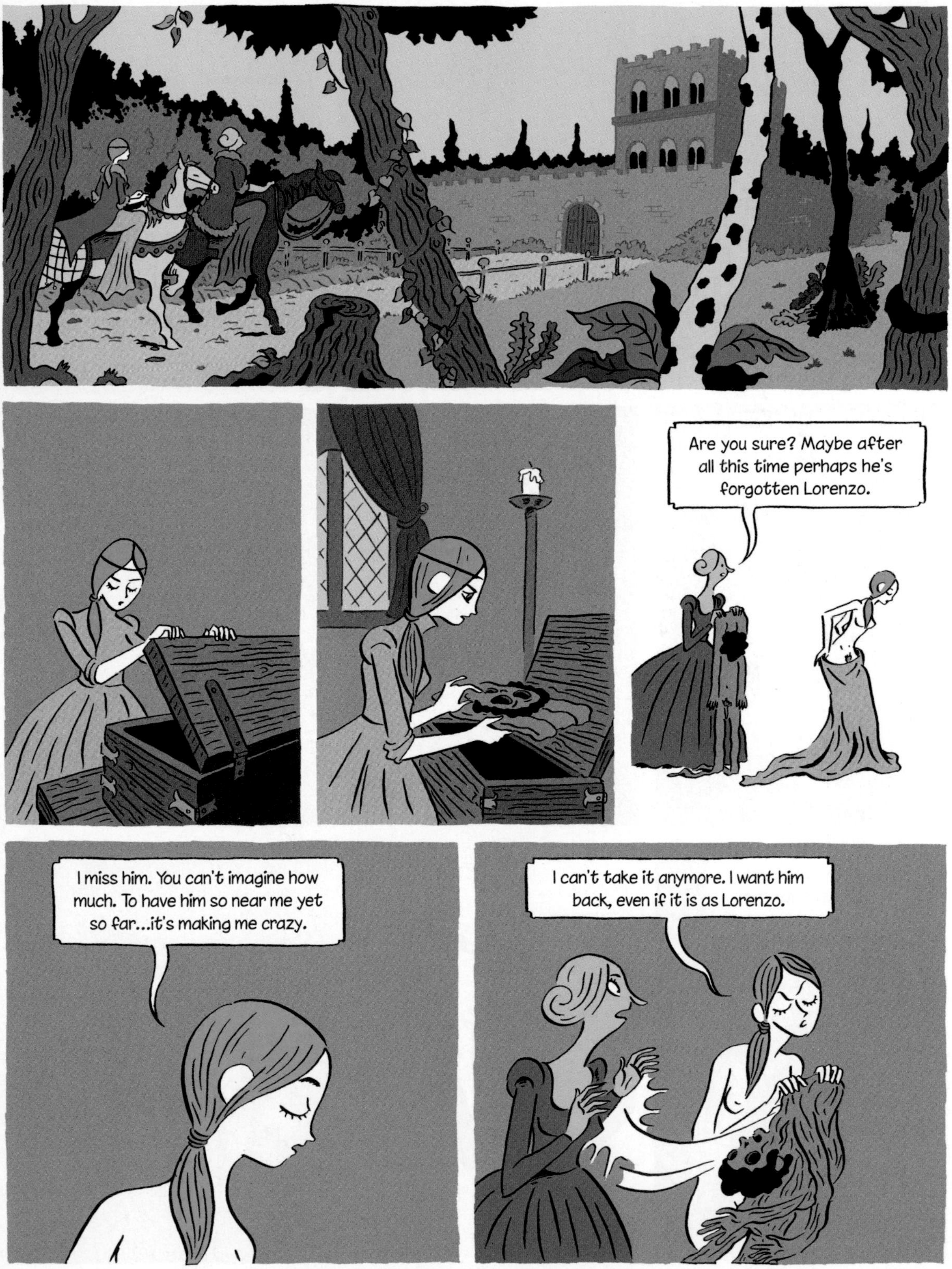
Are you sure? Maybe after all this time perhaps he's forgotten Lorenzo.
I miss him. You can't imagine how much. To have him so near me yet so far...it's making me crazy.
I can't take it anymore. I want him back, even if it is as Lorenzo.

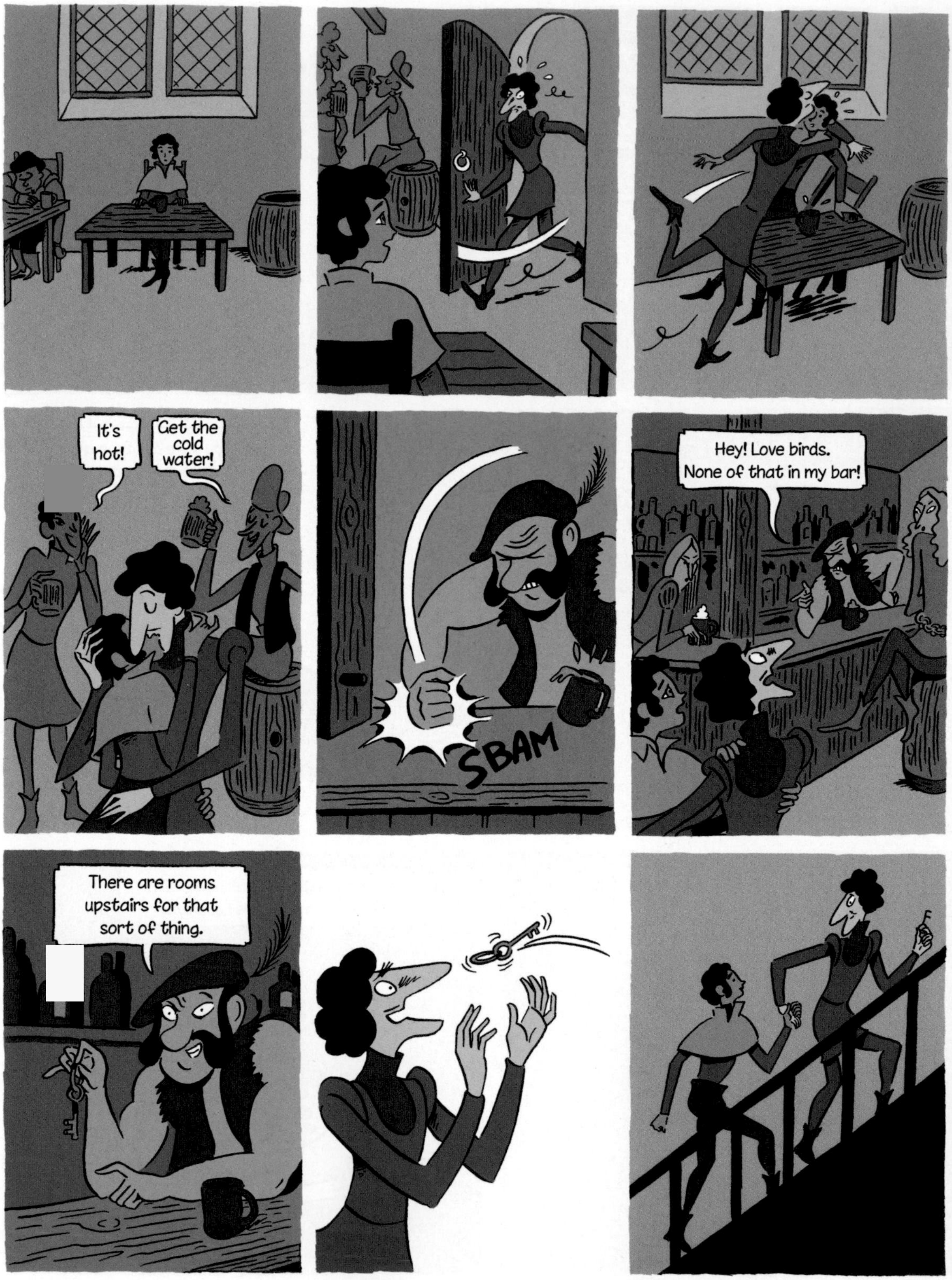
It's hot!
Get the cold water!
SBAM
Hey! Love birds. None of that in my bar!
There are rooms upstairs for that sort of thing.

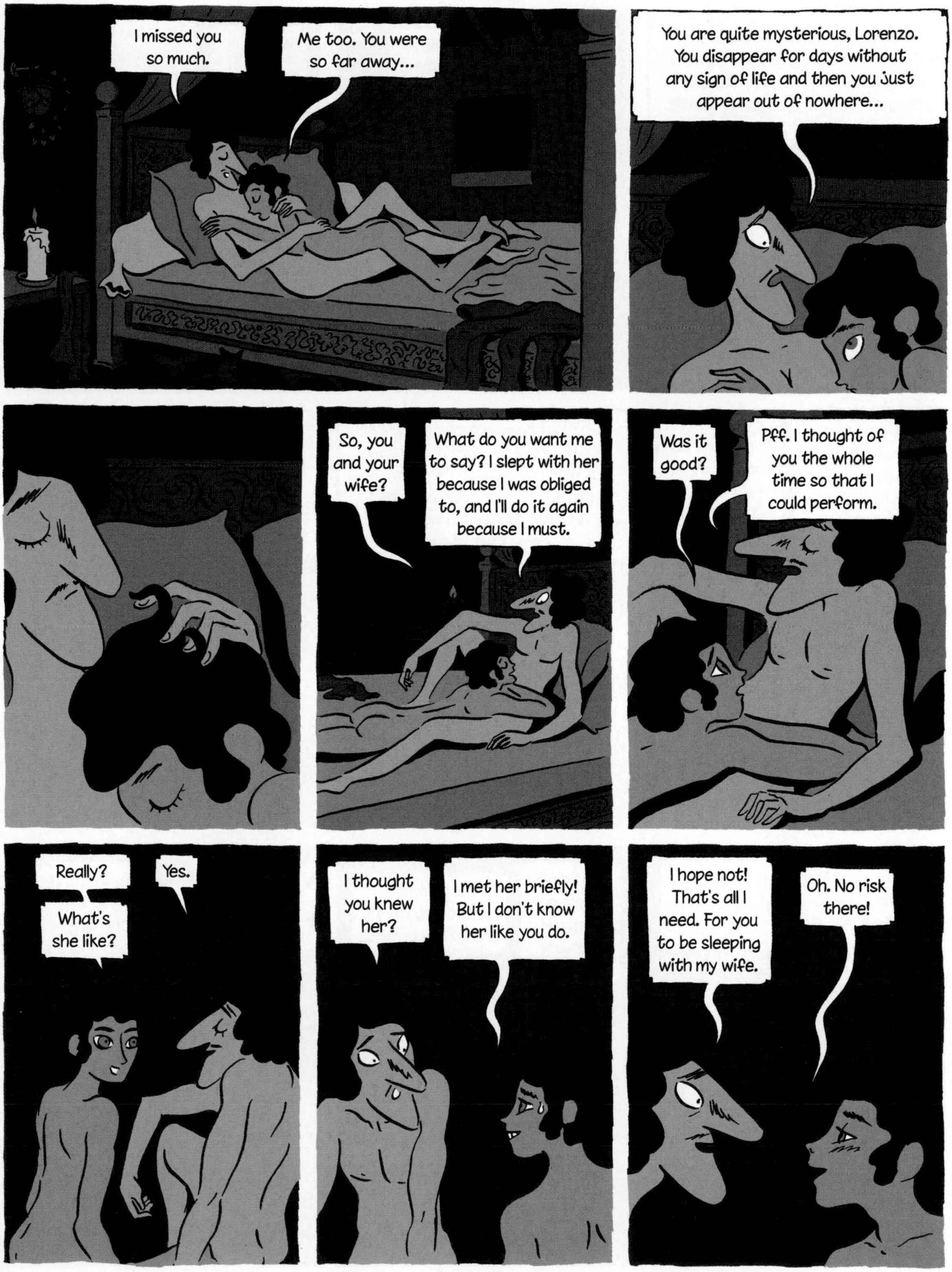
I missed you so much.
Me too. You were so far away...
You are quite mysterious, Lorenzo. You disappear for days without any sign of life and then you just appear out of nowhere...
So, you and your wife?
What do you want me to say? I slept with her because I was obliged to, and I'll do it again because I must.
Was it good?
Pff. I thought of you the whole time so that I could perform.
Really?
Yes.
What's she like?
I thought you knew her?
I met her briefly! But I don't know her like you do.
I hope not! That's all I need. For you to be sleeping with my wife.
Oh. No risk there!

There's not much to say. She's my wife. You could say she's pretty. She's very gracious and open minded for a young girl from that type of family.

But I think she guessed my preferences...

Really? Poor thing.

Why poor thing?

That can't be easy to not be desired by your husband.

It would be worse if I were a womanizer, wouldn't it? At least she knows it's not her.

That's one way to look at it. But I wouldn't want to be her.

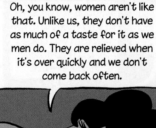

Oh, you know, women aren't like that. Unlike us, they don't have as much of a taste for it as we men do. They are relieved when it's over quickly and we don't come back often.

It's a good thing though! How could a husband be sure of his wife's fidelity if she likes to get it on? She may take it anywhere she can get it!

A woman can like making love to the one she loves without it being dirty...

Don't be silly. You don't know women.

I've heard there are woman who actually enjoy it.

Lost women, unnatural, they'll end up in a brothel.

DING DONG

Oh, this isn't good. Tonio only rings when there's trouble.

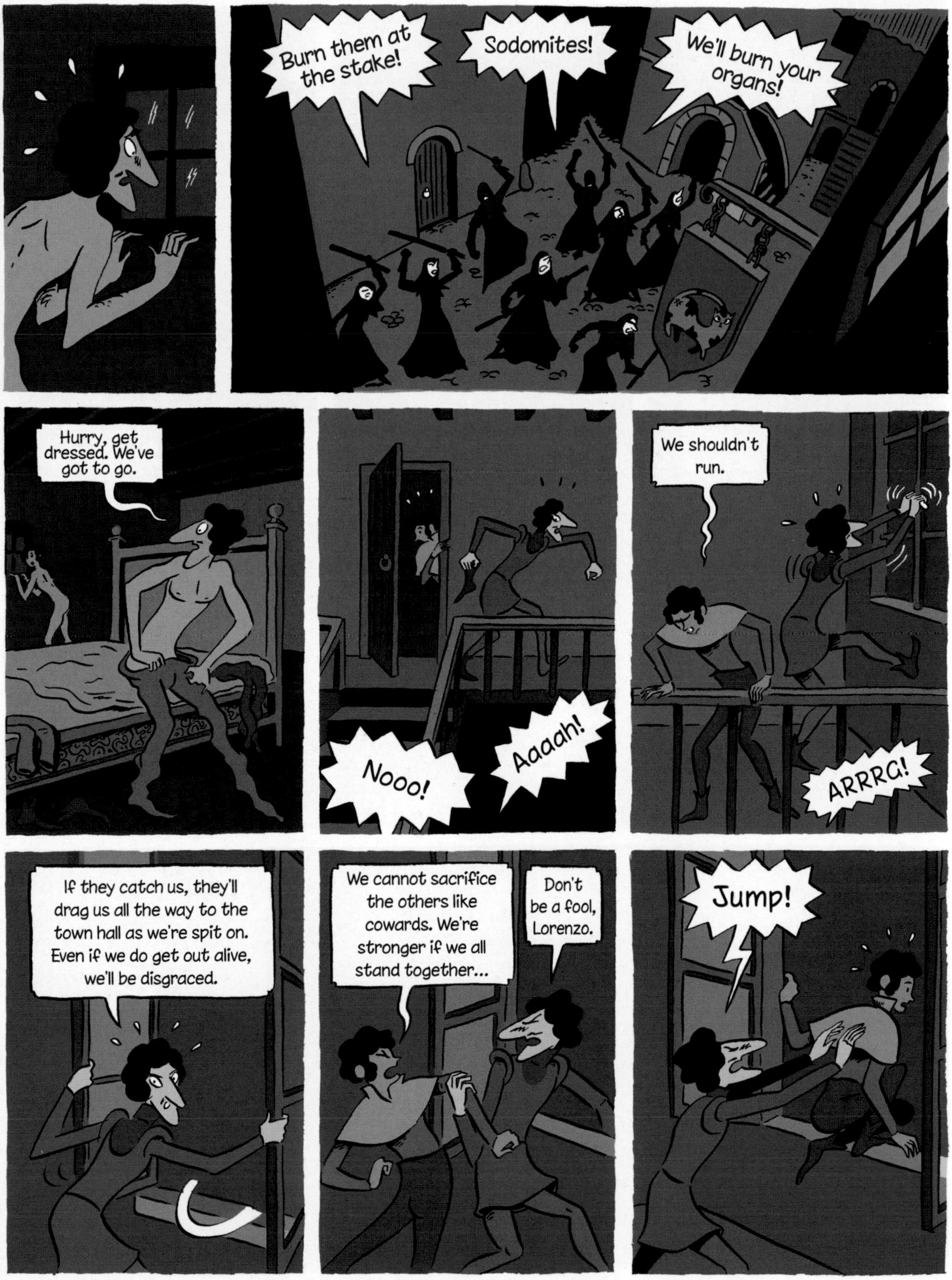
Burn them at the stake!
Sodomites!
We'll burn your organs!
Hurry, get dressed. We've got to go.
Nooo!
Aaaah!
We shouldn't run.
ARRRG!
If they catch us, they'll drag us all the way to the town hall as we're spit on. Even if we do get out alive, we'll be disgraced.
We cannot sacrifice the others like cowards. We're stronger if we all stand together...
Don't be a fool, Lorenzo.
Jump!

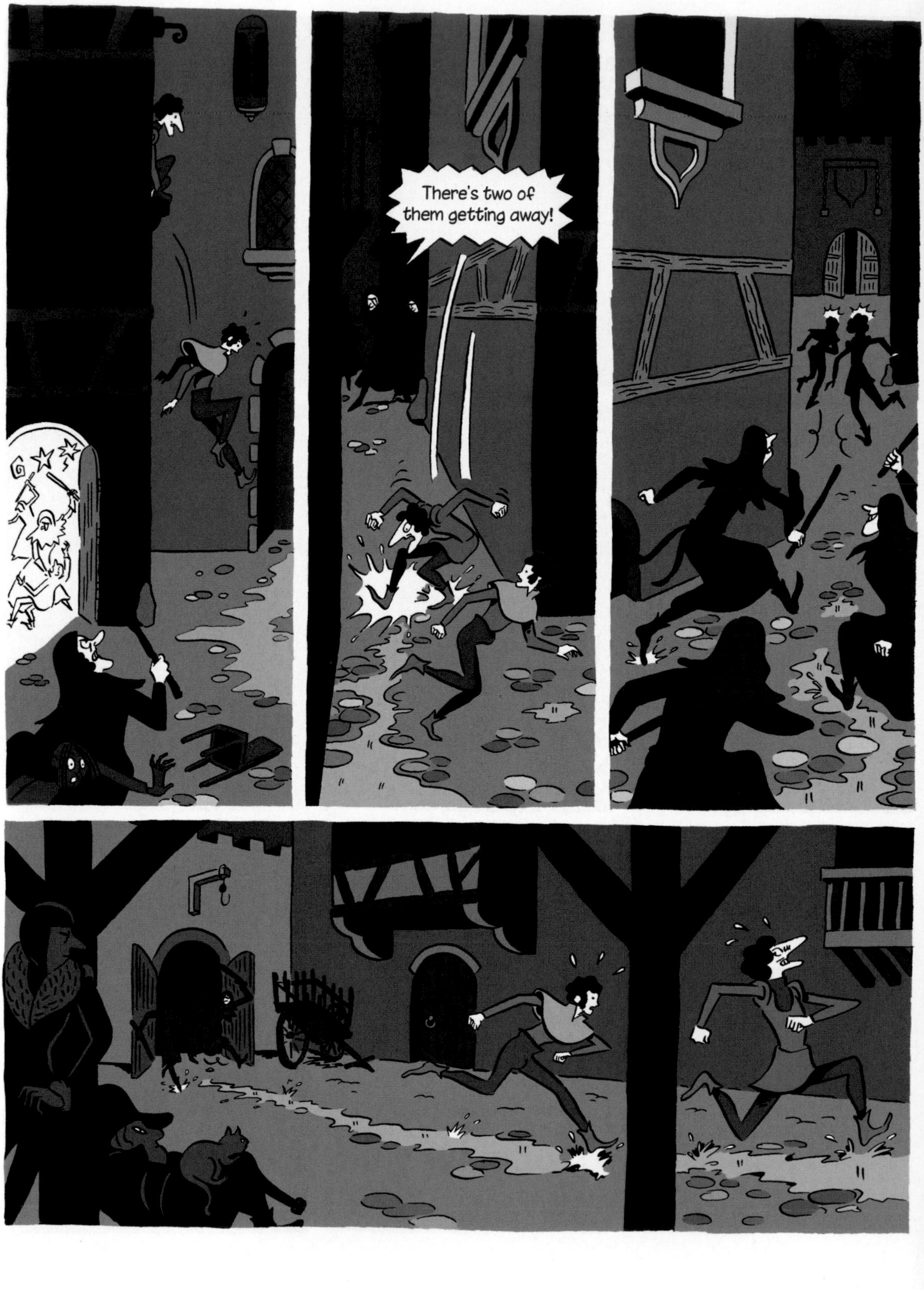
There's two of them getting away!

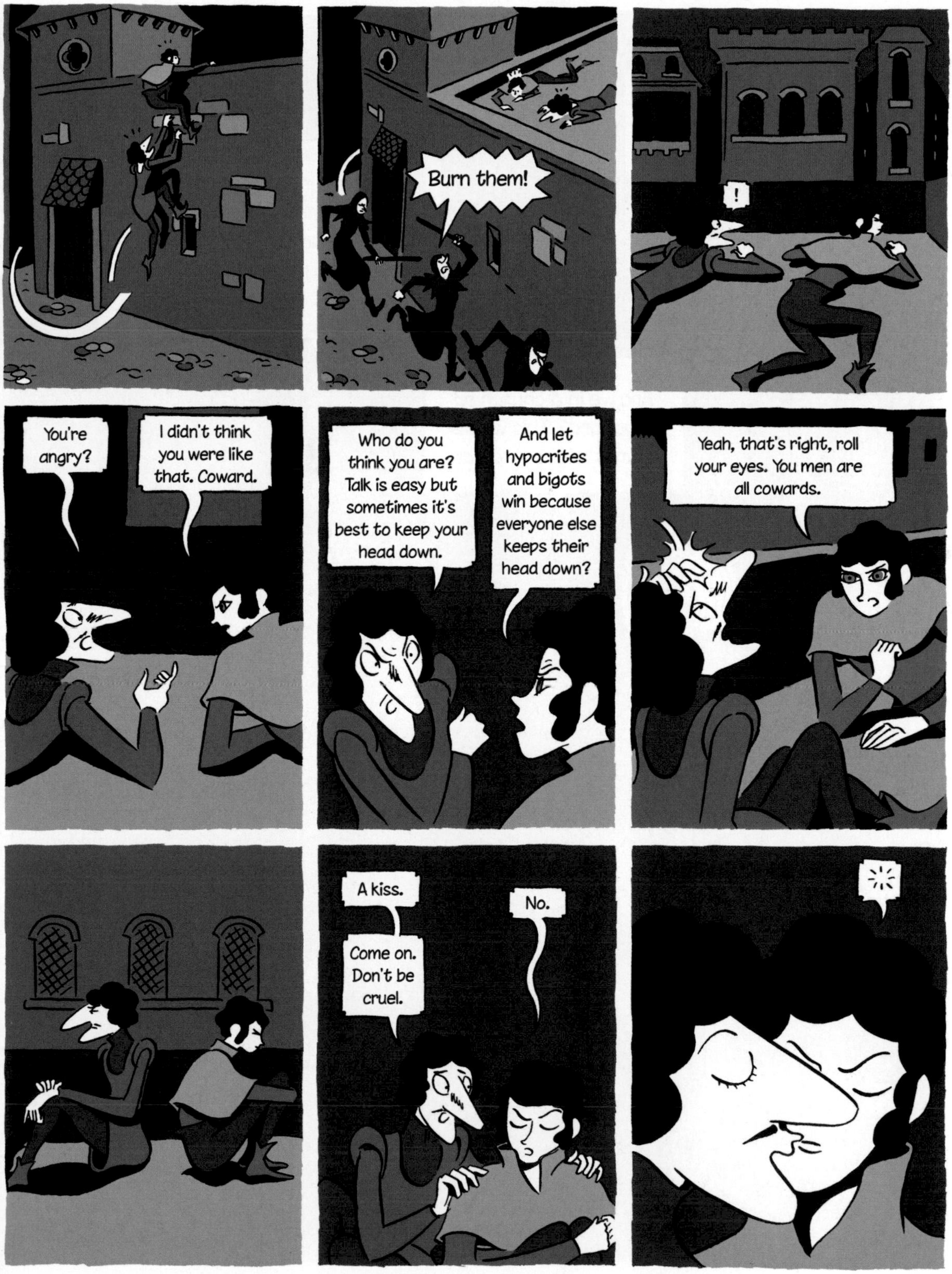
Burn them!
!
You're angry?
I didn't think you were like that. Coward.
Who do you think you are? Talk is easy but sometimes it's best to keep your head down.
And let hypocrites and bigots win because everyone else keeps their head down?
Yeah, that's right, roll your eyes. You men are all cowards.
A kiss.
Come on. Don't be cruel.
No.

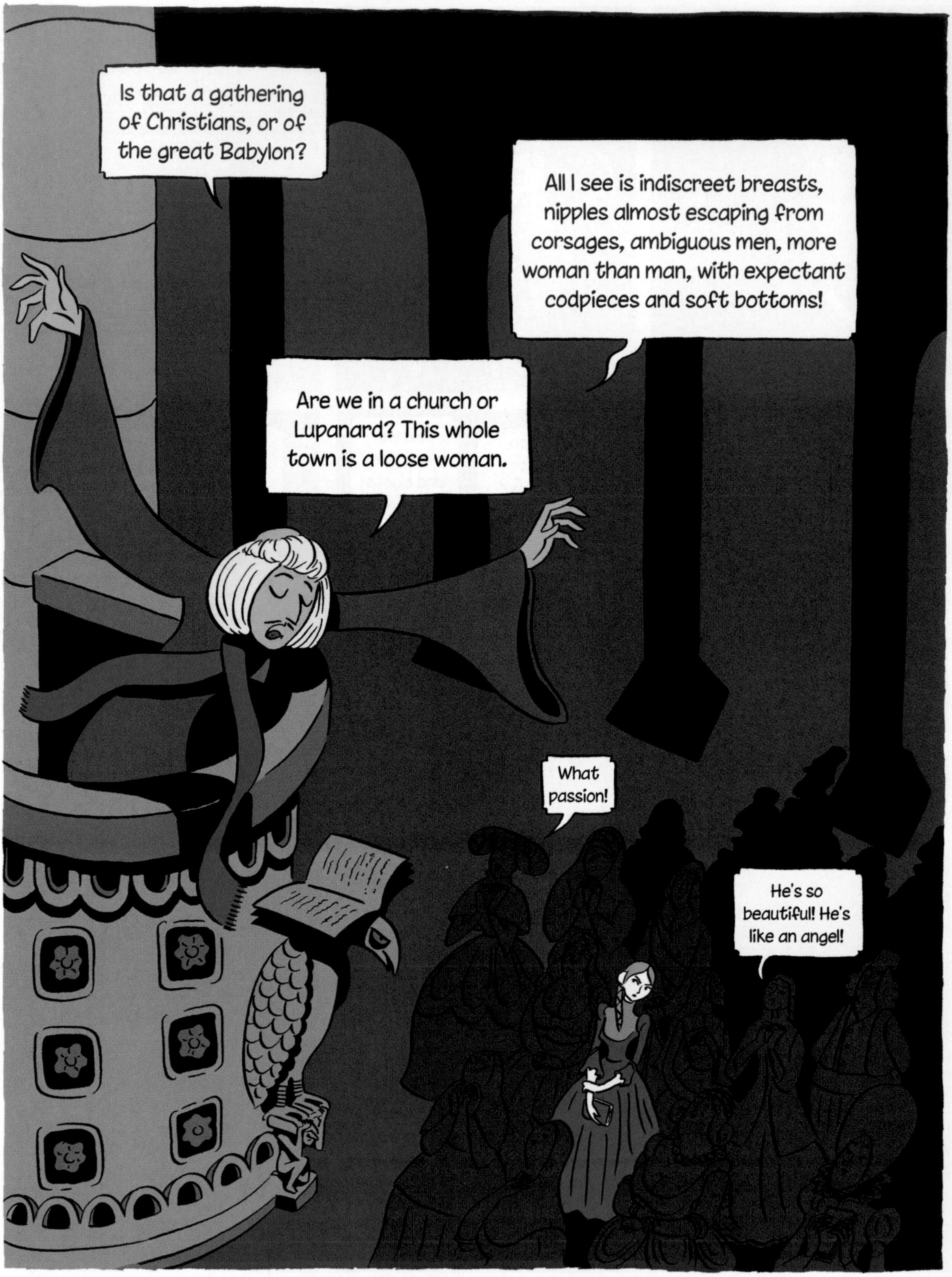
Is that a gathering of Christians, or of the great Babylon?
All I see is indiscreet breasts, nipples almost escaping from corsages, ambiguous men, more woman than man, with expectant codpieces and soft bottoms!
Are we in a church or Lupanard? This whole town is a loose woman.
What passion!
He's so beautiful! He's like an angel!

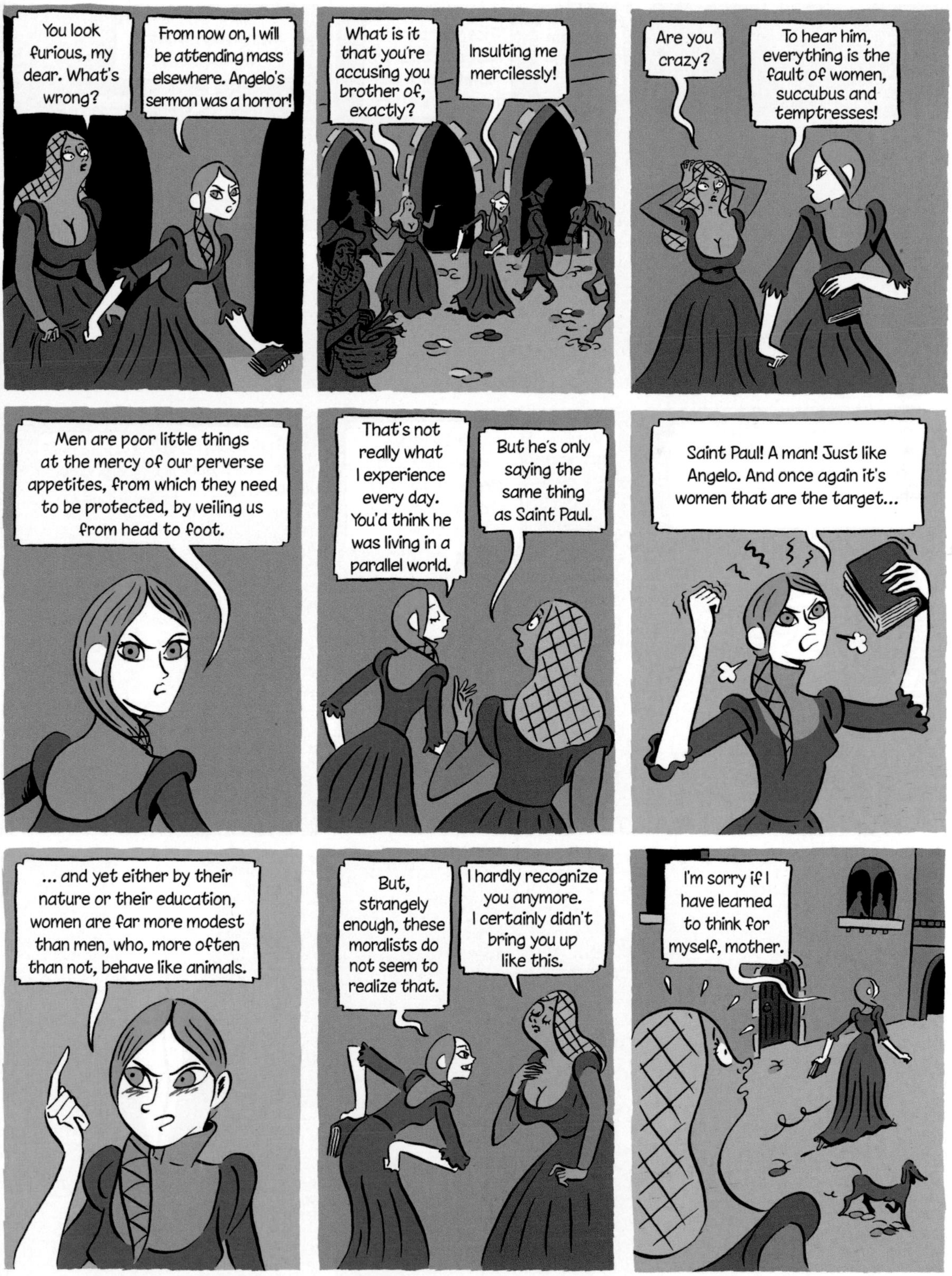
You look furious, my dear. What's wrong?
From now on, I will be attending mass elsewhere. Angelo's sermon was a horror!
What is it that you're accusing you brother of, exactly?
Insulting me mercilessly!
Are you crazy?
To hear him, everything is the fault of women, succubus and temptresses!
Men are poor little things at the mercy of our perverse appetites, from which they need to be protected, by veiling us from head to foot.
That's not really what I experience every day. You'd think he was living in a parallel world.
But he's only saying the same thing as Saint Paul.
Saint Paul! A man! Just like Angelo. And once again it's women that are the target...
... and yet either by their nature or their education, women are far more modest than men, who, more often than not, behave like animals.
But, strangely enough, these moralists do not seem to realize that.
I hardly recognize you anymore. I certainly didn't bring you up like this.
I'm sorry if I have learned to think for myself, mother.

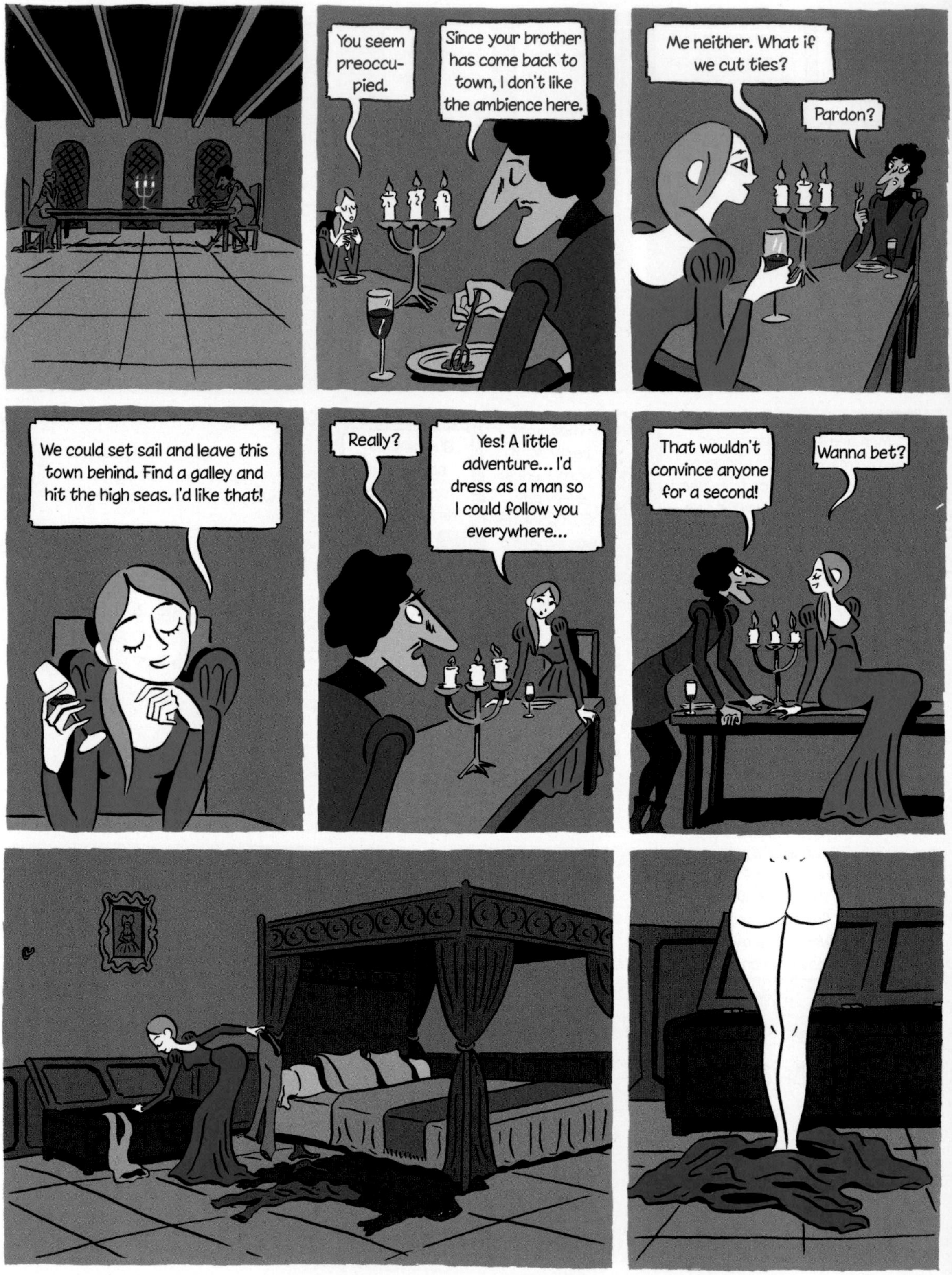
You seem preoccu-pied.
Since your brother has come back to town, I don't like the ambience here.
Me neither. What if we cut ties?
Pardon?
We could set sail and leave this town behind. Find a galley and hit the high seas. I'd like that!
Really?
Yes! A little adventure... I'd dress as a man so I could follow you everywhere...
That wouldn't convince anyone for a second!
Wanna bet?

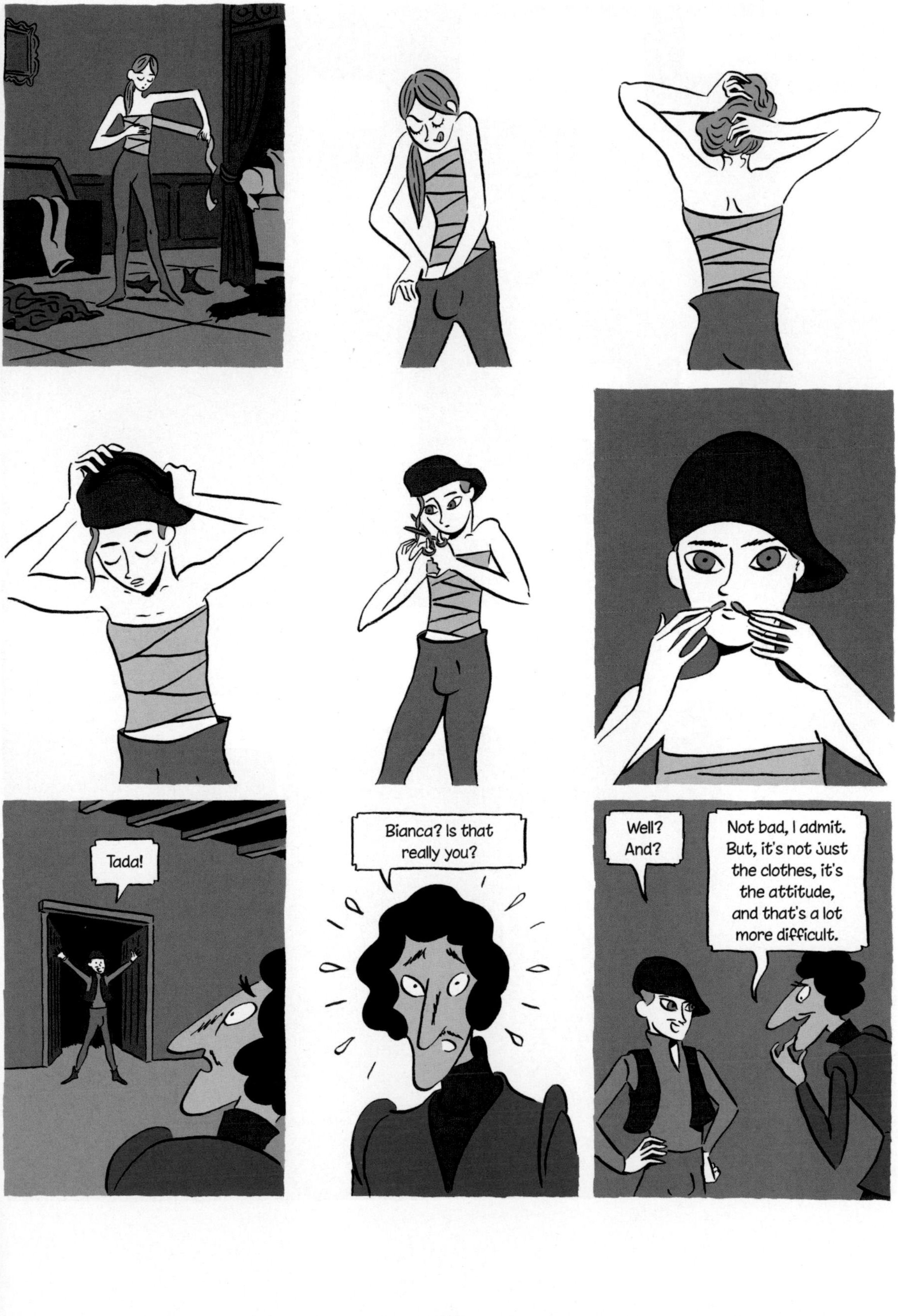
Tada!
Bianca? Is that really you?
Well? And?
Not bad, I admit. But, it's not just the clothes, it's the attitude, and that's a lot more difficult.

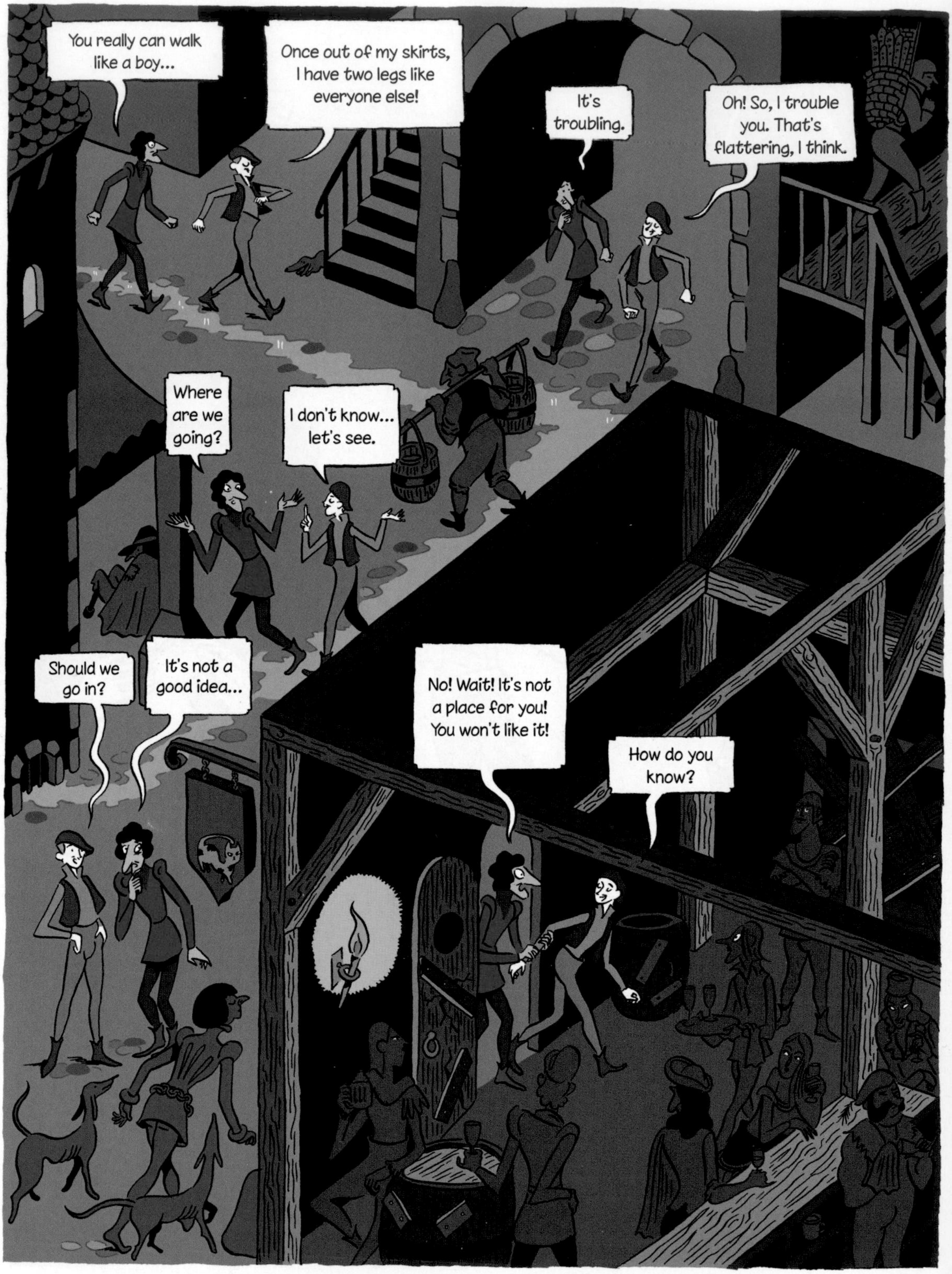
You really can walk like a boy...
Once out of my skirts, I have two legs like everyone else!
It's troubling.
Oh! So, I trouble you. That's flattering, I think.
Where are we going?
I don't know... let's see.
Should we go in?
It's not a good idea...
No! Wait! It's not a place for you! You won't like it!
How do you know?

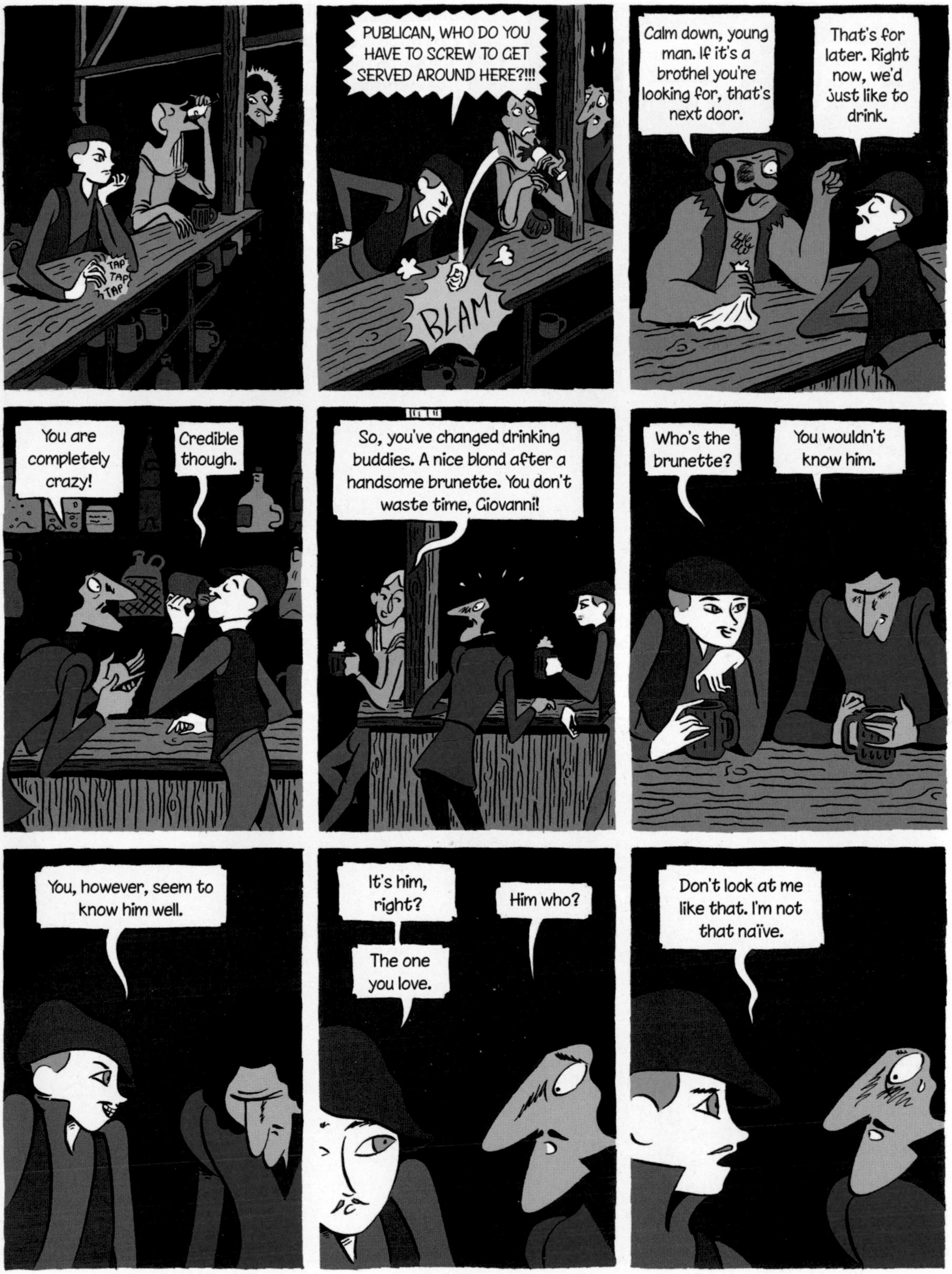

TAP TAP TAP
PUBLICAN, WHO DO YOU HAVE TO SCREW TO GET SERVED AROUND HERE?!!!
BLAM
Calm down, young man. If it's a brothel you're looking for, that's next door.
That's for later. Right now, we'd just like to drink.
You are completely crazy!
Credible though.
So, you've changed drinking buddies. A nice blond after a handsome brunette. You don't waste time, Giovanni!
Who's the brunette?
You wouldn't know him.
You, however, seem to know him well.
It's him, right?
The one you love.
Him who?
Don't look at me like that. I'm not that naïve.

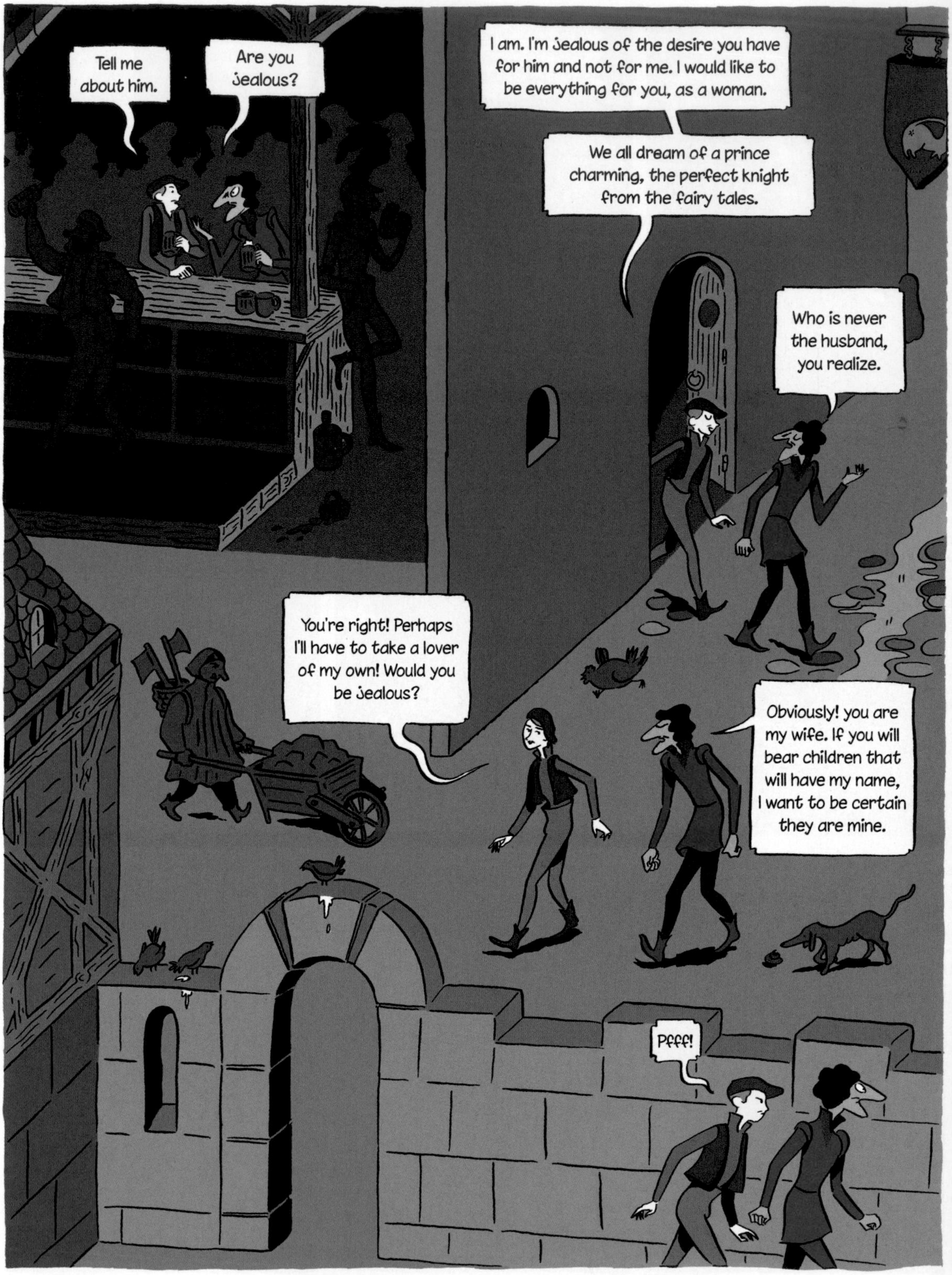
Tell me about him.
Are you jealous?
I am. I'm jealous of the desire you have for him and not for me. I would like to be everything for you, as a woman.
We all dream of a prince charming, the perfect knight from the fairy tales.
Who is never the husband, you realize.
You're right! Perhaps I'll have to take a lover of my own! Would you be jealous?
Obviously! you are my wife. If you will bear children that will have my name, I want to be certain they are mine.
Pfff!

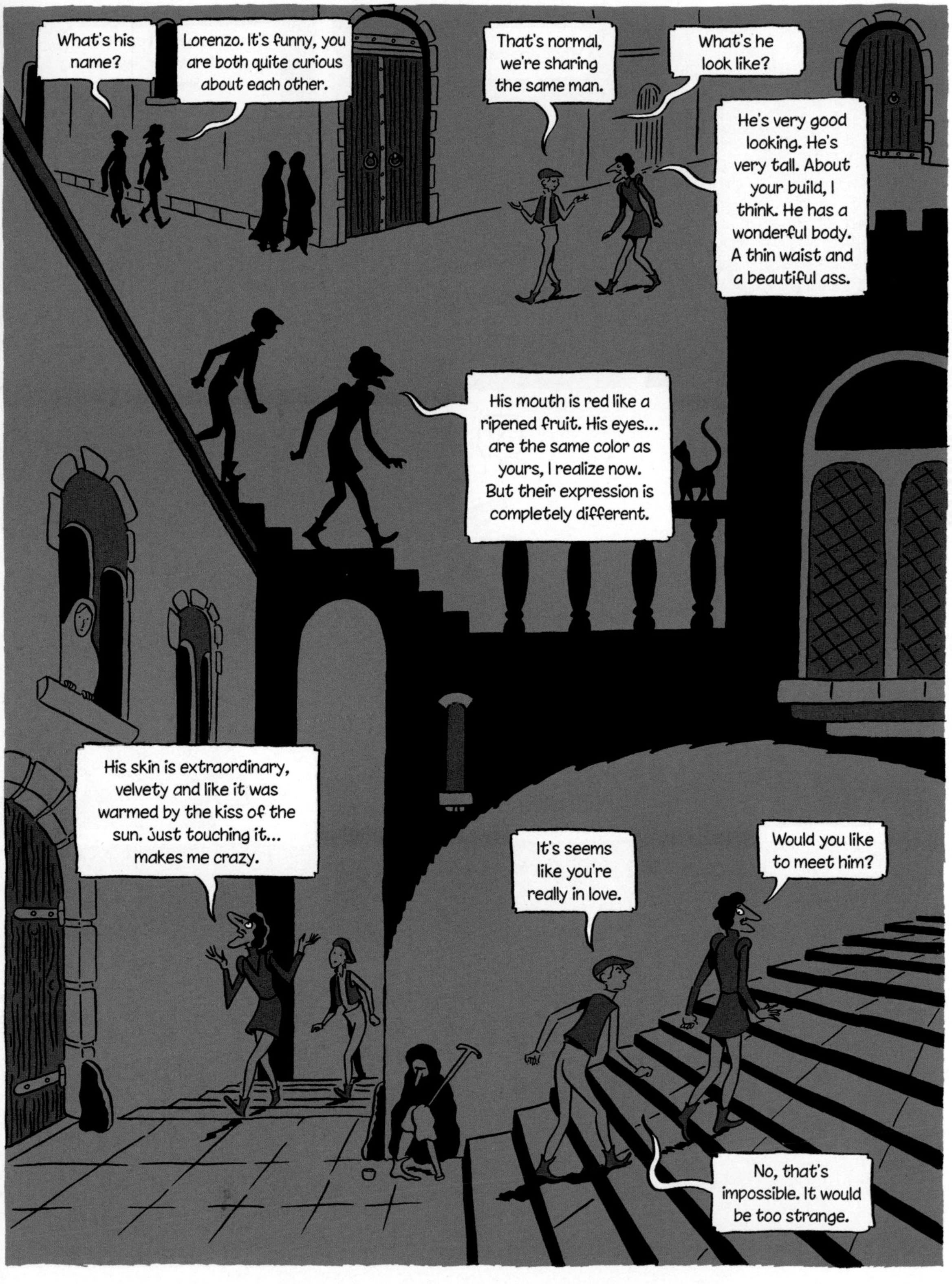
What's his name?
Lorenzo. It's funny, you are both quite curious about each other.
That's normal, we're sharing the same man.
What's he look like?
He's very good looking. He's very tall. About your build, I think. He has a wonderful body. A thin waist and a beautiful ass.
His mouth is red like a ripened fruit. His eyes... are the same color as yours, I realize now. But their expression is completely different.
His skin is extraordinary, velvety and like it was warmed by the kiss of the sun. Just touching it... makes me crazy.
It's seems like you're really in love.
Would you like to meet him?
No, that's impossible. It would be too strange.

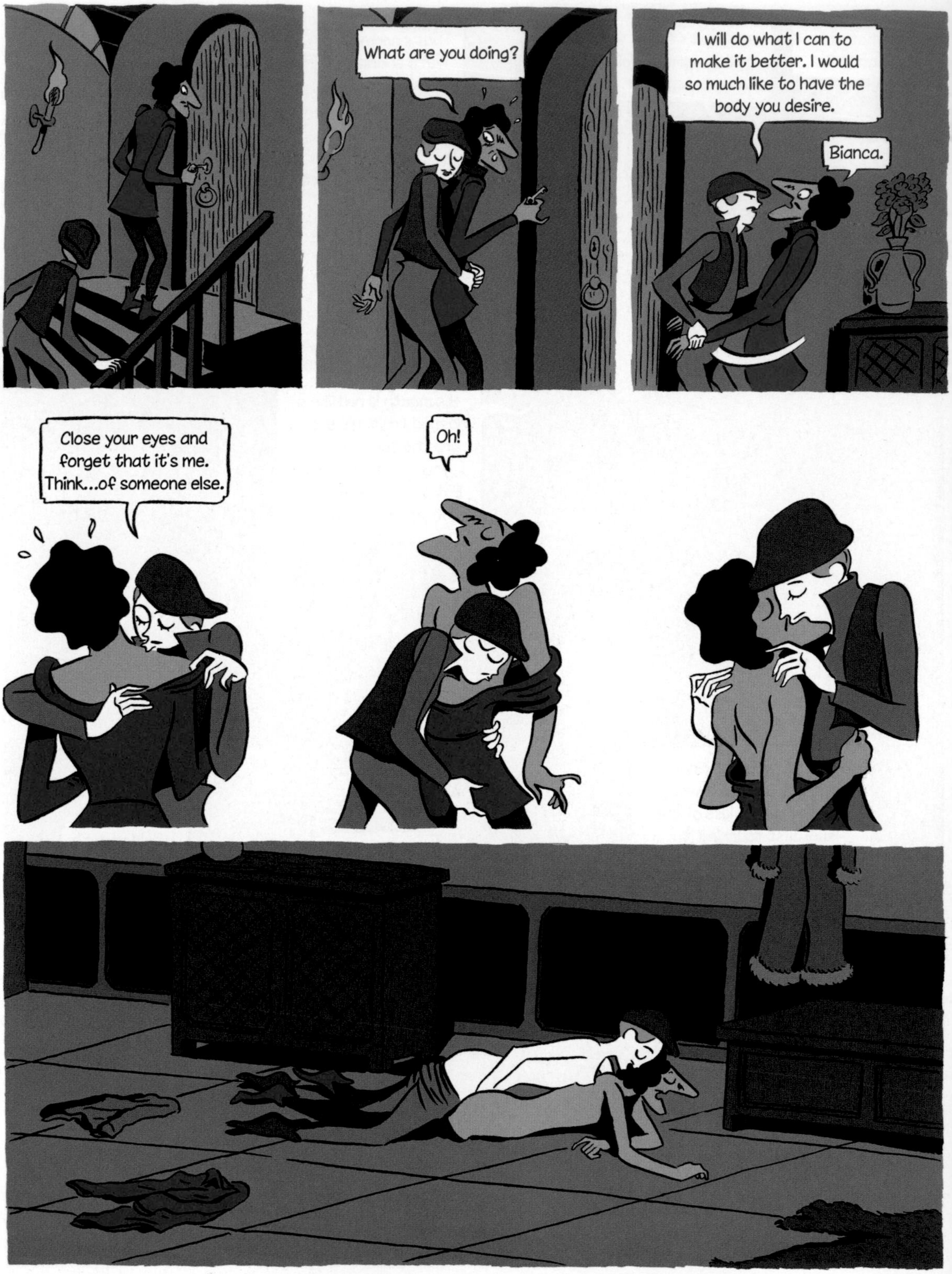
What are you doing?
I will do what I can to make it better. I would so much like to have the body you desire.
Bianca.
Close your eyes and forget that it's me. Think...of someone else.
Oh!

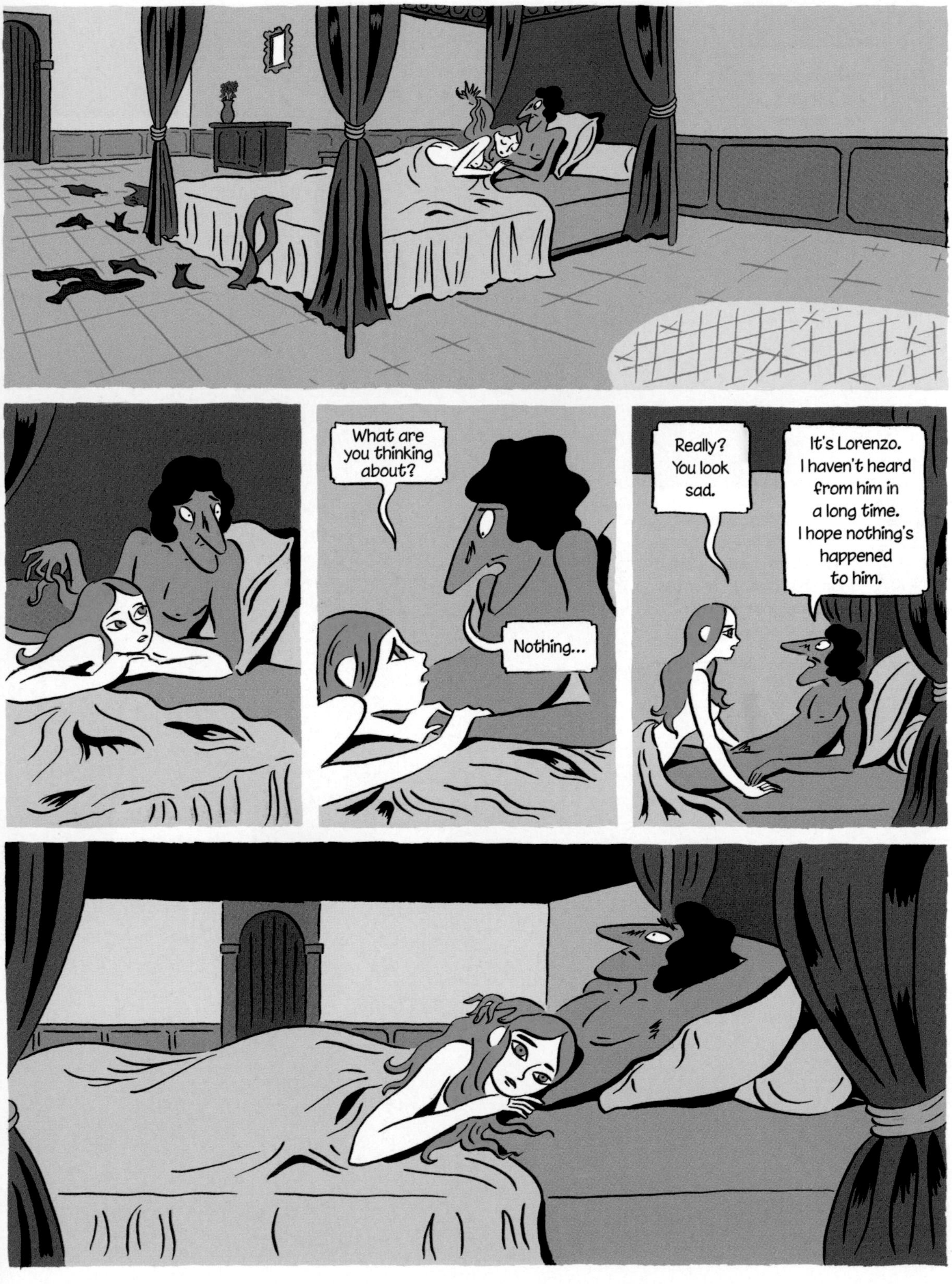
What are you thinking about?
Nothing...
Really? You look sad.
It's Lorenzo. I haven't heard from him in a long time. I hope nothing's happened to him.

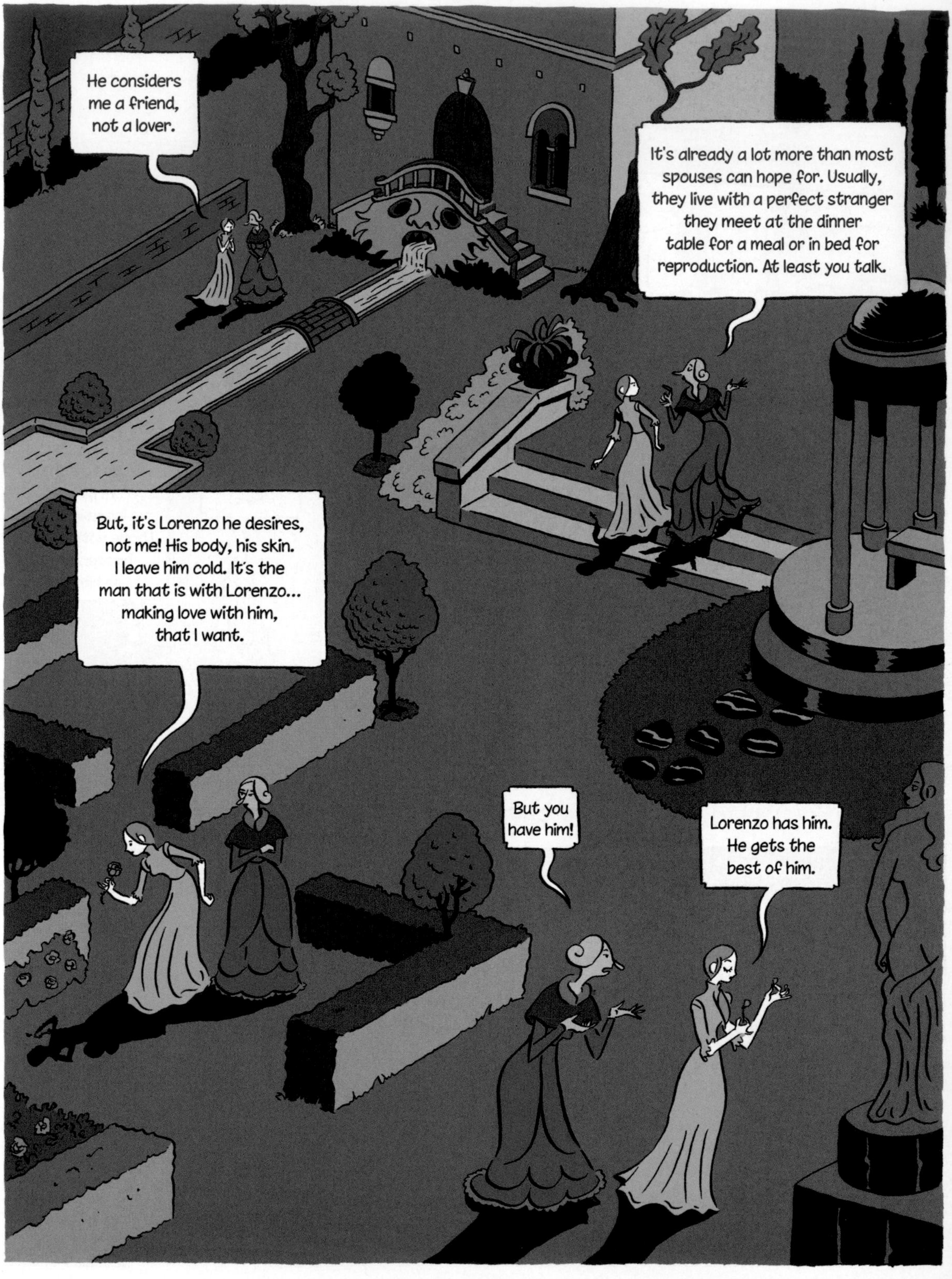
He considers me a friend, not a lover.
It's already a lot more than most spouses can hope for. Usually, they live with a perfect stranger they meet at the dinner table for a meal or in bed for reproduction. At least you talk.
But, it's Lorenzo he desires, not me! His body, his skin. I leave him cold. It's the man that is with Lorenzo... making love with him, that I want.
But you have him!
Lorenzo has him. He gets the best of him.

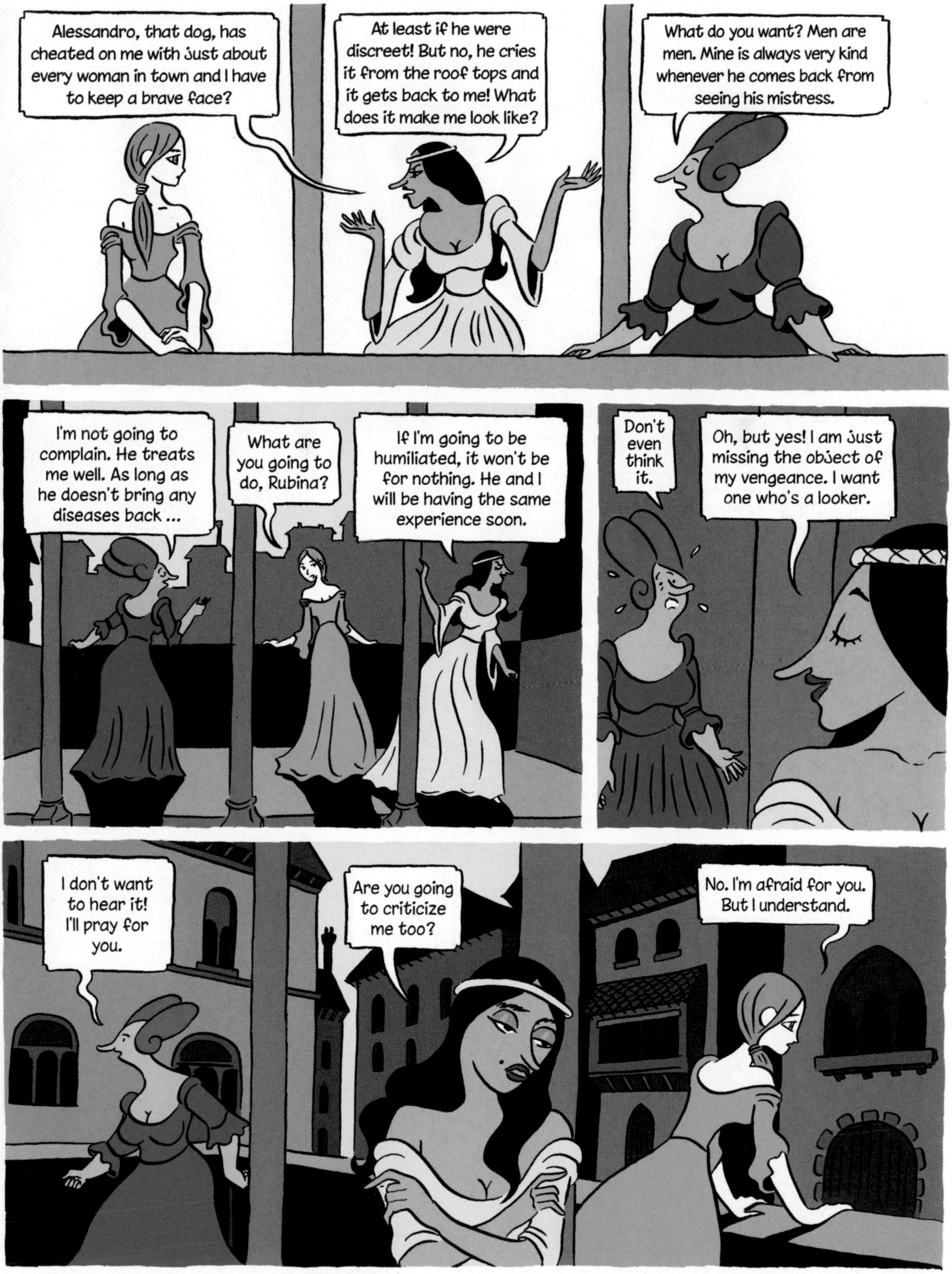
Alessandro, that dog, has cheated on me with just about every woman in town and I have to keep a brave face?
At least if he were discreet! But no, he cries it from the roof tops and it gets back to me! What does it make me look like?
What do you want? Men are men. Mine is always very kind whenever he comes back from seeing his mistress.
I'm not going to complain. He treats me well. As long as he doesn't bring any diseases back ...
What are you going to do, Rubina?
If I'm going to be humiliated, it won't be for nothing. He and I will be having the same experience soon.
Don't even think it.
Oh, but yes! I am just missing the object of my vengeance. I want one who's a looker.
I don't want to hear it! I'll pray for you.
Are you going to criticize me too?
No. I'm afraid for you. But I understand.

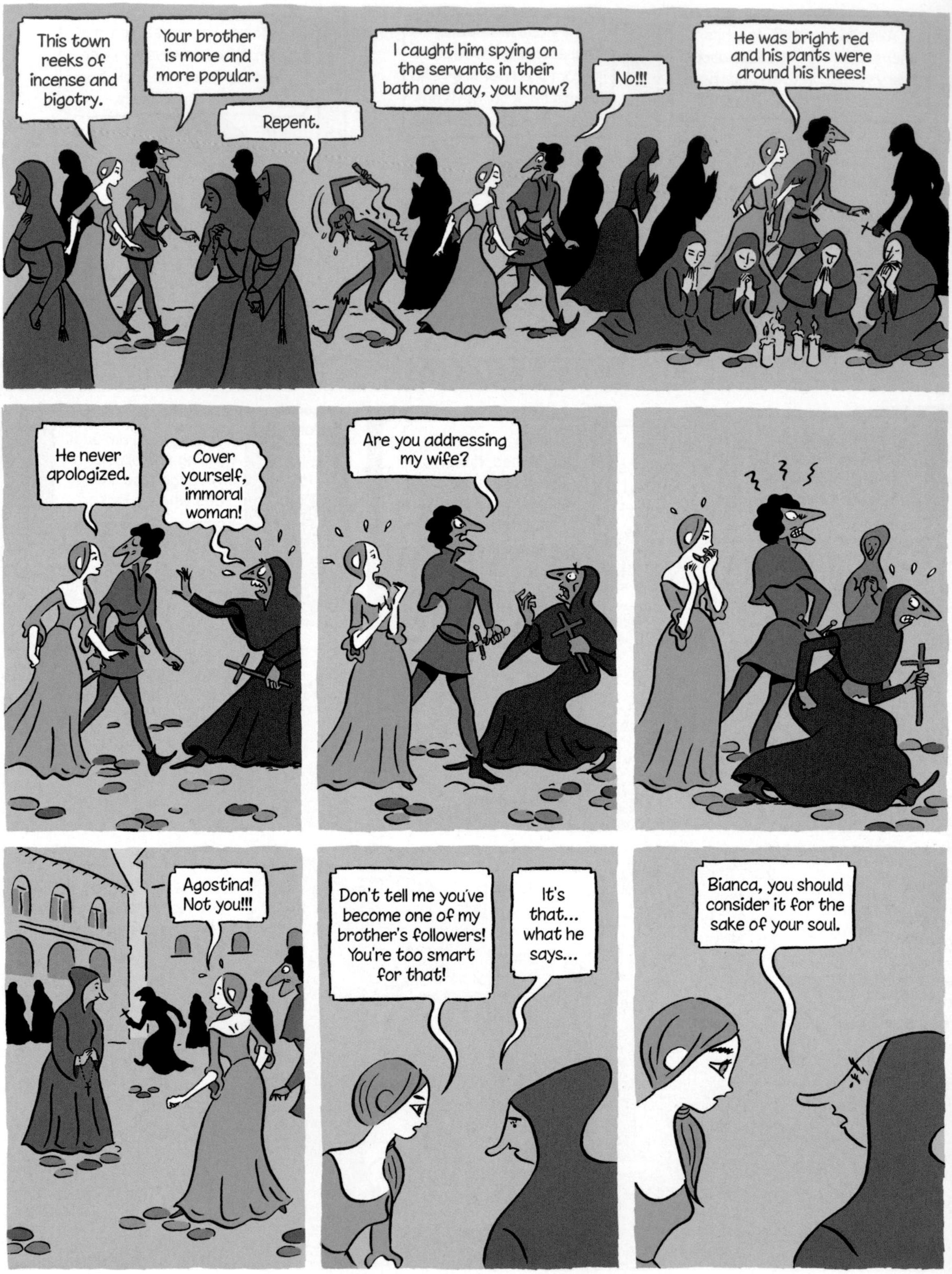
This town reeks of incense and bigotry.
Your brother is more and more popular.
Repent.
I caught him spying on the servants in their bath one day, you know?
No!!!
He was bright red and his pants were around his knees!
He never apologized.
Cover yourself, immoral woman!
Are you addressing my wife?
Agostina! Not you!!!
Don't tell me you've become one of my brother's followers! You're too smart for that!
It's that... what he says...
Bianca, you should consider it for the sake of your soul.

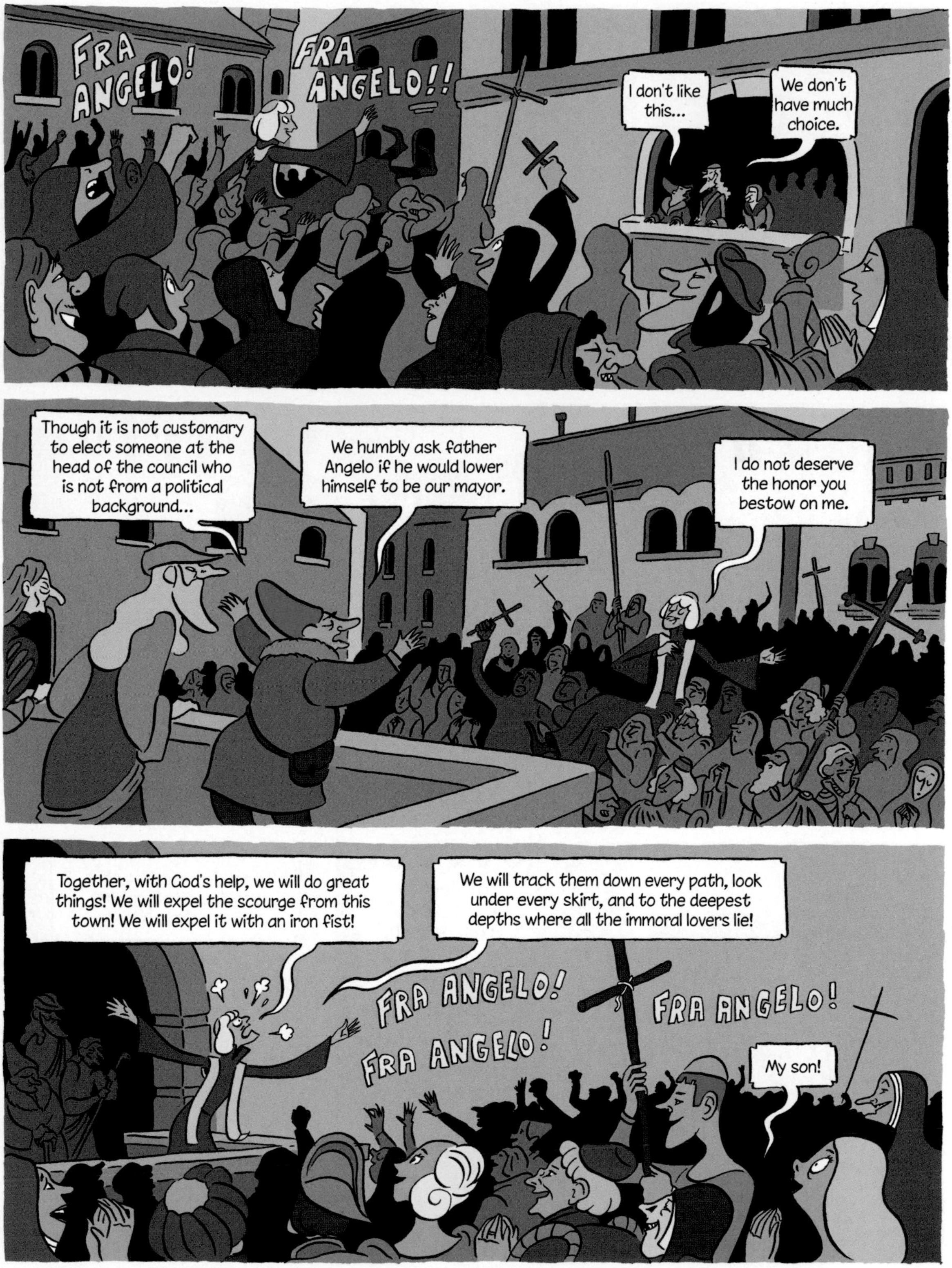
FRA ANGELO!
FRA ANGELO!!
I don't like this...
We don't have much choice.
Though it is not customary to elect someone at the head of the council who is not from a political background...
We humbly ask father Angelo if he would lower himself to be our mayor.
I do not deserve the honor you bestow on me.
Together, with God's help, we will do great things! We will expel the scourge from this town! We will expel it with an iron fist!
We will track them down every path, look under every skirt, and to the deepest depths where all the immoral lovers lie!
FRA ANGELO!
FRA ANGELO!
FRA ANGELO!
My son!

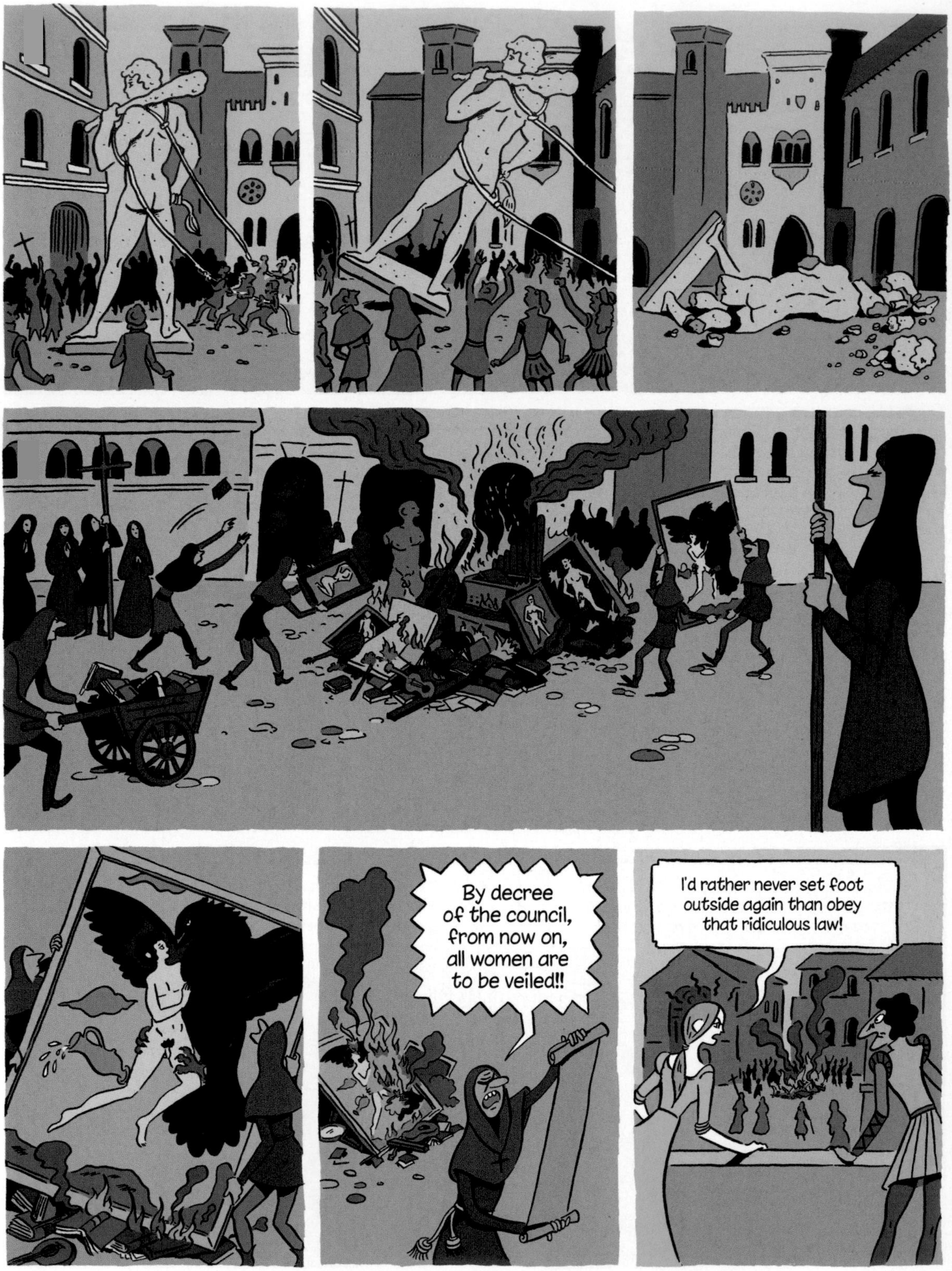
By decree of the council, from now on, all women are to be veiled!!
I'd rather never set foot outside again than obey that ridiculous law!

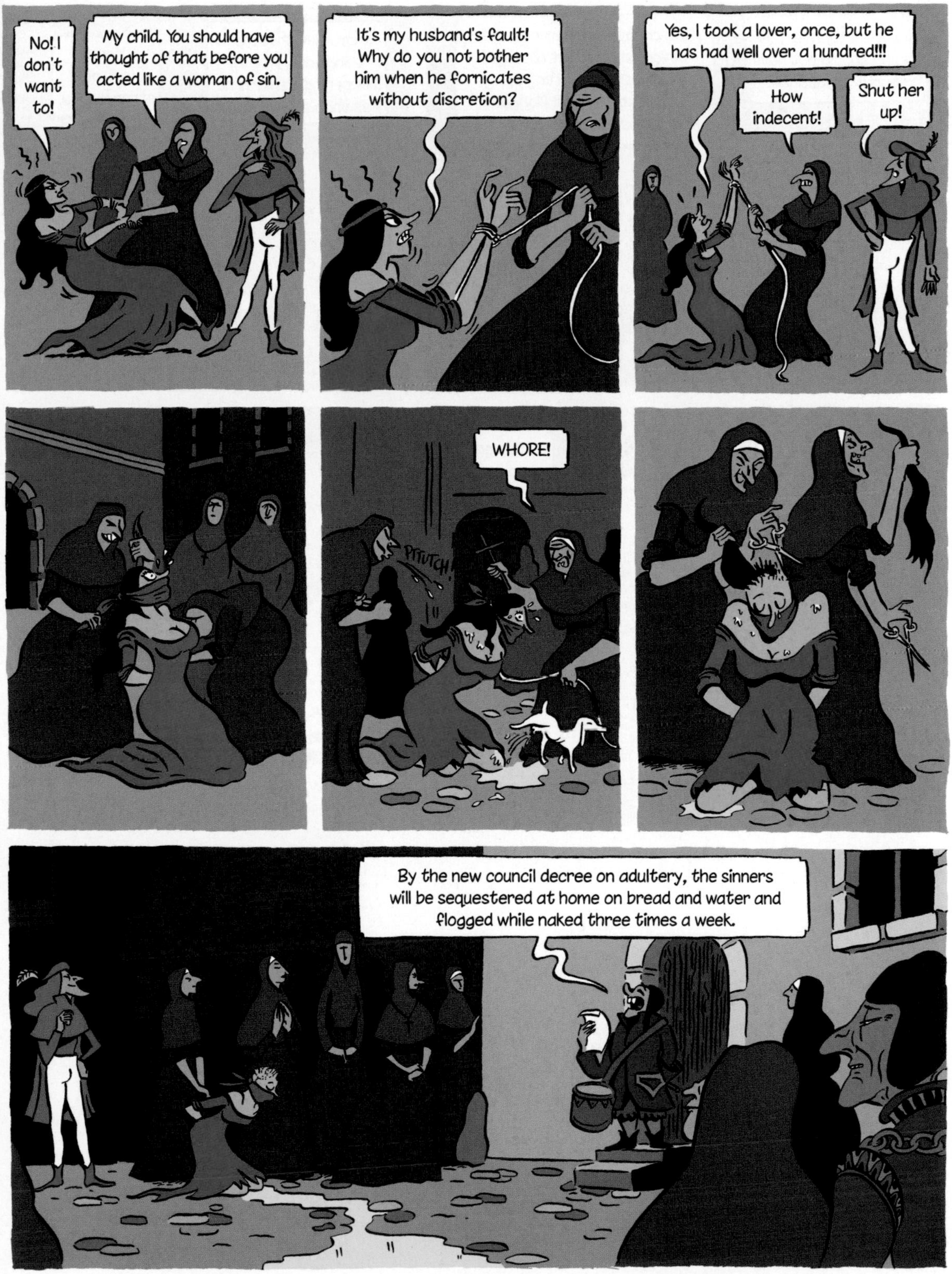
No! I don't want to!
My child. You should have thought of that before you acted like a woman of sin.
It's my husband's fault! Why do you not bother him when he fornicates without discretion?
Yes, I took a lover, once, but he has had well over a hundred!!!
How indecent!
Shut her up!
WHORE!
PFFUTCH!
By the new council decree on adultery, the sinners will be sequestered at home on bread and water and flogged while naked three times a week.

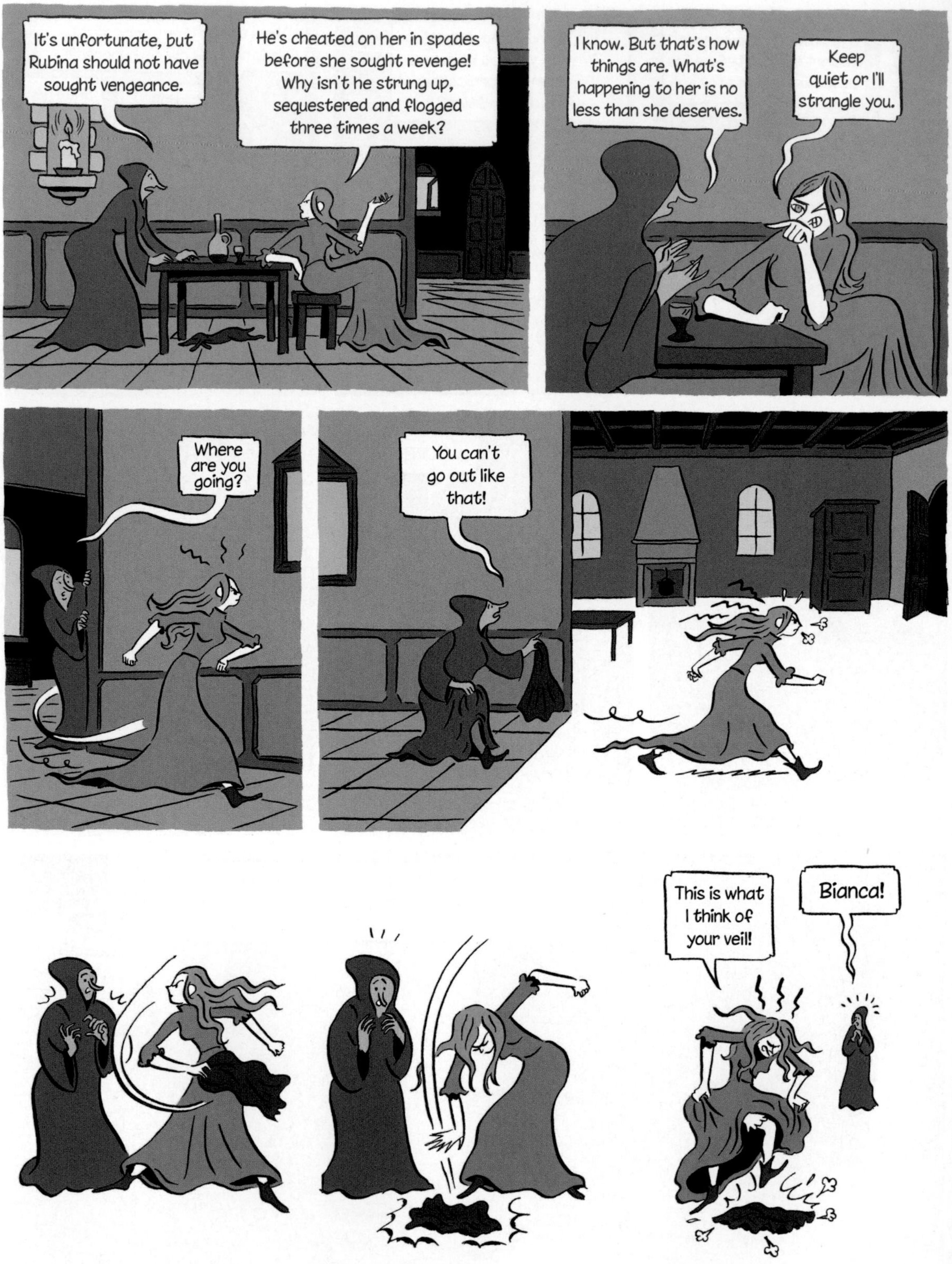
It's unfortunate, but Rubina should not have sought vengeance.
He's cheated on her in spades before she sought revenge! Why isn't he strung up, sequestered and flogged three times a week?
I know. But that's how things are. What's happening to her is no less than she deserves.
Keep quiet or I'll strangle you.
Where are you going?
You can't go out like that!
This is what I think of your veil!
Bianca!

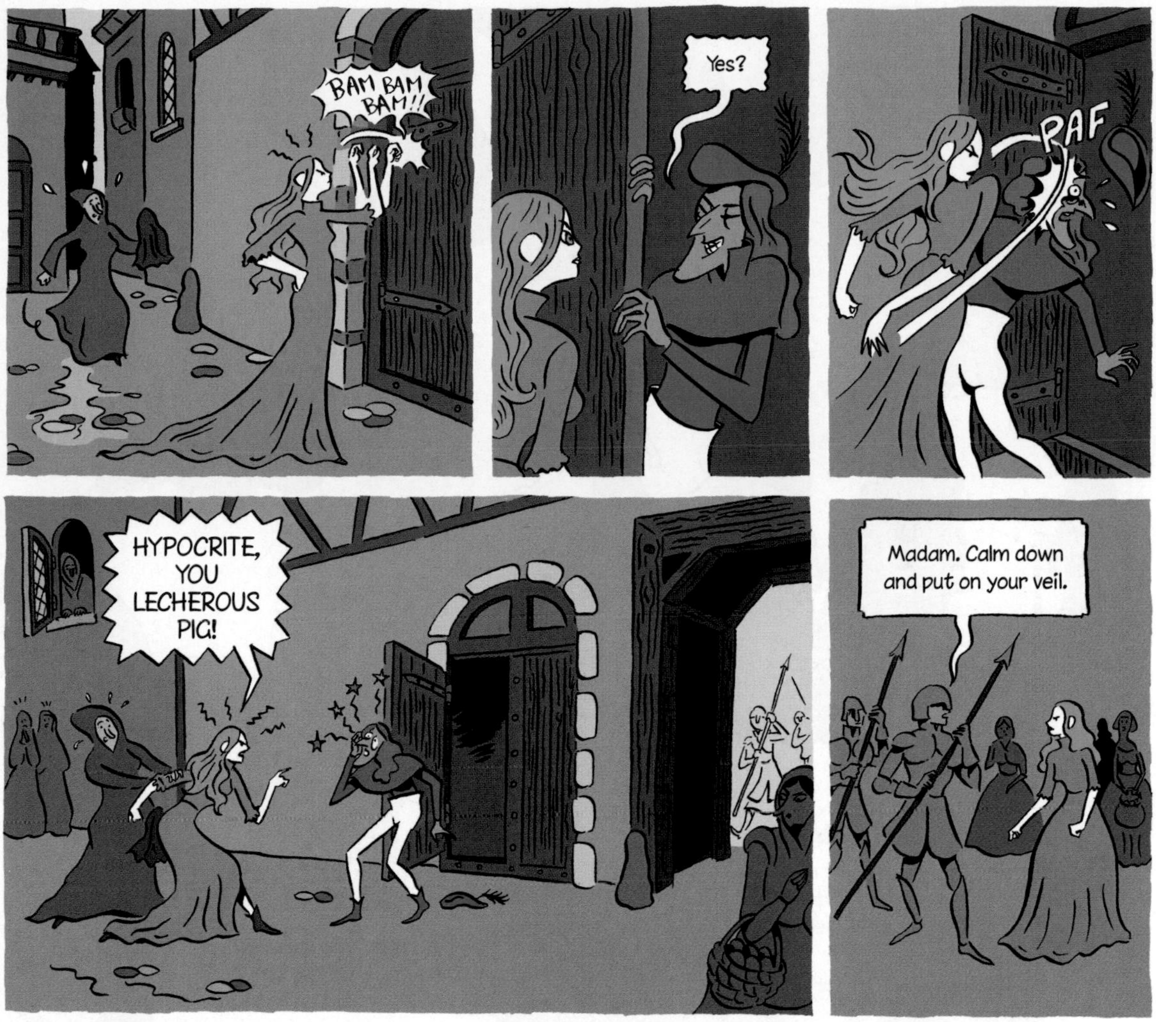
BAM BAM BAM!!
Yes?
PAF
HYPOCRITE, YOU LECHEROUS PIG!
Madam. Calm down and put on your veil.

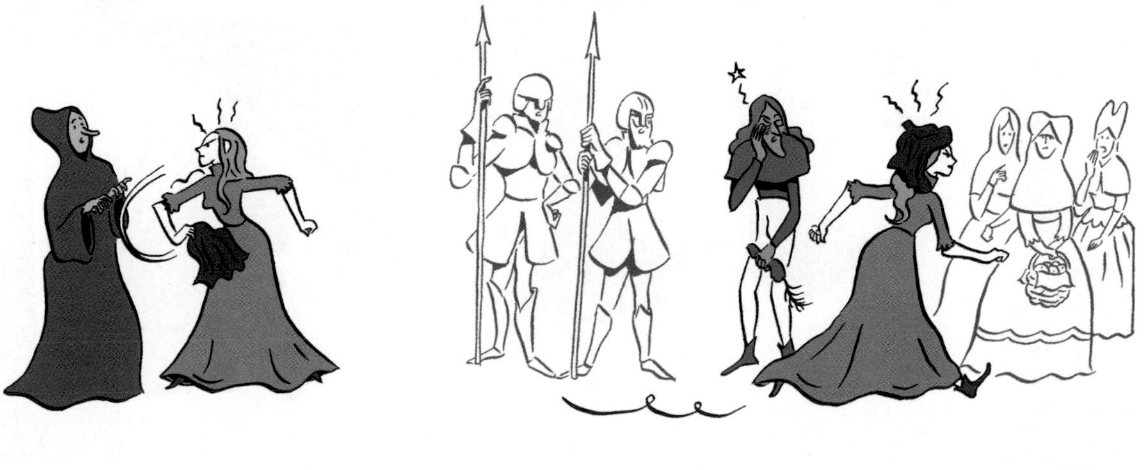

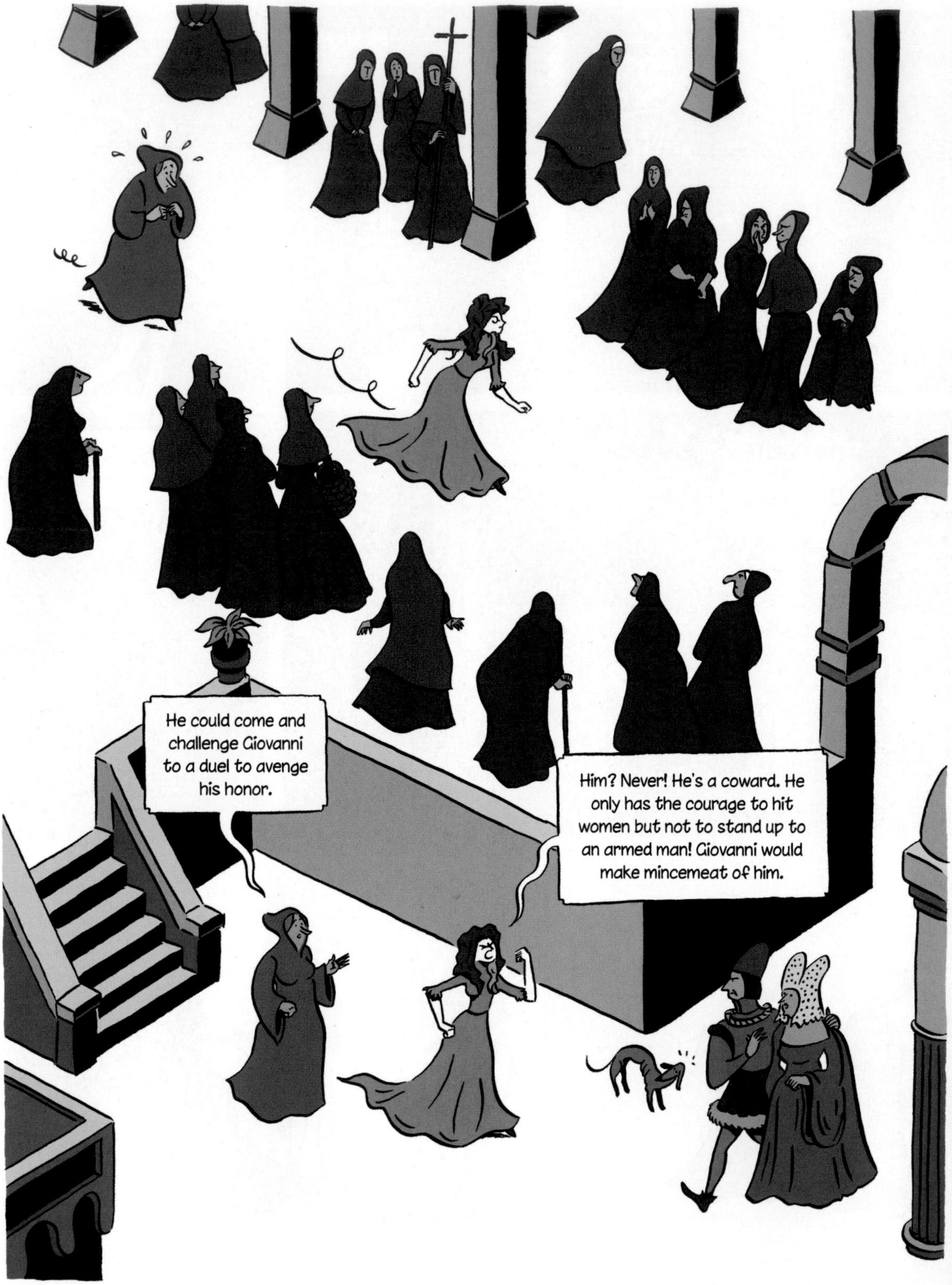
He could come and challenge Giovanni to a duel to avenge his honor.
Him? Never! He's a coward. He only has the courage to hit women but not to stand up to an armed man! Giovanni would make mincemeat of him.

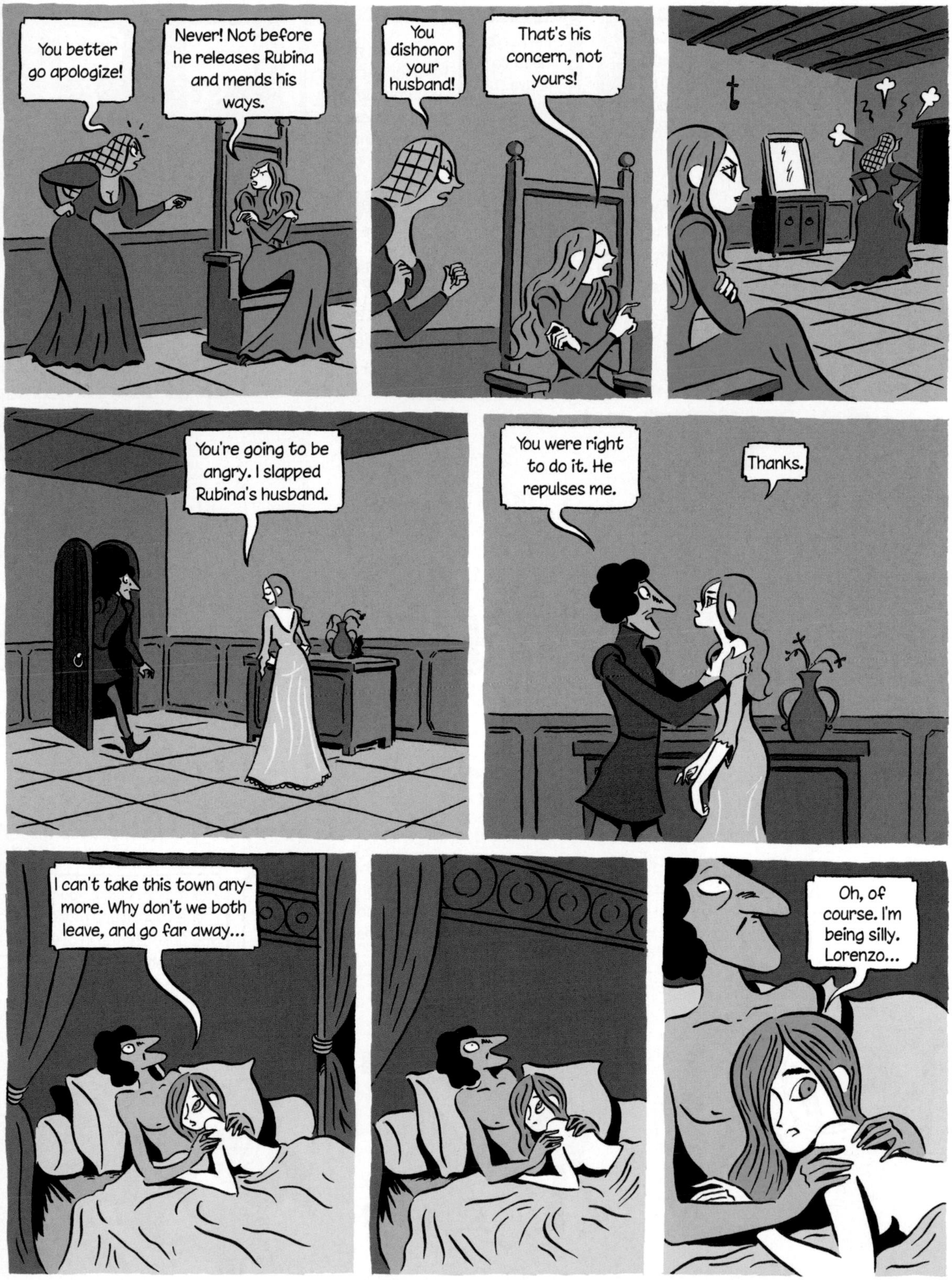
You better go apologize!
Never! Not before he releases Rubina and mends his ways.
You dishonor your husband!
That's his concern, not yours!
You're going to be angry. I slapped Rubina's husband.
You were right to do it. He repulses me.
Thanks.
I can't take this town any-more. Why don't we both leave, and go far away...
Oh, of course. I'm being silly. Lorenzo...

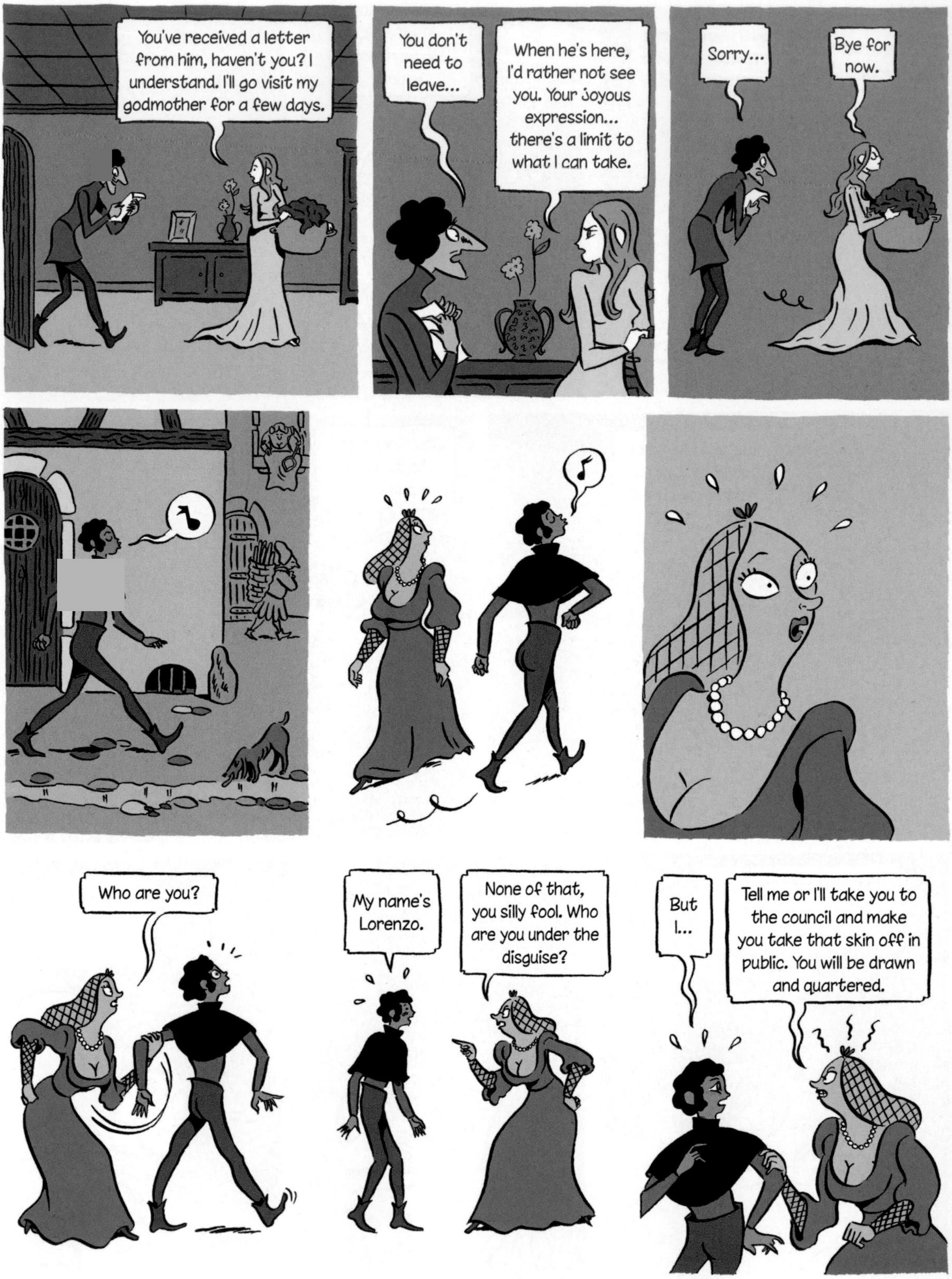
You've received a letter from him, haven't you? I understand. I'll go visit my godmother for a few days.
You don't need to leave...
When he's here, I'd rather not see you. Your joyous expression... there's a limit to what I can take.
Sorry...
Bye for now.
Who are you?
My name's Lorenzo.
None of that, you silly fool. Who are you under the disguise?
But I...
Tell me or I'll take you to the council and make you take that skin off in public. You will be drawn and quartered.

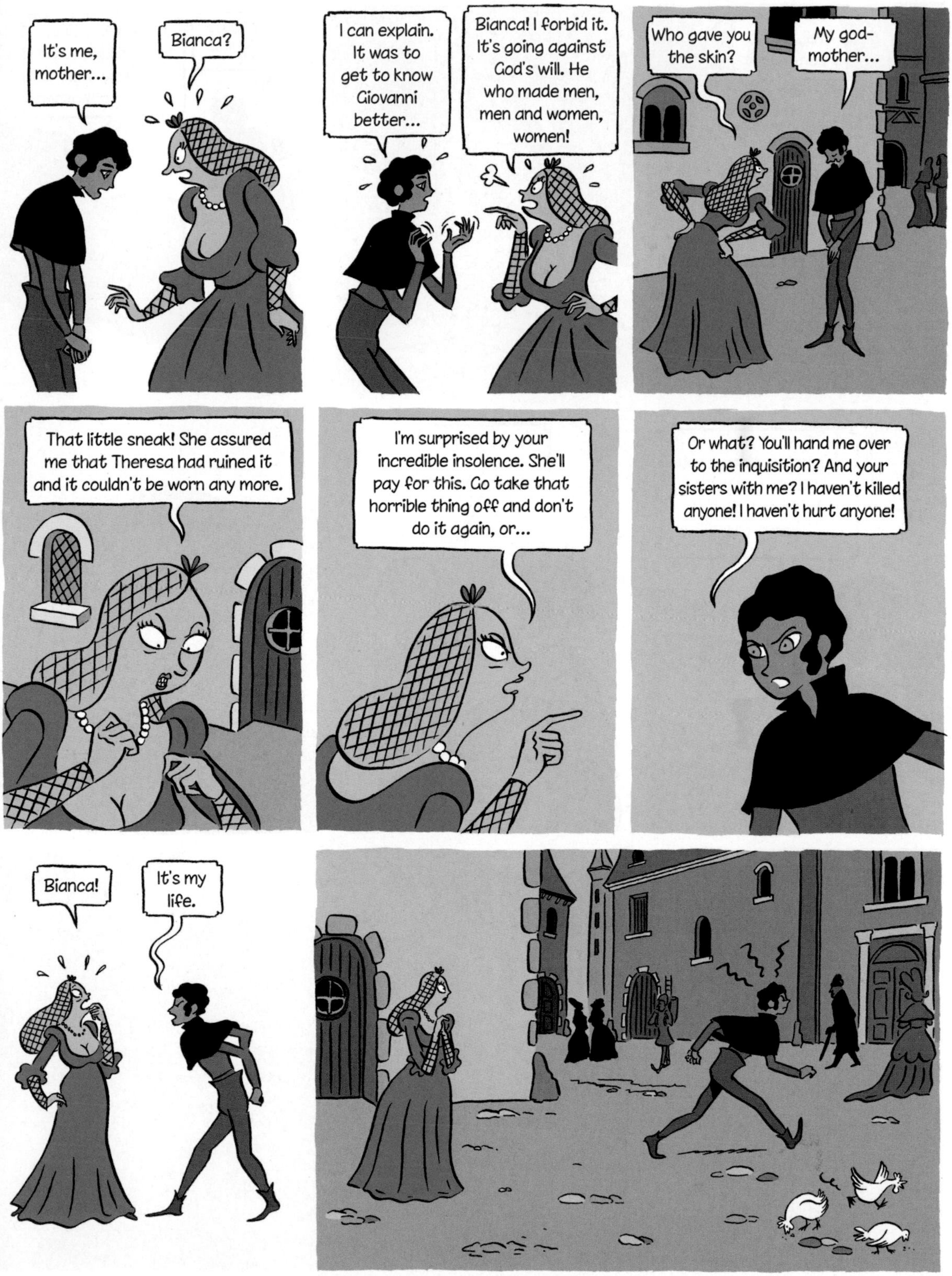

It's me, mother...
Bianca?
I can explain. It was to get to know Giovanni better...
Bianca! I forbid it. It's going against God's will. He who made men, men and women, women!
Who gave you the skin?
My god-mother...
That little sneak! She assured me that Theresa had ruined it and it couldn't be worn any more.
I'm surprised by your incredible insolence. She'll pay for this. Go take that horrible thing off and don't do it again, or...
Or what? You'll hand me over to the inquisition? And your sisters with me? I haven't killed anyone! I haven't hurt anyone!
Bianca!
It's my life.

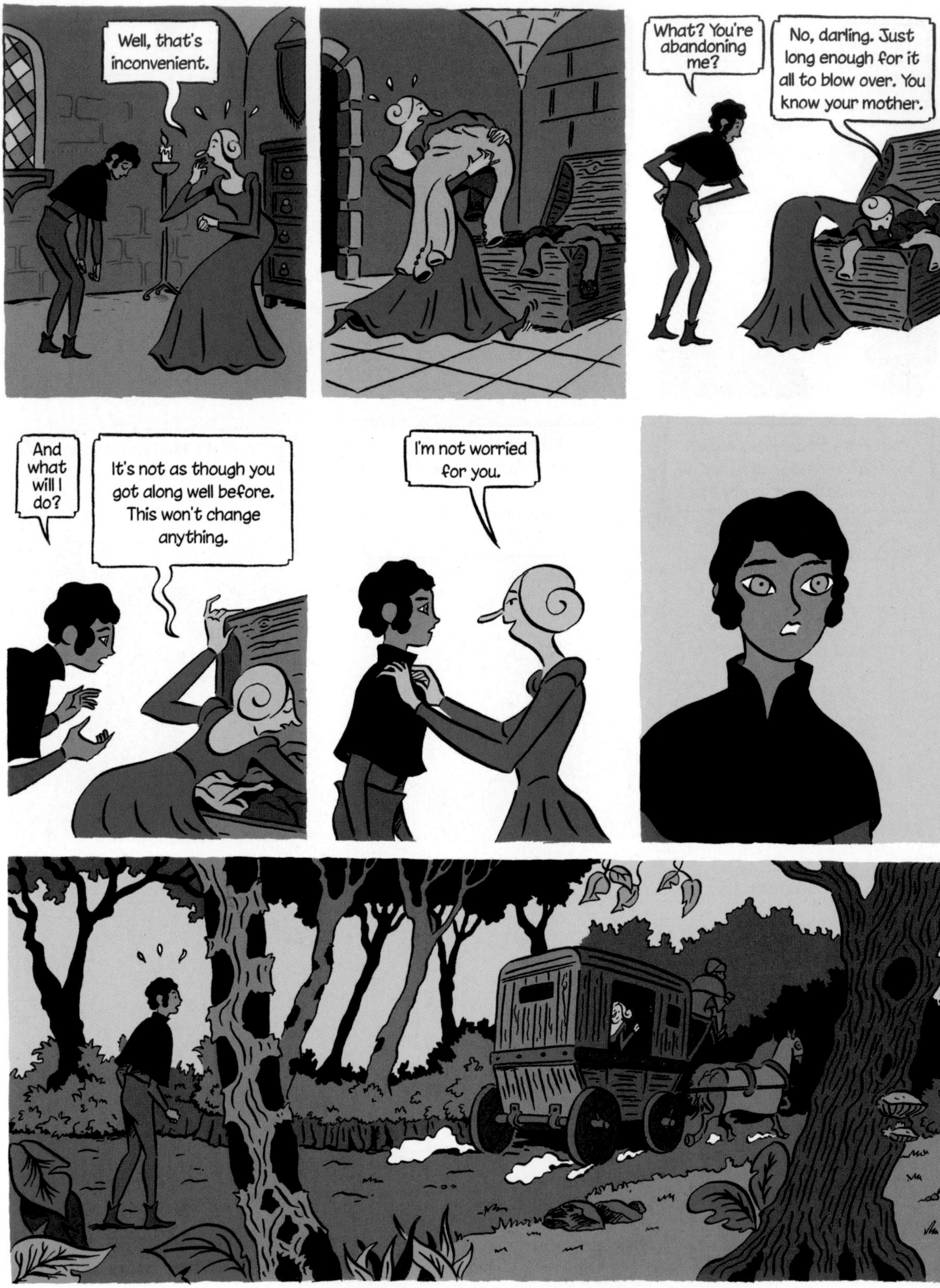
Well, that's inconvenient.
What? You're abandoning me?
No, darling. Just long enough for it all to blow over. You know your mother.
And what will I do?
It's not as though you got along well before. This won't change anything.
I'm not worried for you.

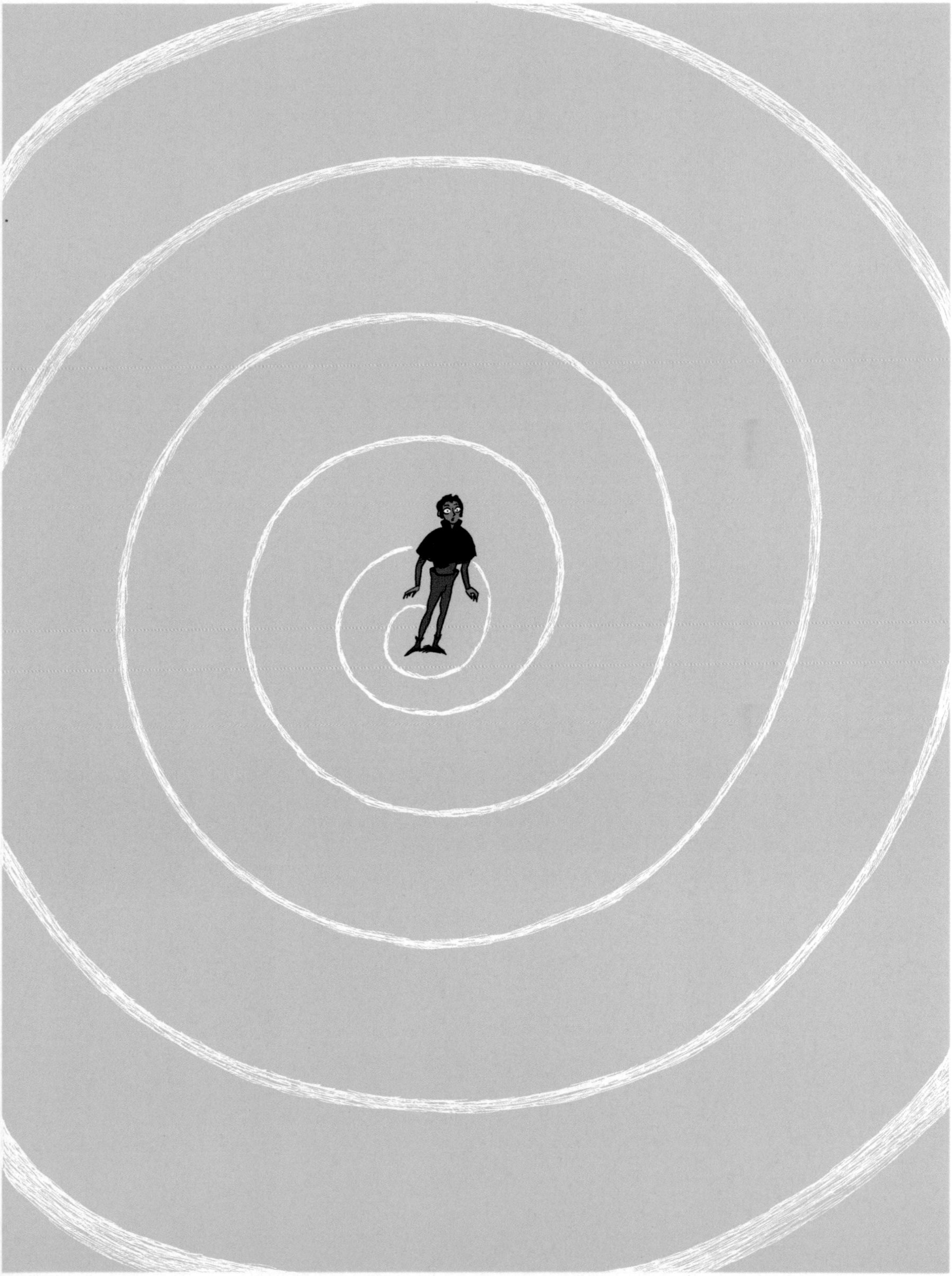

Chapter IV

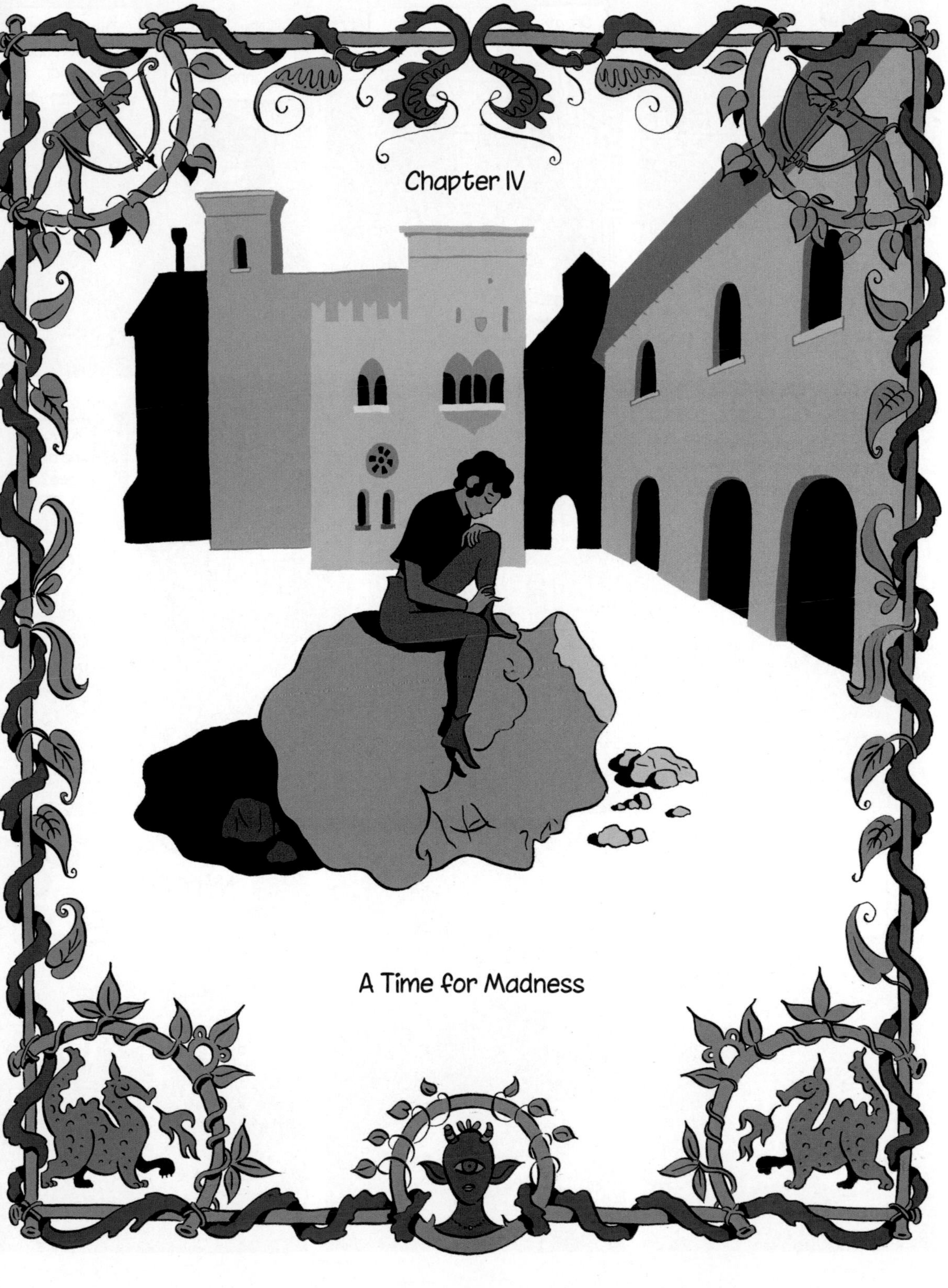

A Time for Madness

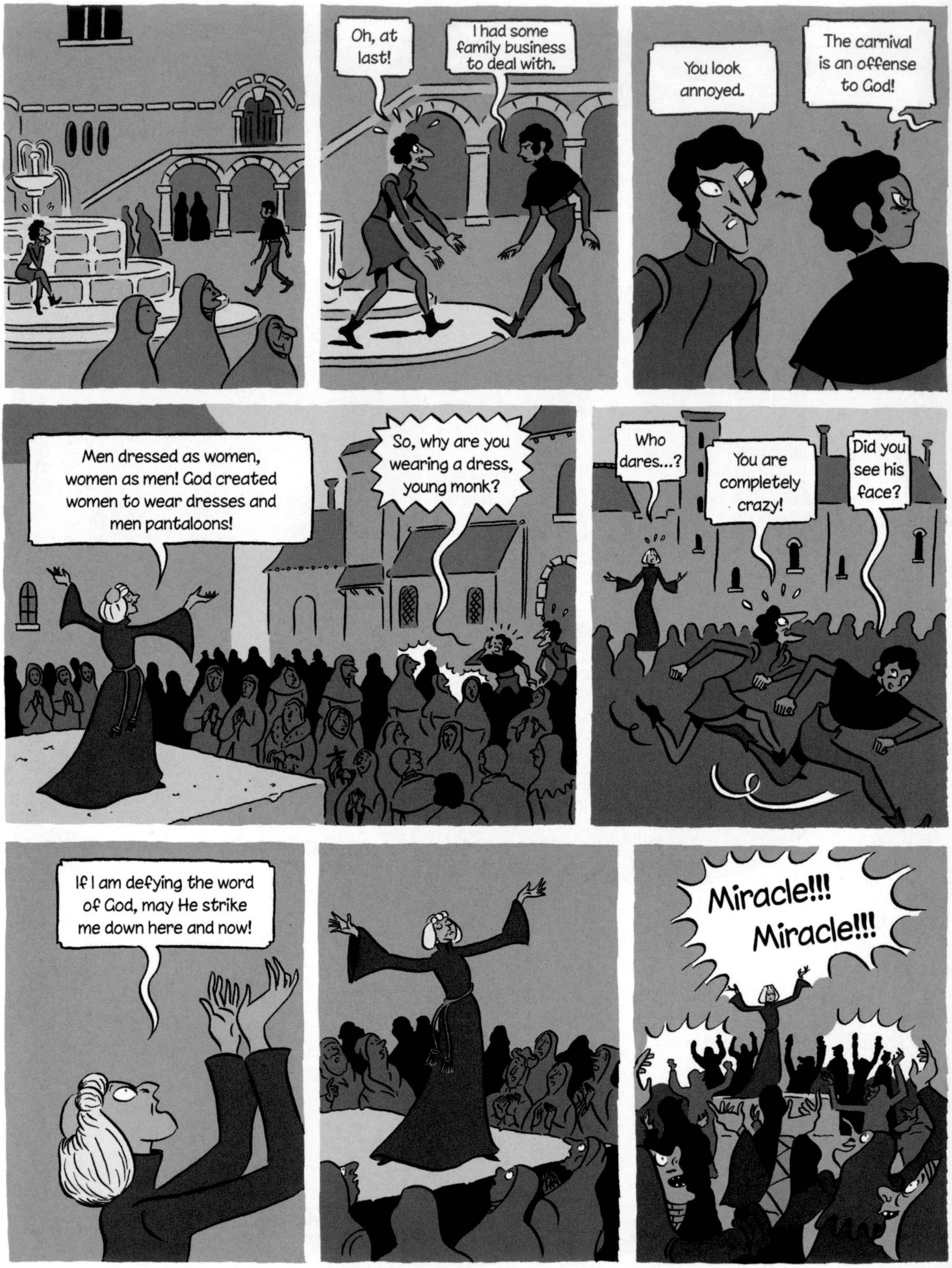
Oh, at last!
I had some family business to deal with.
You look annoyed.
The carnival is an offense to God!
Men dressed as women, women as men! God created women to wear dresses and men pantaloons!
So, why are you wearing a dress, young monk?
Who dares...?
You are completely crazy!
Did you see his face?
If I am defying the word of God, may He strike me down here and now!
Miracle!!! Miracle!!!

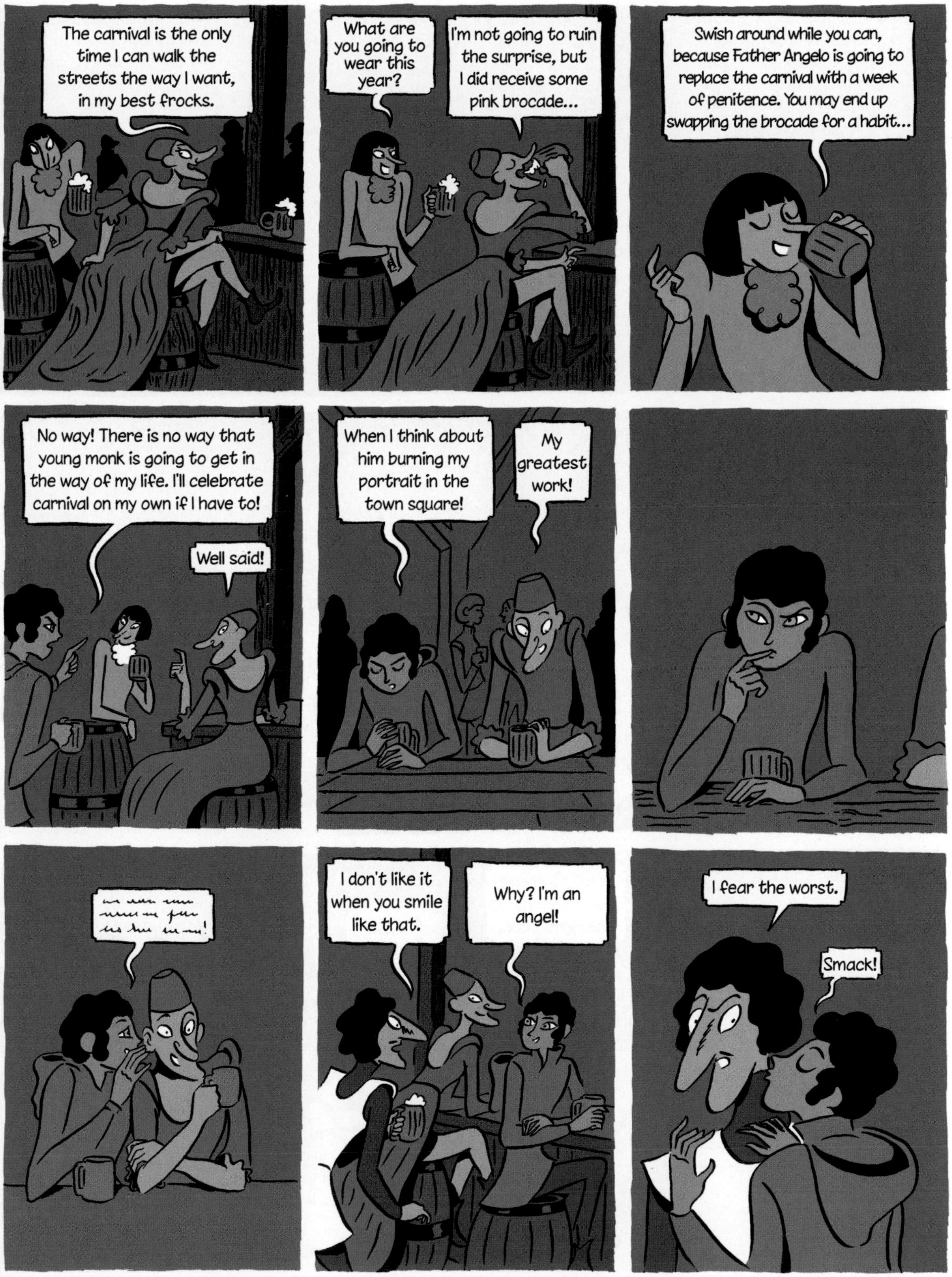
The carnival is the only time I can walk the streets the way I want, in my best frocks.
What are you going to wear this year?
I'm not going to ruin the surprise, but I did receive some pink brocade...
Swish around while you can, because Father Angelo is going to replace the carnival with a week of penitence. You may end up swapping the brocade for a habit...
No way! There is no way that young monk is going to get in the way of my life. I'll celebrate carnival on my own if I have to!
Well said!
When I think about him burning my portrait in the town square!
My greatest work!
I don't like it when you smile like that.
Why? I'm an angel!
I fear the worst.
Smack!

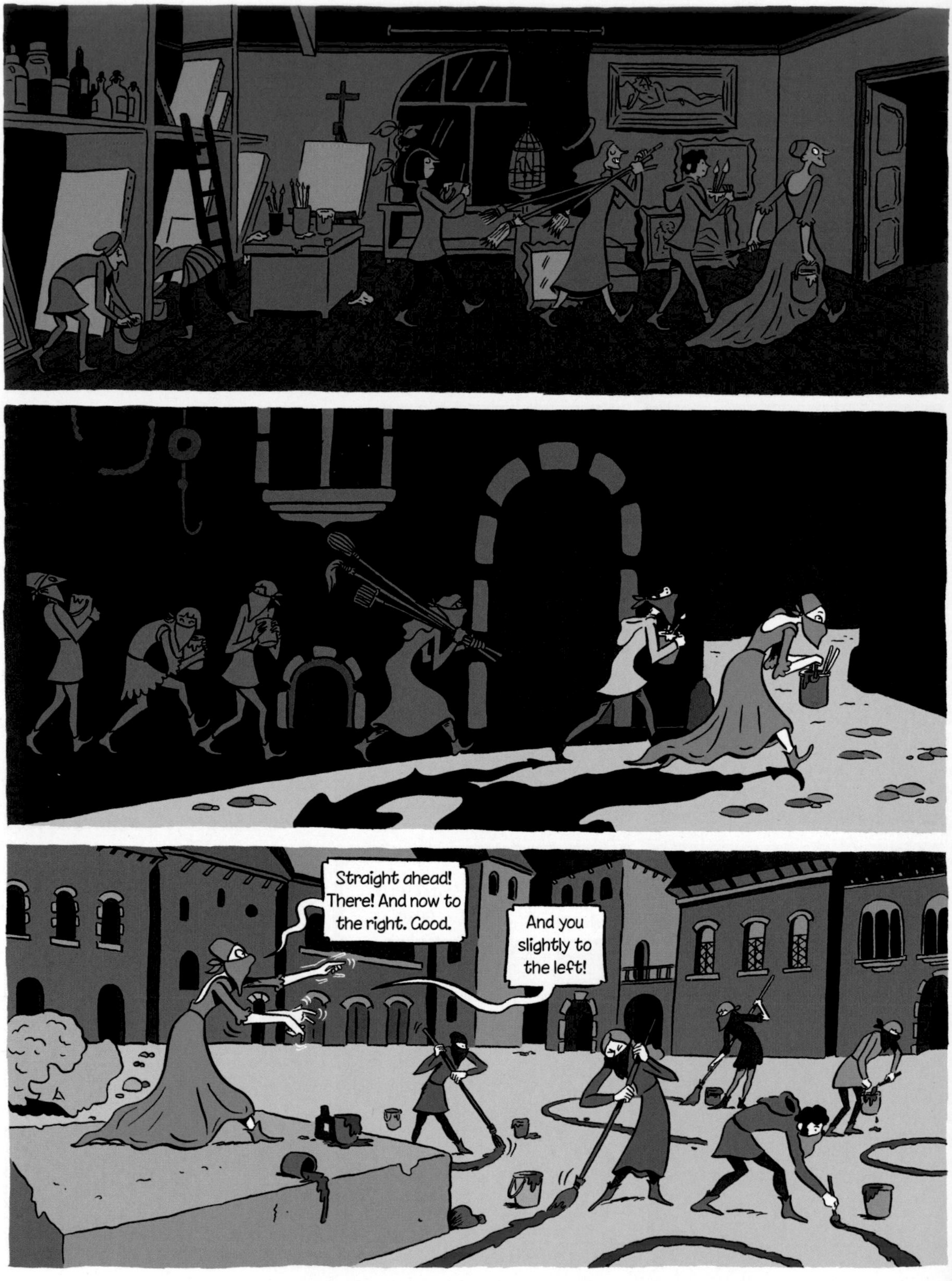
Straight ahead! There! And now to the right. Good.
And you slightly to the left!

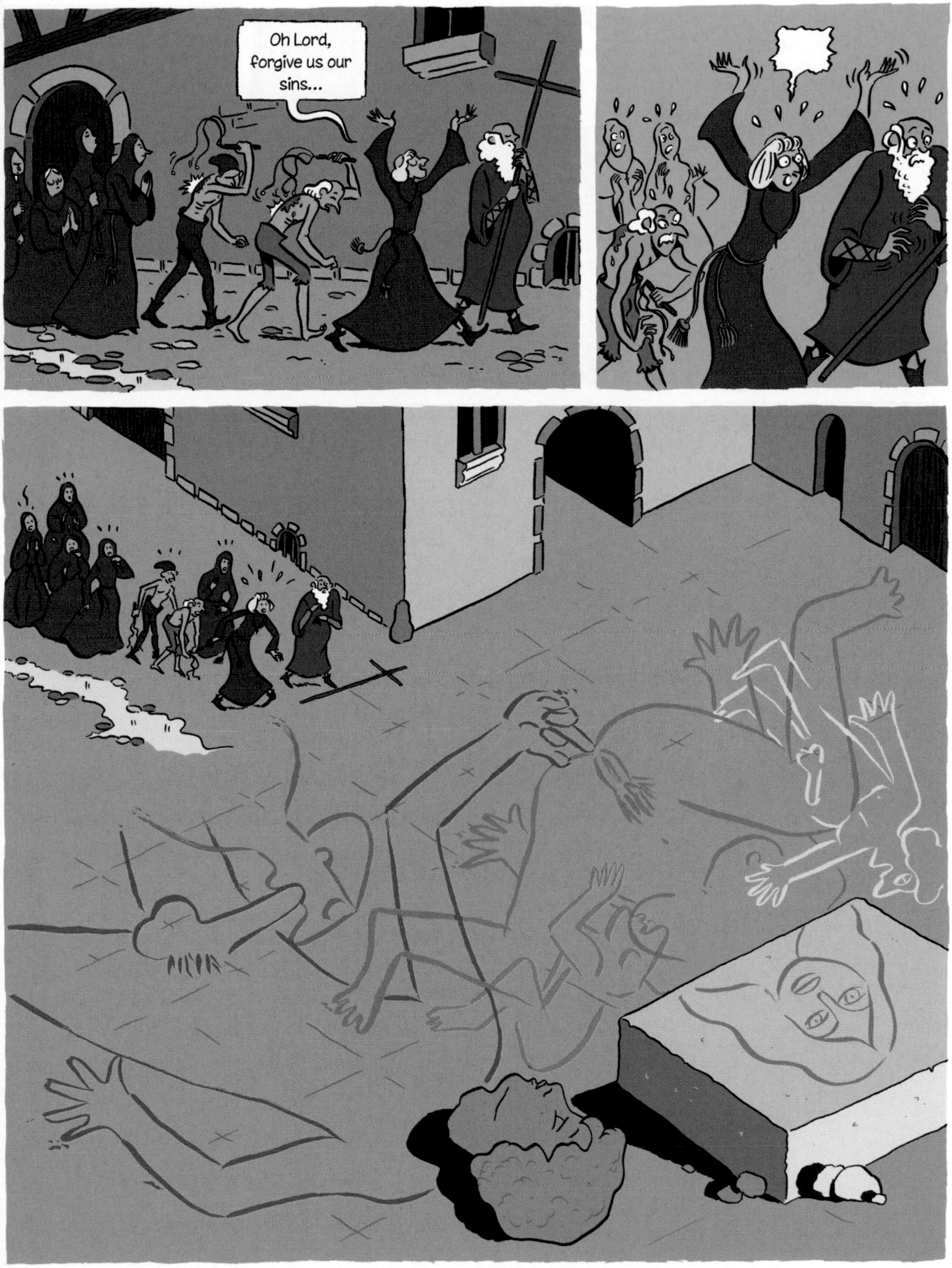
Oh Lord, forgive us our sins...

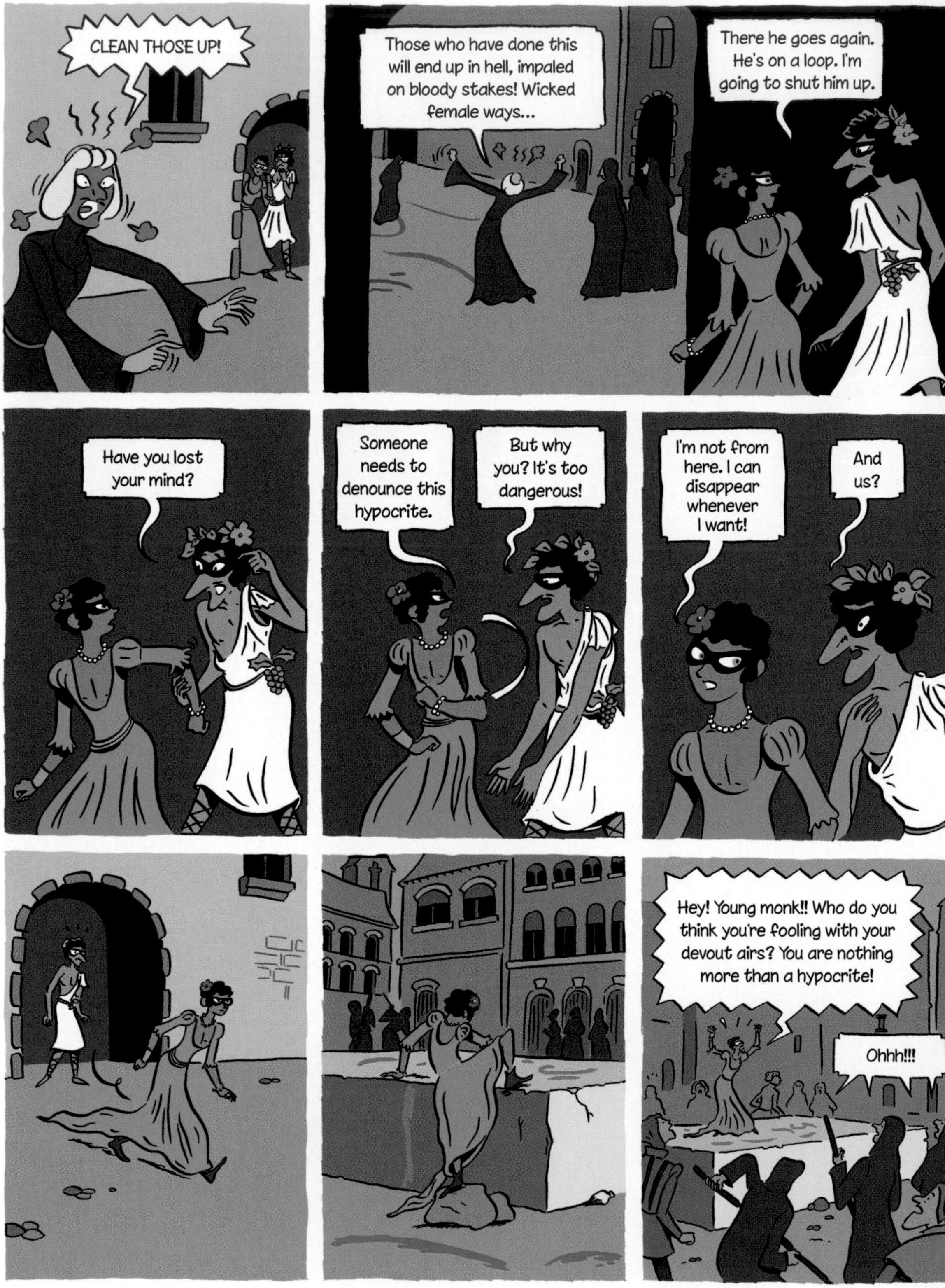
CLEAN THOSE UP!
Those who have done this will end up in hell, impaled on bloody stakes! Wicked female ways...
There he goes again. He's on a loop. I'm going to shut him up.
Have you lost your mind?
Someone needs to denounce this hypocrite.
But why you? It's too dangerous!
I'm not from here. I can disappear whenever I want!
And us?
Hey! Young monk!! Who do you think you're fooling with your devout airs? You are nothing more than a hypocrite!
Ohhh!!!

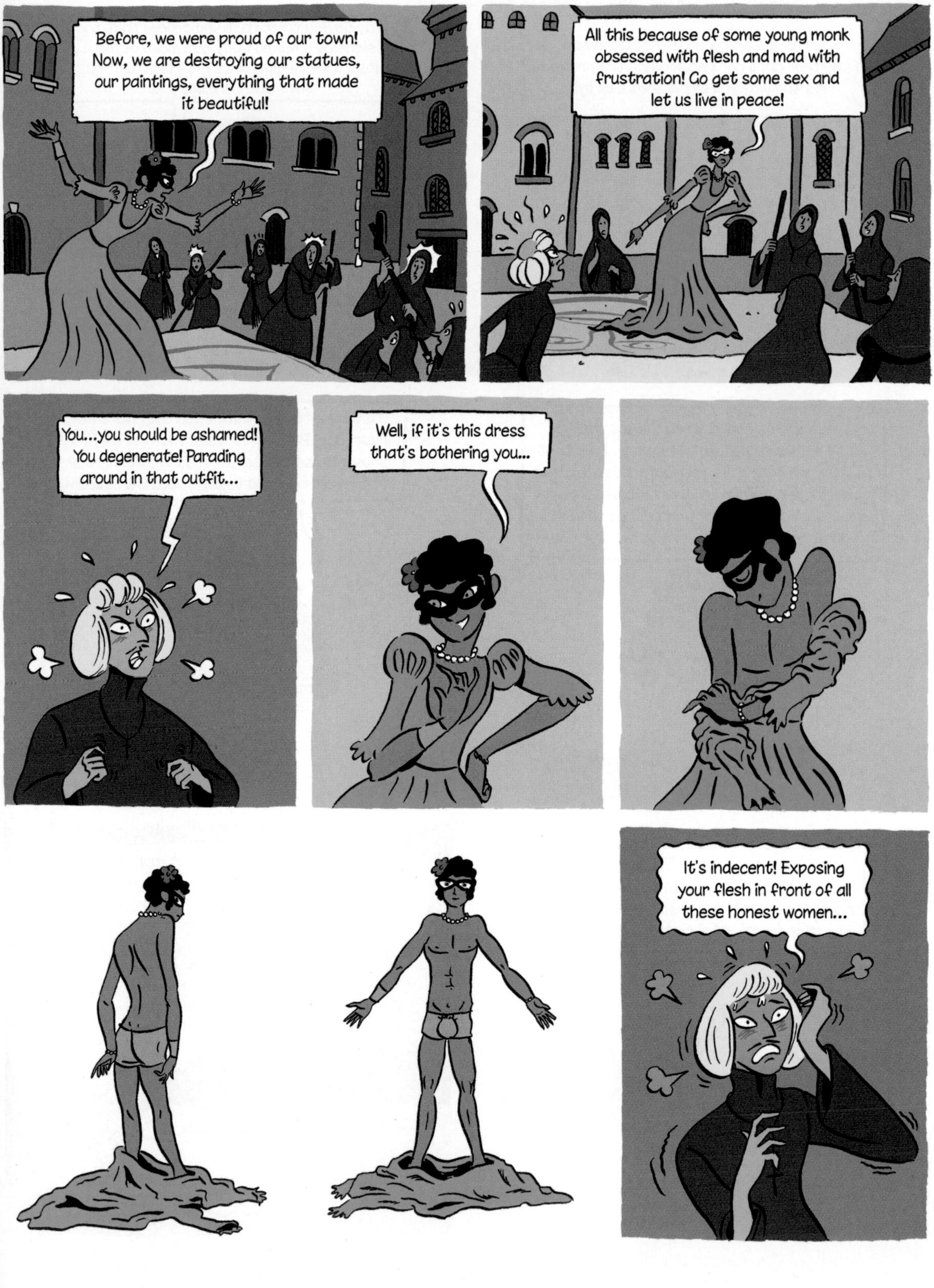
Before, we were proud of our town! Now, we are destroying our statues, our paintings, everything that made it beautiful!
All this because of some young monk obsessed with flesh and mad with frustration! Go get some sex and let us live in peace!
You...you should be ashamed! You degenerate! Parading around in that outfit...
Well, if it's this dress that's bothering you...
It's indecent! Exposing your flesh in front of all these honest women...

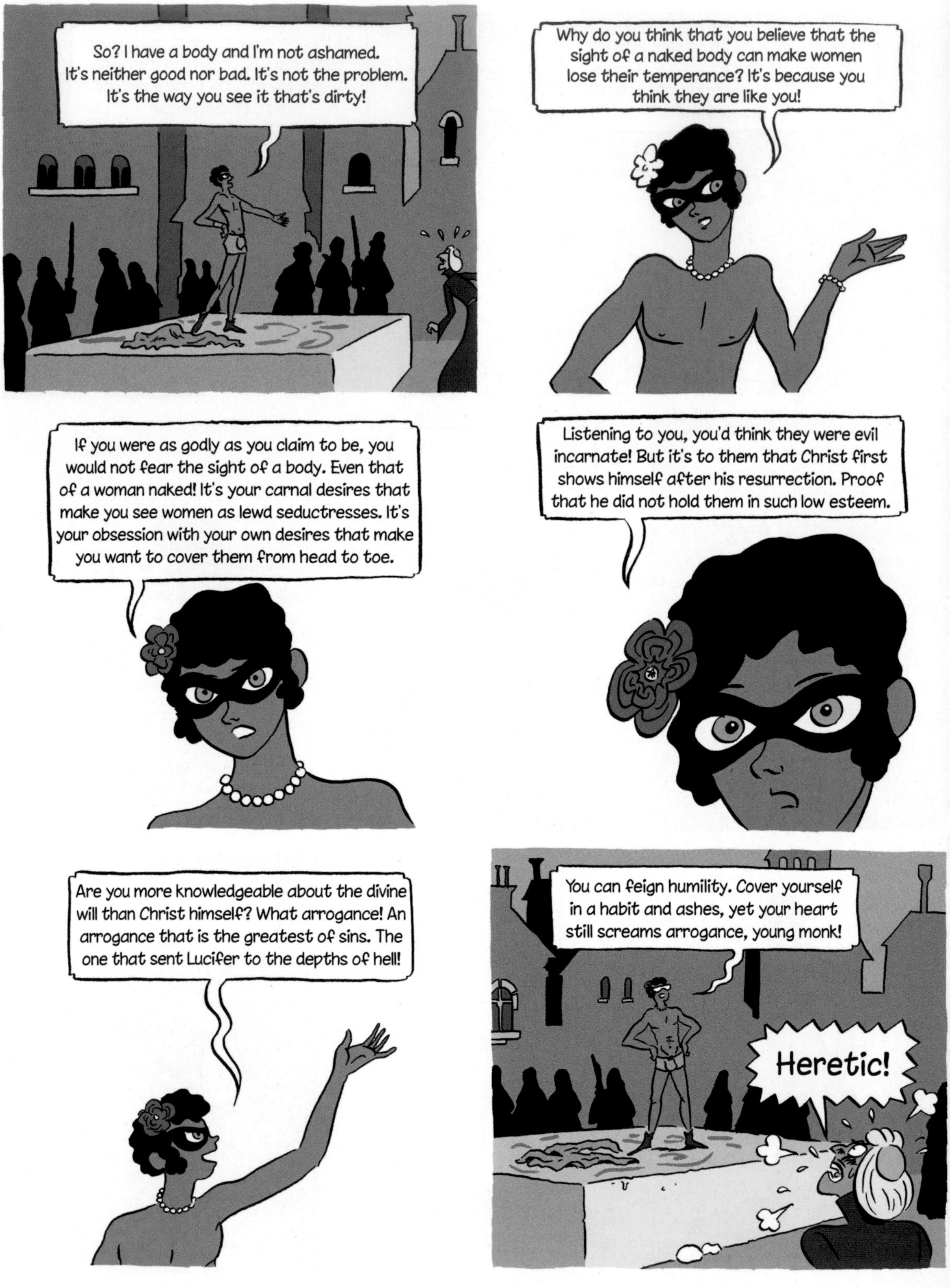
So? I have a body and I'm not ashamed. It's neither good nor bad. It's not the problem. It's the way you see it that's dirty!
Why do you think that you believe that the sight of a naked body can make women lose their temperance? It's because you think they are like you!
If you were as godly as you claim to be, you would not fear the sight of a body. Even that of a woman naked! It's your carnal desires that make you see women as lewd seductresses. It's your obsession with your own desires that make you want to cover them from head to toe.
Listening to you, you'd think they were evil incarnate! But it's to them that Christ first shows himself after his resurrection. Proof that he did not hold them in such low esteem.
Are you more knowledgeable about the divine will than Christ himself? What arrogance! An arrogance that is the greatest of sins. The one that sent Lucifer to the depths of hell!
You can feign humility. Cover yourself in a habit and ashes, yet your heart still screams arrogance, young monk!
Heretic!

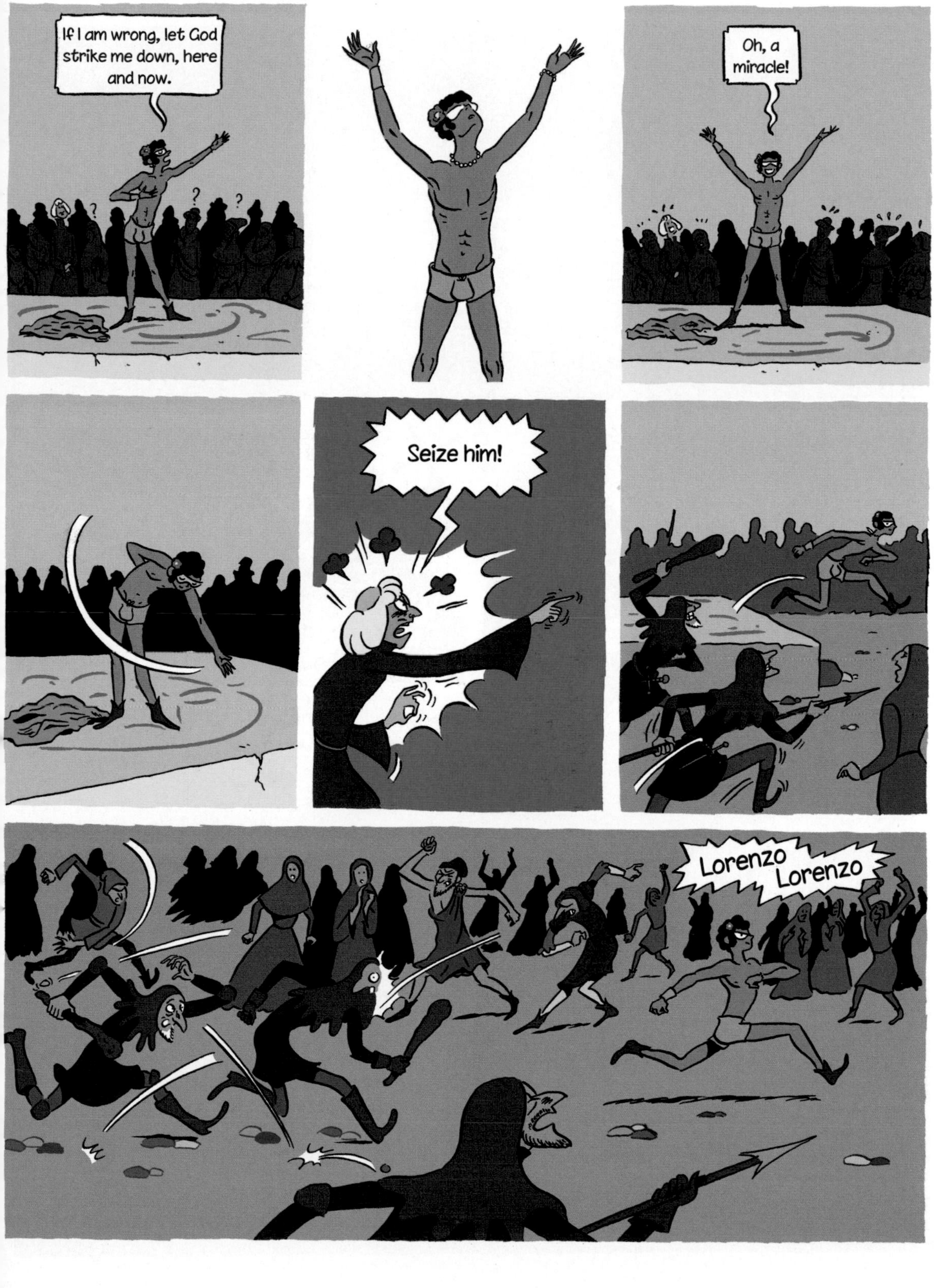
If I am wrong, let God strike me down, here and now.
Oh, a miracle!
Seize him!
Lorenzo
Lorenzo

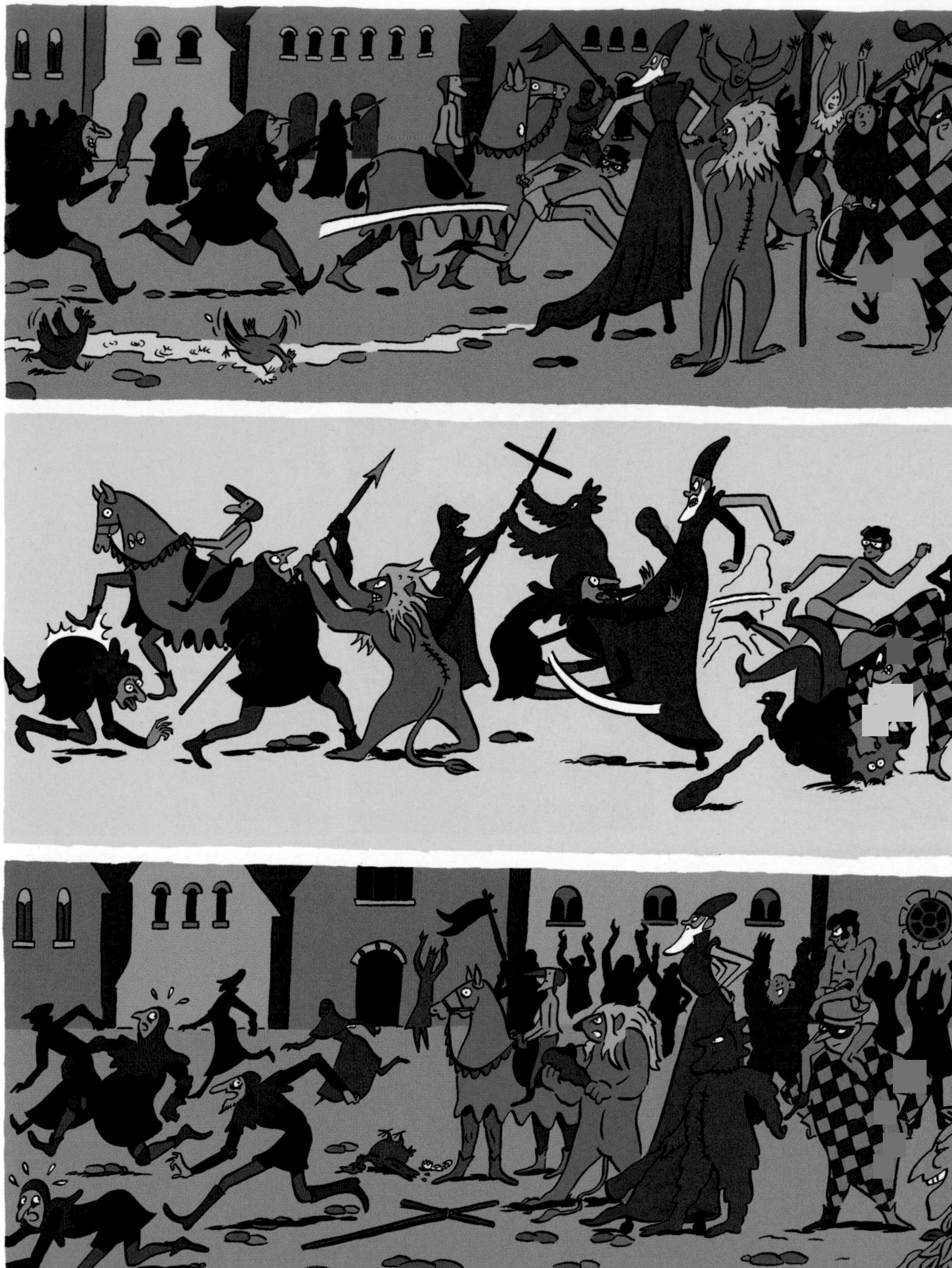

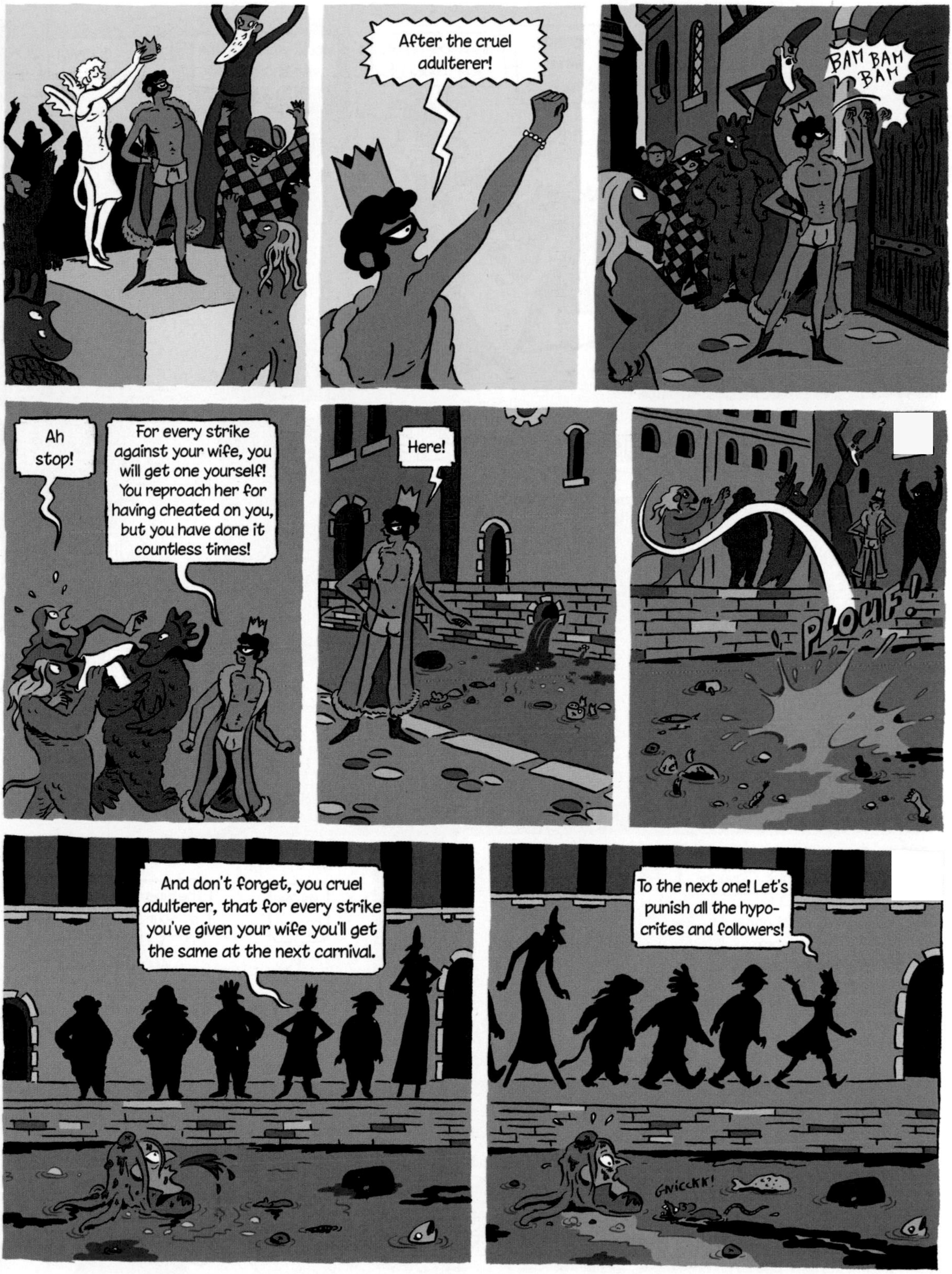
After the cruel adulterer!
BAM BAM BAM
Ah stop!
For every strike against your wife, you will get one yourself! You reproach her for having cheated on you, but you have done it countless times!
Here!
PLOUF!
And don't forget, you cruel adulterer, that for every strike you've given your wife you'll get the same at the next carnival.
To the next one! Let's punish all the hypocrites and followers!
GNICCKK!

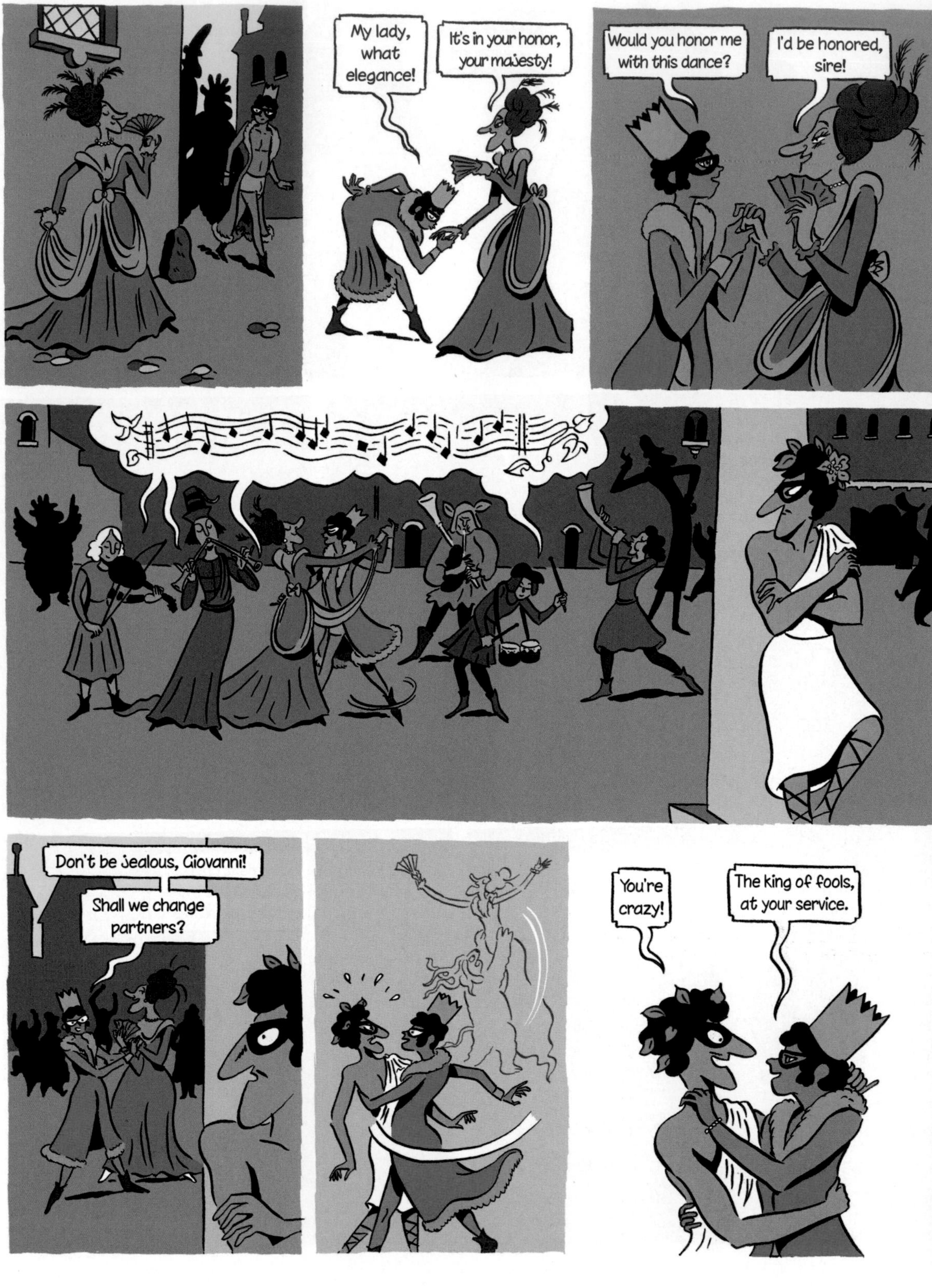

My lady, what elegance!
It's in your honor, your majesty!
Would you honor me with this dance?
I'd be honored, sire!
Don't be jealous, Giovanni!
Shall we change partners?
You're crazy!
The king of fools, at your service.

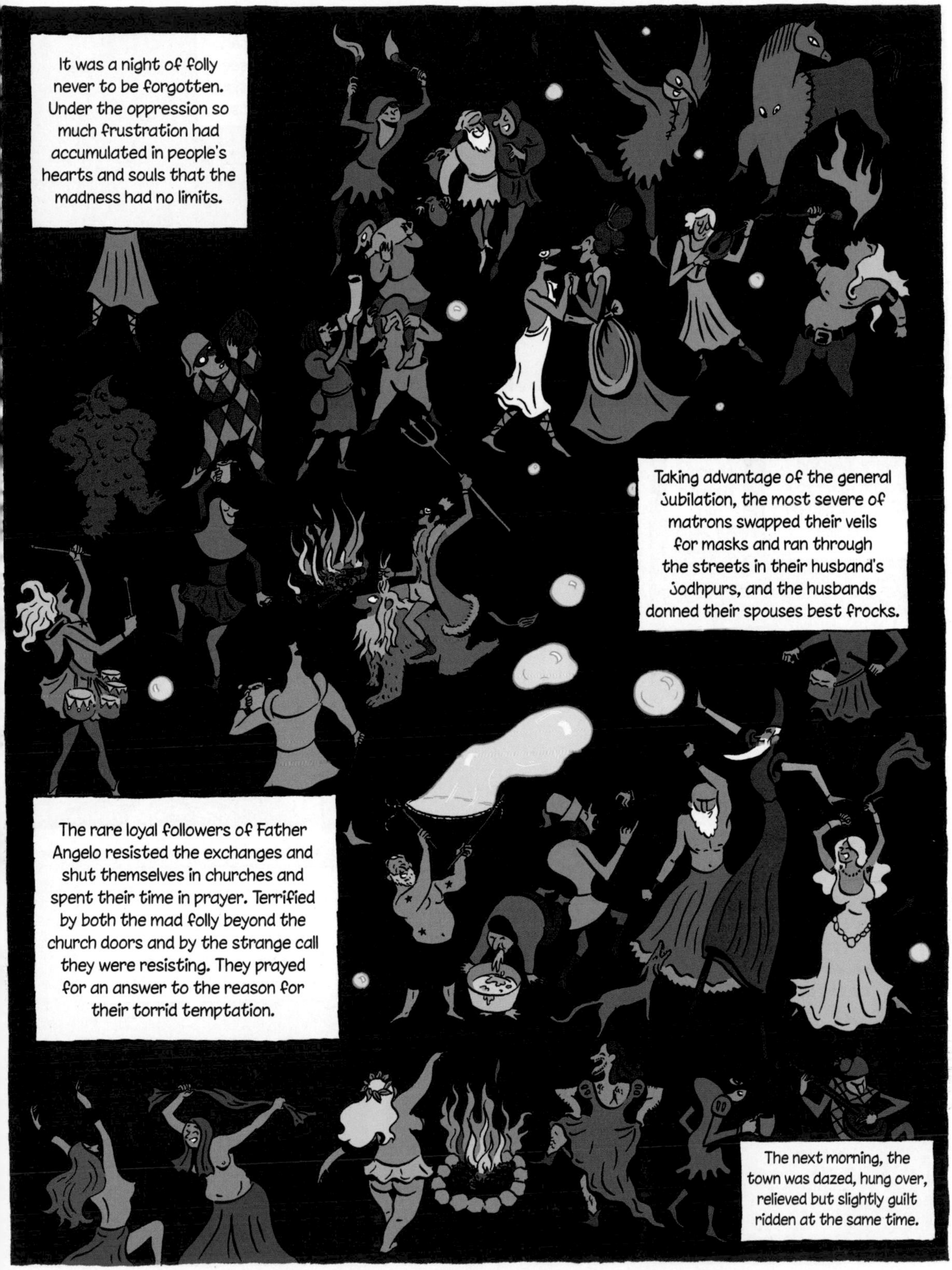
It was a night of folly never to be forgotten. Under the oppression so much frustration had accumulated in people's hearts and souls that the madness had no limits.
Taking advantage of the general jubilation, the most severe of matrons swapped their veils for masks and ran through the streets in their husband's jodhpurs, and the husbands donned their spouses best frocks.
The rare loyal followers of Father Angelo resisted the exchanges and shut themselves in churches and spent their time in prayer. Terrified by both the mad folly beyond the church doors and by the strange call they were resisting. They prayed for an answer to the reason for their torrid temptation.
The next morning, the town was dazed, hung over, relieved but slightly guilt ridden at the same time.

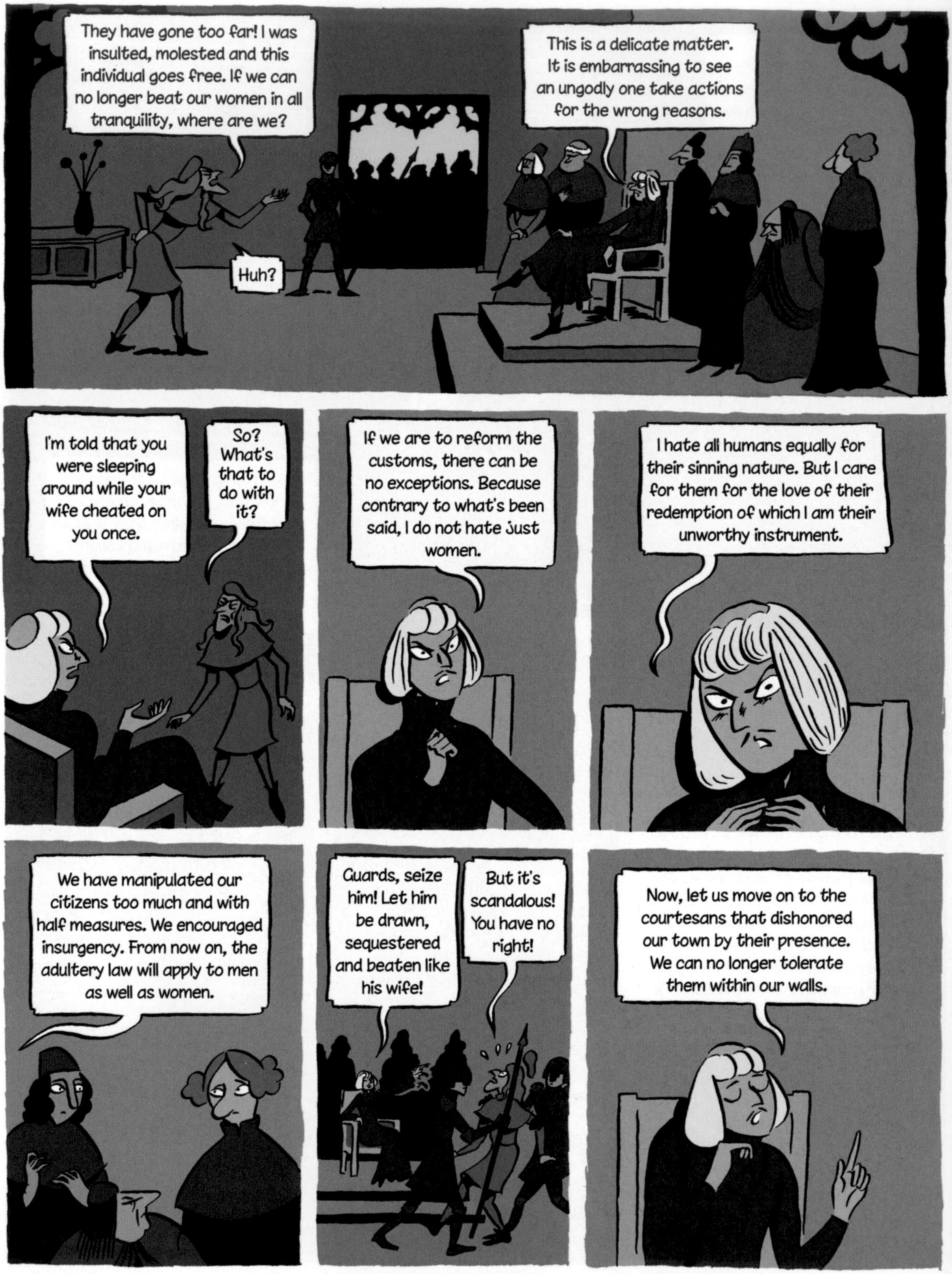
They have gone too far! I was insulted, molested and this individual goes free. If we can no longer beat our women in all tranquility, where are we?
Huh?
This is a delicate matter. It is embarrassing to see an ungodly one take actions for the wrong reasons.
I'm told that you were sleeping around while your wife cheated on you once.
So? What's that to do with it?
If we are to reform the customs, there can be no exceptions. Because contrary to what's been said, I do not hate just women.
I hate all humans equally for their sinning nature. But I care for them for the love of their redemption of which I am their unworthy instrument.
We have manipulated our citizens too much and with half measures. We encouraged insurgency. From now on, the adultery law will apply to men as well as women.
Guards, seize him! Let him be drawn, sequestered and beaten like his wife!
But it's scandalous! You have no right!
Now, let us move on to the courtesans that dishonored our town by their presence. We can no longer tolerate them within our walls.

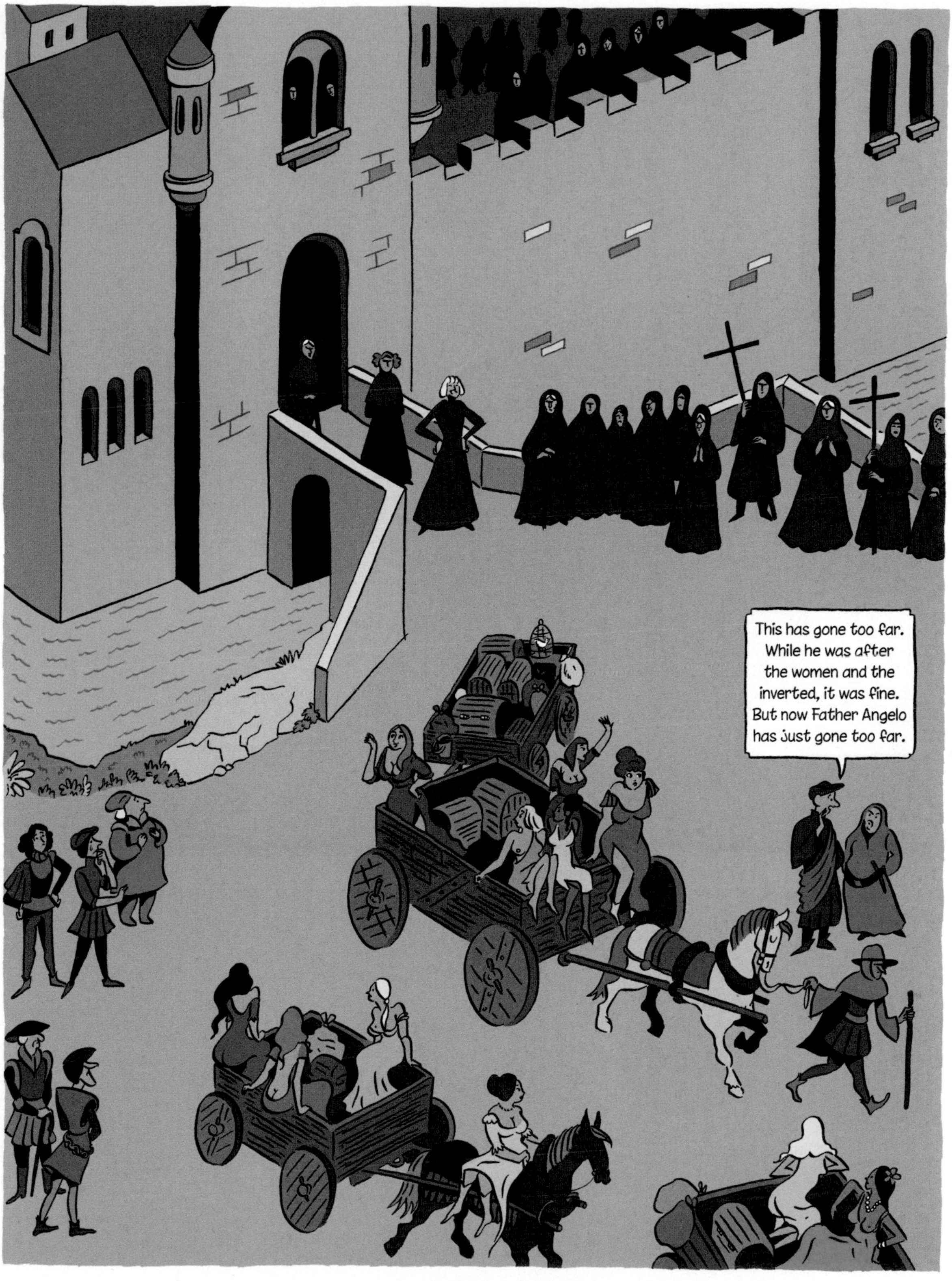
This has gone too far. While he was after the women and the inverted, it was fine. But now Father Angelo has just gone too far.

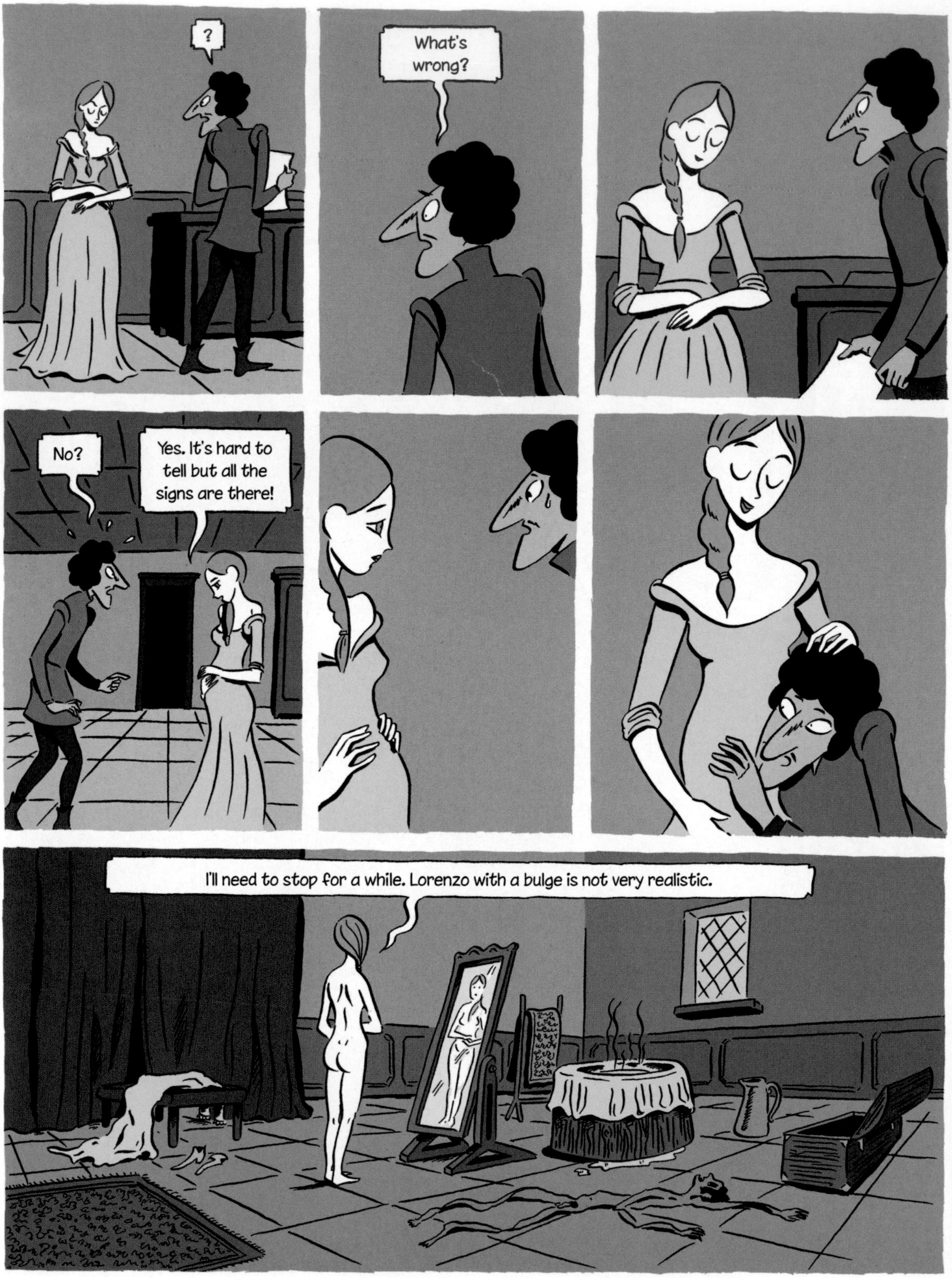
?
What's wrong?
No?
Yes. It's hard to tell but all the signs are there!
I'll need to stop for a while. Lorenzo with a bulge is not very realistic.

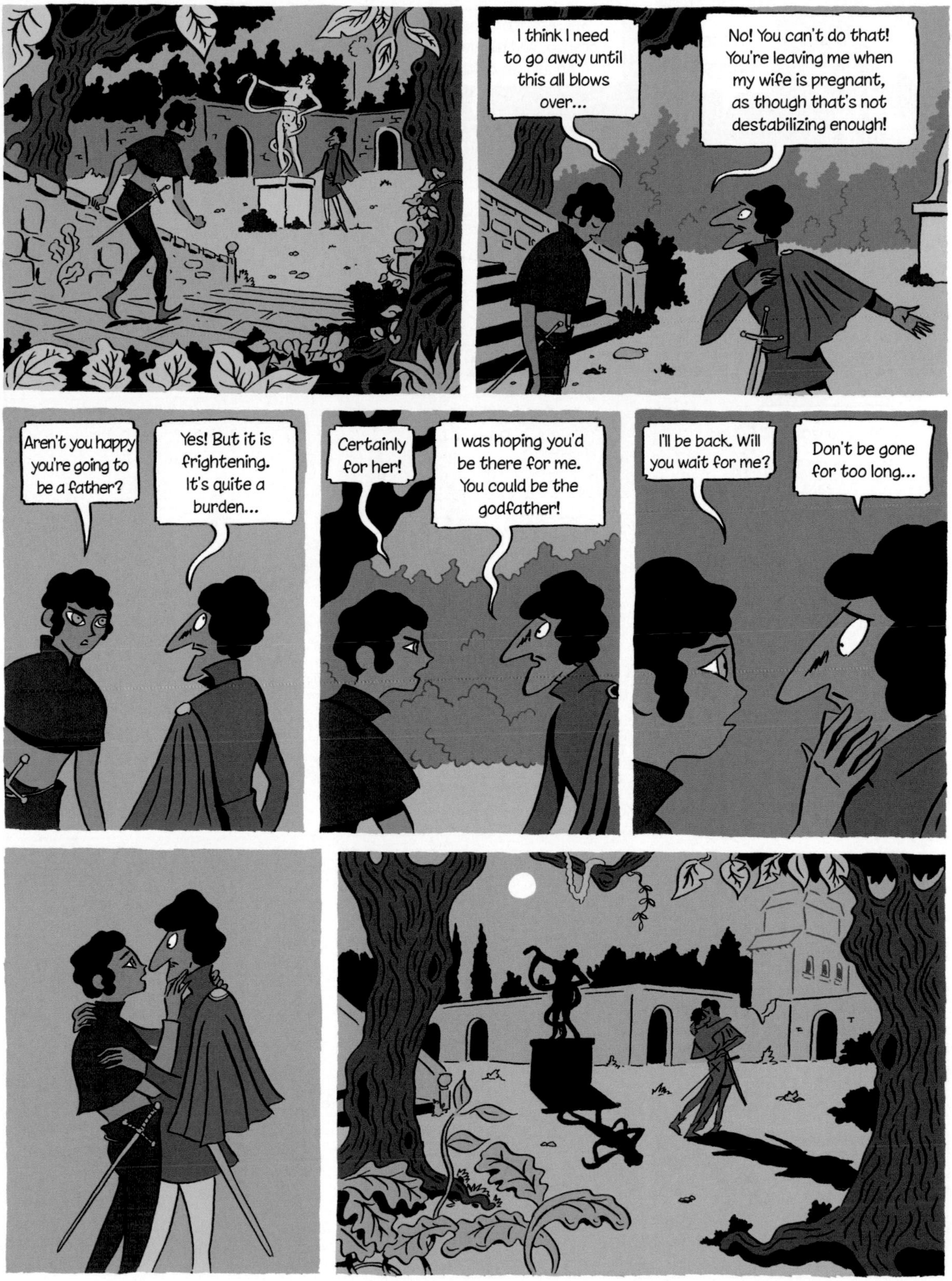
I think I need to go away until this all blows over...
No! You can't do that! You're leaving me when my wife is pregnant, as though that's not destabilizing enough!
Aren't you happy you're going to be a father?
Yes! But it is frightening. It's quite a burden...
Certainly for her!
I was hoping you'd be there for me. You could be the godfather!
I'll be back. Will you wait for me?
Don't be gone for too long...

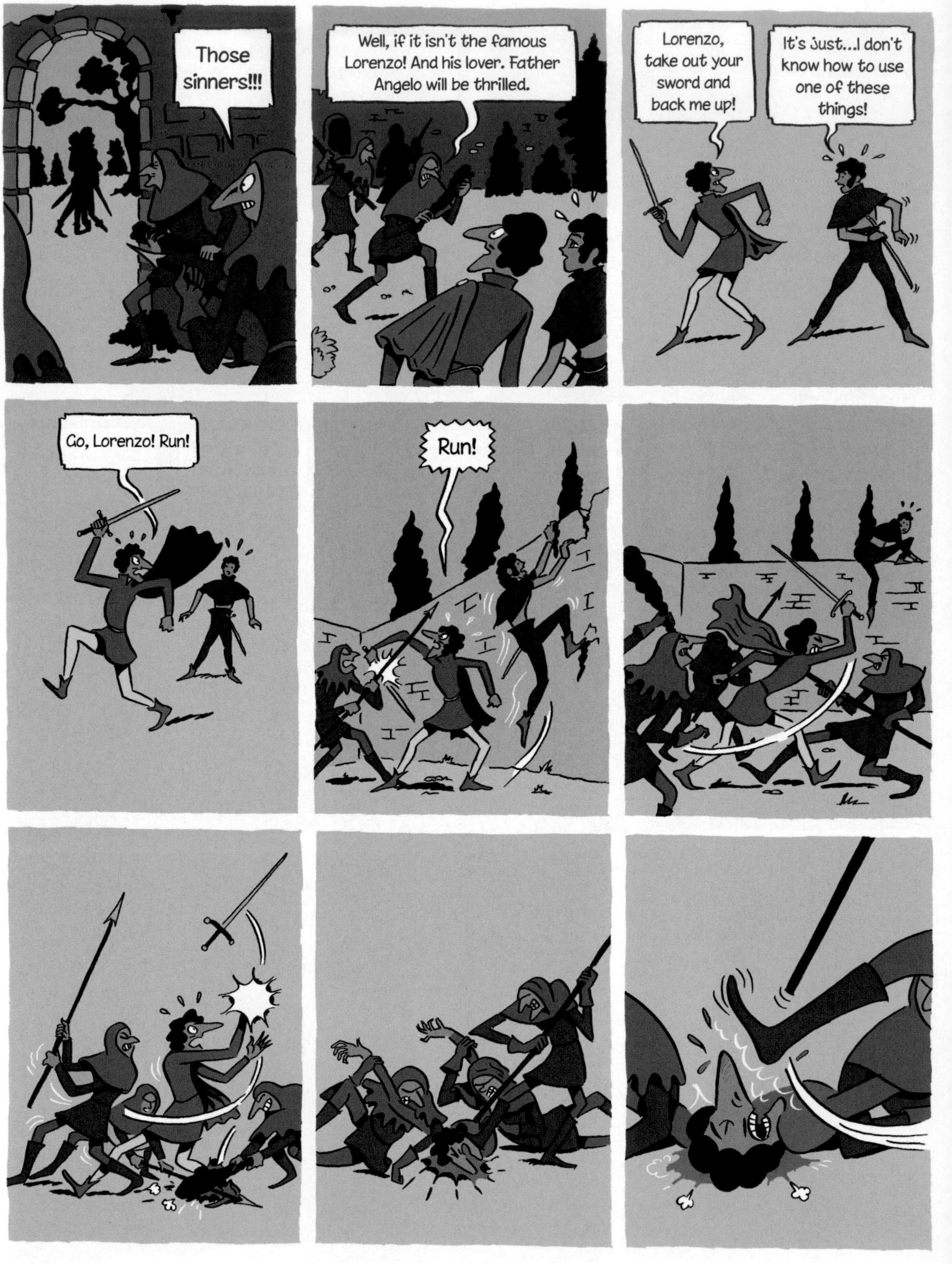
Those sinners!!!
Well, if it isn't the famous Lorenzo! And his lover. Father Angelo will be thrilled.
Lorenzo, take out your sword and back me up!
It's just...I don't know how to use one of these things!
Go, Lorenzo! Run!
Run!

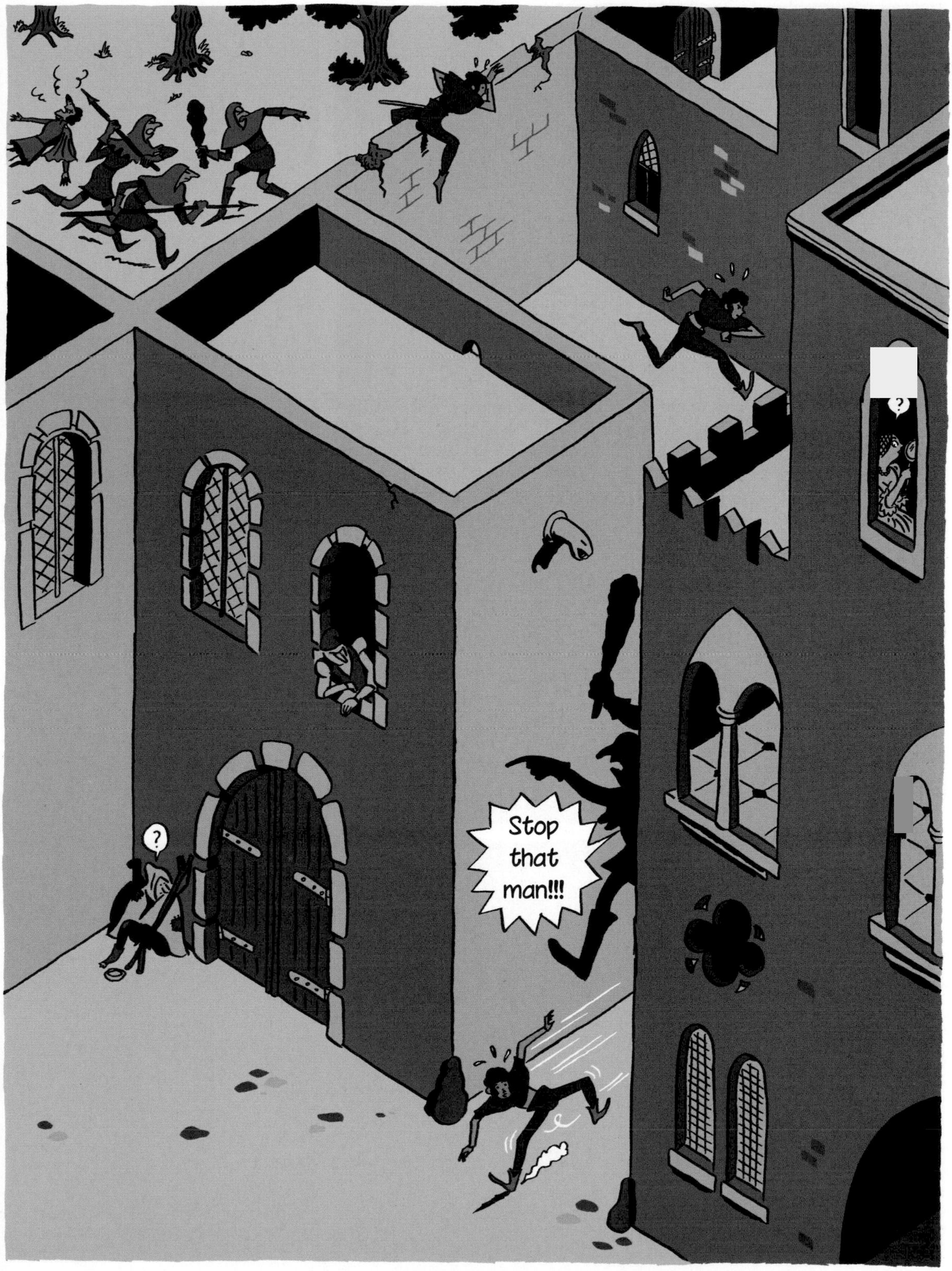
?
?
Stop that man!!!

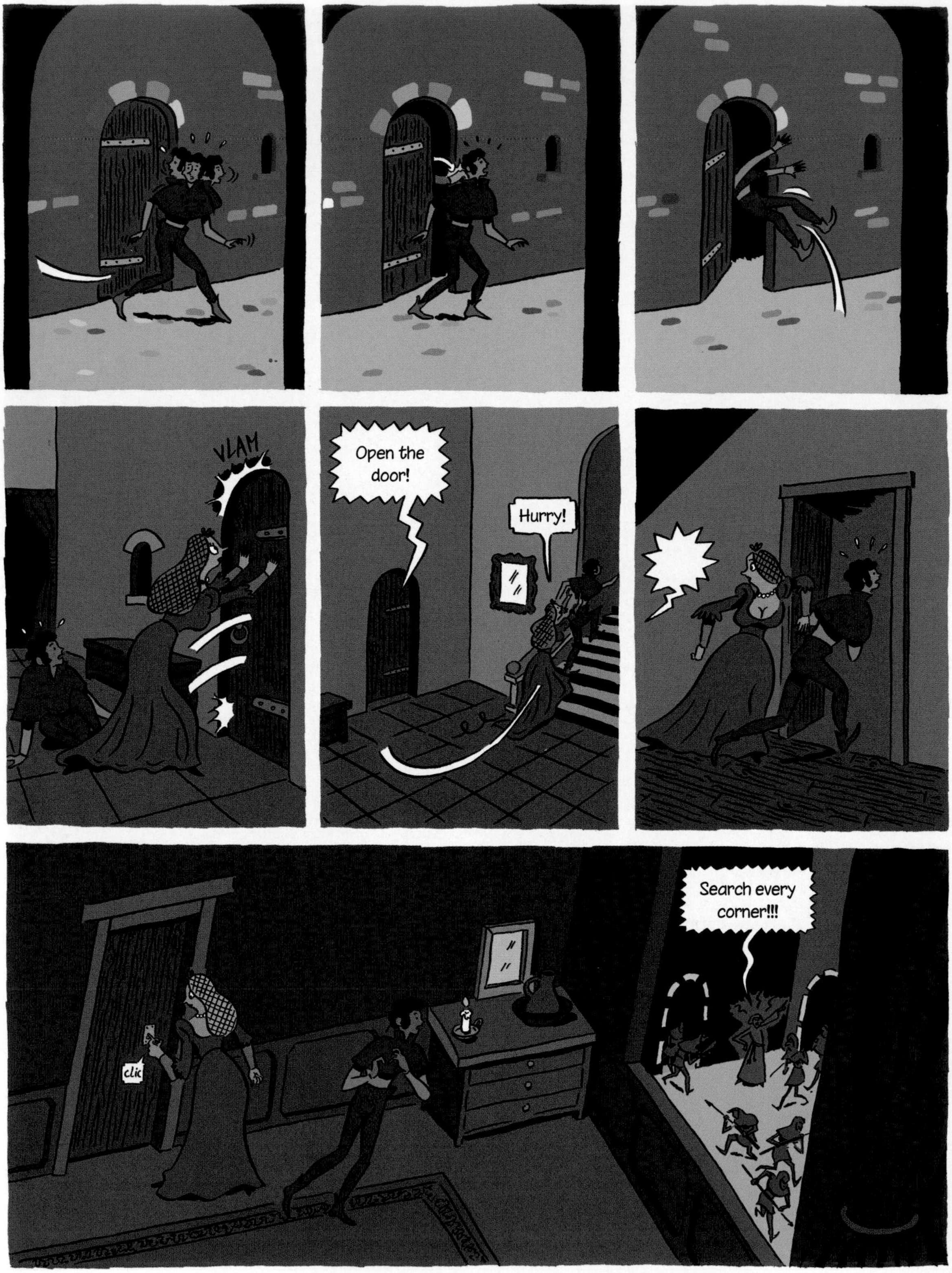
VLAM
Open the door!
Hurry!
Search every corner!!!
clic

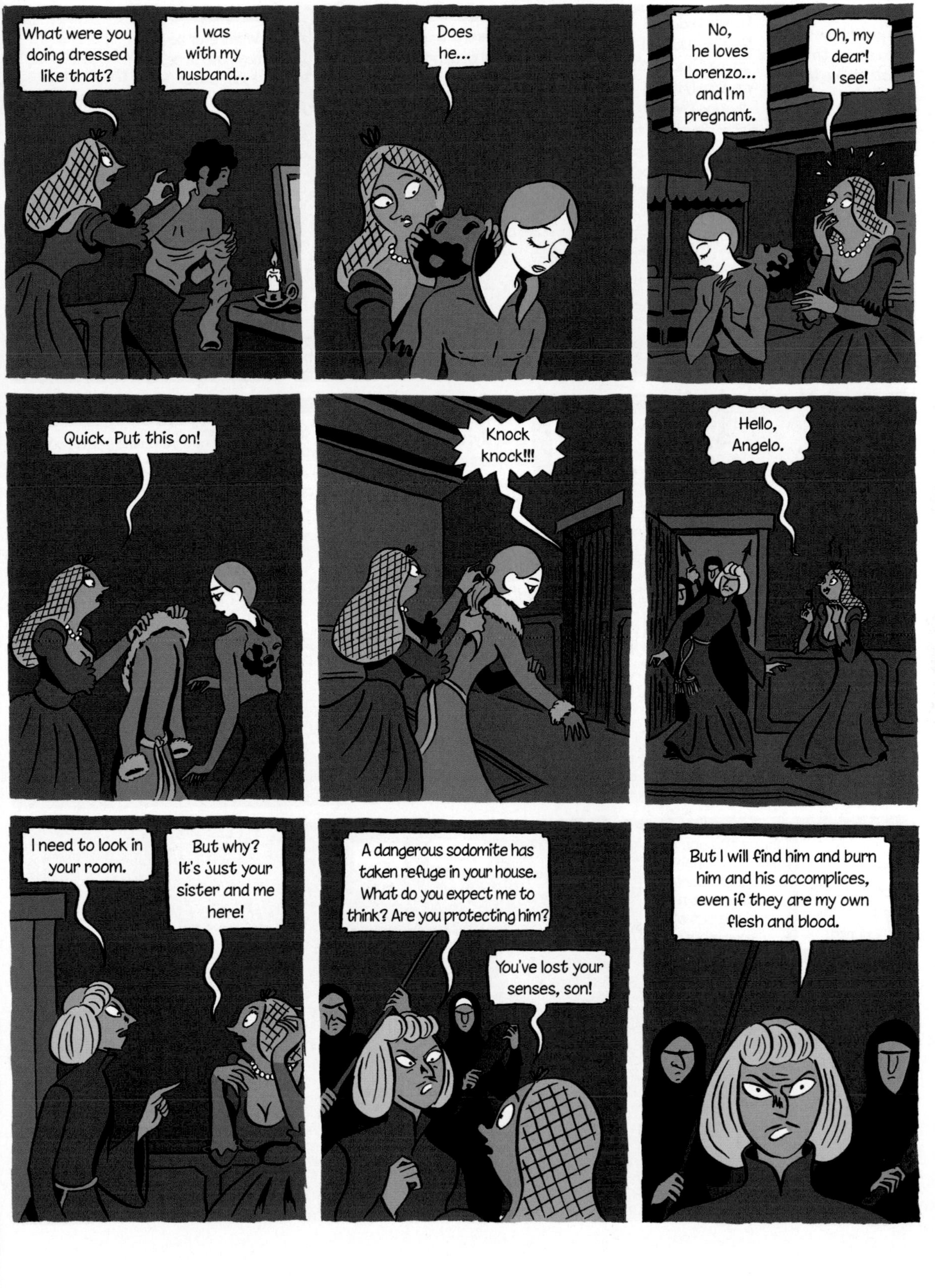
What were you doing dressed like that?
I was with my husband...
Does he...
No, he loves Lorenzo... and I'm pregnant.
Oh, my dear! I see!
Quick. Put this on!
Knock knock!!!
Hello, Angelo.
I need to look in your room.
But why? It's just your sister and me here!
A dangerous sodomite has taken refuge in your house. What do you expect me to think? Are you protecting him?
You've lost your senses, son!
But I will find him and burn him and his accomplices, even if they are my own flesh and blood.

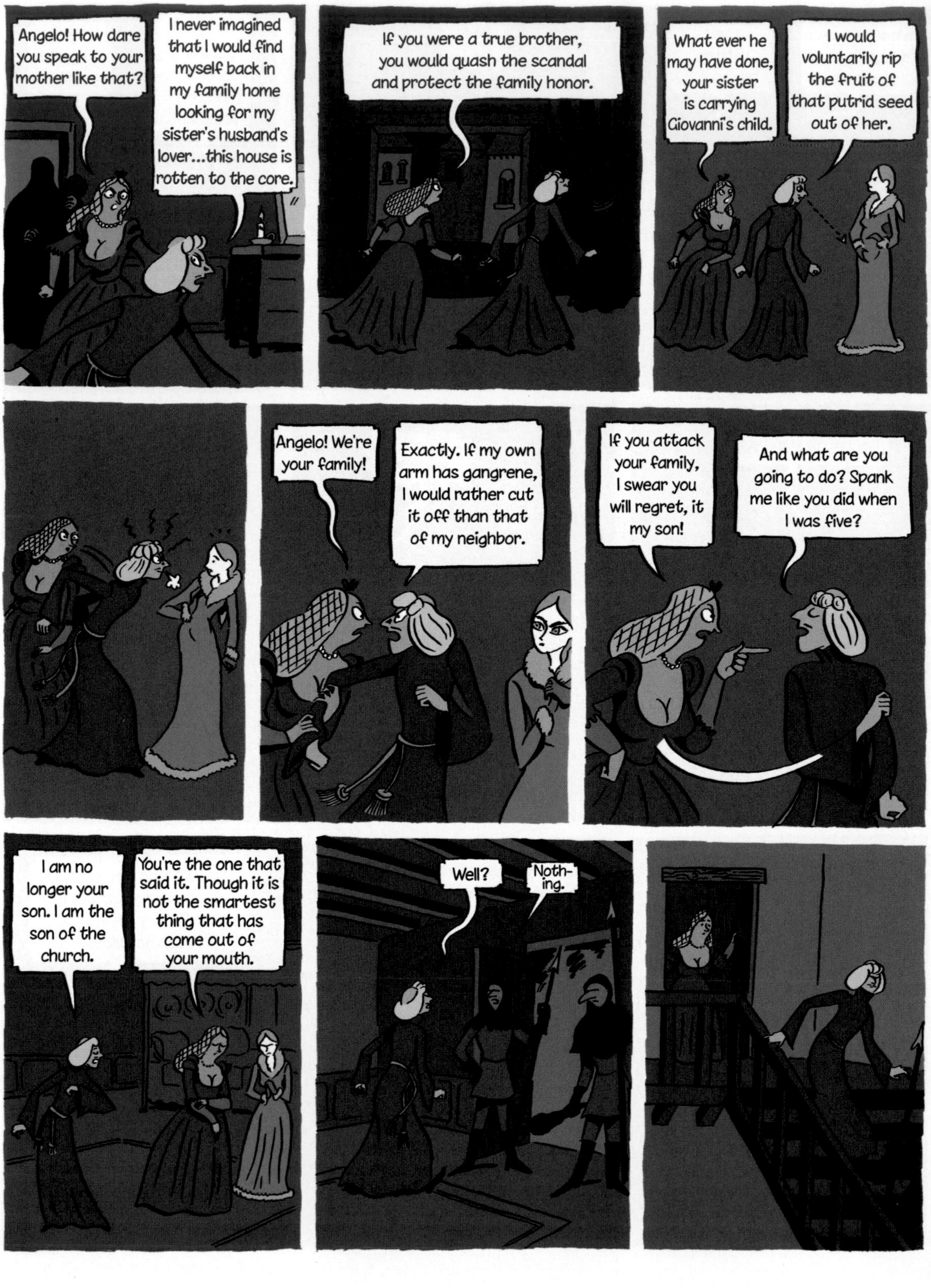
Angelo! How dare you speak to your mother like that?
I never imagined that I would find myself back in my family home looking for my sister's husband's lover...this house is rotten to the core.
If you were a true brother, you would quash the scandal and protect the family honor.
What ever he may have done, your sister is carrying Giovanni's child.
I would voluntarily rip the fruit of that putrid seed out of her.
Angelo! We're your family!
Exactly. If my own arm has gangrene, I would rather cut it off than that of my neighbor.
If you attack your family, I swear you will regret, it my son!
And what are you going to do? Spank me like you did when I was five?
I am no longer your son. I am the son of the church.
You're the one that said it. Though it is not the smartest thing that has come out of your mouth.
Well?
Noth-ing.

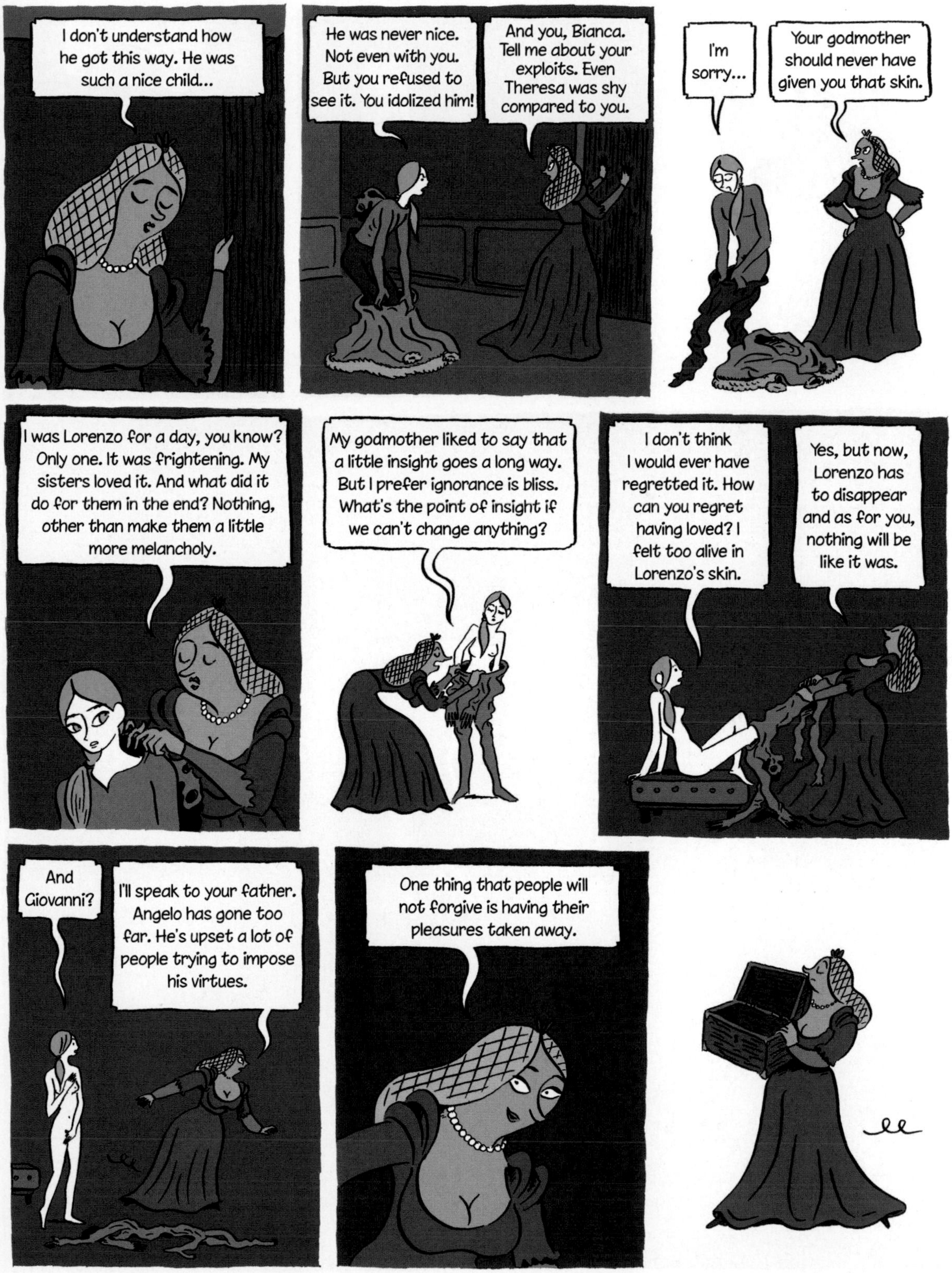
I don't understand how he got this way. He was such a nice child...
He was never nice. Not even with you. But you refused to see it. You idolized him!
And you, Bianca. Tell me about your exploits. Even Theresa was shy compared to you.
I'm sorry...
Your godmother should never have given you that skin.
I was Lorenzo for a day, you know? Only one. It was frightening. My sisters loved it. And what did it do for them in the end? Nothing, other than make them a little more melancholy.
My godmother liked to say that a little insight goes a long way. But I prefer ignorance is bliss. What's the point of insight if we can't change anything?
I don't think I would ever have regretted it. How can you regret having loved? I felt too alive in Lorenzo's skin.
Yes, but now, Lorenzo has to disappear and as for you, nothing will be like it was.
And Giovanni?
I'll speak to your father. Angelo has gone too far. He's upset a lot of people trying to impose his virtues.
One thing that people will not forgive is having their pleasures taken away.

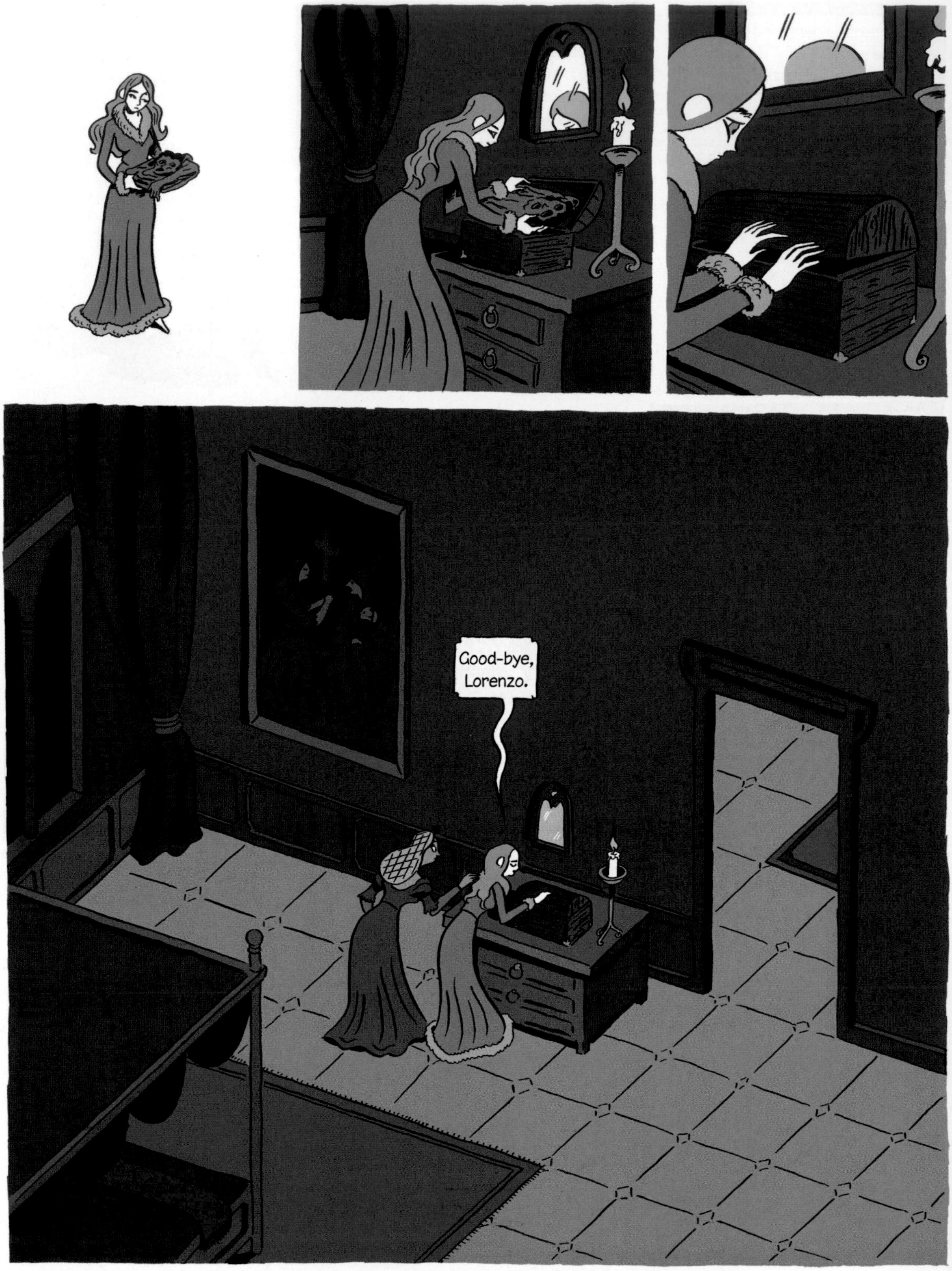
Good-bye, Lorenzo.

My son's health is a worry. Angelo seems down. Sin revolts him to such a degree that it makes him ill. I'm not sure that his living in a town like ours is good for him and vice versa.

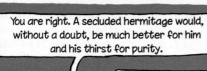
You are right. A secluded hermitage would, without a doubt, be much better for him and his thirst for purity.

I agree with that.

And that would reassure the foreign merchants that seem to have forgotten the way to our town.

You've taken the words right out of my mouth.

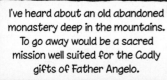
I've heard about an old abandoned monastery deep in the mountains. To go away would be a sacred mission well suited for the Godly gifts of Father Angelo.

I'm sure that the bishop would not be opposed to a generous donation from us.

Very good idea!

The resolution has been voted in unanimously.

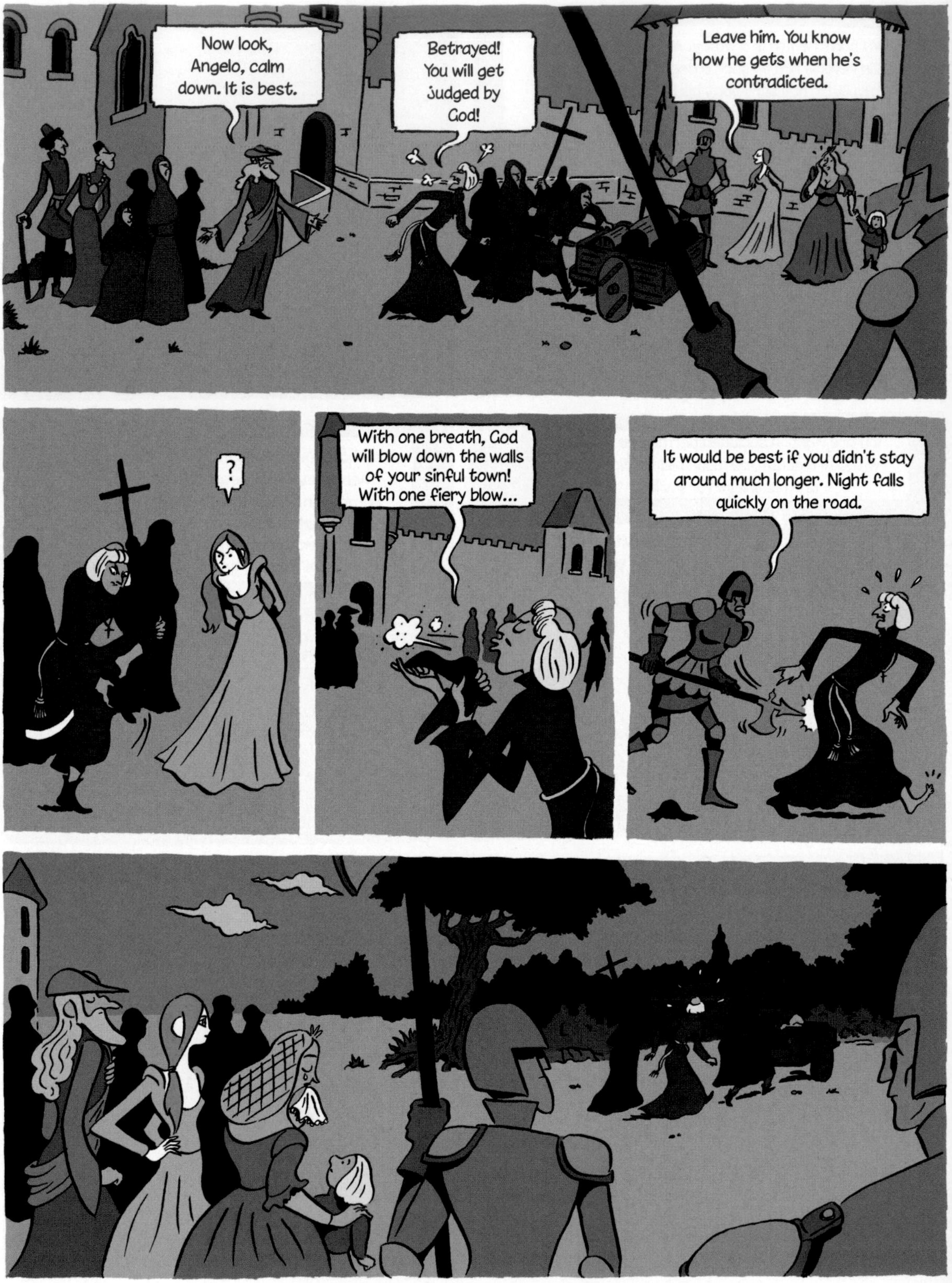
Now look, Angelo, calm down. It is best.
Betrayed! You will get judged by God!
Leave him. You know how he gets when he's contradicted.
?
With one breath, God will blow down the walls of your sinful town! With one fiery blow...
It would be best if you didn't stay around much longer. Night falls quickly on the road.

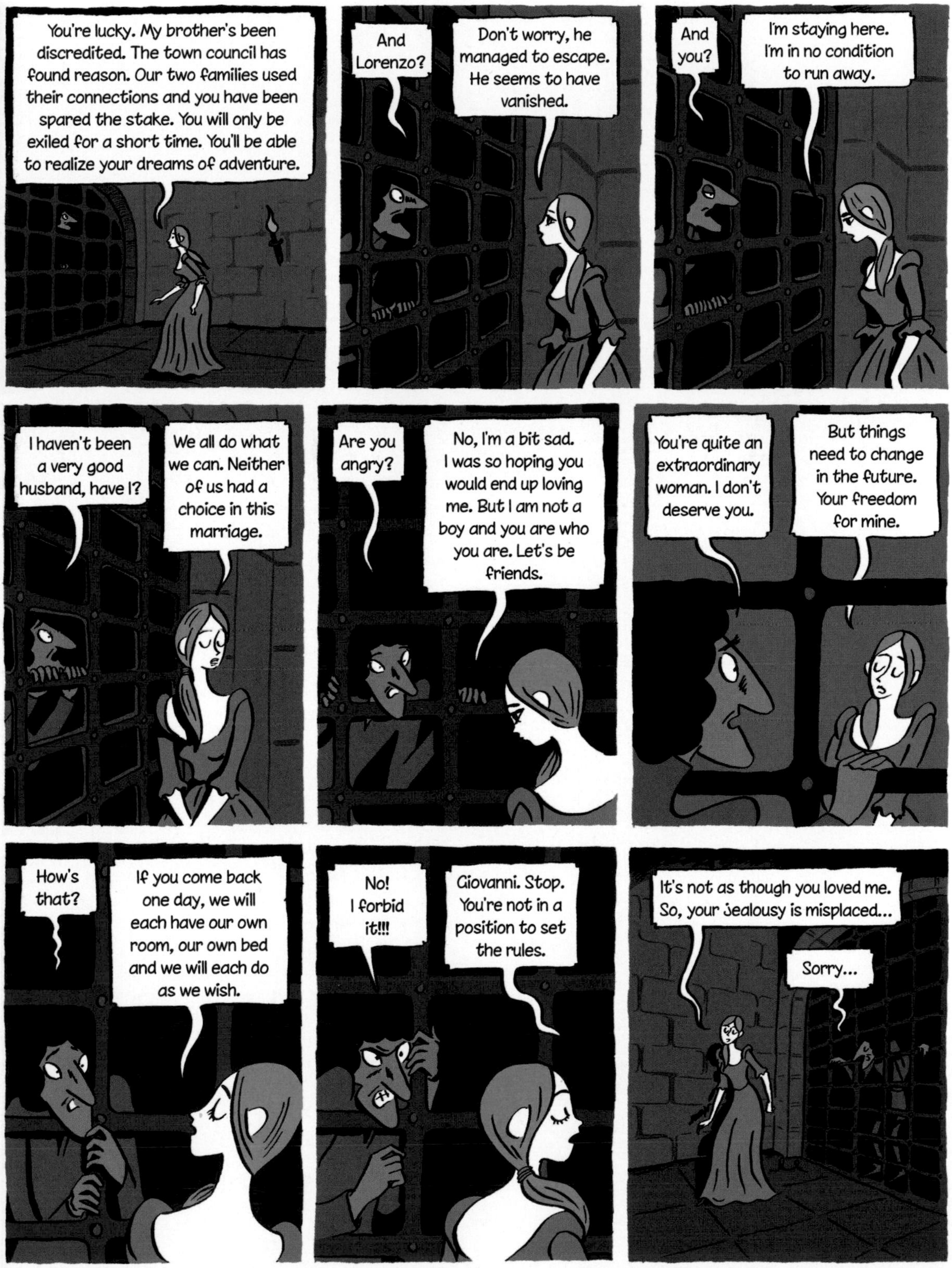
You're lucky. My brother's been discredited. The town council has found reason. Our two families used their connections and you have been spared the stake. You will only be exiled for a short time. You'll be able to realize your dreams of adventure.
And Lorenzo?
Don't worry, he managed to escape. He seems to have vanished.
And you?
I'm staying here. I'm in no condition to run away.
I haven't been a very good husband, have I?
We all do what we can. Neither of us had a choice in this marriage.
Are you angry?
No, I'm a bit sad. I was so hoping you would end up loving me. But I am not a boy and you are who you are. Let's be friends.
You're quite an extraordinary woman. I don't deserve you.
But things need to change in the future. Your freedom for mine.
How's that?
If you come back one day, we will each have our own room, our own bed and we will each do as we wish.
No! I forbid it!!!
Giovanni. Stop. You're not in a position to set the rules.
It's not as though you loved me. So, your jealousy is misplaced...
Sorry...

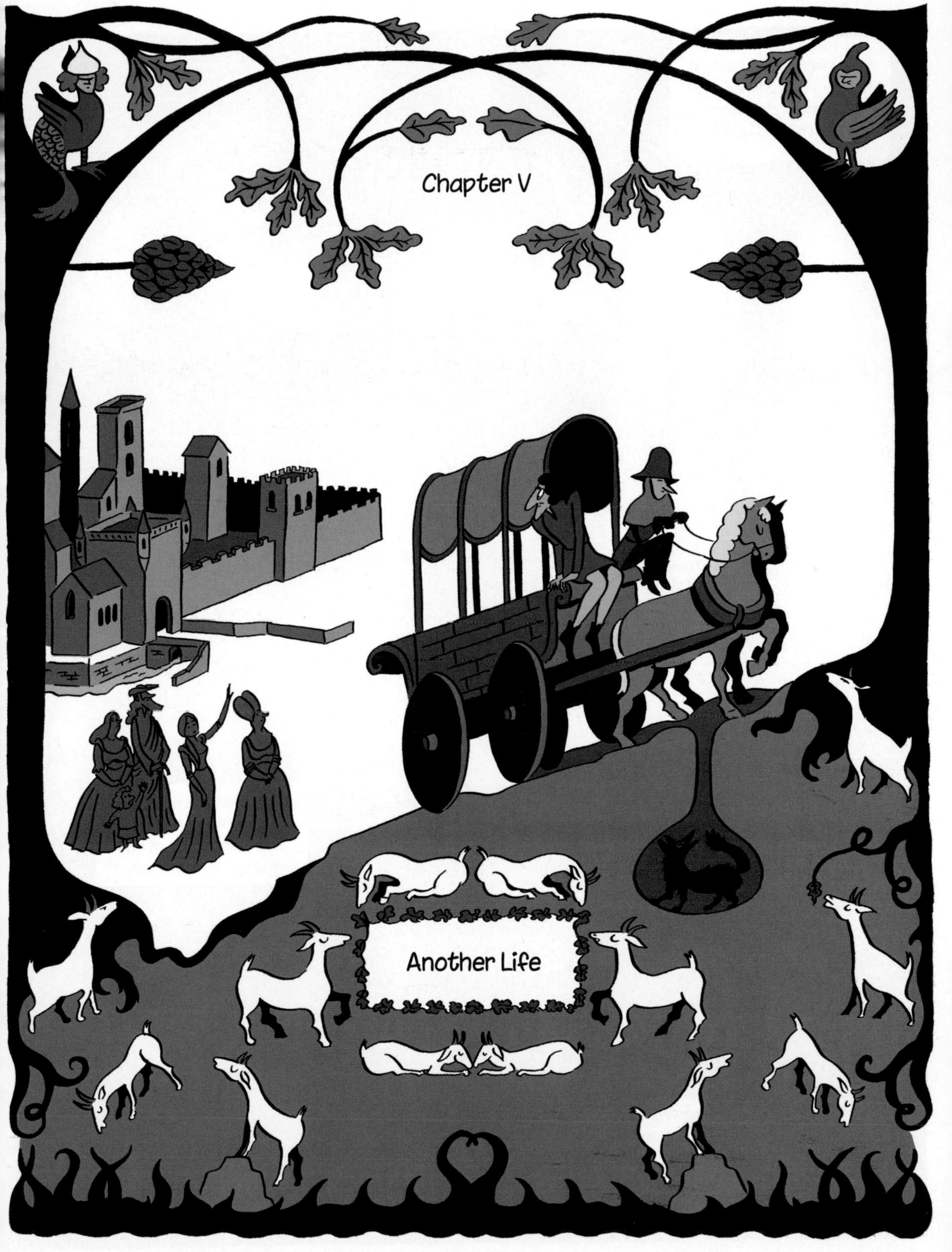
Chapter V
Another Life

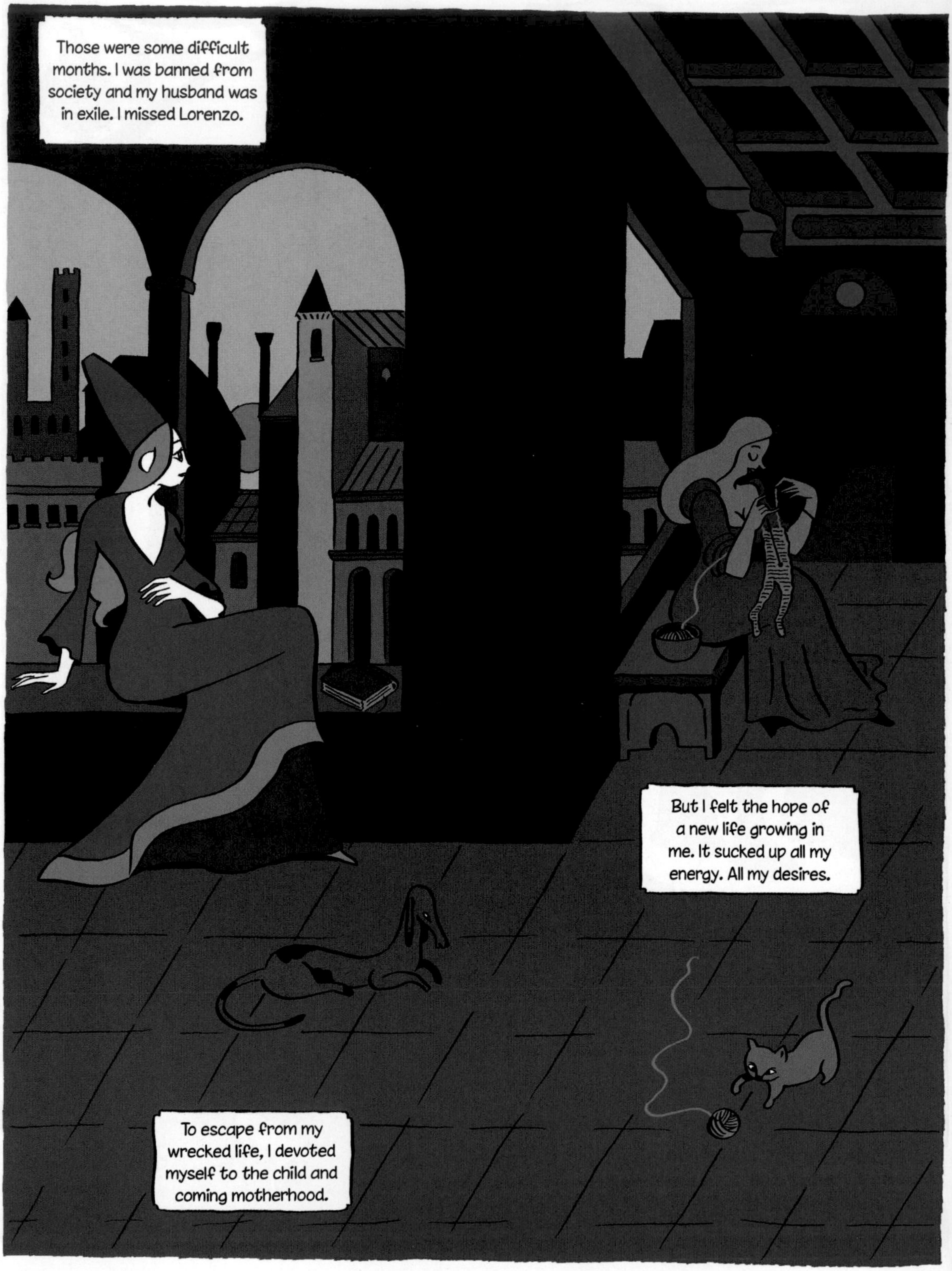
Those were some difficult months. I was banned from society and my husband was in exile. I missed Lorenzo.
But I felt the hope of a new life growing in me. It sucked up all my energy. All my desires.
To escape from my wrecked life, I devoted myself to the child and coming motherhood.

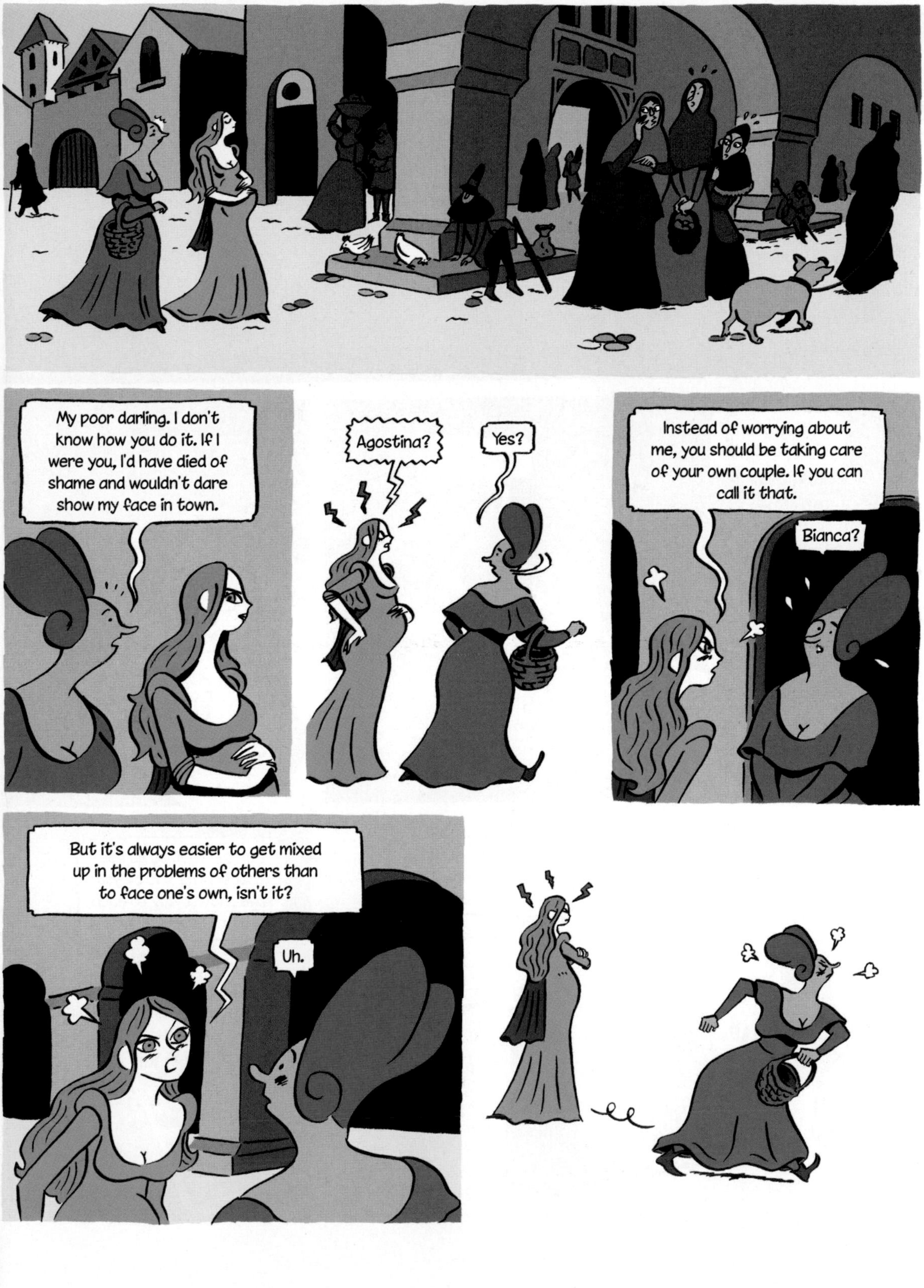
My poor darling. I don't know how you do it. If I were you, I'd have died of shame and wouldn't dare show my face in town.
Agostina?
Yes?
Instead of worrying about me, you should be taking care of your own couple. If you can call it that.
Bianca?
But it's always easier to get mixed up in the problems of others than to face one's own, isn't it?
Uh.

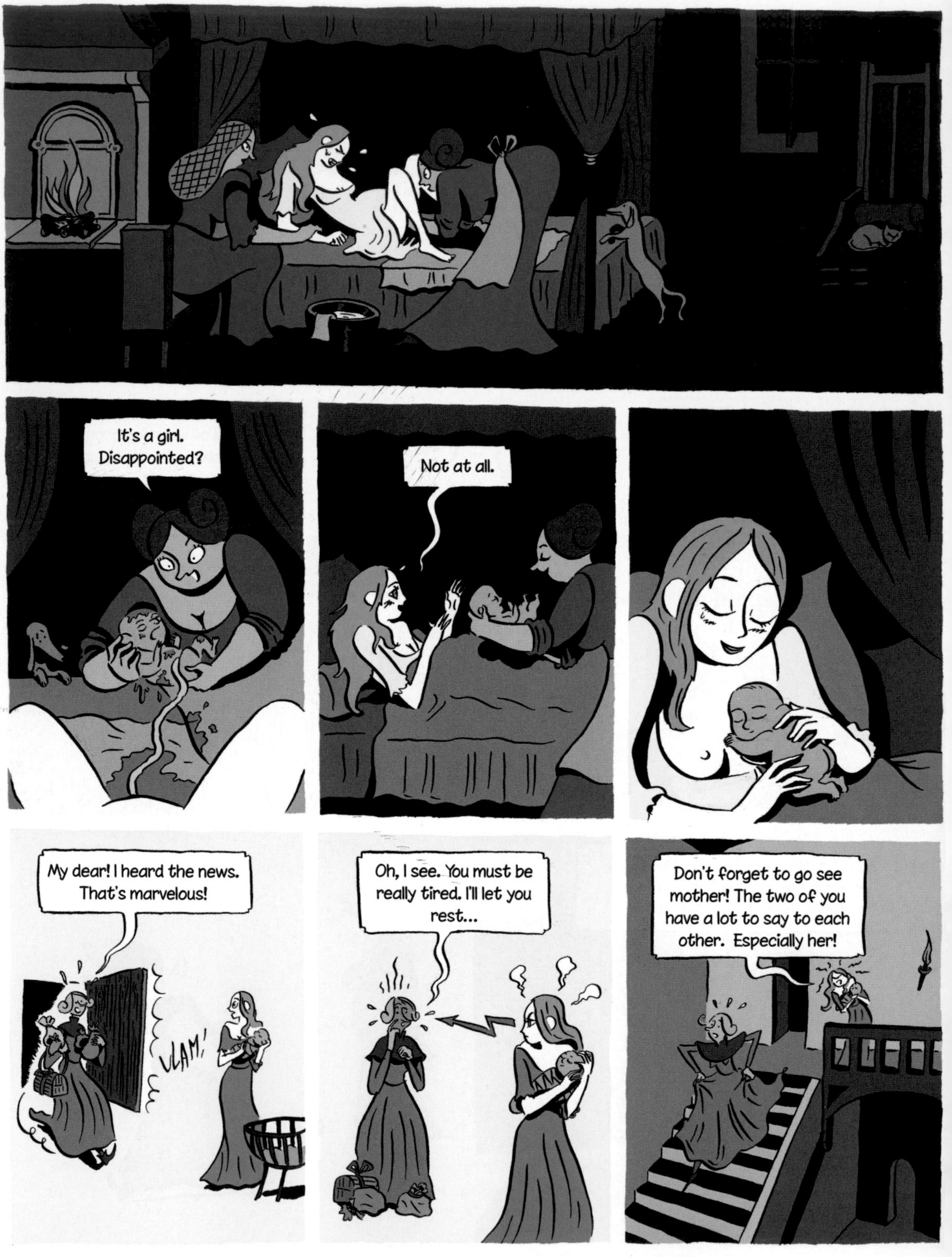
It's a girl. Disappointed?
Not at all.
My dear! I heard the news. That's marvelous!
VLAM!
Oh, I see. You must be really tired. I'll let you rest...
Don't forget to go see mother! The two of you have a lot to say to each other. Especially her!

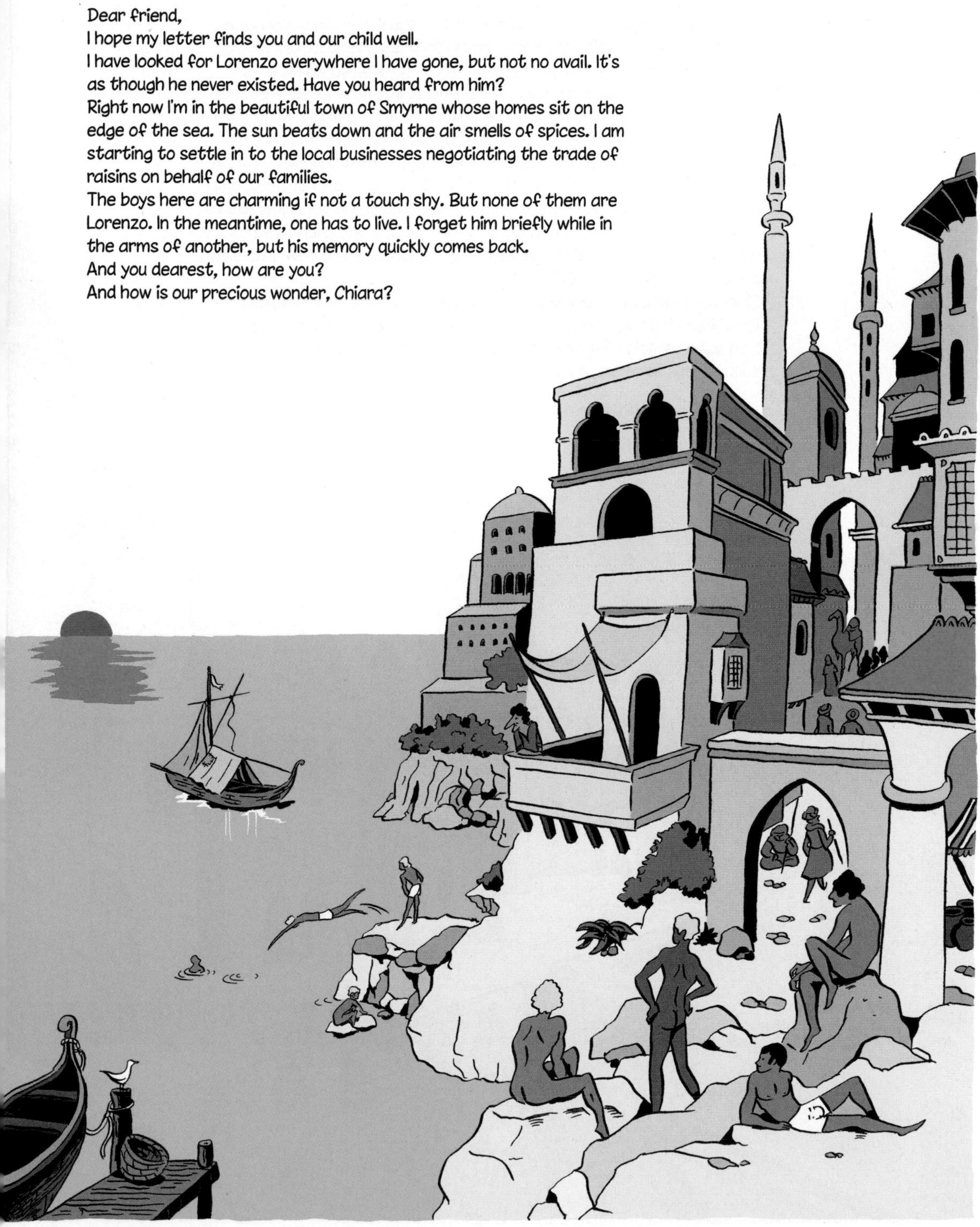
Dear friend,
I hope my letter finds you and our child well.
I have looked for Lorenzo everywhere I have gone, but not no avail. It's as though he never existed. Have you heard from him?
Right now I'm in the beautiful town of Smyrne whose homes sit on the edge of the sea. The sun beats down and the air smells of spices. I am starting to settle in to the local businesses negotiating the trade of raisins on behalf of our families.
The boys here are charming if not a touch shy. But none of them are Lorenzo. In the meantime, one has to live. I forget him briefly while in the arms of another, but his memory quickly comes back.
And you dearest, how are you?
And how is our precious wonder, Chiara?

Dear friend,
Chiara is growing fast. She is as beautiful as the sun and an angel when she's not confronted by demons! I send with this letter a locket with a portrait of her painted by your friend Peccorino, who sends his love.
Rubina's husband died in the arms of a whore. Rubina is finally free, but she left town. I hope that she will be able to start a new life. No one here has seen or heard from Lorenzo. But, from time to time, Vive Lorenzo appears on the walls of a church and the priests cross themselves wildly before setting off to clean off the words that only reappear again later. And this year, at the carnival, the most beautiful boy in town was elected this year's Lorenzo. He proudly wore the crown and the enchanted attire, much to the dismay of the priests trying to dissuade this new tradition and the chants of VIVE LORENZO!
Since my brother has left town, things are back to normal. Religious fanaticism is passé and your escapades with Lorenzo would no longer shock. I am quite certain that I will be able to get your exile reversed and you will soon be able to return to us.

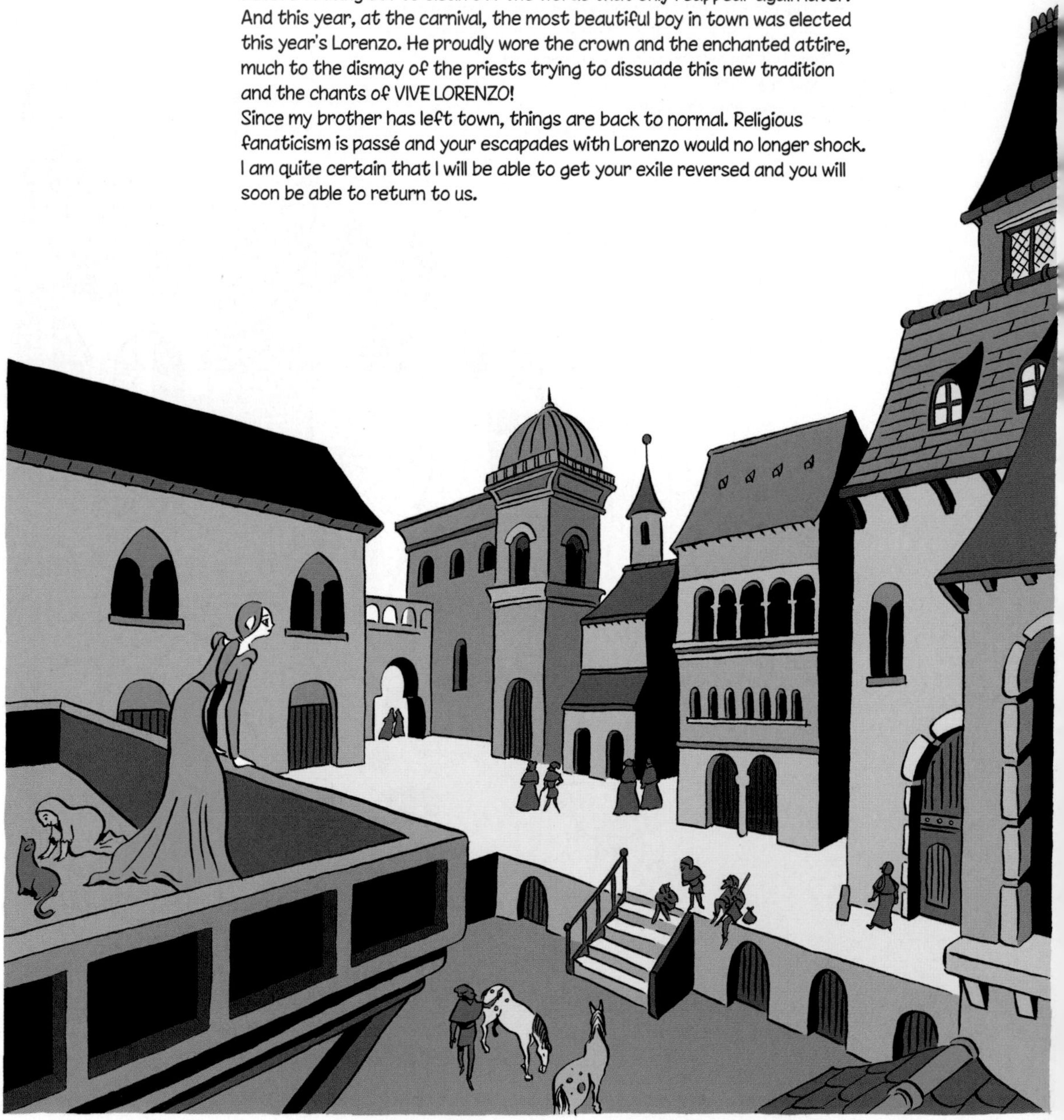

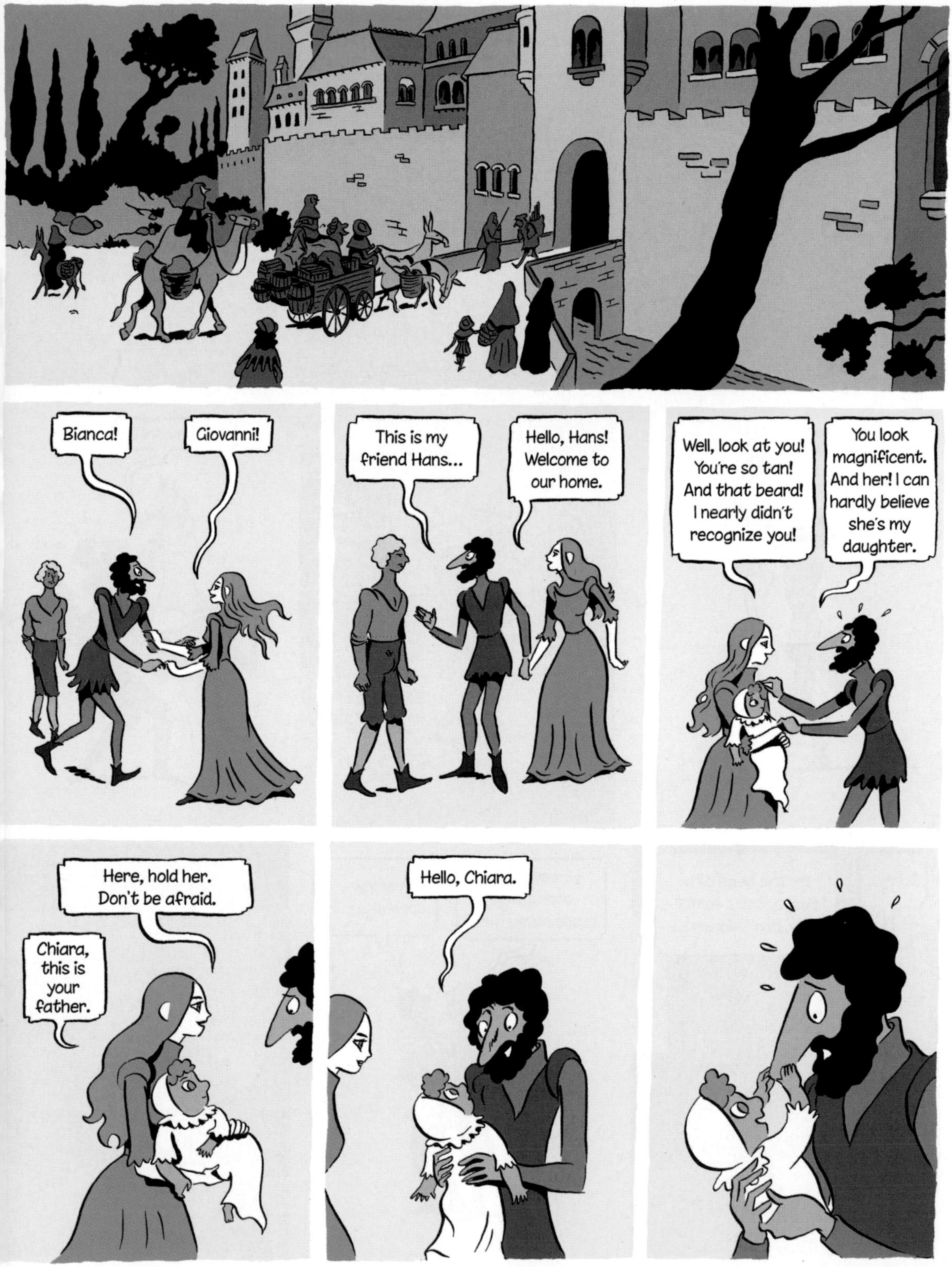
Bianca!
Giovanni!
This is my friend Hans...
Hello, Hans! Welcome to our home.
Well, look at you! You're so tan! And that beard! I nearly didn't recognize you!
You look magnificent. And her! I can hardly believe she's my daughter.
Chiara, this is your father.
Here, hold her. Don't be afraid.
Hello, Chiara.

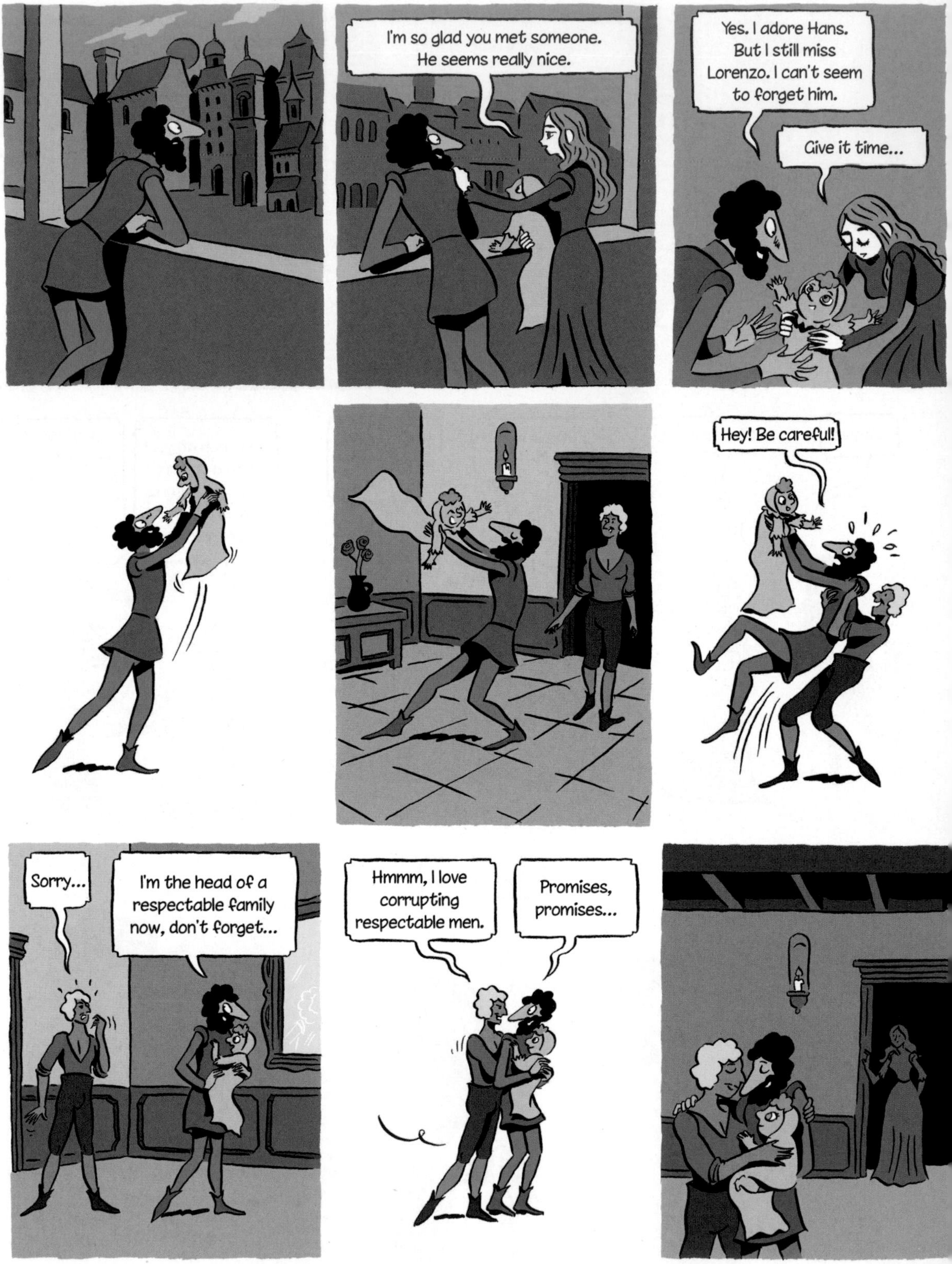
I'm so glad you met someone. He seems really nice.
Yes. I adore Hans. But I still miss Lorenzo. I can't seem to forget him.
Give it time...
Hey! Be careful!
Sorry...
I'm the head of a respectable family now, don't forget...
Hmmm, I love corrupting respectable men.
Promises, promises...

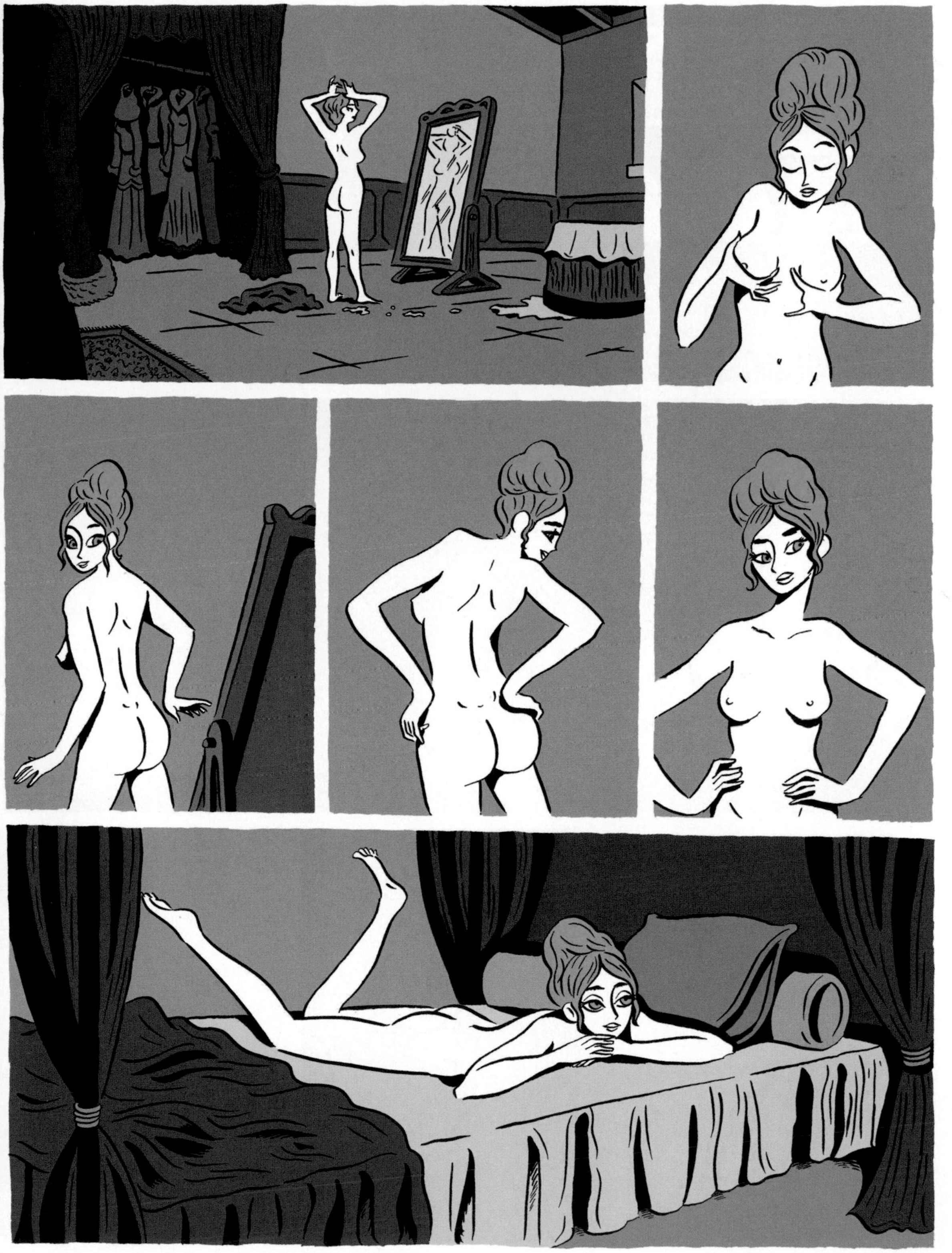

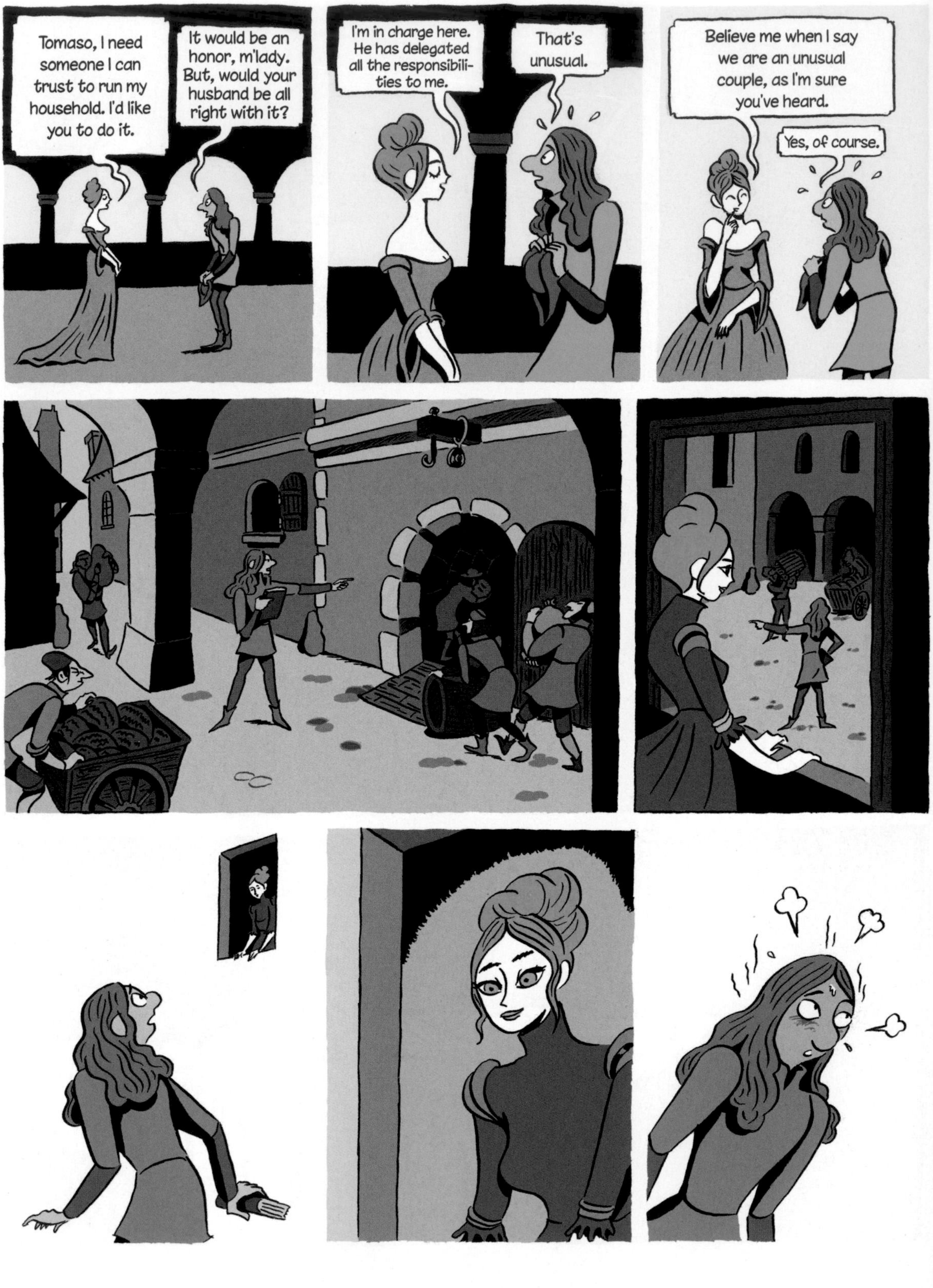
Tomaso, I need someone I can trust to run my household. I'd like you to do it.
It would be an honor, m'lady. But, would your husband be all right with it?
I'm in charge here. He has delegated all the responsibilities to me.
That's unusual.
Believe me when I say we are an unusual couple, as I'm sure you've heard.
Yes, of course.

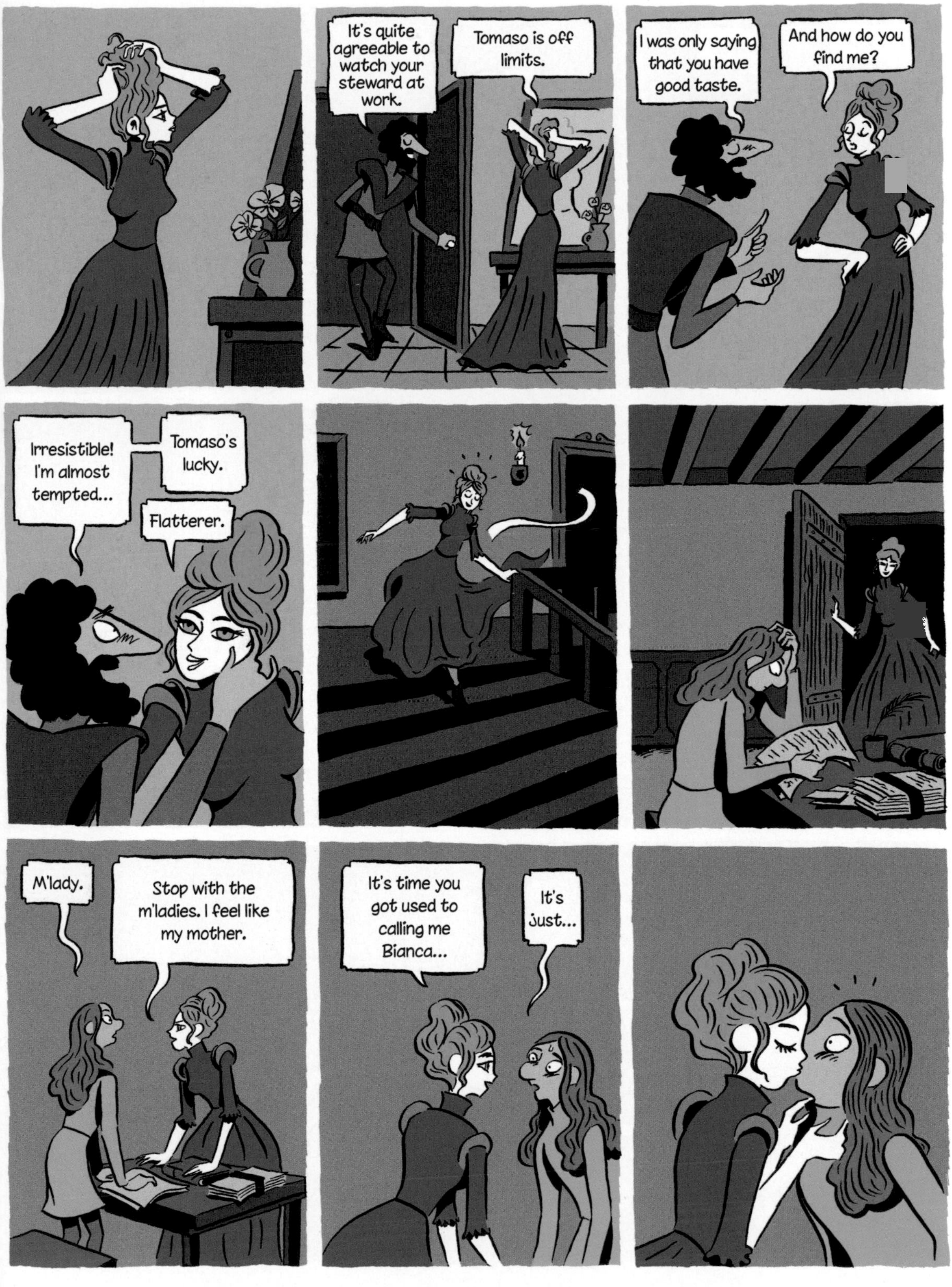
It's quite agreeable to watch your steward at work.
Tomaso is off limits.
I was only saying that you have good taste.
And how do you find me?
Irresistible! I'm almost tempted...
Tomaso's lucky.
Flatterer.
M'lady.
Stop with the m'ladies. I feel like my mother.
It's time you got used to calling me Bianca...
It's just...

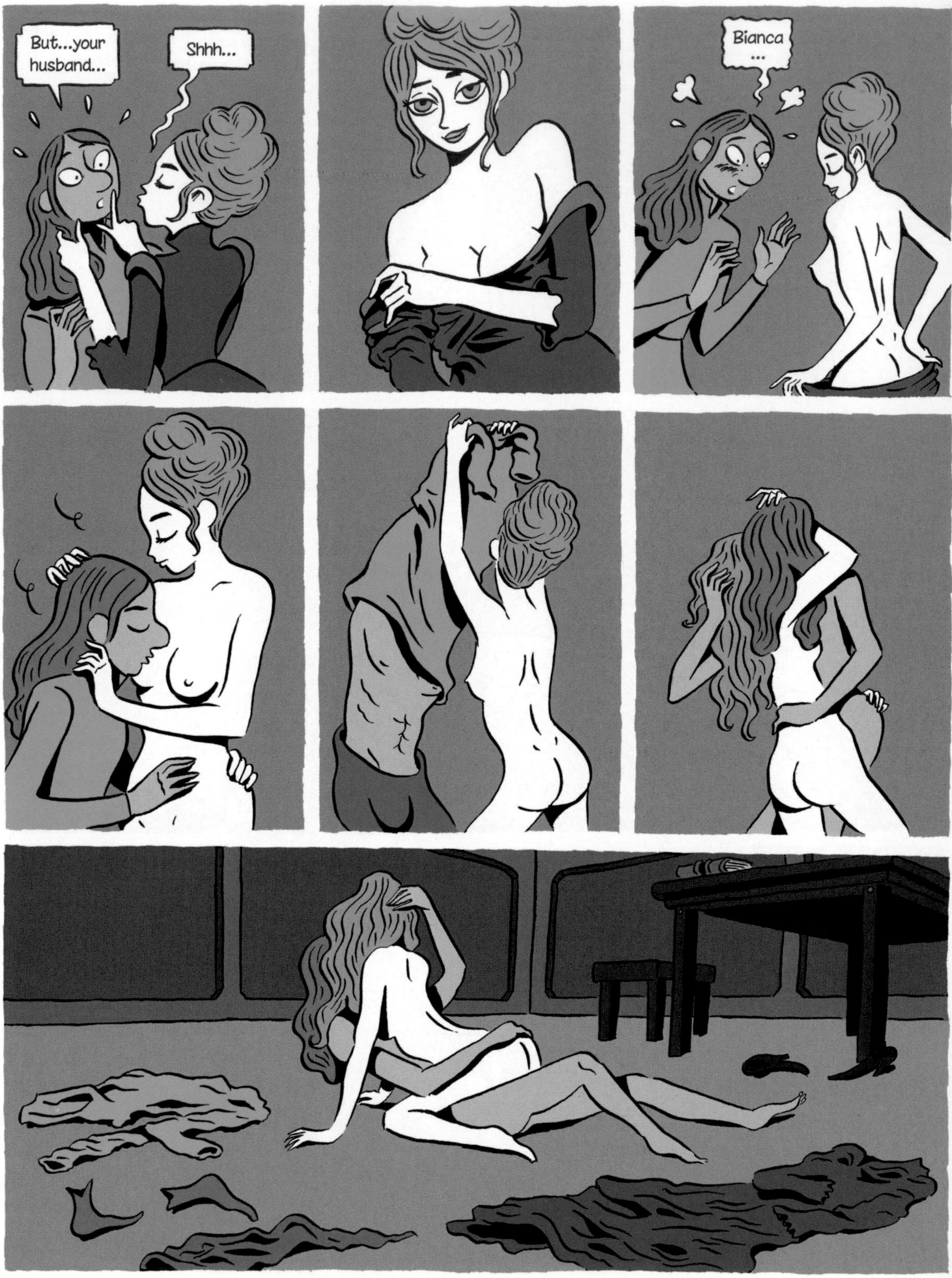

But...your husband...
Shhh...
Bianca ...

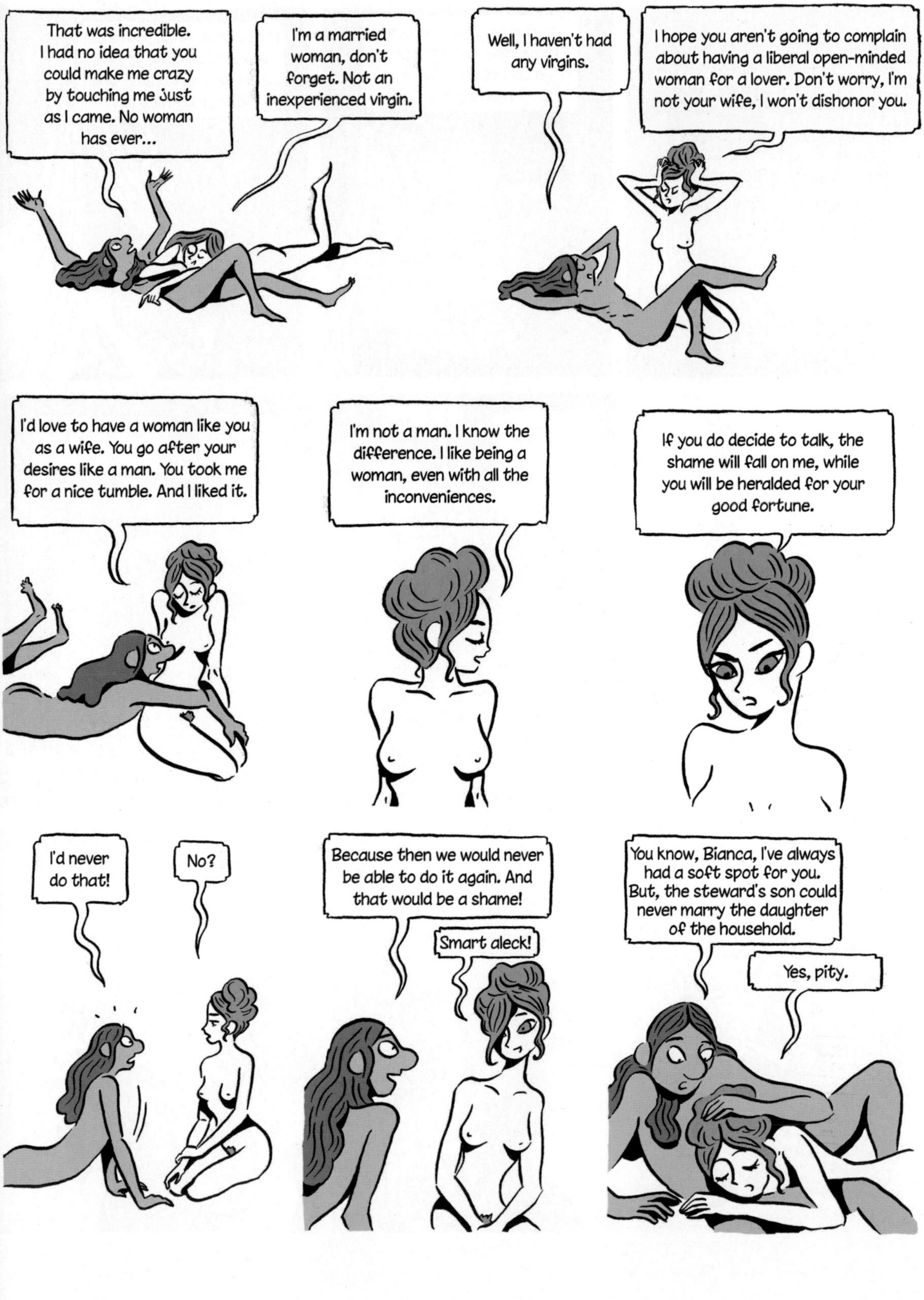
That was incredible. I had no idea that you could make me crazy by touching me just as I came. No woman has ever...
I'm a married woman, don't forget. Not an inexperienced virgin.
Well, I haven't had any virgins.
I hope you aren't going to complain about having a liberal open-minded woman for a lover. Don't worry, I'm not your wife, I won't dishonor you.
I'd love to have a woman like you as a wife. You go after your desires like a man. You took me for a nice tumble. And I liked it.
I'm not a man. I know the difference. I like being a woman, even with all the inconveniences.
If you do decide to talk, the shame will fall on me, while you will be heralded for your good fortune.
I'd never do that!
No?
Because then we would never be able to do it again. And that would be a shame!
Smart aleck!
You know, Bianca, I've always had a soft spot for you. But, the steward's son could never marry the daughter of the household.
Yes, pity.

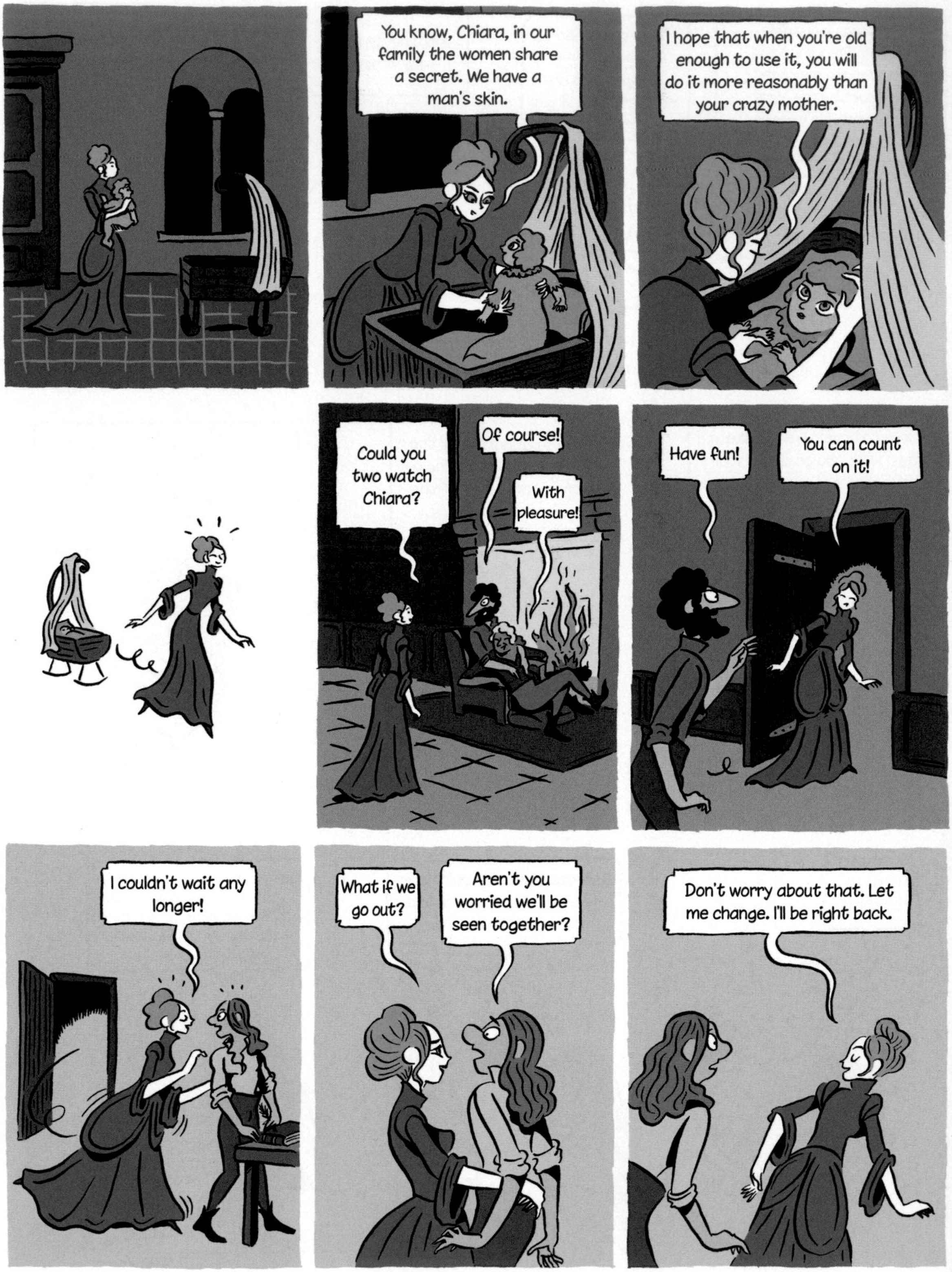
You know, Chiara, in our family the women share a secret. We have a man's skin.
I hope that when you're old enough to use it, you will do it more reasonably than your crazy mother.
Could you two watch Chiara?
Of course!
With pleasure!
Have fun!
You can count on it!
I couldn't wait any longer!
What if we go out?
Aren't you worried we'll be seen together?
Don't worry about that. Let me change. I'll be right back.

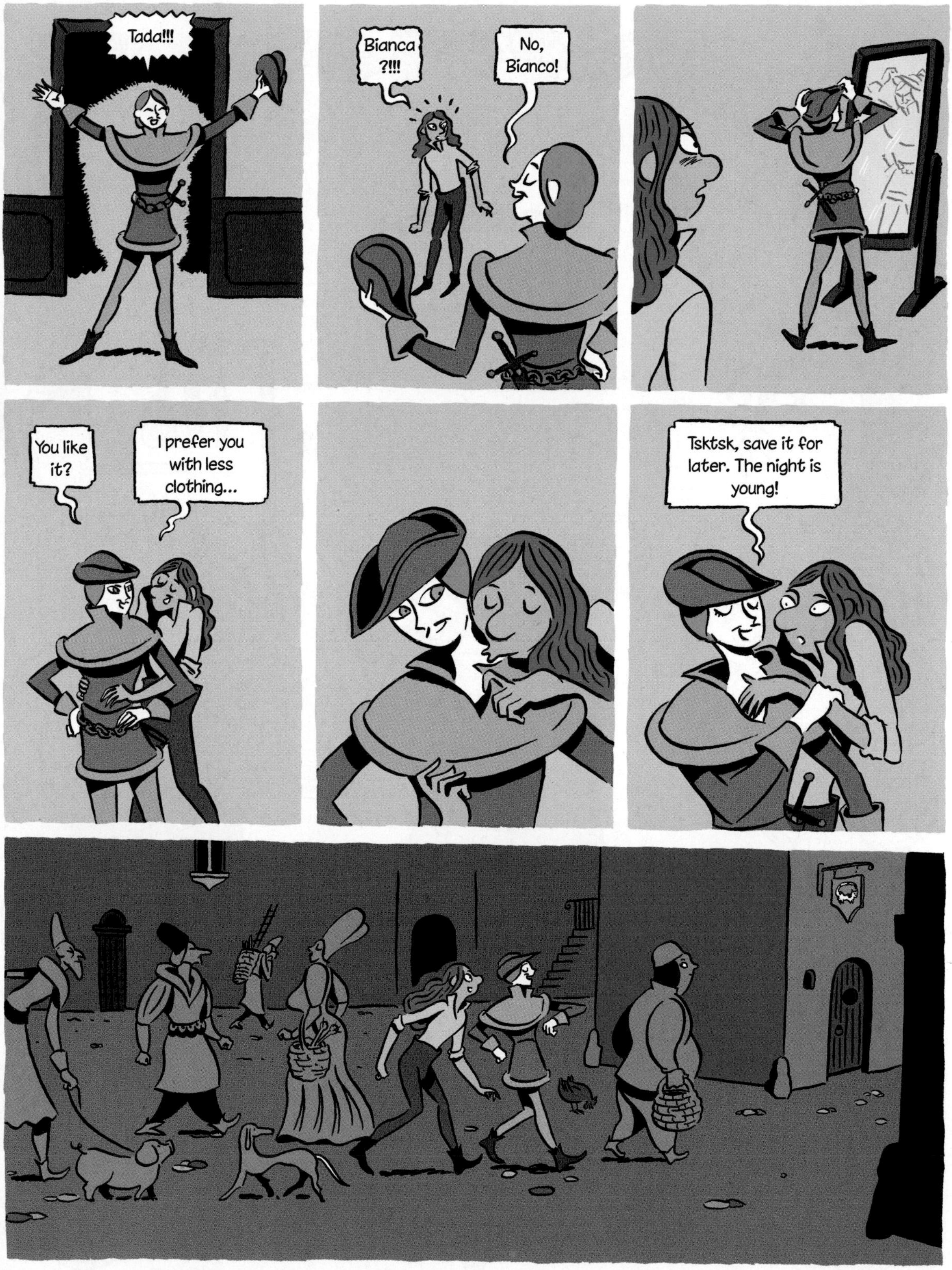
Tada!!!
Bianca ?!!!
No, Bianco!
You like it?
I prefer you with less clothing...
Tsktsk, save it for later. The night is young!

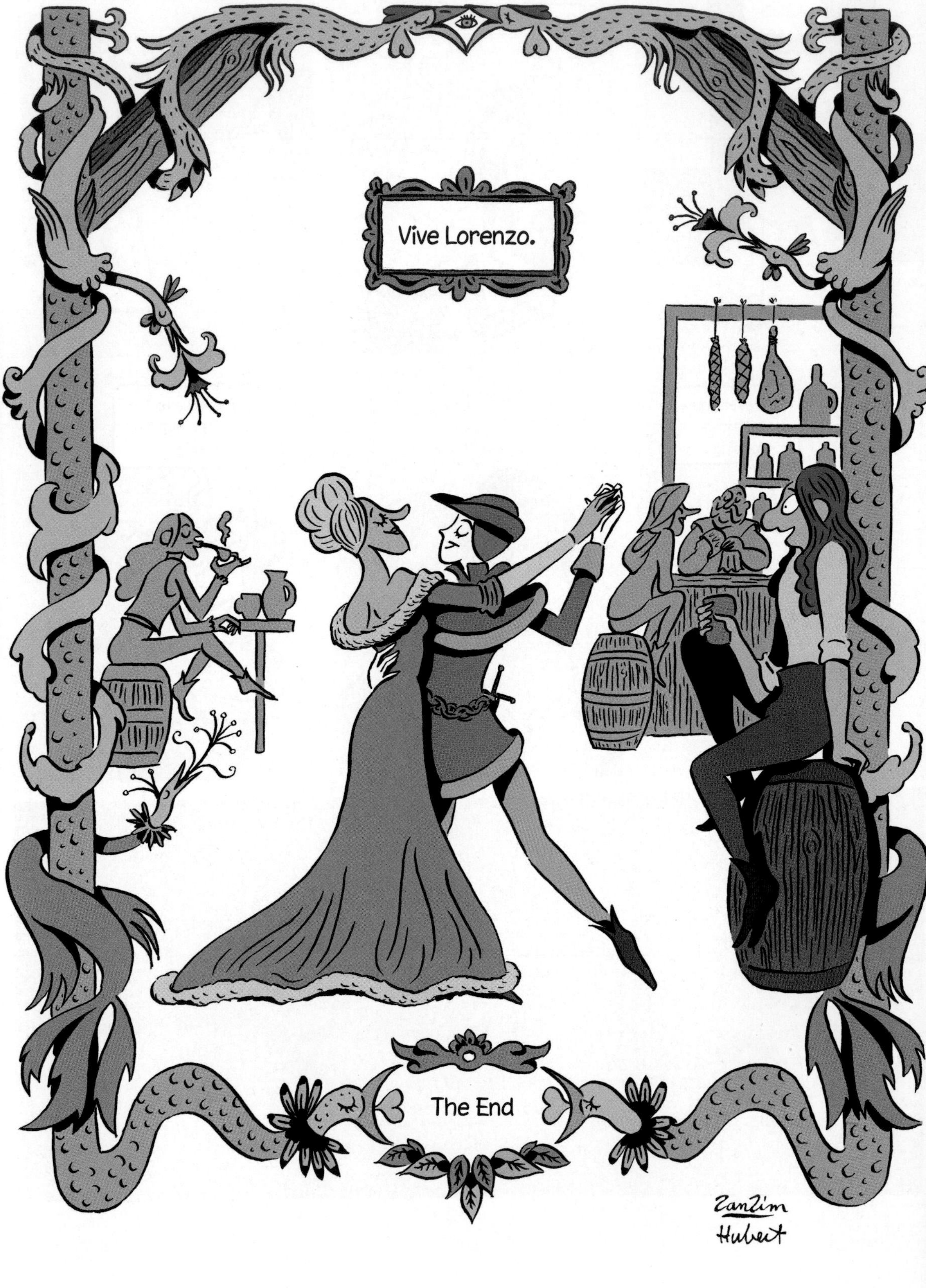
Vive Lorenzo.
The End
ZanZim
Hubert

A MAN'S SKIN DISCUSSION GUIDE
A Man's Skin by Hubert and Zanzim
DISCUSSION GUIDE BY *MATTHEW NOE, MSLS*

Synopsis

Bianca has reached marrying age and in Renaissance Italy that means marrying as best suits her family. In this case, that means Giovanni, a young, pleasantly attractive heir of a merchant family. Yearning to know her fiancé before they are wed, Bianca learns that she can do just that. By donning her family's secret — a "man's skin" long-named Lorenzo — she can move freely about the world as a man, free of the limits placed upon women. Along the way she learns of Giovanni's own secret, her own desires, and what she will do to live life how she wishes — even if that puts her at great odds with her brother, Father Angelo.

Major Characters

Bianca (Lorenzo), Giovanni, Angelo, Rubina, Agostina, Tomaso, Bianca's Mother, Bianca's Godmother

Themes

Love, Gender, Sexuality, Compassion, Understanding, Religion, Morality

Discussion Questions

1. Clothing is a major point of contention throughout the comic. Discuss how appearances weave through the narrative and motivate actions by characters like Bianca, Angelo, and Peccorina.

2. In comics, time is often conveyed through the arrangement of panels and management of the space between them (the gutter). In *A Man's Skin*, however, we also see time manipulated in other ways. How else do we see time pass?

3. Set in Renaissance Italy, among families of wealth, color is everywhere — richly embroidered clothing, paintings, building, and even saturating entire panels. Explain how this background color saturation helps influence the ways scenes are interpreted by the reader.

4. "To hear him, everything is the fault of women, succubus and temptresses! Men are poor little things at the mercy of our perverse appetites which they need to be protected from by veiling us from head to foot. That's not really what I experience every day. You'd think he was living in a parallel world." In this speech against the preaching of her brother, Bianca is challenging notions of gender roles often enforced by (mis)interpretations of scripture. In what ways do these (mis)interpretations continue to impact society today?

5. Even as Giovanni navigates a world that hates him for his sexuality, he still clings to many of the roles assigned to his gender. What are some of those roles and why might he cling so strongly to some of them, while rejecting others?

6. The moment Angelo becomes mayor, he sets about destroying all artwork he decrees is indecent. How does one determine what counts as "appropriate" and who should be allowed to make those decisions?

7. "I would voluntarily rip the fruit of that putrid seed out of her," says Angelo when finding out about Bianca's pregnancy. How does this violent suggestion of abortion square with his claims of piety?

8. Both Bianca and Lorenzo are schooled on how to ensure a male child is conceived, and though one has the air of superstition, the other the air of science, in our modern age we know them both to be false. And yet many today still hold to misconceptions like this. What myths about conception, sex, and gender have you heard recently?

9. "One thing that people will not forgive is having their pleasures taken away," says Bianca's mother, and yet there seem to be limits to whose pleasures are taken into consideration. What do Bianca's adventures as Lorenzo tell us about those limits?

10. Men and women in *A Man's Skin* seemingly live in different versions of reality. The skin of Lorenzo allows Bianca to cross the barrier and experience both — but are there only two ways to live in the world? Bianca certainly seems to find a different road, but are there other characters making their own way?

11. Both in her own skin and in Lorenzo's, Bianca is drawn and described as beautiful and desirable. How might her experiences have been different if she were considered less attractive in her time?

12. What does Bianca and Giovanni's journey from betrothal to open marriage teach us about compassion, friendship, and romantic love?

13. A fable with such a strong moral perspective could easily fall into preachiness. How do Hubert and Zanzim navigate this risk? (Hint: think about humor.)

Project Ideas

- Practice your observation skills by recording a journal every day for a week or two, making note of the day's interactions with expectations built on gender, sex, and sexuality. Feel free to write about these observations in prose, but also be certain to include illustrations or short comics as well, especially when it comes to notes about fashion and modesty. At the end of your observation period, reflect on what you've recorded. Did you learn anything new? Do any of your observations inspire you to make changes in your own life? Are there norms that you want to see changed? Consider how you might help make those changes.

- Engage with your local community by seeking out organizations advocating for the rights of the LGBTQ+ community. Learn about the challenges happening where you live and consider how you might contribute to solving them. You might even propose hosting a book club for *A Man's Skin*!

- We got to see Bianca and Giovanni's happy endings, but what came next for Rubina or Angelo or Peccorina? Flex your creativity by creating a comic about what comes next for one of the many characters in *A Man's Skin*.

- Imagine that your family has inherited a suit — a "skin" — that allows you to transform into another sex while wearing it. What would your skin look like? What would your name be while donning it? Draw it and a wardrobe to go along with your temporary change!

- Religion plays a crucial role throughout *A Man's Skin*, advancing the plot, as well as providing the inspiration for much of the art throughout the comic. Research what role the church played during Renaissance Italy and its influence on the art of the time. How have these roles changed over time? How does religion influence the art of your time?

A Man's Skin
sketches

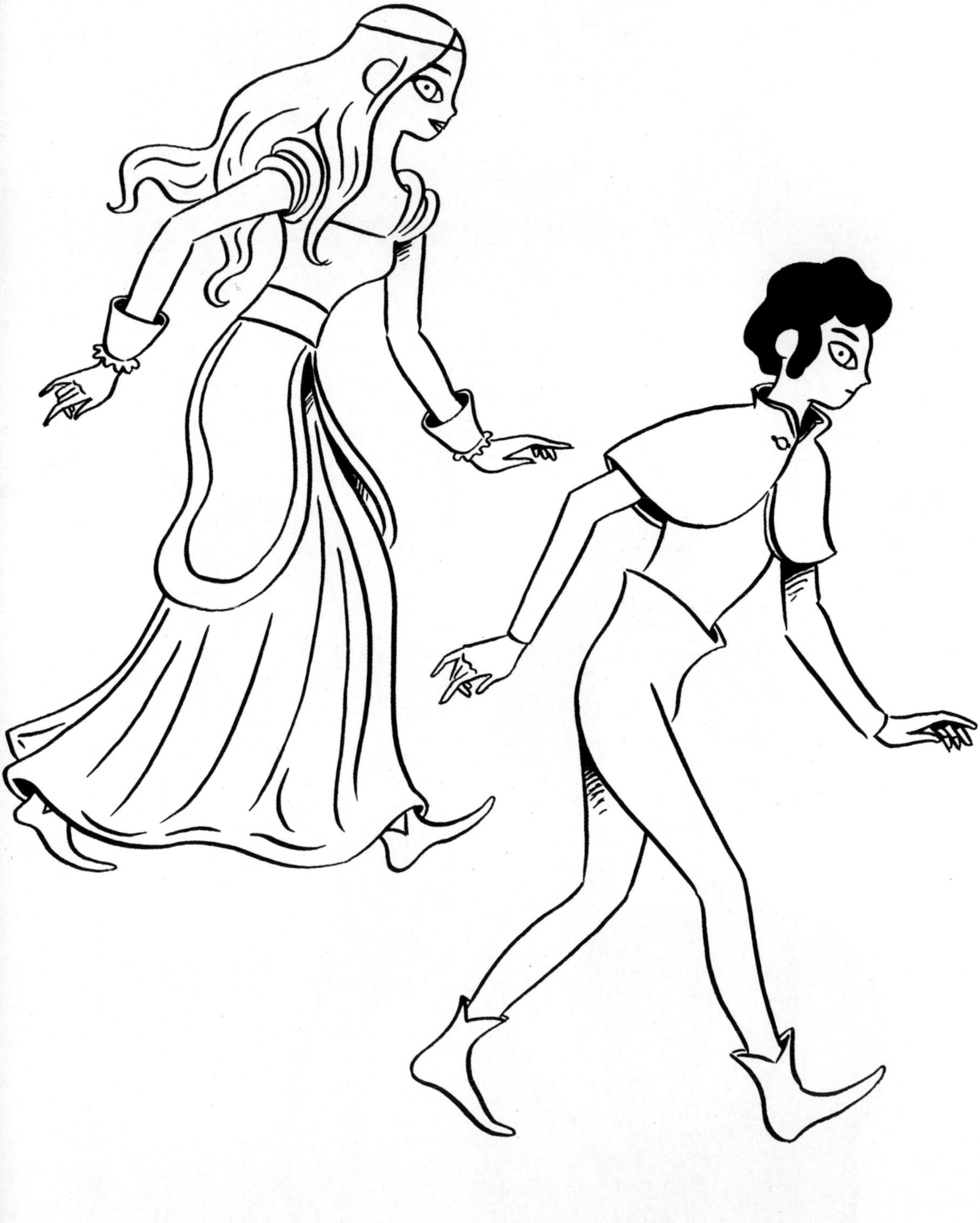

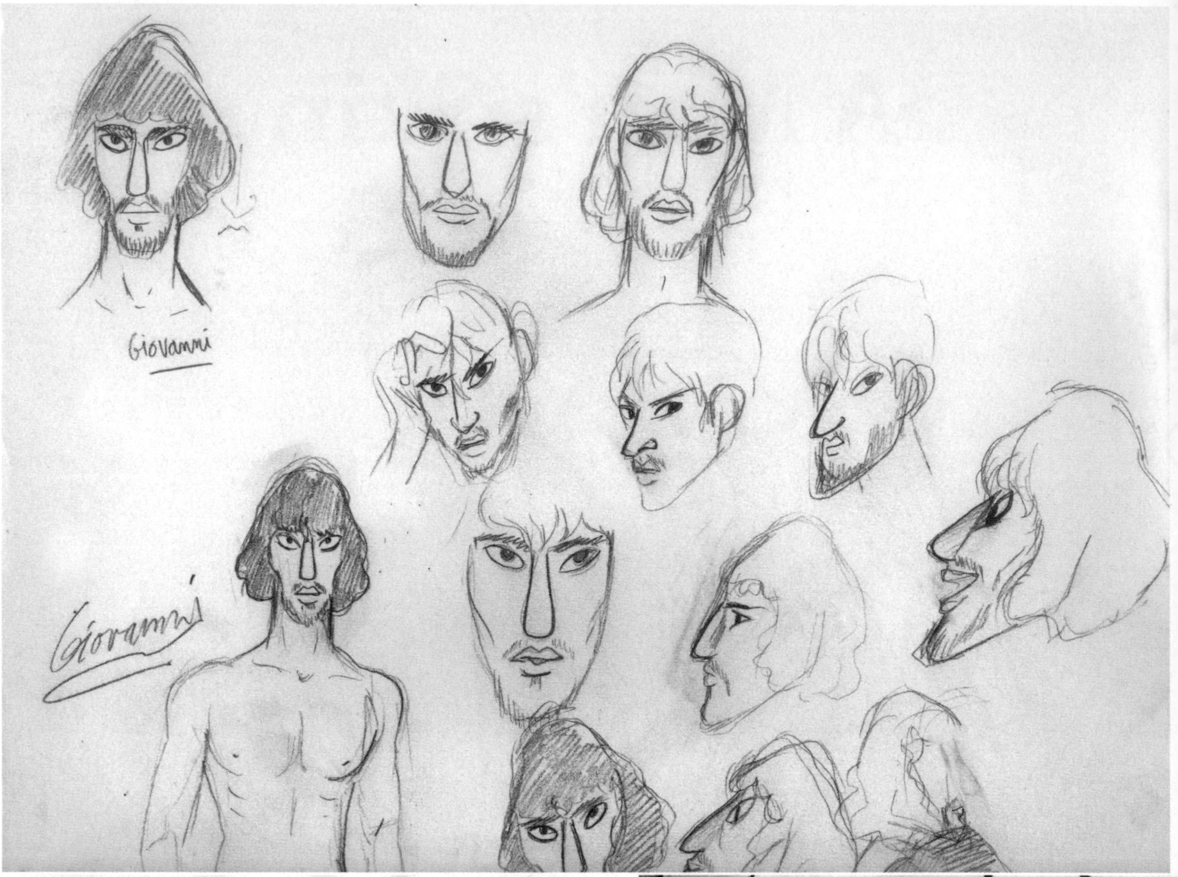
Giovanni
Giovanni

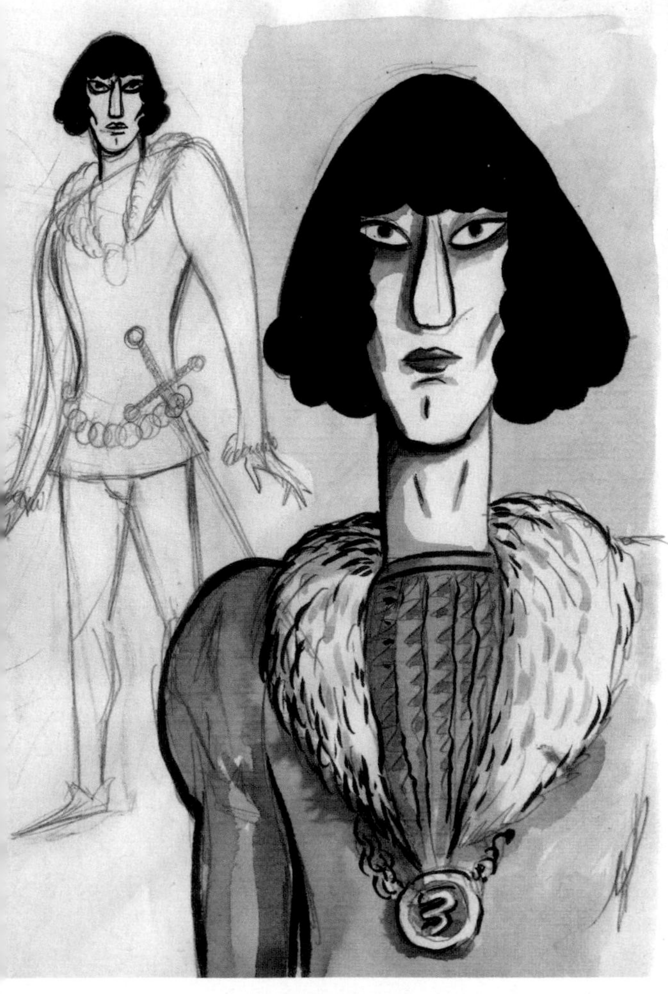

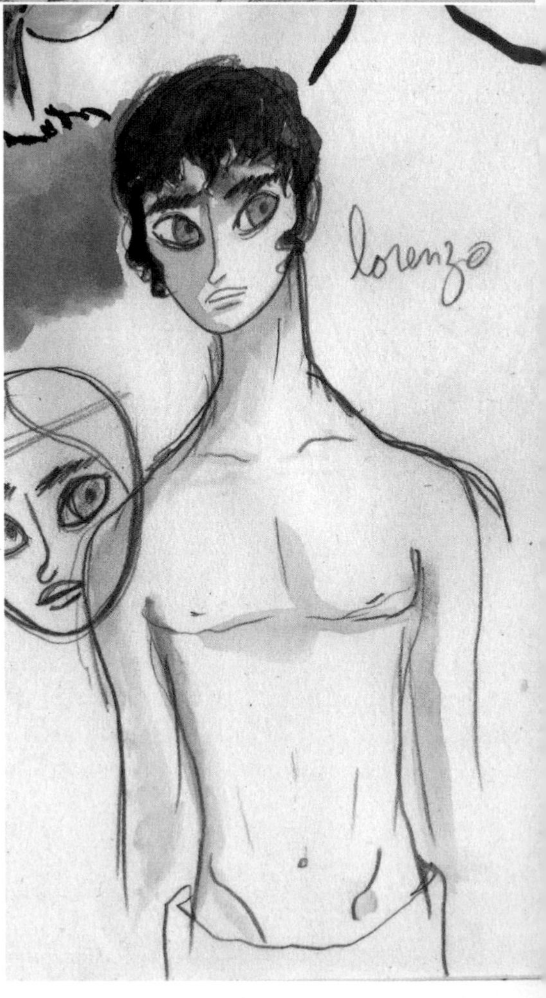
lorenzo

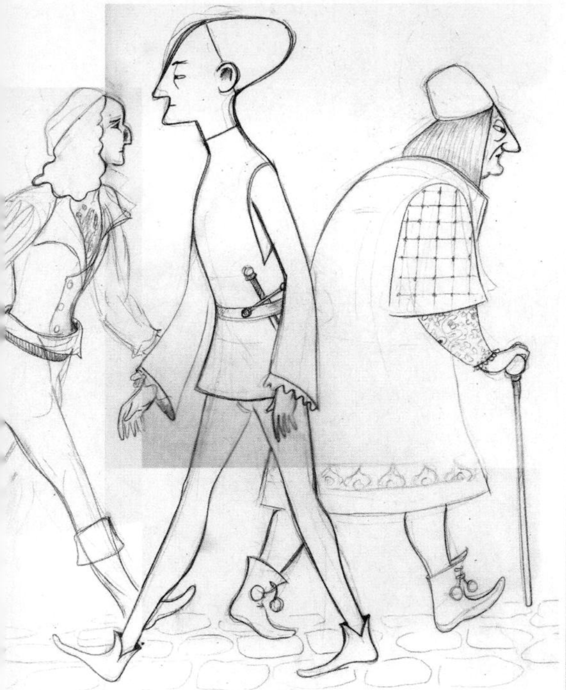
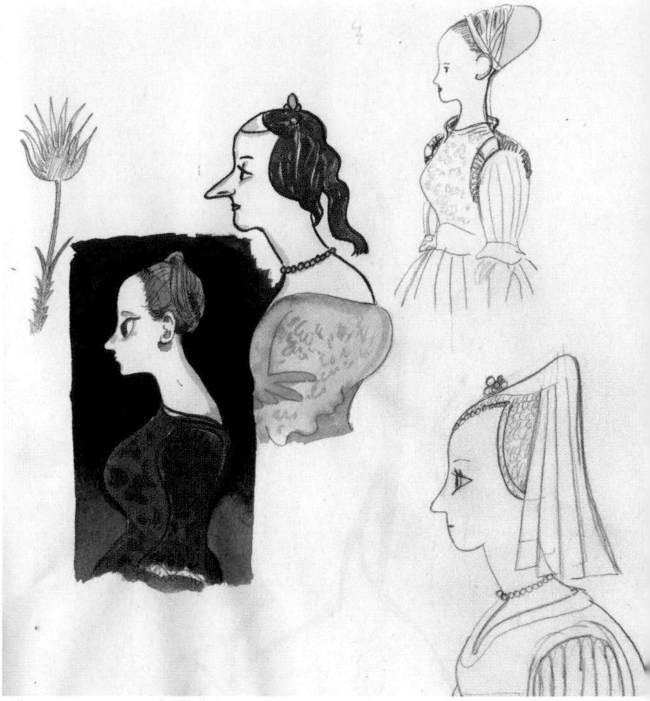
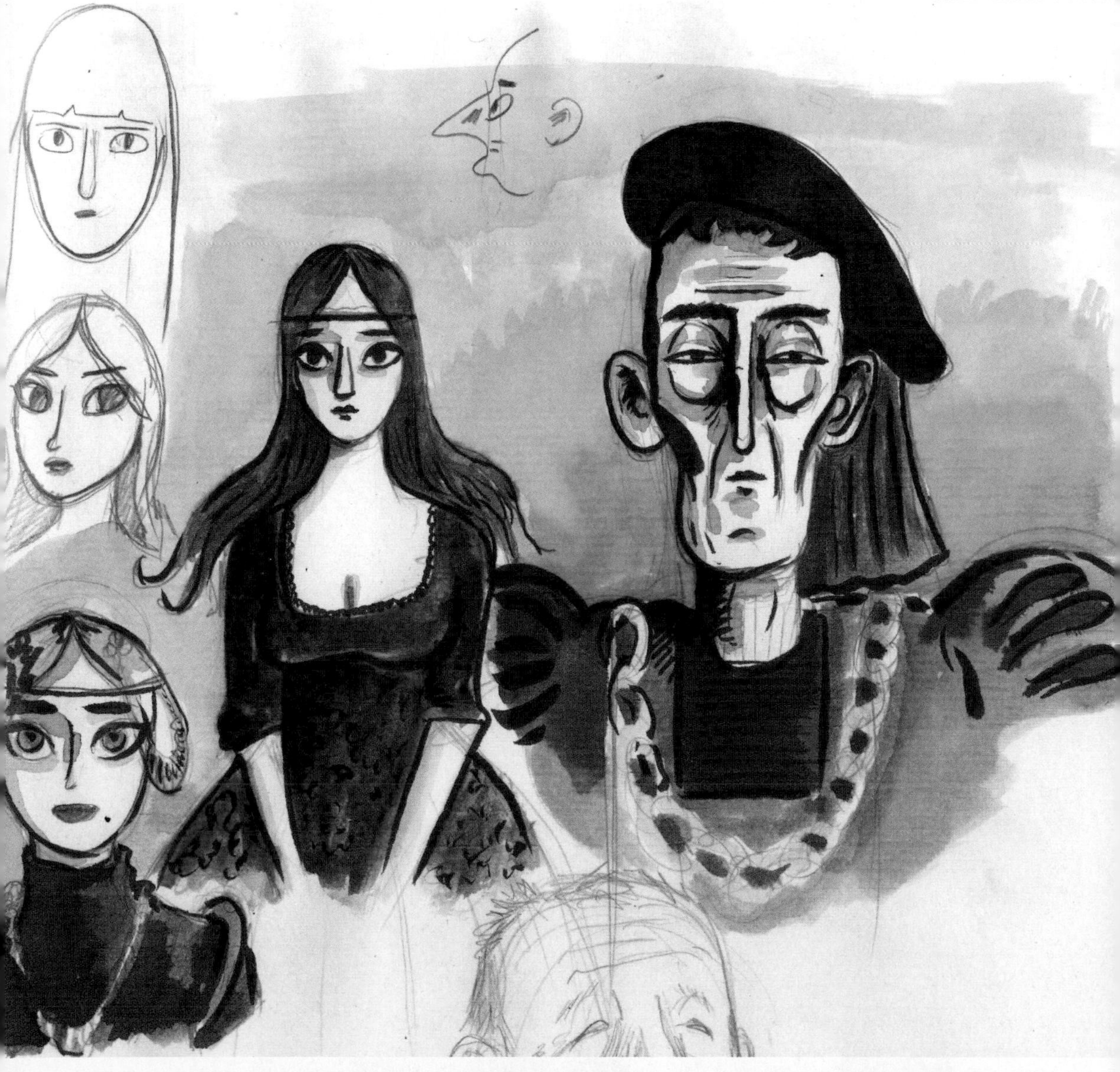

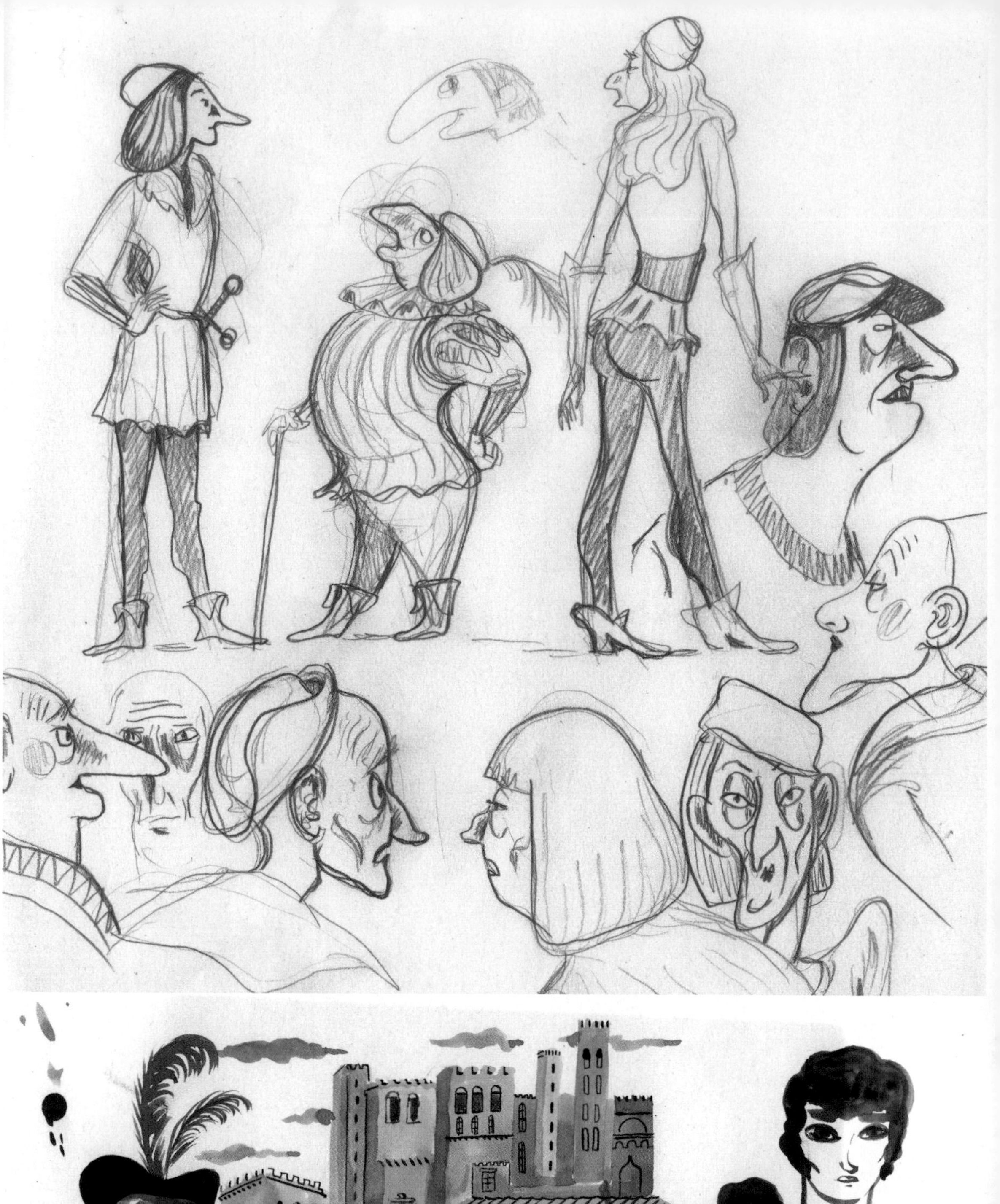

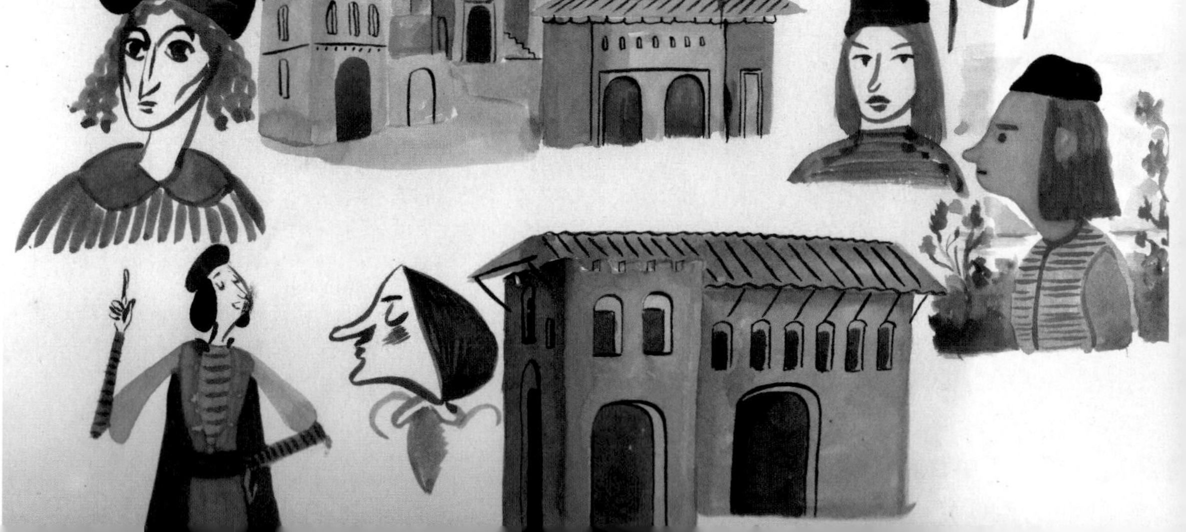

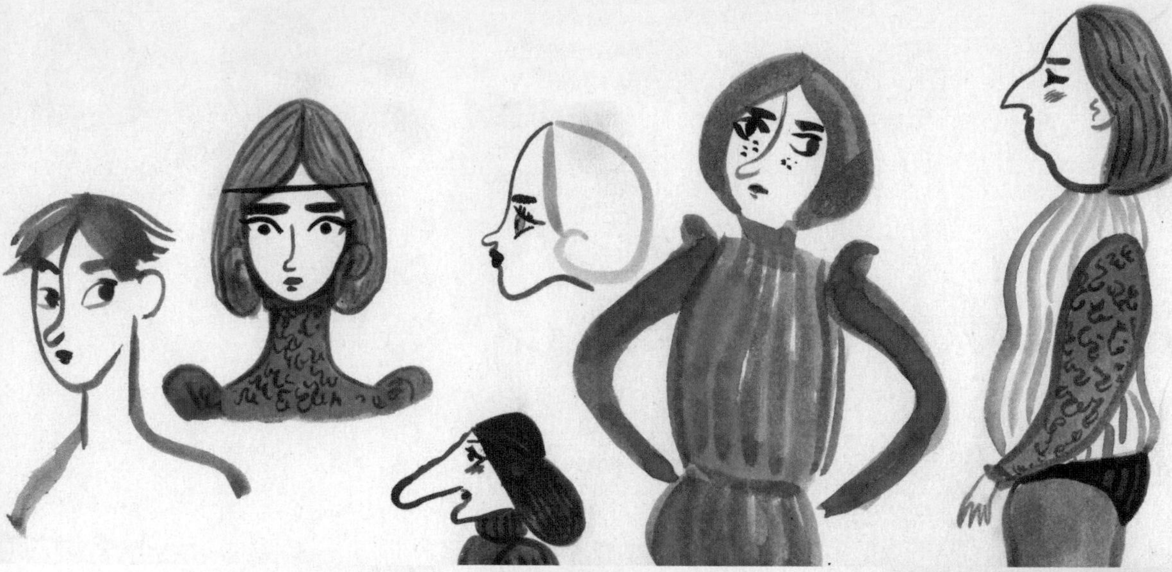
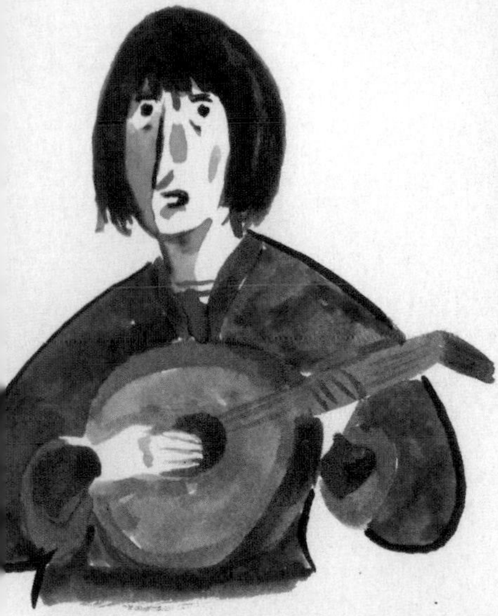
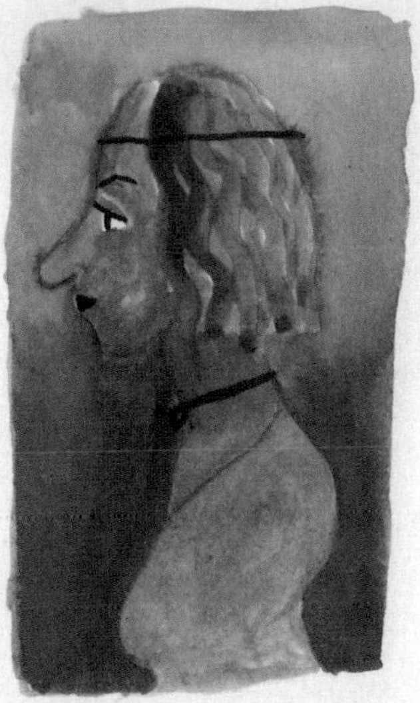
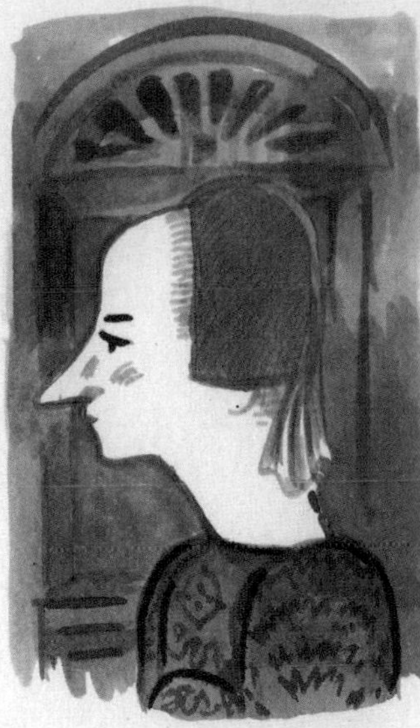
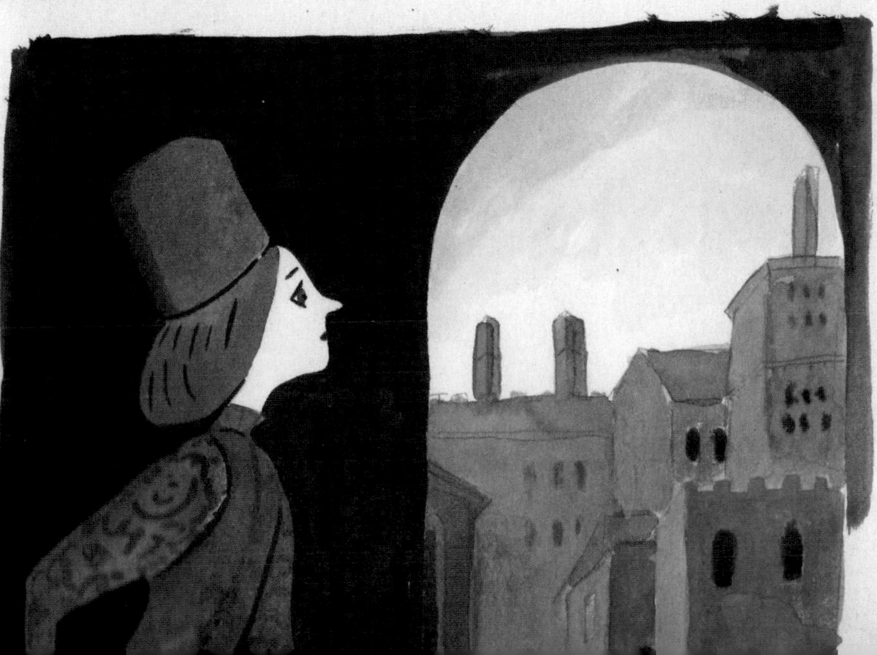
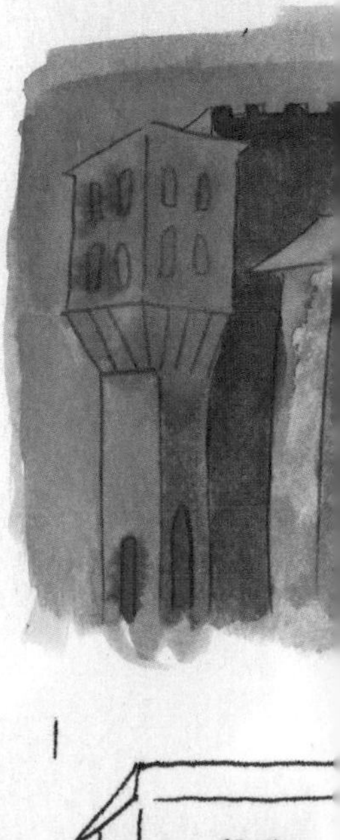
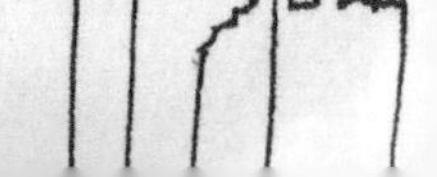

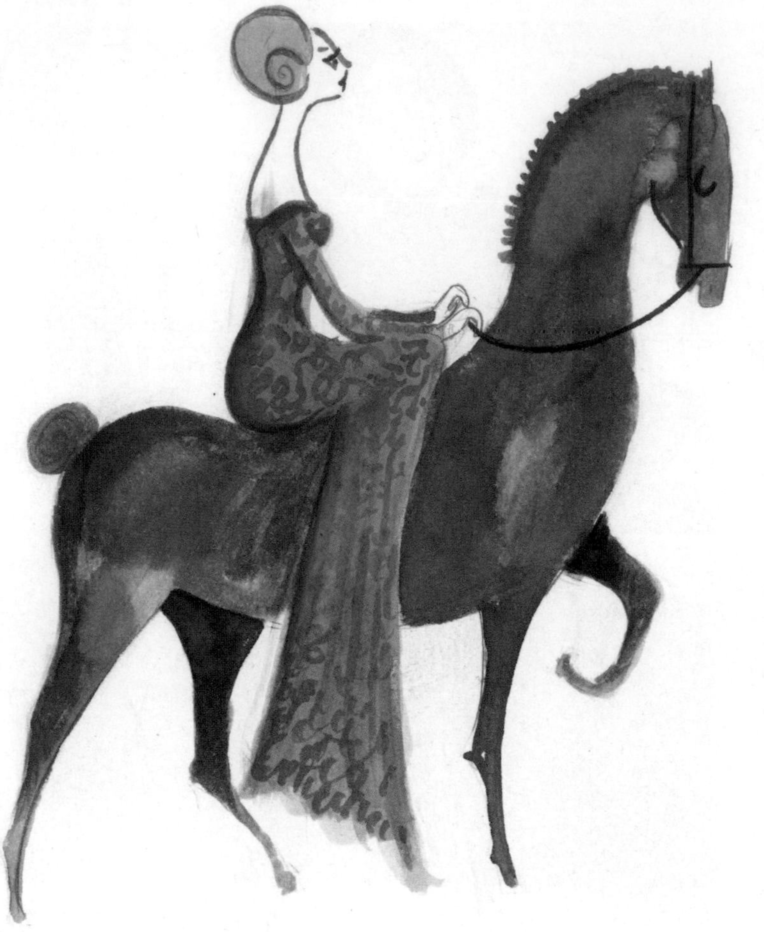

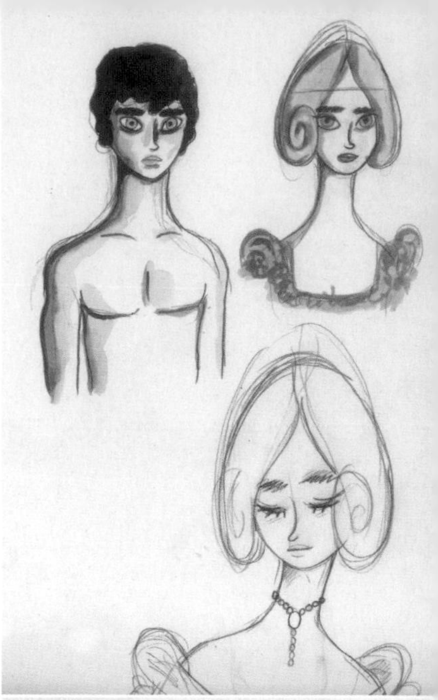

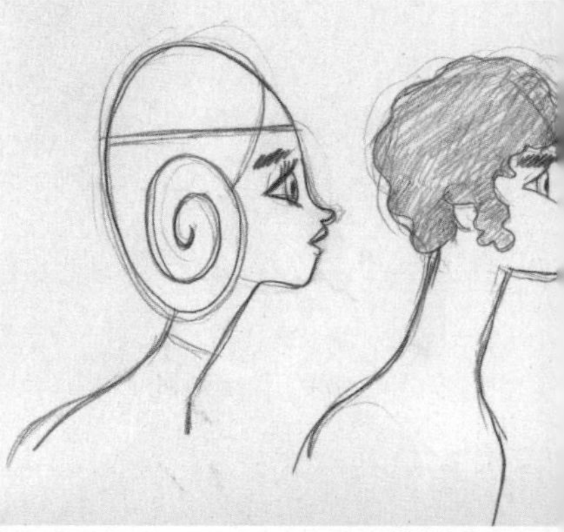

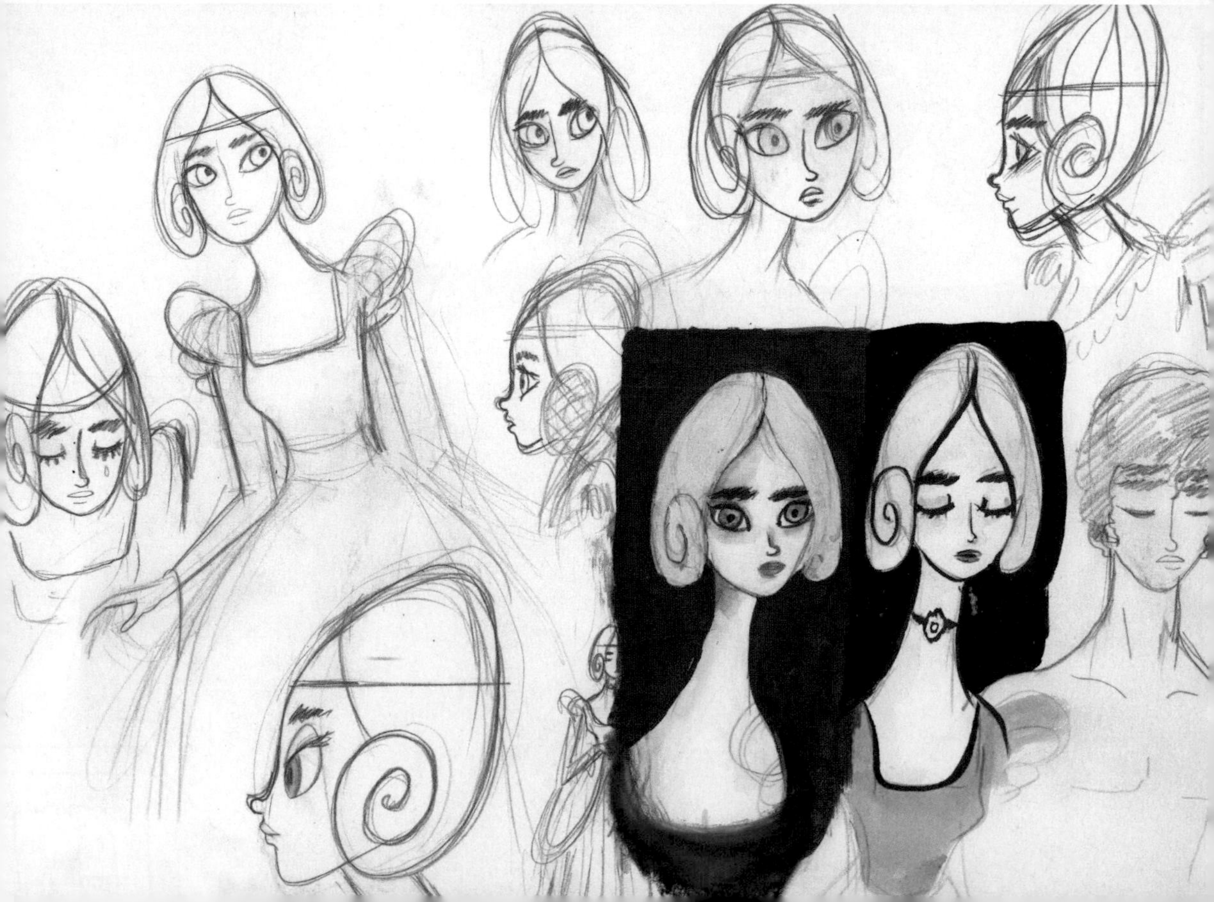

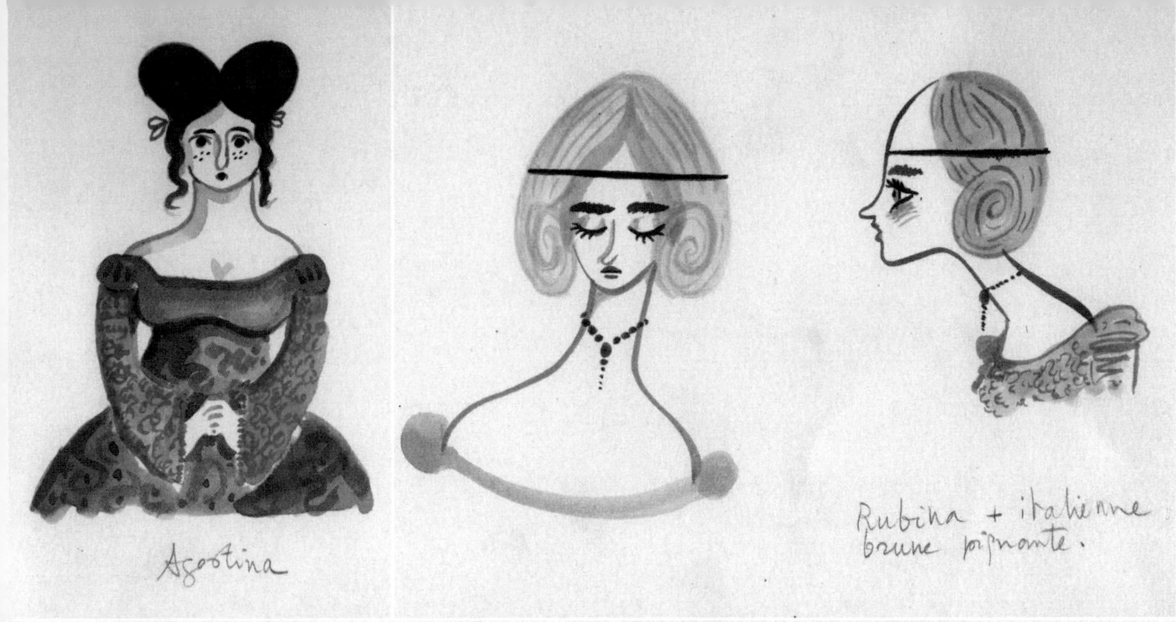
Agostina
Rubina + italienne
brune piquante.
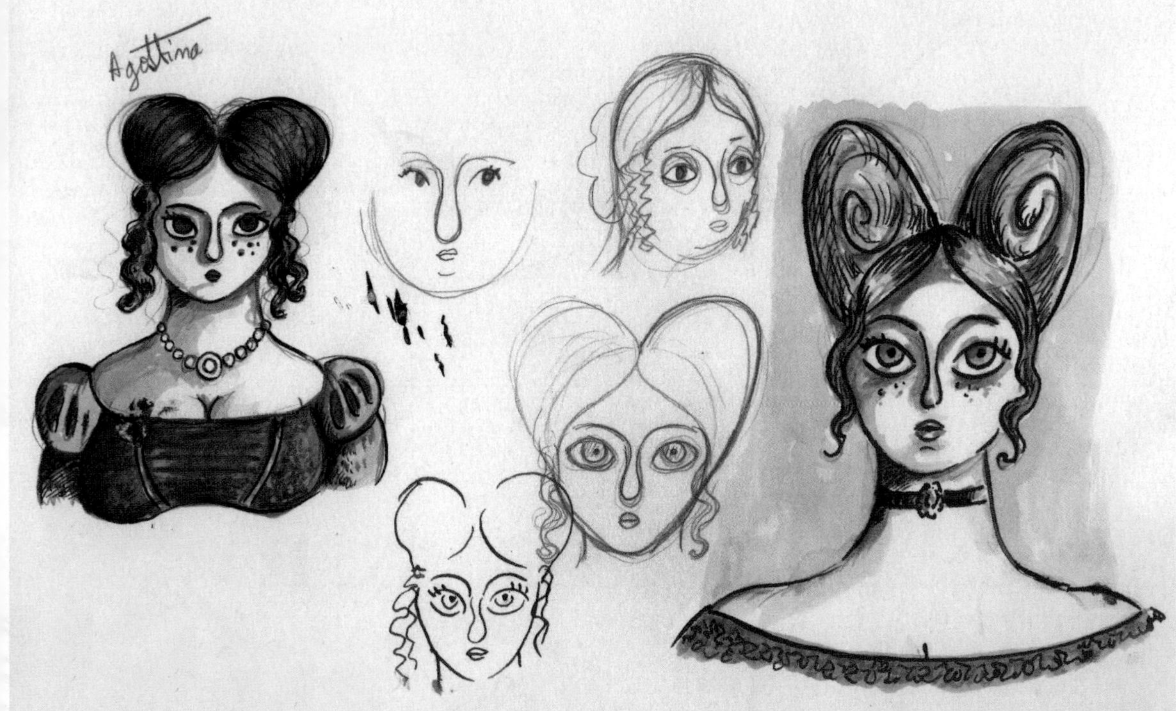
Agostina
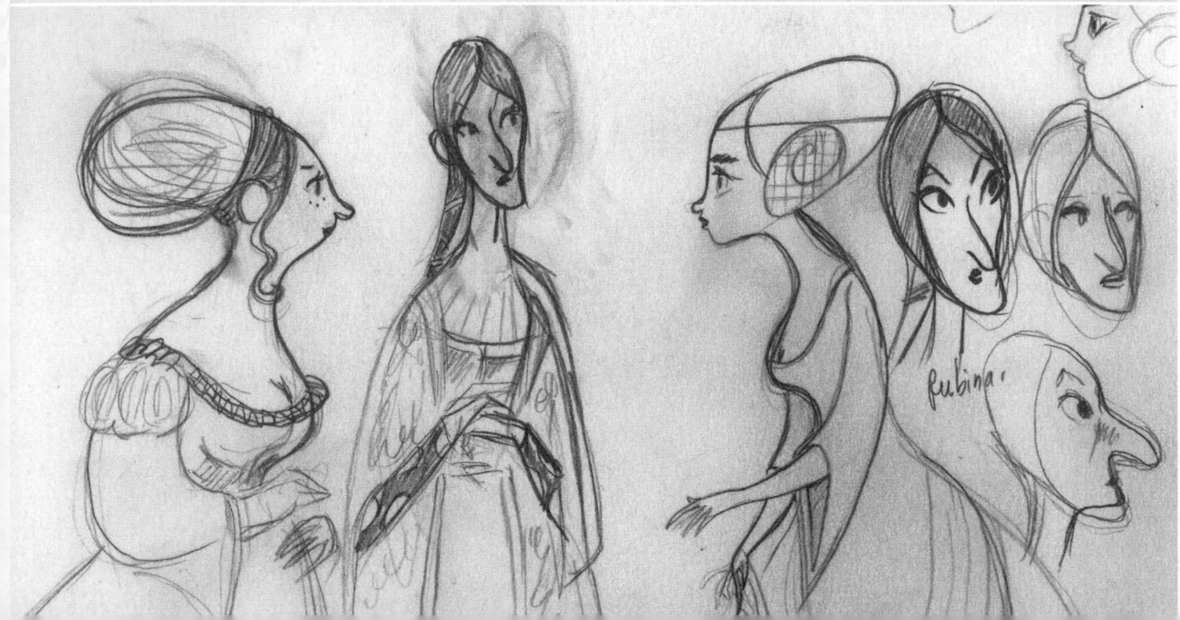
Rubina.

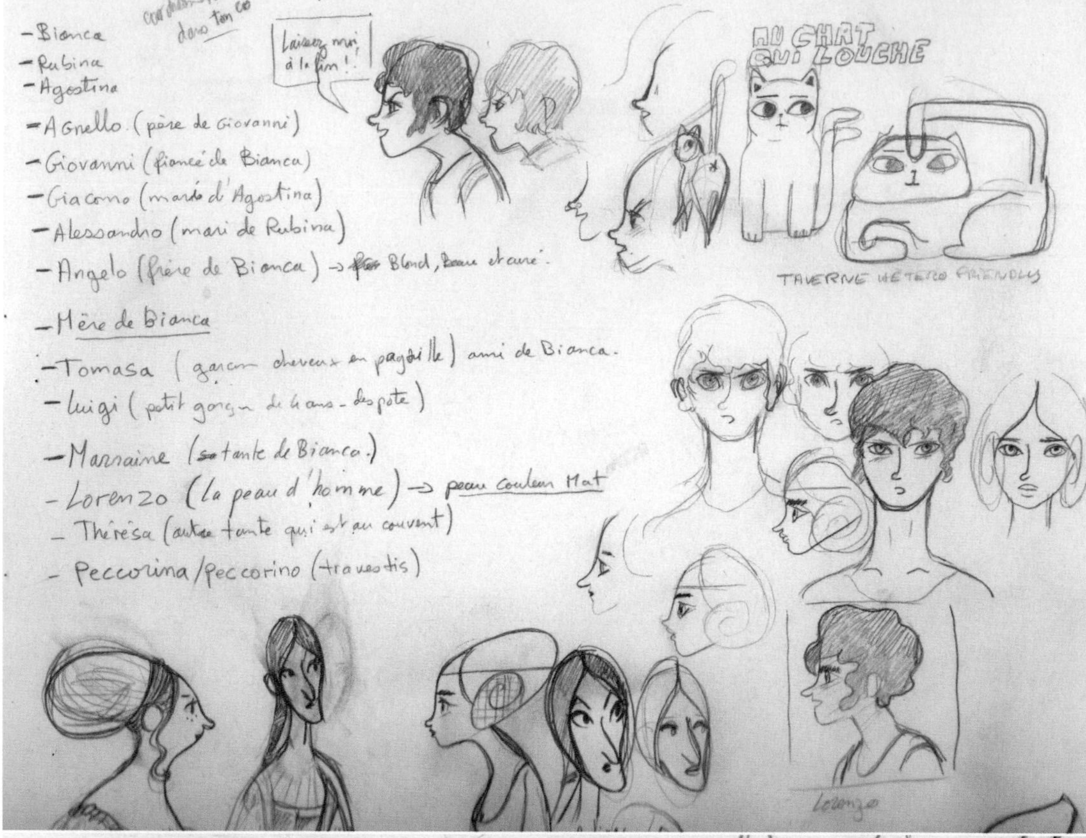
- Bianca
- Rubina
- Agostina
- Agnello (père de Giovanni)
- Giovanni (fiancé de Bianca)
- Giacomo (mari d'Agostina)
- Alessandro (mari de Rubina)
- Angelo (frère de Bianca) → Blond, beau et carré.
- Mère de Bianca
- Tomasa (garçon cheveux en pagaille) ami de Bianca.
- Luigi (petit garçon de la mans-despote)
- Marraine (tante de Bianca.)
- Lorenzo (la peau d'homme) → peau couleur Mat
- Thérèsa (autre tante qui est au couvent)
- Peccorina/Peccorino (travestis)
Laissez-moi, à la fin !
AU CHAT QUI LOUCHE
TAVERNE HETERO FRIENDLY
Lorenzo

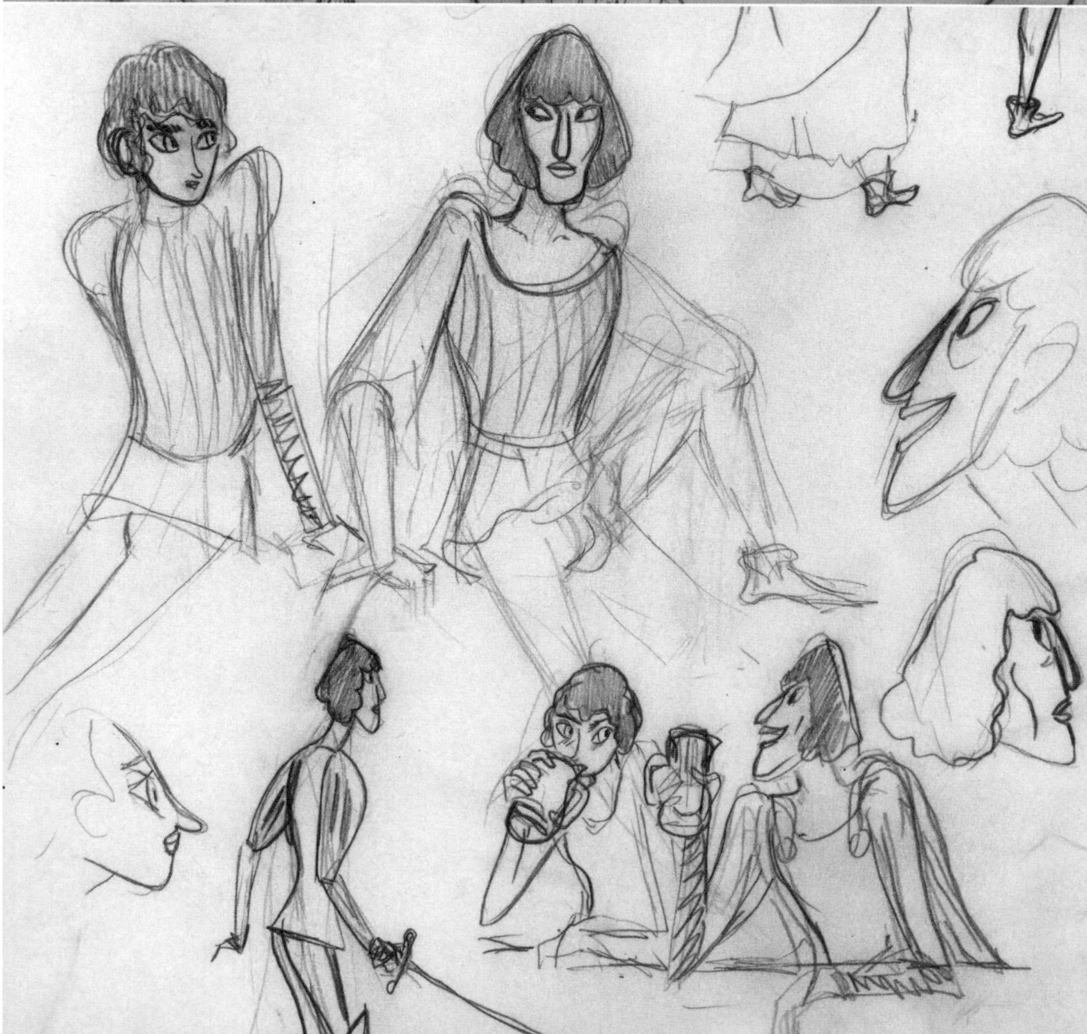

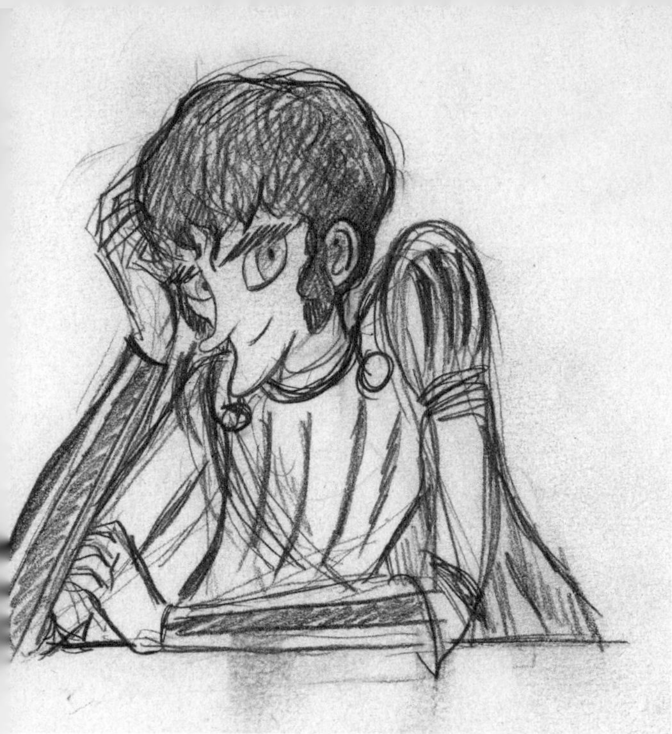

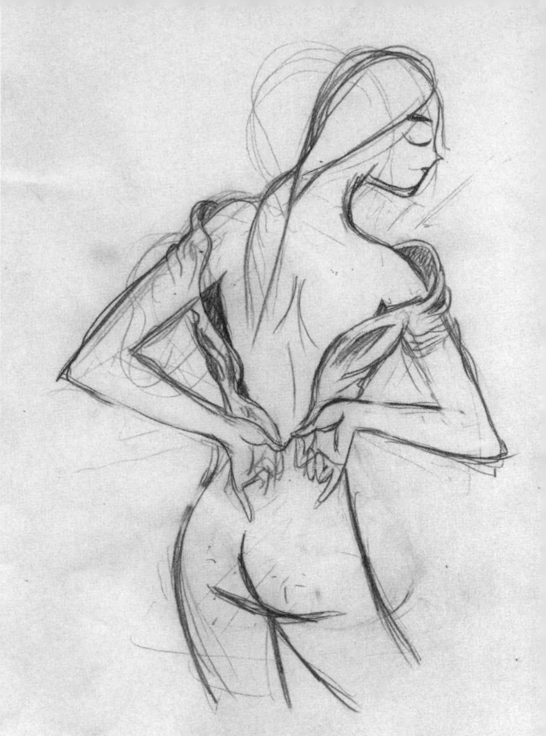

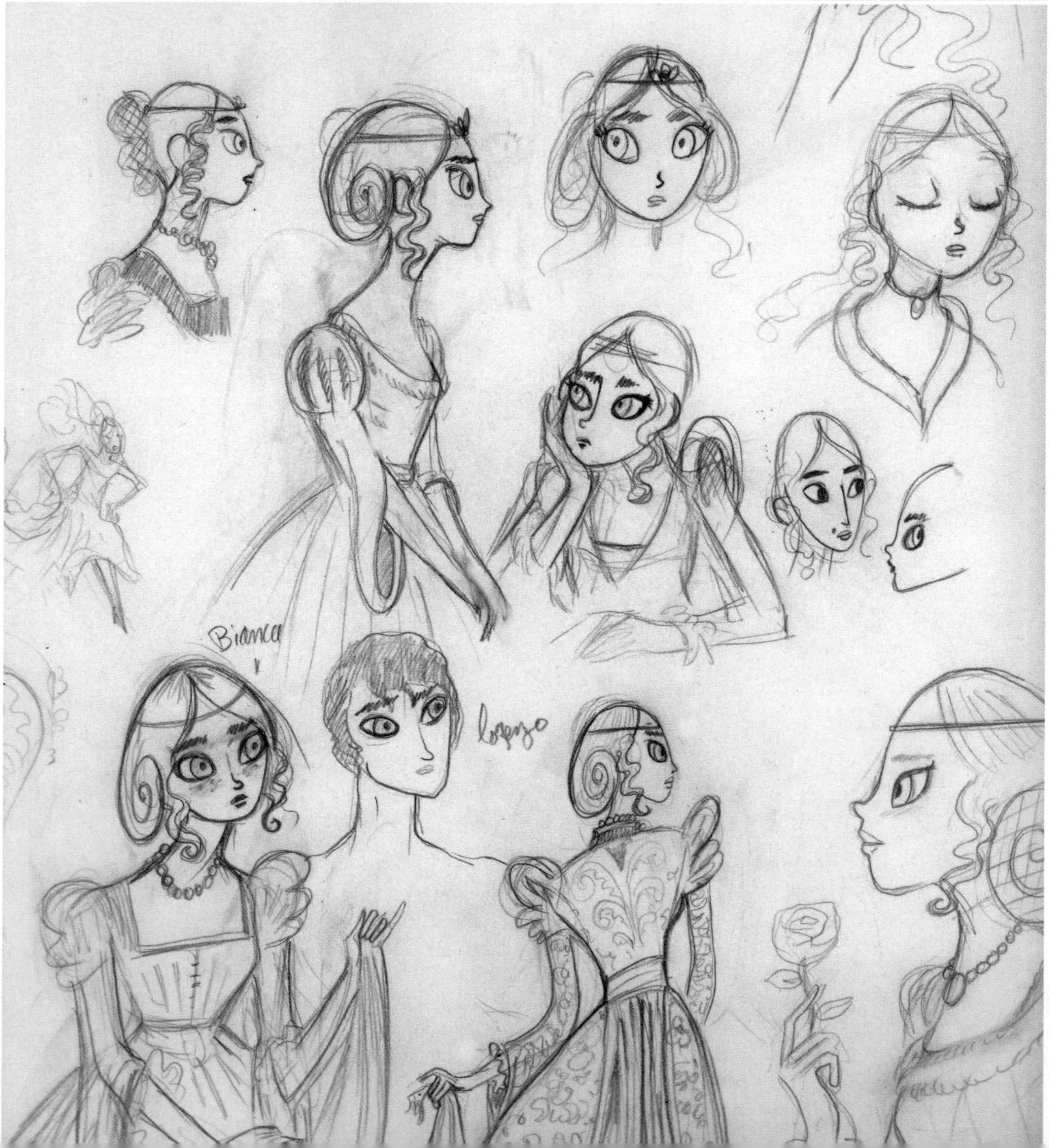
Bianca
lorenzo

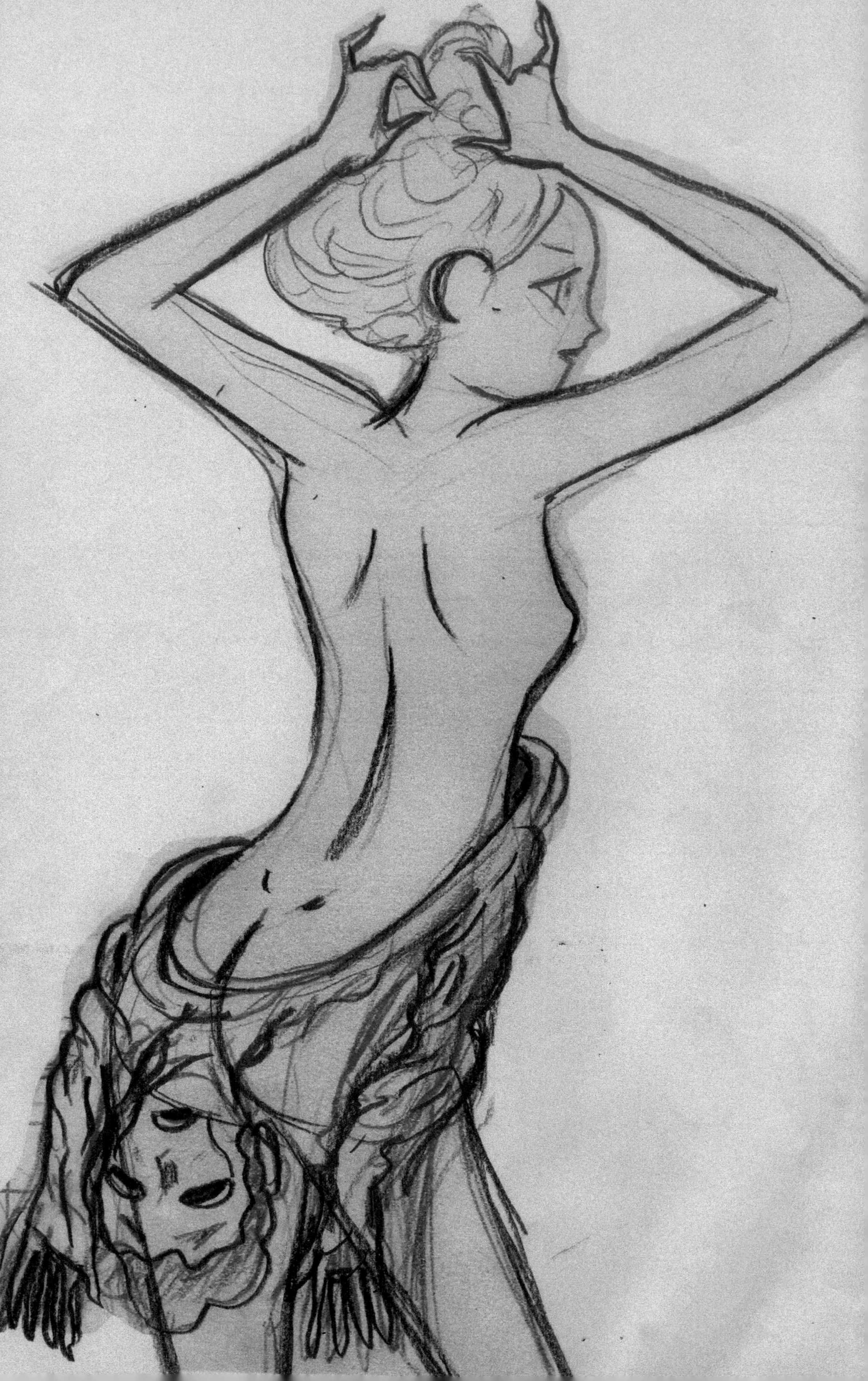

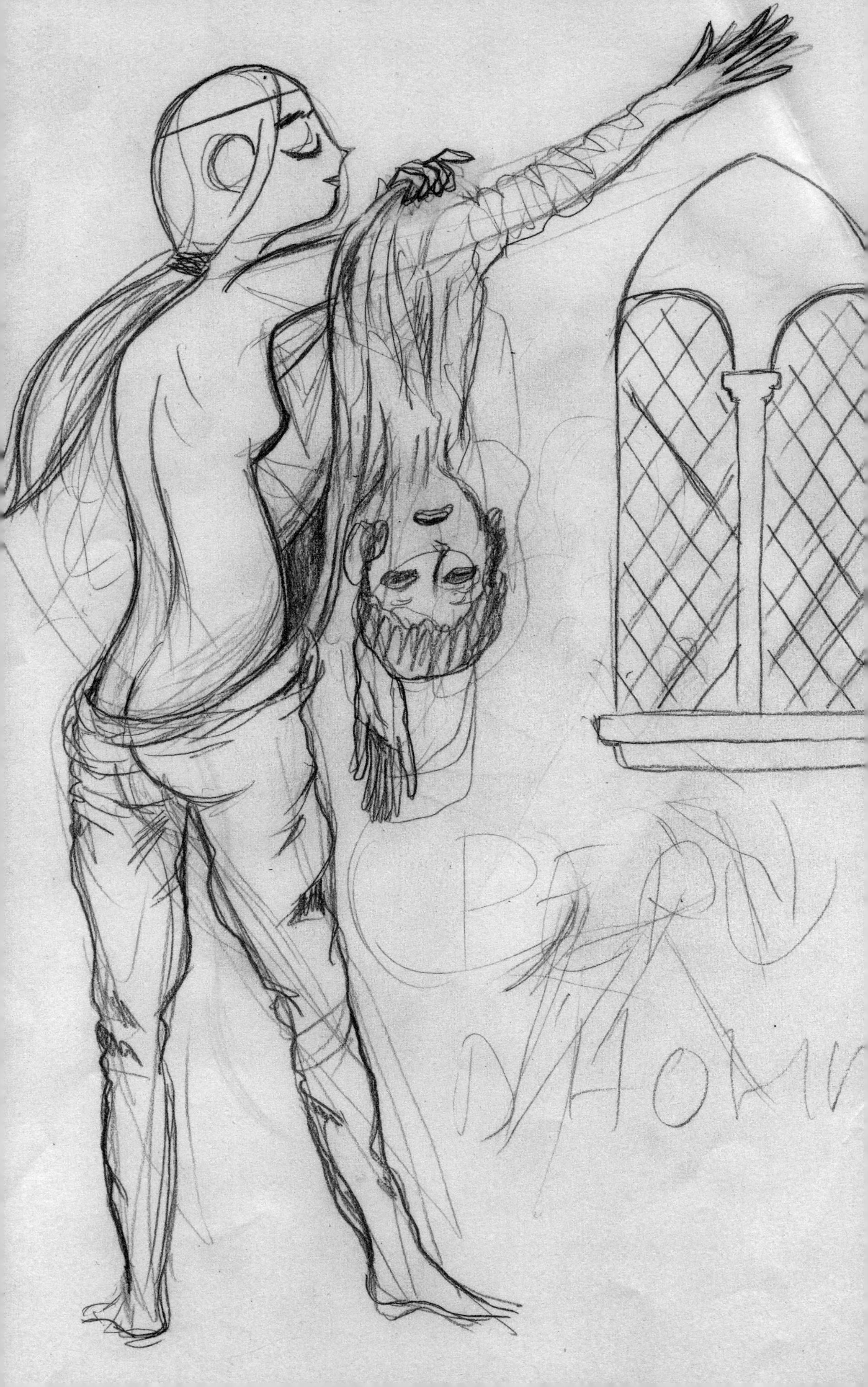

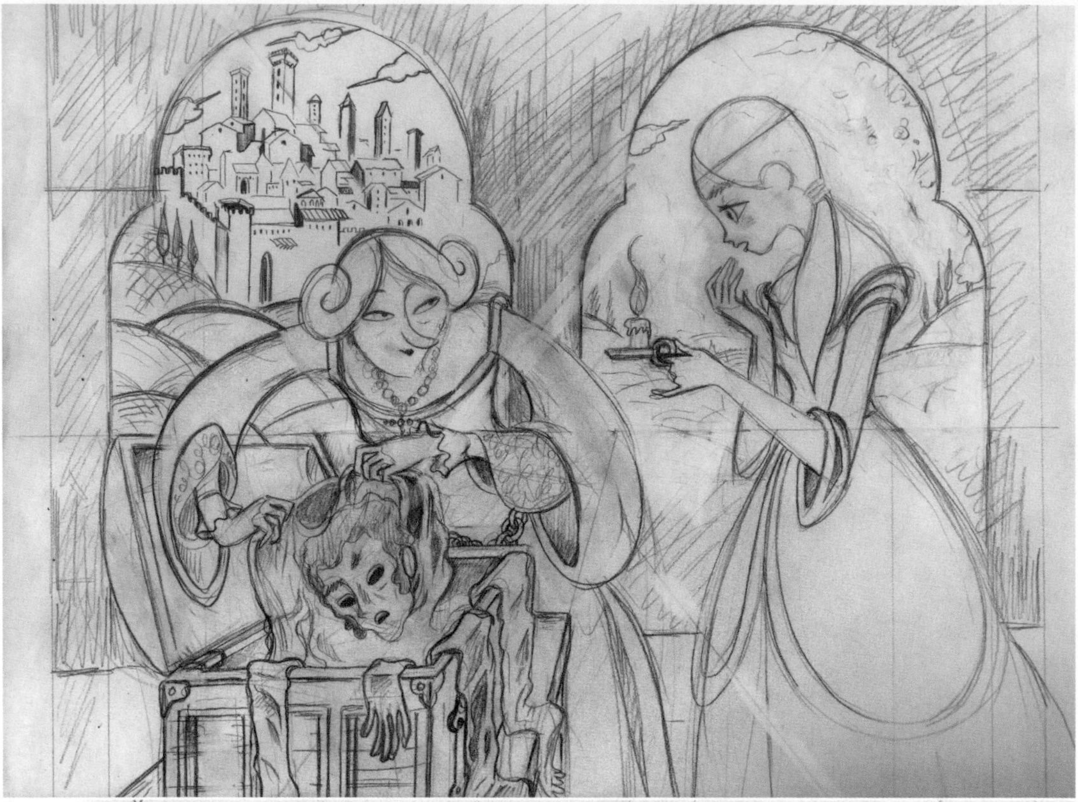

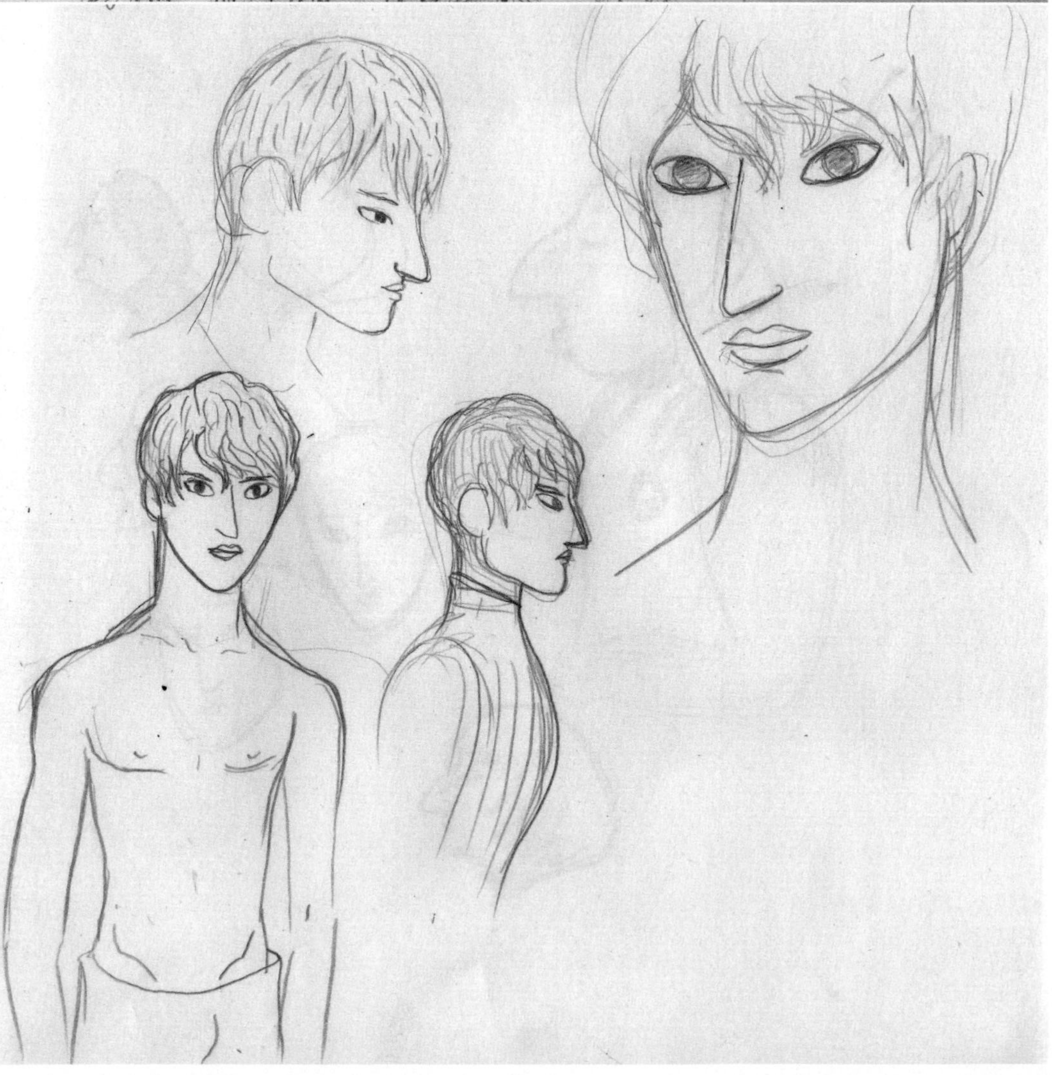

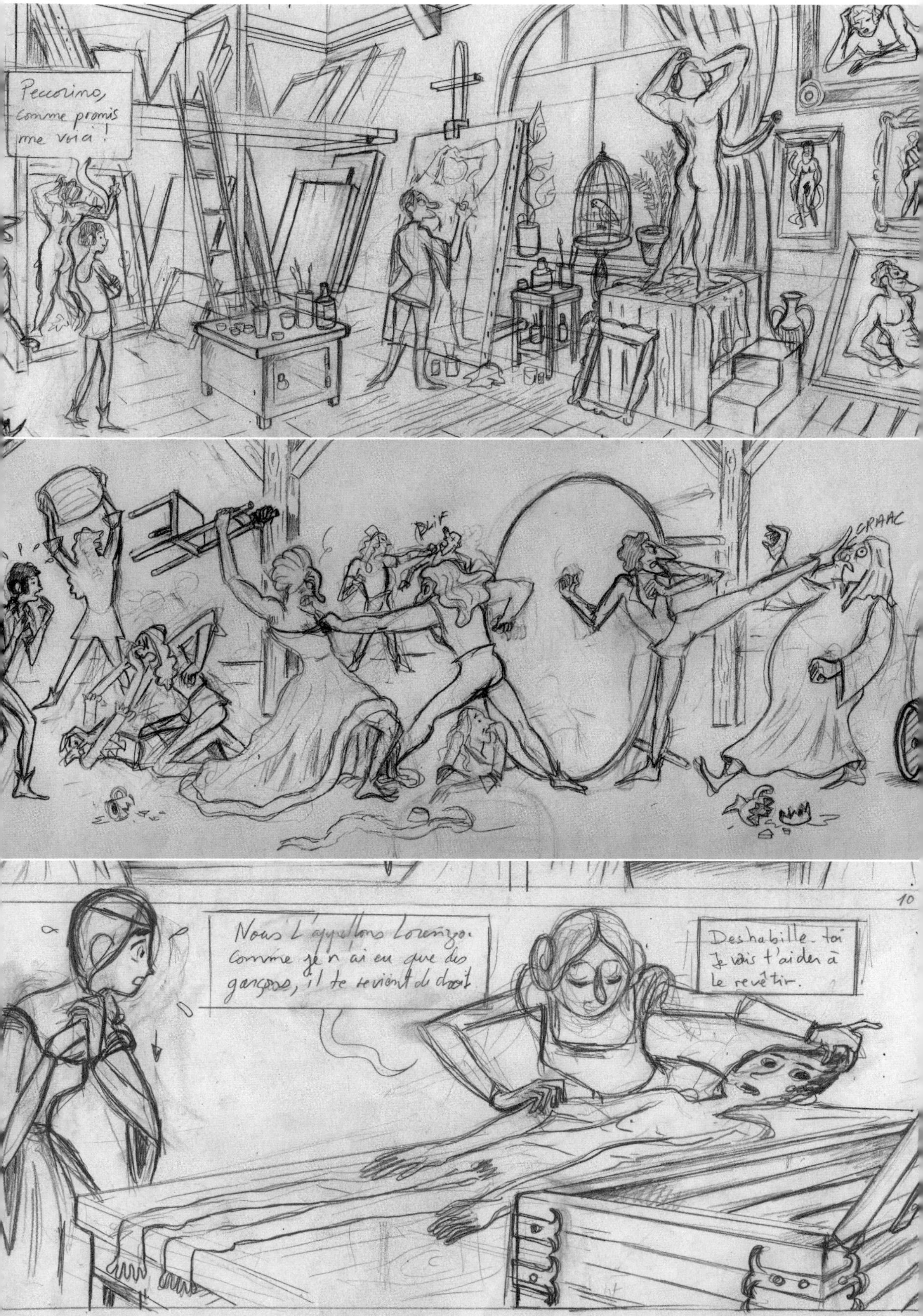
Peccorino, Comme promis me voià !
PLIF
CRAAC
10
Nous L'appellons Lorenzo. Comme je n'ai eu que des garçons, il te revient de droit
Deshabille-toi Je vais t'aider à le revêtir.